SEVEN HUNDRED
YEARS OF
ENGLISH COOKING

We all look on with anxious eyes
  When father carves the duck,
And mother almost always sighs
  When father carves the duck.
Then all of us prepare to rise
And hold our bibs before our eyes
And be prepared for some surprise
  When father carves the duck.

He braces up and grabs a fork
  Whene'er he carves a duck,
And won't allow a soul to talk
  Until he's carved the duck.
The fork is jabbed into the sides,
Across the breast the knife he slides,
And every careful person hides
  From flying chips of duck.

The platter always seems to slip
  When father carves a duck,
And how it makes the dishes skip.
  Potatoes fly amock—
The squash and cabbage leap in space,
We get some gravy on our face,
And father mutters Hindu grace
  Whene'er he carves a duck.

We thus have learned to walk around
  The dining-room and pluck
From off the window-sills and walls
  Our share of father's duck:
While father growls and blows and jaws,
And swears the knife was full of flaws,
And mother jaws at him because
  He couldn't carve a duck.

By an anonymous bard, requote from
The Pleasures of the Table by George
H. Ellwanger.

SEVEN HUNDRED YEARS OF ENGLISH COOKING

MAXIME McKENDRY

Edited by Arabella Boxer

Exeter Books

NEW YORK

Published in USA 1983
by Exeter Books
Distributed by Bookthrift
Exeter is a trademark of Simon & Schuster
Bookthrift is a registered trademark of Simon & Schuster
New York, New York

ISBN 0-671-05973-4

Printed in Czechoslovakia

CONTENTS

ACKNOWLEDGMENTS

The historical notes in this book would never have been accomplished without the assistance in editing and research given by Lorraine Davis.

Tina Cassel contributed both ingenuity and her practical skills in testing the recipes, many of which may not have been tasted for many centuries.

Arabella Boxer must be especially thanked, if not also sympathized with, as to her fell the the arduous task of reducing to a reasonable number the recipes I longed to include. She courageously excised twenty-five apple pies from one century alone! And she also conscientiously retested most of the recipes.

I should also like to thank my husband John McKendry, Curator of Prints at the Metropolitan Museum, New York, for his endless encouragement, and his patience with a messy kitchen and a disrupted household; I am grateful to him and to my friends who bravely sat down to meals of strange origins and unusual spices, and who gave me their honest opinions of the various dishes.

My thanks to Smirk's masterpiece, the Reading Room at the British Museum for its very existence, its whispering peace; its staff who were mysteriously able to conjure up an ancient tome despite enormous difficulties and the frequent sad reminder: 'Destroyed by enemy action.'

To the book dealers who allowed me to copy down recipes from their rare books whose value was way beyond my means.

To all the cooks, scribes and prelates of bygone days who transcribed their culinary achievements so that we may enjoy them and take pride in our country's cooking so many centuries later.

To the New York Society Library for giving me free run of their stacks, a room to work in and patience with my long delay in returning books!

To the staff of the Cloisters in New York, for their interest, their confidence in using me as a medieval caterer for the Feast of St Polycarp and for the free hand they gave me to plunder their exquisite medieval Herb Garden.

To Elizabeth Roth at the New York Public Library for introducing me to their cookbook collection and invaluable range of reference material.

To Sir George Weidenfeld for constantly encouraging me to write and his willingness to publish a new author, a habit for which he is well known and loved.

To my mother, Rhoda Birley, who has certainly inspired me to try out anything in the kitchen, at any time of day or night.

To my children Louise and Alexis who since childhood have been inflicted with experimental dishes; who have somehow survived and flourished and now 'mess it forth' pretty well themselves.

To Culpeper House in England for their long list of herbs that can be bought at their two shops in London; to the Meadowbrook Herb Farm in Rhode Island, on the outskirts of Newport, U.S.A. for their excellent supply of herbs, both potted, dried and in seed packets and which include hyssop, much used in medieval times; to a shop called Aphrodisia, 28 Carmine St., N.Y., U.S.A. where to my great surprise and joy I found galingale and cubebs.

FOREWORD

THIS BOOK LOOKS at English food from medieval times to the present. First, I should like to give Anglo-Saxon people a feeling for the flavours, spices and typical dishes of the progressing centuries, enable them to recognize in themselves not only the family nose or red hair, the voice or mannerism, but their inherited attraction towards saffron, mace, nutmeg, cinnamon, anchovies, mushrooms, sharp sauces, citrus tastes, puddings, cream, butter, jam, pickles, dripping, bread and butter and boiled eggs that is also part of their nature and history. Second, the book should enable readers, in a romantic way, to feel history through one of the senses: taste. Once you have it in your power to cook the rudiments of a medieval royal banquet, an Elizabethan nursery breakfast, an eighteenth-century tavern lunch, or a savoury ice, you begin to see the people, their clothes, their furniture; you can almost hear their conversations as you eat their food. Pastures, crops, herds, great halls and palaces, boats bearing luxuries on rivers and seas, town houses and tea dances – all become as clear as a film.

Many of the dishes in this book are real additions to modern fare and are simple to make. Others have been included for the imaginative cook who will take a flavour from the past, some detail or seasoning that appeals to her, and adapt it in her own kitchen in a personal way. No amateur cooking enthusiast could read all the books from which the recipes were gleaned; no cook tries out all the recipes in the books she so obsessively buys; but recipes are often read with pleasure, even if they are not used. This is why the majority of the earlier dishes have been included in their original texts, some of them sufficiently translated to make sense today. They have been tested and interpreted in terms of modern quantities and methods where the results seemed worthwhile.

Certain herbs, vegetables and spices are now truly obsolete, but surprisingly few. Some produce is unavailable in the mechanized city, or seems so. But more and more people of all ages are returning to the farms, villages and country houses of England where pickling, potting, collaring and home baking are once again acts of hospitality and love – as they have been in the past.

PROLOGUE

THE OLD STONE Age Briton relied on hunting and fishing to bring in the first English meals. Some Neolithic remains found at Whitehawk even suggest that cannibal feasts washed down with beer may have been the menu. In the third millennium before Christ, invading Stone Age farmers crossed the Channel to bring about the country's first culinary revolution. They sowed grain: corn and wheat; they bred animals for food: cattle, pigs and sheep. Marrow bones were eaten and in 330 BC a Roman visitor saw wheat being threshed in covered barns.

About that time the weather took a turn for the better; the prevailing winds followed the Gulf Stream, giving Britain a warmer climate than one would expect at her latitude. That climate and the moderate rainfall are the foundations of English farming. The long coastline meant fishing and ocean trade. Boats sailed as far as the Levant. The farmers, living in hut villages, brewed beer and mead from wheat and honey and flavoured them with cranberries and bog myrtle. Already wine and spices were being imported.

The invasions of Julius Caesar (55–4 BC) and Aulus Plautius (AD 43) brought Roman foods and customs to the Britons. The Romans are thought to have brought cherries and apples and English anchovy sauce is said to be the descendant of Roman *garum*, a sauce made of anchovies and fish gut, steeped in the sun. For three centuries of the Roman occupation, wines were all imported, but the Emperor Probus gave permission for the Britons to cultivate vines and to make their own wine. The English custom of town houses and country estates began with the Romans and the urban Briton may have lived more comfortably under their rule than at any other time until the nineteenth century.

The last Roman soldier left England in AD 407, to be replaced by invaders from the north: Angles, Saxons, Jutes. The Saxons knew about herbs and in their huge halls a hearty dinner was served once a day, with lavish feasts on special occasions. At one end of the hall the chief sat at a table on a raised platform, while trestle tables were set up for the rest of the diners along the sides. Grain was stone-ground to make flour and the bread was baked in earth ovens or under an iron pot on the hearth. Mutton was eaten roasted or boiled with herbs. There were greens and milk puddings made with barley, oats or wheat and honey, cheeses and oatcakes.

Dishes served in Saxon times must have been a delight: crawfish, watercress, wild strawberries, pork chops with apple sauce and ale.

When he died in 735, the Venerable Bede, Britain's most ancient historian, divided his prized supply of spices and delicacies among the brethren: lavender, aniseed, buckwheat, cinnamon, cloves, cubebs, cumin, coriander, cardamom (called grains of paradise), cypress roots (called garmgale, galmgale or galyngale), ginger (both raw and preserved), gromic, liquorice, dried prunes, raisins, pepper and sugar, which was thought of as a spice and used medicinally. Sugar was expensive, having been brought with the rest of these food treasures from the Far East by caravan and by Genoese and Venetian vessels from Alexandria.

Alfred of Wessex's halting of the Danes in 871 saved England's Anglo-Saxon identity and paved the way for the Danes' assimilation into English life. The Danes, who were good farmers, added many agricultural and culinary skills to the English repertoire, such as methods for storing butter and cheese, recipes for drinks made of honey and herbs, and for making fermented wheys and 'hung beef', which was pressed and smoke-dried.

William, Duke of Normandy, is said to have lain down on the beach after victoriously landing on English soil and swallowed two mouthfuls of sand, but the Bayeux Tapestry, stitched about ten years later to commemorate the Battle of Hastings, shows the duke and his brothers enjoying a richer feast. Meat is stewing in a pot hung on a bar between forked sticks; the fire

beneath is in a kind of iron grate. Another huge pot stands on its own three legs over a bonfire. Serving men are handing round meat roasted on spits; the diners have bowls for food and shallow cups of wine. The Bishop of Bayeux (the King's half-brother) says grace. And, most important in those forkless days, a servant kneels with finger bowl and napkins.

William I introduced the language and manners of the French court to Englishmen. Under the Normans the feudal system grew. Wealth was now based on land-holding and the manor was an almost self-sustaining economic unit: big house, grazing lands, common fields, mill, blacksmith shop, village. The English preference for mutton or beef over lamb or veal dates from the Saxon's careful nurture of his herd; cattle or sheep were killed only as needed or in the autumn – there was no way to feed them over the winter – and the meat could be salted or pickled. The term 'powdered meat' in old recipes refers to the salting process. William's nobles, wanting the best animals for meat, clashed with the Saxon farmers, who wanted to keep them for breeding.

The Normans still ate one big meal each day in the vast hall with the owner and his guests at the raised table and the rest of the diners along the sides, with the 'hall fire' in between. The smoke curled to the rooftop where meats were hung to cure – fireplaces with chimneys did not appear until about the thirteenth century. The first tablecloths were seen on these manor-house tables: narrow strips of linen draping the front, back, top and ends, consisting of five separate pieces designed to shield the knees of those at the head table from draughts and from the eyes of their social inferiors. Each diner had his own 'nef' – a set of spoons, knife and spike. Salt, finely crushed, was offered in a handsome silver-gilt saltcellar on the high table and in lesser vessels on the side tables. The downgrading of the lesser guests from the high to the side tables led to the salt marking a social boundary: 'below the salt' was the equivalent of a modern '*maître d'hôtel*'s 'Siberia' tables. Those elaborately folded napkins that old-fashioned waiters still produce – shoes, water-lilies, fleurs-de-lis – began on eleventh-century tables. The groom who served the bread to each cover (a platter for two people) wrapped the loaf 'in a stately way' in a napkin.

Roasted joints were borne in smoking on their spits, and the carved pieces were handed round on the tip of the knife. Boiled or stewed dishes were served on platters; sauces, of course, in saucers, to be dipped into – with pages standing by with basins of water and towels when needed. The flat bread that served as the diner's actual plate was renewed between courses.

William I so much enjoyed a soup or stew prepared by his cook that he rewarded the man with a manor, recorded in the Domesday Book: 'Robert Argyllon holdeth one carucate of land in Addington in the county of Surry, by the service of making one mess in an earthen pot in the kitchen of our Lord the King, on the day of his coronation, called *De la Groute*'. Seven centuries later, at the coronation of George IV, the Court of Claims record for 12 July 1820 reads: 'The petition of the Archbishop of Canterbury, which was presented by Sir G. Nayler, claiming to perform the service, of presenting a dish of *De la Groute* to the King at the Banquet, was considered by the Court, and decided to be allowed'. The dish was said to be a kind of plum porridge or water gruel with plums in it, and Sir G. Naylor was the lord of the same manor of Addington.

The failure of the Crusades forced the development of sea routes to the Orient and built up the land trade with the Middle East. Towns and commerce flourished, and with trade came new spices and wines. The Moorish occupation of Spain influenced not only the arts but cooking too. Dishes popular in the fourteenth and fifteenth centuries are still served in the Middle East. Pepper and spices from the East were so costly that rents could be paid in peppercorns – though now a 'peppercorn rent' means one that is just a token.

FROM THE FOURTEENTH TO THE SIXTEENTH CENTURY

T HE VERY FIRST English cookery book seems to be one written in the twelfth century by Alexander-Neckham, but the oldest really usable document of this kind is *The Forme of Cury*, compiled by the chief master-cooks of Richard II late in the fourteenth century. Other culinary writings of the time were called *Bokes of Kervyne*, which consisted of instructions in the knightly art of carving meats. At the king's or duke's table the carving was done by an honoured retainer and had a complex code. Some of the verbs are intriguing: 'slat a pike', 'spoil a hen', 'unbrace a mallard', 'fin a chub', 'untache a curlew', 'barb a lobster', 'border a pasty', 'thigh small birds', 'dysfygure that pecake'. The carver must know 'the fair handling of a knife'; he should place on the knife only two fingers and a thumb and the same on the bird or animal to be carved, and he must wipe the knife on a napkin – not the tablecloth. Here are two examples from *Babees Book*:

Displaye that crane: Take a crane, and unfolde his legges, and cut off his wynges and his legges, and sauce him with poudres of gynger, mustard, vynegre, and salte.

Dismembre that heron: Take a heron, and reyse his legges and his wynges as a crane, and sauce him with vynegre, poudre of gynger and salte.

Among the important books were *Liber Cure Cocorum* (1430), and *Boke of Nurture*, by John Russell (1450), usher and marshal to Humphrey, Duke of Gloucester.

Two fifteenth-century cookery books have provided us with recipes from the days of the Lancaster Henrys (Henry IV, Henry V, Henry VI) and the York monarchs – Edward IV, Edward V and Richard III – who came after them. The first is divided into three parts: *Kalendare de Potages dyuers*, *Kalendare de Leche Metys* and *Dyuerse bake metis*. Written in 1430 or 1440, it contains the bills of fare for several monumental banquets along with the recipes. The second book exists in the form of two early manuscripts, almost identical, with only a few recipes in each that are left out of the other. Many of the recipes in these books are French in

origin, but their French names have taken strange and wonderful forms that are amusing to decipher.

Many of these medieval dishes are delightfully spiced and seasoned with cinnamon, pepper, ginger, cloves, garlic, galingale, vinegar, verjuice and wine. Ale was widely used in cooking, and almond milk is so frequent in these recipes that any cook venturing to reproduce a medieval banquet might start by preparing a good supply (see p. 53).

Whale, porpoise, seal, sturgeon, swan, crane, heron, peacock – all appear on those fifteenth-century pages. Whale was served on the royal table and that of the Lord Mayor of London, roasted on a spit or boiled and sent down with peas. The tongue and the tail were the favoured parts. Porpoise was carried in whole, carved and eaten with mustard. (When the Tudor period began at the end of the century, Henry VII still thought porpoise a good dish to serve to an ambassador).

Medieval cooks were imaginative in preparing other fish too. Turbot was roasted on a spit, basted with verjuice and spices; haddock was cooked with garlic; skate was served with a sauce of the fish liver and mustard (later the English thought that skate were musical and played fiddles over the water to lure them); plaice was boiled with herbs in ale and served with a mustard sauce. Oyster and mussels were plentiful (oysters sold for four pence a bushel in 1491); the oysters were served on a bed of parsley that had been soaked in vinegar, a pleasant variation on today's squeeze of lemon juice.

The earliest written reference to English apples has survived in a tenure in Norfolk in the year 1200, requiring that two hundred 'pearmains' and four hogsheads of pearmain cider should be paid yearly at Michaelmas. There are about fifteen hundred early varieties of apples, including the golden pippins that Catherine the Great of Russia had sent to her every year from England, each apple wrapped in silver paper. The medieval custom of cooking fruit with spices survives not only in English pies and puddings but also whenever we grind a bit of pepper on to strawberries or melon to bring out the flavour.

These early cooks used eggs in every possible way. They made omelettes, fritters, pancakes, stuffings of hard-boiled eggs and herbs, and used eggs as thickeners in sauces and stews. Scrambled eggs cooked with fried onions were called 'hanoney'; a giant fried egg made with a number of whites centred with several yokes (it would still delight any child) was known as 'towres'. The large number of eggs called for in these old recipes results from their small size. Commercial egg farming has increased the size of hens' eggs, if not the flavour. The eggs of gulls, plovers and quail have always been considered delicacies in England and are almost always eaten hard-boiled.

Medieval cooks were also very fond of colour. Saffron's brilliant yellow (this was grown in the southern counties, hence the names of towns such as Saffron Walden) and the reddish hue of saunders (powdered sandalwood) were used along with green spinach or parsley juice to colour soups in stripes or to give marbleized effects; this is an attractive way to serve a creamy soup such as vichysoisse.

The variety and gargantuan quantities of food served at the great feasts and banquets of the kings, nobles and rich churchmen were truly overwhelming. Dinner, the chief meal, was eaten between eleven and twelve noon, while supper came at about five in the afternoon. At formal banquets, royal and otherwise, three meat courses were followed by three fish courses. Each of these six courses was brought to a close by something sweet: a pastry, a sweetmeat (called 'doucetye') or an elaborate device known as a 'soltelte', a subtlety. This was a construction of sugar and paste, sometimes combined with jelly or 'blamange', gorgeous to behold but made to be eaten. It might represent a hunting scene, or perhaps a ship fully armed; one depicted the interior of an abbey church with its various altars. Gilding was often used. This cook's sculpture or edible showpiece was designed to flatter the honoured guest, often in a way that we might not think of as particularly subtle.

Here is an excerpt from the *Noble Boke of Curtasye* by William Caxton, from *The Babees Book*: the do's and don'ts for the medieval table, many of them still the stock-in-trade of English nannies: 'Do not stuff mouth with bread or you will look like an ape.' 'Do not slurp soup.' 'Do not pat the dog.' (Pets roamed freely in medieval halls.) 'Do not spit in the basin when washing hands, especially if a prelate is present.'

Medieval farming, both on the king's lands and on those of his nobles, and on the common lands had not changed much since Roman times. Wheat, barley, oats, rye, vetches and beans were grown in the fields, which were divided into strips to give each serf a fair share. The manors and the monasteries had herb gardens and orchards and the monasteries often had

vineyards. Crops included plums, apples, cherries (brought in by the Romans); onions, garlic, leeks; cabbages, turnips, parsnips. Mayster Ion Gardener, who wrote the earliest English gardening book in about 1440, mentions radishes, spinach and lettuce. Kitchen gardens supplied herbs: sage, marjoram, rosemary, bugloss, borage, fennel, 'chykynweed' and 'rokett'.

Early in the fourteenth century gardening had reached a remarkably high level of skill in Flanders; by the sixteenth century Alva's reign of terror had driven many refugees to England, where Elizabeth I was on the throne. Their Flemish influence was felt in English gardens and at Elizabethan tables, where new flowers, vegetables and fruits began to appear: 'wardeines, quynces, peches, medlers, chestnottes'. In the other direction, native 'peres and aples' were exported to France in the form of 'pirry and sydre'.

In 1564 Mr John Hawkins, captain of the *Jesus of Lübeck*, brought back from his voyage to 'the coast of Guinea, and the Indies of Nova Hispania' the first sweet potato, *ipomea batata*. According to Richard Hakluyt in his *Principall Navigations . . . of the English Nation*: 'These potatoes be the most delicate rootes that may be eaten, and doe farre exceed our passeneps or carets. Their pines be of the bignes of two fists . . . and the inside eateth like an apple, but it is more delicious than any sweet apple sugred'. The arrival of the common potato, *solanum tuberosum*, is more obscure. It seems likely that the plant originated in Peru and reached Englishmen's hands by way of Virginia. Thomas Harriott, a geographer appointed by Sir Walter Raleigh to accompany Sir Richard Greville to the colony, returned with Sir Francis Drake and may have brought potatoes back to Raleigh. In any case, Raleigh planted them on his lands at Youghal in Ireland in about 1586. Some even say that it was ships from the Spanish Armada foundering off the coast of Ireland that brought 'Ireland's lazy root', as William Cobbett, writing in 1830, called it. Actually two hundred years went by before the potato became an English field crop.

Imported fruits were treats for those who could afford them. Catherine Parr, Henry VIII's last wife, sent messengers to Holland when she wanted a good fruit salad. Dried fruits, raisins, prunes had been coming from Portugal and the Levant since the thirteenth century; by the reign of Elizabeth I every large household had dates, figs and raisins for making sweet puddings.

In the reigns of the Tudor kings – Henry VII, Henry VIII, Edward VI – both lords and villagers kept livestock: oxen, cows, sheep, pigs and poultry. So little was known yet about winter feeding of farm animals that all the old or weakly had to be slaughtered in the autumn, and dried, salted or pickled to preserve the meat for the winter months.

At all times all manner of birds and beasts were hunted, snared and trapped. At Ingatestone Hall, built by Sir William Petre, then Secretary of State, in 1540, a wide variety of birds were eaten. His careful household accounts for the year 1552 give us a view of his larder; mallards, widgeons, wild ducks, teals, cranes, shovelards and shellfowls; woodcocks, snipes (or snites), marles, curlews, praines, plovers, redshanks, one goodwin (a New Year gift), and partridges; wild pigeons and those from the dovecote, larks, blackbirds, starlings and sparrows. Since meat and poultry were not eaten during Lent or on Fridays and Saturdays – as well as on other fast days, both sacred and secular – fresh and salt fish were important. The fish from the Hall ponds are not recorded in the account books, but we know of gifts of fish included carp, bream, roach, perch, tench and pike. Sea fish were purchased: sole, plaice, flounder, whiting, choyt (or cheyt), rochet, mullet, bret, smelt and cod; mackerel, gurnard, butt, bass, salmon and thornback. Oysters were eaten at Ingatestone Hall by the barrel from early July to late March and occasionally crabs, whelks and mussels would appear. Salt fish eked out the Lenten supply: ling, stockfish, haberdin. Stockfish, or cod, was dried and beaten by the cook with a club – or stock. Fish was important under Elizabeth. Statute laws were passed for its consumption in Lent: on Fridays and Saturdays, to encourage shipping and because of meat shortage; there were heavy penalties for non-obedience.

Since freshness is all-important in fish, transport has always been crucial to fish eating. Until rapid transport became possible, fish was eaten where it was caught. In Tudor times fresh fish for London came from neighbouring ponds and streams; all other fish were salted or

smoked before they arrived at Queenhythe, the chief watergate of the City of London. Nets were set in the Thames near London Bridge, and the size of the mesh was carefully regulated to let the young fish slip through, so as to avoid depleting the supply. The punishment for taking too-small fish was appropriate: in 1561 a woman caught 'bryngyng younge frye of dyvers kynd unlafull' was paraded round the town wearing a fragrant crown of tiny fishes.

Dried fish and salt bacon were sometimes hung from the yardarm on sailing vessels at sea. Fish were sold 'by the yard' in country markets; the damaged specimens were lined up on wooden boards a foot long and half a foot wide and sold off for 'a penny a boardful'.

Because it was hard to keep meat fresh and because only the big houses had hearths for roasting and baking, cook-shops where pies, puddings and baked meats were prepared began to spring up. The customer could buy a hot dish or bring in his own joint to be cooked. The prices for these services were regulated by law. William Fitz Stephen, in his preface to a biography of Thomas Becket, described one of these public cook-shops:

.... upon the river bank amid the wine that is sold from ships and wine cellars there daily according to the season, you may find viands, dishes roast, fried and boiled, fish great and small, the coarser food for the poor, the more delicate for the rich, such as venison and birds both big and little. If friends, weary with travel, should of a sudden come to any of the citizens ... they hasten to the river bank, and there all things desirable are ready to their hand.

They remained popular until the nineteenth century.

18

In the shops and at home, spices and onions or garlic improved the flavour of meat or fish that might not be perfectly fresh or that had lost some of its savour in being salted or pickled. The importance of the spice trade with the East was such that the Guild of Pepperers, already organized in the eleventh century, ultimately gave their name – Grossarii, from *peso grosso*, 'great beam', the weights given into their charge in the fourteenth century are the basis of our avoirdupois system – to the modern Grocer.

Bread, made in every home in medieval times, was sometimes baked in a communal oven. In eleventh-century London two companies – the White Bakers and the Brown Bakers – were incorporated in about 1307. The two finally got together two hundred years later. In early Tudor times the whitest flour – with most of the bran screened out through linen cloths (a process known as 'bolting') – was used to make 'paindemaigne', which by the fifteenth century was called 'manchet'. Flours 'bolted' through coarser cloths, so that more of the bran passed through, made the darker breads called 'cheat', 'cocket', or the whole-grain or rye mixtures known as 'tourte', 'brown', 'black', 'bis' or 'trete'. Oats were used for bread in the north; in the first edition of Samuel Johnson's dictionary they are defined as 'a grain, which in England is generally given to horses, but in Scotland supports the people'.

Bread was truly the staff of life and as far back as King John's reign there were laws controlling the price of bread, the most famous being the Assize of Bread of 1266.

Tudor drinks were ale, cider, perry, metheglin (a kind of mead, made from honey) or wine. All except the wine were made on the estate and well-to-do villagers also brewed their own ale, as did tenant farmers. The owners of inns and hostelries had their special brews; but the end of the Tudor period saw the decline of the monastery vineyards and most wine was imported.

The Flemish influence was again felt at English tables early in the fifteenth century when hops were added to the brewing of ale to make beer. Like any other new idea, this innovation was viewed with suspicion. King Henry VI in 1436 tried to soothe these fears with a commendation of 'biere' as 'notable, healthy, and temperate'; but it took years to catch on. Henry VIII went so far as to forbid the use of hops in beer (his own brewer was to use neither hops nor brimstone), but the practice continued. Wormwood was also used to give a bitter cast. Beer finally did replace ale, probably because the hops had a preservative effect, whereas ale would keep for only a few days in warm weather unless the alcoholic content was high.

Henry VIII, with both Lancastrian and Yorkist blood, took after his pleasure-loving grandfather, Edward IV. Although his father, Henry VII, was a wiry lightweight, he inherited from his mother a fine body 6 feet 2 inches tall. His love of good food and the size of the meals served to him resulted, by his fiftieth birthday, in a chest that measured 57 inches and a 54-inch waist.

Henry's household staff was impressive. The medieval division of authority between the Lord Chamberlain and the Lord Steward persisted. 'Abovestairs' was the Lord Chamberlain's realm, while the Lord Steward had a 'belowstairs' staff who saw to the king's comforts and nurture: bakehouse and pantry, cellar and buttery, saucery and spicery, wafery and confectionery, scullery and laundry, boiling house and scalding house. Food supplies were handled by the acatary and the poultry. Altogether the Lord Steward commanded in 1509 a staff of 220 and – at least in peacetime – controlled more funds than anyone else in the kingdom. Here is an Italian visitor's account of a banquet this staff produced at Greenwich for one thousand diners:

The guests remained at table for seven hours by the clock. All the viands placed before the King were borne by an 'elephant', or by 'lions', or 'panthers' or other 'animals', marvellously designed . . . The removal and replacing of dishes the whole time was incessant, the hall in every direction being full of fresh viands on their way to table. Every imaginable sort of meat known in the Kingdom was served, and fish in like manner, even down to prawn pasties. But the jellies of some twenty sorts perhaps, surpassed everything, being made in the shape of castles and animals of various descriptions, as beautiful and as admirable as can be imagined. (Anon., from Neville Williams, *Henry VIII and his Court*, 1971).

At one feast, celebrating the betrothal between the French Dauphin and Henry VIII's two-year-old daughter, Princess Mary, the guests were seated at a huge horseshoe-shaped table, the ladies alternating with the men – an arrangement that attracted attention. The service was glittering: 'On the buffet were eighty-two vases of pure gold of various sorts, the smallest being the size of a tall glass, one foot high, and drinking cups four foot high'. And the food was equally impressive: 'Beeves and muttons, porkers and fat hogs; capons and chickens by the dozen, six salmon, fifteen swans, four peacocks, fifty-four dozen larks; lashings of butter; green ginger, marmalades, quinces; gallons of cream and "frumenty".'

One Corpus Christi Day, when Henry VIII went to France and embraced Francis I upon the Field of the Cloth of Gold the English ladies watching the jousts drank rather freely, passing the wine flask and large cups among themselves and the French nobles. This English custom of sharing the same cup shocked the French. After one day of jousting both kings had hearty appetites, and a chef called Merryman provided for Henry's table in the first serving: soup, cygnets, venison, pike, heron; pies of pears, custard and fruit; in the second serving: soup, kid, sturgeon, peacock, quails, baked venison and tarts; in the third serving: soup, pheasant, agrets, kid, 'German haggis' and oranges. 'Beefs, veals and hogges' were provided in huge amounts for the rest of the entourage. Hypocras, a spiced wine, was the chief drink.

Banqueting on this scale was provided by Henry's own nobility, too. Here is the menu offered to the king and his group when they visited the marquess of Exeter at Horsley in Surrey, in the summer of 1533:

The first course consisted of salads of damsons, artichokes, cabbage lettuces, purslane and cucumbers, with which were served cold dishes of stewed sparrows, carp, capons in lemon, larded pheasant, duck, gulls, brews, forced rabbit, pasty of venison from fallow deer and pear pasty. This was followed by a hot course of stork, gannet, heron, pullets, quail, partridge, fresh sturgeon, pasty of venison from red deer, chickens baked in caudle and fritters. Once these dishes were removed the third and last course was served, consisting of jelly, blancmange, apples with pistachios, pears with carraway, filberts, scraped cheese with sugar, clotted cream with sugar, quince pie, marchpane and rounded off with the customary wafers and hippocras, the cordial of spiced wine that was the Tudor equivalent of a glass of port. (Neville Williams, *Henry VIII and his Court*, 1971).

A little later, in 1541, when inflation had begun to plague the English economy, the Lord Mayor of London was instructed to proclaim a price ceiling on sugar and arbitrary laws restricted the extravagance of the rich: at one 'messe' an archbishop, duke, marquis or earl could have seven main dishes; viscounts, barons or bishops might have six; substantial knights and squires were limited to five; and all others had to make do with four – though soup, salad, eggs, tripe, calves' feet and entrails, puddings and fruits, did not count.

The tables of royalty and the rich were well supplied with beef, mutton, pork, veal, game and venison; carp, pike, eels and lampreys; their bread was the finest manchet; they drank red and white French and German table wines, sweet wines from the Levant, ale, beer and cider. Englishmen of every class were thought by foreign visitors to eat better than their counterparts abroad, particularly when it came to meat. A Venetian ambassador wrote that English gentlemen, great epicures and avaricious by nature, served themselves the most delicate fare and gave their households the coarsest bread, beer and cold meat – baked on Sunday to last the week – but all of this in great abundance. The diet of the ordinary country people was 'black' bread, milk, cheese, eggs and occasionally bacon or fowl. Medieval English men of all classes had relished 'white meats' – dairy products – but in the prosperous early sixteenth century these were considered common fare. A depression late in the sixteenth century cut the meat supply for country people, but soups were popular; and one glorious English dish, bacon or ham ('collops') and eggs, may well date from this time.

Elizabeth I's eligibility brought glittering suitors to England's shores, and the diaries and letters of their retinues are a rich source of domestic details of the Elizabethan age. This was the first period of truly domestic building in England. Onto the medieval hall – a common meeting-place for all – were grafted family quarters on one side, servants' quarters on the other. Joint-stools – like little tables – were still used to sit on at mealtimes. But in royal and well-to-do households standing tables replaced the old trestle-tables that had been taken down after dinner and stacked against the wall in Medieval times. These new tables even had draw-tops, with extra leaves at each end. The Elizabethans loved fine table linen and each place would be set with a trencher, a napkin and a spoon.

As in former times, wine, ale and drinking vessels stood on the sideboard and a servant waited at the ready to serve them. In the kitchen the butler carefully chipped any cinders from the crust on the bread. The great saltcellar on the table and the basin, ewer and fine damask were still placed nearby. A great display of gilt or silver plate was essential for anyone with any social standing.

In middle-class households guests still used their own knives at table. During Elizabeth's reign forks were brought back from Italy, but they did not come into general use for some time.

Anthony, Viscount Montague, owner of Cowdray Castle in Sussex, drew up some directions for serving of meals in his household in 1595. The family dined in a chamber adjoining the great Buck Hall. Before the gentleman usher offered his service to his lordship at ten o'clock, the table had been set in an elaborate ritual. The yeoman usher began the ceremony, leading the yeoman of the ewry, with everyone making two bows to his lordship's table. The yeoman usher kissed his hand and placed it on the table to indicate where the cloth should be laid. When the cloth was in place the yeoman of the pantry arranged at each place a trencher, a roll of bread and a silver-hafted knife and spoon, bowing as he did so. The yeoman of the cellar placed the salt on the table and the drinking paraphernalia on the buffet. When the gentleman usher had informed his lordship that all was prepared, and when he had seen the carver and the sewer (table servant) wash their hands at the ewry board, he led the carver to the table – not without stopping twice to bow. The actual calling up of the dinner from the kitchen had to be relayed from the gentleman usher to the yeoman usher and on down through the ranks. Then, as the dishes were solemnly borne in, the whole household stood, reverently. The meat was set before his lordship, and – if it were done to his liking (he had instructed the clerk of the kitchen that no saucy scullion should affront his lordship's joint by turning his back on it while it roasted) – the carver could begin his task.

It has been explained that the elaborate menus of the period, just as complex as those of Henry IV, did not necessarily indicate complete gluttony on the part of Elizabethan diners, for each man chose the dishes he preferred; and the vast number assured that there would be plenty left for the second sitting – the meal for the huge retinue of servants.

One truly English dish – pork and pease – acquired a regal reputation on 10 May 1554 when Princess Elizabeth went to All Hallows Staining church to give thanks for her deliverance from the Tower of London. After her prayer she stepped next door to The King's Head at the Fenchurch Street corner of Mark Lane and ate a hearty meal of pork and pease. The parish clerk ordered the church bells to be rung vigorously during the meal, and Elizabeth is said to have been generous with her gratuity. With this sudden wealth the clerk invited his friends and neighbours in to celebrate the occasion by a pork-and-pease dinner at his house, and this feast became an annual event. After the clerk's death the parishioners changed the date to November, the anniversary of Elizabeth's coming to the throne, and gathered for their pork-and-pease dinner at the tavern, which by then called itself The Queen's Head. The metal dish and cover that held the original pork and pease eaten by Elizabeth (or so the owners say) is preserved today in the Marble Room of The London Tavern.

The rise of tenant farming, begun in the thirteenth century and toppling the feudal system by the middle of the fifteenth, was speeded up by the devastation of the Black Death and the Wars of the Roses. The sixteenth century brought the burgeoning of the wool trade, and the progressive enclosing of the common lands to provide grazing for sheep often deprived the poor of their cows and so of dairy products. Earlier menus include such interesting dishes as porpoise, seal or whale meat, but these seem to have gone out of fashion by the late sixteenth century. Vegetables were not popular and salads were made principally from onions and herbs.

Breakfasts in England consisted of bread, beer or wine, herring or sprats (salted or pickled), boiled beef or mutton. The supper food was much the same. The variety of game was still enormous. Here are the tasty items from the household records of My Lady Margaret and Maister Ingeram Percey: 'cranys, redshankes, fesauntes, sholardes, pacokes, knottes, bustardes, great byreds, hearonsewys, bytterns, reys, kyrlewes, wegions, dottrells, ternes, smale byrdes'.

On the Churche's 'fysshe dayes' salt herrings, salmon, eels, sprats and fresh fish replaced meat. During Elizabeth's reign there were two powerful spurs to extra enforcement of meatless days: first, the need to encourage shipbuilding and the training of sailors; and second, the high price of meat. Englishmen were urged to eat fish on Wednesdays as well as Fridays and on any other fast day that seemed suitable.

The first book to deal with the preparation of food in a general way was written by Andrew Boorde in 1542 and called *A Dyetary of Helth*. Having abandoned his vocation as a monk and studied medicine overseas, Boorde served Henry VIII as doctor and the king sent him on a tour of all the universities of Christendom. After another stay in the charterhouse he set out in 1534 to tour France and Spain on behalf of his monarch, to report on the reactions abroad to Henry's divorce and remarriage. The candid truth-telling in his reports earned him banishment to the university in Glasgow. The next year found him first in Cambridge, then setting off on his longest voyage, which took him all the way to Jersualem. In 1542 Andrew Boorde settled in Montpellier, and there he wrote his most famous works, including *A Dyetary of Helth*, which expounded a theory that is enjoying great vogue today: health depends on diet. It is tempting to quote endlessly from Boorde, but let's content ourselves with his description of the range of meats in his day, not just roast beef but:

Pygges, specially some pygges, is nutrytyve; and made in a gelye it is restoratyve, so be it the pygee be fleed, the skyn taken off and then stewed with restoratyves, as a cocke is stewed to make a gelye. A yonge fatte pygge in physicke is singularly praysed, if it be well ordered in the rostynge, the skyn not eaten.

Fysshe may be sod, rostyd, brulyd and baken, every one after their kynde and use, and fasshyon of the countree, as the coke and the physicyon wiyll agre and devyse. For a good coke is half a physicyon. for the chefe physycke (the counceyll of a physycyon excepte) dothe come from the kytchyn; wherefore the physycyon and coke for sycke men must consult togyther for the preparacion of meate for sycke men.

Boorde's chapter on aphrodisiacs advocates 'artechokes and rockat', and recommends 'quycke-beam, seene, sticados, hartys tongue, mayden here, pulyall mountane, borage, organum; sugar and whyte wyne' to cure melancholy.

Soups

White Bean Soup

For to make a potage feneboiles :
Take white beans and seeth them in water and
bray the beans in a mortar all to nought and let
it seeth in almonds milk and do therein wine
and honey and seeth raisins in wine and do
thereto serve it forth. (The Forme of Cury, 1378)

Serves 4
6 OZ (1 CUP) DRIED WHITE BEANS
½ PT (1–1½ CUPS) ALMOND MILK (*see p.* 53)
¼ PT (½ CUP) WHITE WINE
4 TBS HONEY
1 OZ (¾ CUP) RAISINS, PLUMPED IN HOT VINEGAR
   IN WHICH YOU HAVE DISSOLVED A LITTLE
   BROWN SUGAR

Soak the beans in water for 1 hour, drain, put
them in a saucepan and cover with salted
water. Simmer until tender, for about 1 hour.
Drain, reserving the cooking water. Put the
beans into a saucepan with the almond milk,
wine and honey and simmer for 10 minutes. If
the soup is too thick, dilute it with the cooking
water. Season to taste and add the drained
raisins. Simmer for 5 minutes and serve.

Cold Fennel Soup

Cold brewet :
Take crumb of almonds dry it in a cloth and
when it is dried do it in a vessel, do thereto salt,
sugar, and white powder of ginger and juice of
fennel and wine and let it well stand, lay full
and mix and drip it forth.
(The Forme of Cury, 1378)

Serves 3–4
1¼ PT (3 CUPS) WATER
¼ PT (½ CUP) WHITE WINE
1 HEAD FENNEL, SLICED, WITH SOME OF THE
   FEATHERY TOP RESERVED
1 TSP SUGAR
½ TSP GINGER
2 OZ (½ CUP) GROUND ALMONDS

Bring the water and wine to the boil, add salt
to taste and cook the fennel in the liquid until
tender. Purée in a blender. Return to the cleaned
pan, add the ginger and almonds, season to
taste and simmer for 15 minutes. Leave to cool.
Serve chilled, sprinkled with some of the
feathery top of the fennel, finely chopped.

Slit Leek Soup

Take white leeks and slit them and do them to
seeth in wine, oil and salt, rost bread and lay in
dish and the liquor above and serve it forth.
(The Forme of Cury, 1378)

Serves 3–4
6–8 LEEKS, THE WHITE PART ONLY, SLICED
   LENGTHWAYS
2 TBS OIL
1 BOTTLE WHITE WINE, OR HALF WINE AND HALF
   VEGETABLE STOCK
6–8 SMALL SLICES FRENCH BREAD, TOASTED

Season the finely slivered leeks and sauté in
the oil until tender, but do not burn them.
Add the wine (or wine and stock) and simmer,
partially covered, for 30–45 minutes, seasoning
to taste. Arrange the crisp toast slices in a
warmed tureen and pour the soup over them.
Serve at once.

Onion Soup with Almonds

Dorry, Soupes Dorrye: endored or 'gilded'
soups glazed with almond milk. The term
'endoring' covered any method which gave the
food a golden appearance: by the use of egg
yolks, saffron, or in this case a crusty surface
made of bread and almonds, such as the cheese
and bread we are used to in French onion soup.

For to make soupes dorry :
Nym onions and mince them small and fry them in
oil d'olif – Nym wine and boil it with the onions
toast white bread and do it in dishes and good
almond milk also and do them about and serve
it forth. (Two Fifteenth-century Cookery Books)

Serves 4
6 OZ (2 CUPS) FINELY CHOPPED ONION
2–3 TBS OLIVE OIL
I PT (2½ CUPS) WHITE WINE
I PT (2½ CUPS) ALMOND MILK (*see p.* 53)
3 TBS COARSELY GROUND ALMONDS
8 SLICES FRENCH BREAD, LIGHTLY TOASTED
A LITTLE EXTRA OIL AND BUTTER

Sauté the onions in the oil until golden; add the wine and almond milk and season to taste. Simmer for 20–30 minutes. Meanwhile sauté the ground almonds in a little extra oil until they are golden but not too crisp. Spoon the soup into individual fireproof bowls, or into a large bowl shallow enough to fit under the grill. Lay a slice of toast on top of the soup in each bowl or spread all the slices out on the larger one. Scatter the oily almonds on top of the toast, dot with butter and grill very lightly.

Split Pea Soup with Beans and Onions

Lange wortes de pesoun:
Take grene pesyn, an washe hem clene an caste hem on a putte, an boyle hem tyl they breste, an thanne take hem vyppe of the potte, an put hem with brothe yn a-nother potte, an lete hem kele; than draw hem thorw a straynowre in-to a fayre potte, an than take oynonys, an screde hem in to or thre, an take hole wortys and boyle hem in fayre water: and take hem vyppe, an ley hem on a fayre bord, an cytte on iij or iiij, an key hem to the oynonys in the potte, to be drawyd pesyn; an let hem boyle tyl they ben tendyr; an thanne tak fayre oyle and frye hem, or ellys sum fresche brothe of sum maner fresche fysshe, an caste there-to, an Safron, an salt a quantyte, and serue it forth.
(*Two Fifteenth-century Cookery Books*)

Serves 4
6 OZ (I CUP) SPLIT GREEN PEAS
2 PT (5 CUPS) WATER
¼ LB STRING BEANS
3 ONIONS, SLICED
4 TBS OLIVE OIL
I TSP SALT
¼ TSP GROUND PEPPER

Put the peas into a saucepan with the water. Bring to the boil and cook gently for 1½ hours, partially covered. Meanwhile boil the string beans until tender but still crisp. Fry the sliced onions in the oil until golden. Chop the drained string beans and add to the onions in the pan. Cook for a few minutes. Drain off the oil and add the onions and the beans to the pea soup. Taste and season with salt and pepper.

Soup in Three Colours

Medieval English people were very visual about their food. They loved strange shapes and particularly enjoyed dishes of unusual colours. This is my version of a popular multicoloured soup.

Serves 4–6
1½–2 PTS (4 CUPS) CREAMY BLENDED POTATO SOUP
⅛ TSP SAFFRON
4 TBS (¼ CUP) COOKED SPINACH OR FRESH PARSLEY, CHOPPED

Divide the soup into three portions. Leave the first portion white and chill. Infuse the second portion with the saffron, over very low heat, until it is brightly coloured. Strain and chill. Then infuse the third portion with the chopped spinach or parsley, over low heat, straining when it has turned a good green. Chill. When you are ready to serve, put some soup of each colour into each individual bowl, making a pattern of the three colours and keeping them as distinct as possible.

Saffron Soup

For to make eyerin in bruet:
Nym water and welle it and break eyerin and cast them in and grind pepper and saffron and temper up with sweet milk and boil it and hack cheese small and cast therein and mix it forth.
(*The Forme of Cury, 1378*)

Serves 2–3

1 PT (2½ CUPS) MILK
⅛ TSP SAFFRON
⅛ TSP GROUND PEPPER
½ TSP SALT
½ EGGS
2 OZ (½ CUP) GRATED CHEESE

Heat the milk, saffron, pepper and salt to boiling point. Stir in the cheese and cook, still stirring, for 1 minute. Beat the eggs in a bowl and blend into the soup, stirring constantly with a fork. Serve as soon as the eggs are set.

Vegetable Marrow Soup

Gourdes in potage :
Take young gourdes pare them and cut them in pieces. Cast them in gode broth and do it to a good party of oynons minced ; take pork soden, grind it and mix it with yolkes of eggs, do it to saffron and salt and mix it forth with sweet aromatic powder.
(*The Forme of Cury, 1378*)

Serves 4
5 OZ (1 CUP) PEELED, DICED VEGETABLE MARROW
   (OR SQUASH)
2 PT (5 CUPS) VEGETABLE STOCK
2 ONIONS, CHOPPED
1 TSP CINNAMON
¼ TSP NUTMEG
½ TSP GINGER
½ LB (½ CUP) LEAN PORK, MINCED (GROUND)
4 EGG YOLKS

Simmer the squash in the stock with the onions and spices for 20 minutes or until tender. Add the pork and cook until the meat is no longer pink. Beat the egg yolks in a bowl and blend in some of the hot stock, then stir back into the soup and cook very gently, stirring, until thickened. Do not let it boil. Season to taste and serve.

Chicken Soup with Pork

(*A Noble Boke of Cookery*)

Serves 4–6
A 2½ LB CHICKEN
2½ LB BONELESS PORK (IN ONE PIECE)
1 TSP CUMIN
¼ TSP SAFFRON
4–5 SPRIGS PARSLEY
4 OZ (2 CUPS) BREADCRUMBS

Put the chicken and pork into a stewing-pan with water, seasonings and spices. Bring to the boil and simmer briskly for 45 minutes. Lift out the chicken and remove bones and skin, returning these to the pot to add extra flavour. Continue to simmer until the pork is very tender. Remove the pork, mince it and the chicken meat and toss and mix them in a bowl with the breadcrumbs. Put them in a saucepan and gradually strain in the cooking broth, stirring until the soup takes on a rich creamy consistency. Bring to the boil and simmer for another 5–10 minutes. A piece of butter added just before serving improves the flavour. Add extra pepper and salt if needed.

You may need extra chicken broth (made with a cube if necessary) if the soup is too thick; it should be like light cream.

Fish Soup with Saffron

This is quite like the Marseilles *bouillabaisse* and shows the Mediterranean influence prevalent in England at this time.

Tenche in cyueye :
Take a tenche, an skalde hym, roste hym, grynde Pepir an Safroun, Brede an Ale, & melle it to-gederys ; take Oynonys, hakke hem, an frye hem in Oyle, & do hem ther-to, and messe hem forth. (Two Fifteenth-century Cookery Books)

Serves 2
2–3 LB TENCH OR CARP, FILLETED
1 PT (2½ CUPS) FISH STOCK
½ PT (1 CUP) LIGHT ALE
¼ TSP SAFFRON

¼ TSP PEPPER
2 SLICES BREAD, CRUMBLED
2 ONIONS, SLICED THINLY
3 TBS OLIVE OIL

Lightly rub the fish with oil or butter and grill. Meanwhile heat the stock and ale in a saucepan and add the saffron and pepper; simmer briskly for 15 minutes. Stir in the bread to thicken and cook for another 5 minutes. Fry the onions in oil until soft and golden and add them, drained, to the soup. Purée in a blender or rub through a sieve to give a smooth consistency. Arrange the fish on a dish and pour the soup over it. Taste and add salt and pepper if needed.

Oyster Broth

This soup has a curious, rather oriental flavour and adapts well to mussels, which possibly make an even better soup. Choose small oysters, which have a more suitable texture.

Oystrys in bruette :
Take and schene Oystrys, an kepe the water
that cometh of hem, an strayne it, an put it in a
potte, & Ale ther-to, an a lytil brede ther-to ;
put Gyngere, Canel, Pouder of pepir ther-to,
Safroun an Salt ; an whan it is y-now al-moste,
putte on thin Oystrys : loke that they ben wyl
y-wasshe for the schullys : & than serue forth.
(Two Fifteenth-century Cookery Books)

Serves 4
2 PT (5 CUPS) OYSTERS
½ PT (1 CUP) ALE
½ OZ (¼ CUP) BREADCRUMBS
½ TSP GINGER
1 TSP CINNAMON
¼ TSP PEPPER
½ TSP SALT

Scrub the oysters thoroughly and wash them in cold water. Place them in a frying pan over high heat until the shells open. Remove from the pan; discard the shells and reserve the oysters and liquid. Strain the liquid through muslin or cheesecloth and combine with the ale in a saucepan. Bring to the boil.

Stir in the crumbs, spices and seasonings and simmer for 15 minutes. Add the oysters and cook until they curl. Taste and add salt and pepper if needed.

Eggs

Brie Tart

Take a crust inch deep in a trap ; take yolks of
eggs raw and cheese ruayn and meddle it and
the yolks together and do thereto powder, ginger,
sugar, safron, and salt, do it in a trap, bake it
well and serve it forth.
(The Forme of Cury, 1378)

Serves 5–6
¾ LB FLAKY PASTRY
1 PT (2½ CUPS) CREAM
1 TSP SAFFRON
¼ LB (1 CUP) BRIE CHEESE, WITHOUT RIND
½ TSP GINGER
1 TSP SUGAR
3 EGGS PLUS 2 EXTRA YOLKS

Line a 10-inch quiche dish with the pastry and bake at 400° (Mark 6) for 10 minutes. Put the cream, saffron and cheese in a covered bowl in the oven at 200° (Mark ½) for 20–30 minutes, until the cheese has melted somewhat and the saffron has dissolved and coloured the cream. Transfer the mixture to a blender and blend just long enough to amalgamate properly. Add the ginger, sugar and a seasoning of salt and pepper, tasting carefully after each addition.

Beat the eggs with a fork or rotary beater, in a separate bowl, and pour the contents of the blender into them, still whipping. Pour the resulting mixture into the quiche shell and bake at 350° (Mark 4) for 30 minutes, or until set and puffy.

Serve with a green salad flavoured with herbs, using lemon juice instead of vinegar in the dressing, as it is pleasanter with the sharp taste of the brie.

Eggs in Pastry Cases

Pety Pernollys :
Take fayre Floure, Safroun, Sugre, & Salt,
& make ther-of past ; then make smal cofyns ;
then take yolkys of Eyroun, & trye hem fro tho
whyte ; & lat the yolkys be al hole, & not
to-broke, & ley iij or iiij yolkys in a cofyn ; an
than take marow of bonys, to or iij gobettys, &
cowche in the cofynn ; than take pouder Gyngere,
Sugre, Roysonys of coraunce, & caste a-boue ;
& than kyuere thin cofyn with the same past, &
bake hem, & frye hem in fayre grece, & serue
forth. (Two Fifteenth-century Cookery Books)

Serves 4
4 TBS WATER
⅛ TSP SAFFRON
4½ OZ (1 CUP) FLOUR
2 TBS SUGAR
½ TSP SALT
3 OZ (6 TBS) BUTTER
1 EGG YOLK
ABOUT 1½ TBS BEEF MARROW
ABOUT 1 TSP POWDERED GINGER
ABOUT 1 TSP SUGAR
4 LARGE EGG YOLKS (OR 8 SMALL ONES)

Bring the water to the boil with the saffron, then allow to cool. Chill. Sift the flour with the sugar and salt. Cut in the butter with a pastry blender or two knives. Work in the egg yolk and saffron-tinted water. When the mixture is well blended, roll out on a floured board. Line four patty shells with the pastry and bake for 8–10 minutes at 400° (Mark 6). Lower the oven to 350° (Mark 4). Put 1 tsp chopped marrow, a small pinch of ginger and sugar and 1 large or 2 small egg yolks into each pastry shell and bake in the oven until the egg yolks are just set. This makes an attractive starter for a meal.

Lombardy Quiche

This is a typical dish of the Middle Ages and was served to Henry IV at his coronation feast; it is also mentioned in the *Forme of Cury*. A pinch of saffron can be heated with the cream and added to the eggs, and pepper is included in some versions. It seems to have been a sweet and savoury custard-pie served with poultry and game, rather than as a sweetmeat. As vegetables were not eaten with the main courses, and as there were no forks, a quiche was an easy dish to eat with the fingers, thus making the meat courses seem less tedious. The pastry shells were called 'coffins' or 'traps' in these days. This recipe is clearly an early form of *quiche lorraine* and must have come to England from Lombardy.

Crustade Lombarde :
Take gode creme, & leuys of Percely, & Eyroun,
the yolkys & the whyte, & breke hem ther-to,
& strayne thorwe a straynoure, tyl it be so styf
that it wol bere hym-self ; than take fayre Marwe,
& Datys y-cutte in ij or iij & Prunes ; &
putte the Datys an the Prunes & Marwe on a
fayre Cofynne, y-mad of fayre past, & put the
cofyn on the oven tyl it be a lytel hard ; thanne
draw hem out of the oven ; take the lycour and
putte ther-on, & fylle it vyppe, & caste Sugre
y-now on, & Salt ; than lat bake to-gederys tyl
it be y-now ; & if it be in lente, let the Eyroun
& the Marwe out, & thanne serue it forth.
(Two Fifteenth-century Cookery Books)

1 PT (2 CUPS) THICK CREAM
3 EGGS PLUS 2 YOLKS
4 TBS RAW BEEF MARROW, CHOPPED
2 OZ (½ CUP) DATES, PITTED AND MINCED
2 OZ (½ CUP) PRUNES, PITTED AND MINCED
9-INCH PASTRY SHELL, PRE-BAKED
2 TBS PARSLEY, FINELY CHOPPED

Heat the cream but do not boil. Beat the eggs and the extra yolks in a bowl and then pour in the hot cream, beating as you do so. Arrange the marrow, dates and prunes in the pastry shell and pour in the custard. Stir in the parsley. Bake at 350° (Mark 4) for 25 minutes.

Tansey

Tansey was considered a laxative and blood purifier, and is still grown and eaten for health reasons in parts of the United States. (*Two Fifteenth-century Cookery Books*)

Serves 2–3
6 EGGS
2 TBS TANSEY, CHOPPED AND BLANCHED TO REMOVE BITTER TASTE
1 TBS TANSEY JUICE
1 OZ (2 TBS) BUTTER

Beat the eggs lightly in a bowl. Extract the juice from a little tansey by crushing it in a mortar or putting it through a juice extractor. Stir the chopped herbs and the juice into the eggs and season with pepper and salt. Melt the butter in an omelet pan and make a fluffy omelet in the usual way.

Fish

Mackerel with Mint

Freshe Makrelle :
To dight a freche makerelle tak and draw a makerelle at the gil and let the belly be hole and wesche hym and mak the sauce of water and salt and when it boilithe cast in mynt and parsley and put in the fische and serve it furthe with sorell sauce. (A Noble Boke of Cookery)

Serves 2
2 MACKEREL
1 PT (2½ CUPS) WATER
2 TSP SALT
2–3 OZ (1 CUP) FRESH MINT, ROUGHLY CHOPPED

Take fresh mackerel, draw them through the gills and wash them, but do not slit the belly. Bring the salted water to the boil in a rather shallow pan and put in plenty of fresh mint, enough to make a bed for the fish. Put in the fish, bring to the boil and lower the heat at once. Cook until the fish flakes easily, remove, drain and place on a warmed serving dish. Remove the top skin and cover with sorrel sauce. (Page 53). Serve at once.

Fish Marinade

Gele of fish :
Take Tench, pikes, eels, turbot, and place, carve them to pieces, scald them and wash them clean, dry them with a cloth, do them in a pan, do thereto half vinegar and half wine and seeth it well and take the Fish and pick it clean, cool the broth thro' a cloth into an earthen pan. Do thereto powder of pepper and safron enough, let it seeth and skim it well when it is done, do off the grease clean, lay fishe on chargeours and

cool the sewe thro' a cloth and serve it forth.
(*The Forme of Cury, 1378*)

Serves 4
½ PT (1 CUP) VINEGAR
½ PT (1 CUP) WINE
¼ TSP PEPPER
⅛ TSP SAFFRON
2 LBS TENCH, PIKE, EEL, TURBOT OR PLAICE
   CLEANED AND FILLETED (SEPARATELY OR MIXED)

Combine the vinegar, wine, pepper and saffron
in a saucepan. Bring to the boil and simmer
for 10 minutes. Add fish and poach for a further
10 minutes, or until the fish flakes. Remove and
leave to cool. Strain the marinade and pour
over the fish. Marinate overnight.

Fish Mousse with Aspic

Fish gelye :
*Take newe Pykys, an draw hem, an smyte hem
to pecys, & sethe in the same lycoure that thou
doste Gelye of Fleysshe ; an whan they ben
y-now, take Perchys and Tenchys, & sethe ;
& Elys, an kutte hem in fayre pecys, and
waysshe hem, & putte hem in the same lycoure,
& loke thine lycoure be styf y-now ; & if it
wolle notte cacche, take Soundys of watteryd
Stokkefysshe, or ellys Skynnys, or Plays, an
caste ther-to, & sethe ouer the fyre, & skeme it
wyl ; & when it ys y-now, let nowt the Fysshe
breke ; thenne take the lycoure fro the fyre, & do
as thou dedyst be that other Gelye, saue, pylle
the Fysshe & ley ther-off in dysshis, that is,
perche & suche, and Flowre hem, & serue forthe.*
(*Two Fifteenth-century Cookery Books*)

Serves 4
Fish stock
2 LB FISH BONES AND TRIMMINGS
2 PT (5 CUPS) WATER
1 LARGE ONION
2 BAY LEAVES
1 TBS SALT
½ TSP PEPPER
1 STICK CELERY

6 SPRIGS PARSLEY
1 CARROT
1 TSP THYME

Mousse
½ LB WHITE FISH (PLAICE, WHITING, PIKE, ETC.)
2 TBS WHITE WINE
4 TSP (¼ CUP) STOCK
¼ OZ (½ ENVELOPE) GELATINE
2 TBS WATER
½ TSP TARRAGON
1 SMALL ONION, CHOPPED
1 TSP LEMON JUICE
⅛ TSP PEPPER
¼ TSP SALT
¼ PT (½ CUP) THICK CREAM

Filling
½ OZ (1 PACKAGE) GELATINE
1¼ PT (3 CUPS) FISH STOCK
½ LB FISH FILLETS (SOLE, PLAICE OR HALIBUT)

Make the stock by cooking all the ingredients
together for 30 minutes. Strain.

Poach the fish in the wine and the stock.
Soften the gelatine in the water. When the
fish is cooked, lift it out and stir the softened
gelatine into the strained wine and stock
mixture. Chop the fish and purée in the
blender with the wine and stock, the tarragon
and the chopped onion. Stir in the lemon
juice and seasoning and chill over ice. Beat
the cream until peaks form and fold into the
mousse just before it sets. Pour into a 2-pint
(5-cup) oiled mould.

Dissolve the remaining gelatine in 4
tablespoons (¼ cup) of the fish stock. Poach
the fillets in 1 pint (2 cups) of the stock. When
they are done, remove them, drain and cool.
Place the fillets on top of the mousse mixture
in the mould. Take ½ pint (1 cup) of the
strained stock in which the fillets were cooked
and stir into the softened gelatine. Chill over
ice until the mixture starts to thicken, then pour
over the fish fillets in the mould. Chill again.
Turn out to serve.

Tart of Pickled Fish
Tart de brymlent :

Take figs and raisins and wash them in wine and grind them with apples and pears clean picked, take them up and cast them in a pot with wine and sugar take salmon sodden, or codling or haddock, and bray them small and do thereto white powder and whole spices and salt & seeth it and when it is sodden enough take it up and do it in a vessel and let it cool, make a coffin an inch deep and do the farse therein. Plant it above with prunes and damsyns, take the stones out and with dates quartered and picked clean and cover the coffin and bake it well and serve it forth. (The Forme of Cury, 1378)

Serves 2–4

2 OZ ($\frac{1}{2}$ CUP) FIGS
2 OZ ($\frac{1}{2}$ CUP) RAISINS
4 APPLES, PEELED, CORED AND CHOPPED
2 PEARS, PEELED, CORED AND CHOPPED
$\frac{1}{2}$ PT (I CUP) WINE
2 OZ ($\frac{1}{4}$ CUP) SUGAR
$\frac{1}{2}$ LB PICKLED SALMON, COD OR HADDOCK
$\frac{1}{4}$ TSP EACH GINGER, NUTMEG, WHOLE ALLSPICE
$\frac{1}{2}$ TSP CINNAMON
$\frac{1}{2}$ TSP SALT
10-INCH PASTRY SHELL, I INCH DEEP
4 PRUNES, STONED AND QUARTERED
4 DATES, PITTED AND QUARTERED
4 DAMSONS, STONED AND QUARTERED

Take the figs and raisins, wash them in wine and mince with the apples and pears. Put in a pan with the wine and sugar, pickled salmon, cod or haddock, and chop finely. Mix in the spices and salt and cook together for 15 minutes. Leave to cool. Put the fish and fruit forcemeats into the pastry shell. Arrange the prunes, dates and damsons on top and bake at 375° (Mark 5) for 30–40 minutes.

Spiced Fish

For to make egardusye :
Tak Lucys or Tenches and hack them small in gobbets and fry them in oil de olive and seeth nym vinegar and the third part of sugar and minced onions small and boil altogether and cast therein cloves, maces, & quibibs and serve it forth. (The Forme of Cury, 1378)

Serves 3–4

1$\frac{1}{2}$ LB PIKE OR OTHER FIRM WHITE FISH, CUT INTO
   4 OR 5 CHUNKS
2 TBS FLOUR
4 TBS OLIVE OIL
$\frac{3}{4}$ LB ($\frac{1}{2}$ CUP) HONEY
6 FL OZ ($\frac{3}{4}$ CUP) VINEGAR
I SMALL ONION, CHOPPED
3 CLOVES
$\frac{1}{2}$ TSP GROUND MACE
$\frac{1}{4}$ TSP BLACK PEPPER

Dust the fish chunks in the flour. Fry in the olive oil until crisp and light brown. Put the fish pieces into a 4 pint (2$\frac{1}{2}$ cup) saucepan. Cover with the honey and vinegar, chopped onion, cloves, mace and pepper. Simmer until the fish is tender. Serve.

Crab and Salmon Mould

Vyaunde de Cyprys in Lente :
Take gode thikke mylke of Almaundys, & do it on a potte : & nyme the Fleysshe of gode Crabbys, & gode Samoun, & bray it smal, & tempere yt vppe with the forsayd mylke ; boyle it, an lye it with floure of Rys or Amyndoun, an make it chargeaunt ; when it ys y-boylid, do ther-to whyte Sugre, a gode quantyte of whyte Vernage Pime, with the wyne, Pome-garnade. When it is y-dressyd, straw a-boue the grayne of Pome-garnade.
(Two Fifteenth-century Cookery Books)

Serves 3–4

$\frac{1}{2}$ LB FRESH CRABMEAT, COOKED
$\frac{1}{2}$ LB SALMON, COOKED
$\frac{1}{2}$ PT (I CUP) ALMOND MILK (*see p. 53*)
2 TBS RICE FLOUR
2 TBS WHITE WINE
2 TBS SUGAR
SEEDS FROM I–2 POMEGRANATES

Flake the crab meat and salmon, put them in a blender with the almond milk and purée. Spoon into a saucepan, heat gently and sprinkle in the flour. Stir until thickened and then add the wine and sugar. Stir in the pomegranate seeds and season to taste with a little pepper and salt. Chill in a wetted mould. Turn out to serve.

This dish is such an attractive colour – pale pink studded with the scarlet seeds of the pomegranate – that it seems a nice idea to redden it even further by surrounding the mould with a salad of sliced beetroot, radishes and young beetroot-tops, with a vinaigrette dressing.

Lobster and Rice

This dish was again part of Henry IV's coronation feast.

Blamanger of fyshe :
Take rys, an sethe hem tylle they brekyn & late
hem kele ; than caste ther-to mylke of Almaundys ;
nym Perche or Lobstere, & do ther-to, & melle
it ; than nym Sugre with pouder Gyngere, &
caste ther-to, & make it chargeaunt, an than
serue it forth.
(*Two Fifteenth-century Cookery Books*)

Serves 2–3
2 CUPS COLD BOILED RICE
¼ PT (½ CUP) ALMOND MILK (*see p. 53*)
1 TSP GROUND GINGER
¾ LB COOKED LOBSTER, COLD

Blend the rice, milk and ginger well. Toss lightly with the lobster, then cover and refrigerate covered for 1 hour before serving.

Mussels in Broth

Muskels in bruet :
Take muskels, pick them, seeth them with the
own broth, make a layer of crust and vinegar,
do in onions minced & cast the muskels thereto &
seeth it, and do thereto bread with a little salt &
safron the samewise make of oysters.
(*The Forme of Cury, 1378*)

Serves 2
12 MUSSELS

2 OZ (1 CUP) BREADCRUMBS
4 TBS VINEGAR
1 ONION, CHOPPED
A PINCH OF SAFFRON

Take the mussels, pick them over and clean them. Allow them to open in a hot pan and simmer them for a few seconds in their own juice. Arrange a layer of bread crumbs, soaked in the vinegar, in a fireproof dish and cover with a thin layer of very finely chopped blanched onion. Place the mussels on the half-shell on the bread, sprinkle with a little more onion, salt and the finely ground saffron. Serve cold.

Oysters can be prepared in the same way.

Fish Tart

Tart of fish :
Take Eels and salmon and smite them in pieces,
and stew it in almonds milk and verjuice, draw
up on almonds milk with the stew, pick out the
bones clean of the fish and save the middle piece
whole of the Eels and grind that over fish small
and do thereto powdr sugar and salt & grated
bread and farce the eels therewith as the bones
were meddle them over some of the farse and the
milk together and colour it with sanders make a
crust in a trap as before and bake it therein and
serve it forth. (*The Forme of Cury, 1378*)

Serves 2–3
1 SMALL EEL, SKINNED
1 LB SALMON
1 PT (2½ CUPS) ALMOND MILK (*see p. 53*)
2 TBS VERJUICE (*see p. 53*)
2 TBS SUGAR
½ TSP SALT
2 OZ (1 CUP) BREADCRUMBS
¾ LB SHORT PASTRY

Cut the eel into 2″ pieces, leaving the middle section in a 4-5″ piece. Slice the salmon. Stew in the almond milk and verjuice. Strain off the almond milk and reserve ½ pint (1 cup). Pick out the fish bones. Reserve the middle piece of the eel uncooked and poach the other fish pieces in almond milk and verjuice. Mince the rest of the fish finely, adding sugar, salt and breadcrumbs. Stuff the uncooked eel with the mixture.

Line a 10-inch pie dish with the pastry and place the stuffed eel on it. Cover with some of the remaining stuffing and the reserved almond milk. Bake at 375° (Mark 5) for 30–40 minutes.

Eel in Herb Sauce

Conger in sauce :
Take the conger & scald him and cut him in pieces & seeth him; take parsley, mint, pelletour, rosemary & a little sage, bread & salt, powder fort & a little garlic, & a few cloves, take & grind it well, draw it up with vinegar thro' a cloth, cast the fish in a vessel and make it boil on & serve it forth. (The Forme of Cury, 1378)

Serves 2–3

I EEL, SKINNED
I PT (2½ CUPS) FISH STOCK
4 TBS PARSLEY
2 TBS MINT
I TSP ROSEMARY
½ TSP SAGE
2 CLOVES GARLIC, CRUSHED

I OZ (½ CUP) BREADCRUMBS
½ TSP SALT
POWDERFORT (2 TBS CHIVES CHOPPED WITH ½ TSP
    POWDERED MACE)
4 CLOVES, CRUSHED
4 TBS VINEGAR

Skin the eel, cut it into slices and simmer in the fish stock, using the skin for flavour, until tender.

Chop together the parsley, mint, rosemary and sage. Put in a blender with the crushed garlic, the breadcrumbs, salt, powderfort and crushed cloves. Add a little vinegar and blend well. Rub through a sieve, using a little more vinegar to wash the mixture through.

Arrange the eel slices in a fireproof dish, pour the sauce over them and reheat, spooning the sauce over the fish from time to time so that it can absorb the flavour. Simmer for 10–15 minutes and serve.

Braised Fish

Brasele
(Two Fifteenth-century Cookery Books)

Serves 2

2 TROUT
½ CUP WHITE WINE
I TBS VERJUICE
¼ TSP GINGER
¼ TSP GALINGALE (OPTIONAL)

Grill the fish until brown, then simmer in a chafing dish with the verjuice and the other ingredients until the fish flakes easily and is cooked. Put the fish on a warm serving dish, reduce the cooking liquid by half on a sharp flame and pour over the fish.

A Fish Jelly

This is a good basic fish jelly, with a beautiful colour. It can be used for masking any cold poached fish, and for chopped fish aspic.

Serves 6

½ PT (I CUP) CHICKEN STOCK
I PIKE, FILLETED
3 PT (7½ CUPS) WHITE WINE
3 TBS VINEGAR
I TSP SALT
½ TSP PEPPER
¼ TSP SAFFRON
2 (3–4 CUPS) SLICED FISH: EEL (HELPS TO MAKE
   THE JELLY), PERCH OR TENCH
I TBS GELATINE (IF THE STOCK DOES NOT JELL BY
   ITSELF)*

Garnish
SLIVERED ALMONDS
FRESH GINGER

Put the chicken stock and the pike fillets in a saucepan and poach until the fish is tender; remove and reserve the fillets. Put the stock, white wine, vinegar and seasonings into a pan, bring to the boil and simmer for 10 minutes. Add the sliced fish, bring to the boil again and simmer, uncovered, for 45 minutes to 1 hour. Mix the gelatine with a little cold water and add it to the strained fish stock. Simmer, stirring, until thoroughly dissolved.

Pick out the best pieces from the sliced fish and lay them in a shallow wetted mould. Cover with the pike fillets. Sprinkle with slivered almonds and small pieces of fresh ginger. Cover with the cooled stock and chill until set. Unmould to serve.

Poultry and Game

Chicken with Pine-nuts

Take gode cow milke and do it in a pot, take parsley, sauge, ysop, savoury and other good herbs, hew them and do them in the mylke and seeth them, take capon half roasted and smyte them in pieces and do thereto pynner and honey clarified, salt it and colour it with safron and serve it forth. (The Forme of Cury, 1378)

Serves 6

1½ PT (4 CUPS) MILK
4–5 SPRIGS PARSLEY
I SPRIG SAGE
I SPRIG HYSSOP (OR I TSP DRIED HYSSOP)
1–2 SPRIGS SUMMER SAVOURY OR I TSP DRIED
   SAVOURY
¼ TSP PEPPER
I TSP SALT
I CAPON
2 TBS PINE-NUTS
I TSP SAFFRON
¾ LB (½ CUP) HONEY
1–2 EGG YOLKS

Put the milk in a braising pan with the chopped herbs, pepper and salt. Simmer until the herbs have flavoured the milk and it is reduced by half. Meanwhile cut the chicken into serving pieces, as for fried chicken. Grill them until browned and partly cooked. Pour the milk and herbs into a large sauté pan. Bring to the boil and add the chicken pieces, pine-nuts, saffron and honey. Simmer until the chicken is tender. If the milk needs thickening, whisk the egg yolks with some of the milk, return to the pan and stir until thickened, but do not let the mixture boil.

Chicken and Almond Mould

For to make blancmange :
Nym rys and pick them and wash them clean and do thereto good almond milk and seeth them till they all to burst & then let them cool and nym the flesh of the hens or of capons and grind them small, cast thereto white grease and boil it. Nym blanched almonds and saffron and set hem above in the dyshe and serve it forth.
(The Forme of Cury, 1378)

Serves 4

6 OZ (½ CUP) RICE
½ PT (I CUP) ALMOND MILK (*see p. 53*)
½ PT (I CUP) JELLIED STOCK, MELTED
¼ TSP SAFFRON
4 OZ (½ CUP) DICED CHICKEN BREAST
SLIVERED ALMONDS
½ TSP PAPRIKA (OPTIONAL)

Boil the rice in the almond milk until tender but firm. Drain and leave to cool. Mince the diced chicken breast then purée in the blender. Remove and sauté in butter with pepper, salt and the saffron until tender and coloured by the saffron. Purée in blender. Leave to cool. Add just enough gelatine, softened and melted in hot chicken stock, to allow the chicken mixture to set lightly. Put this into a buttered mould.

Turn out into the centre of a green dish with the rice arranged round it. Decorate with blanched almonds and scatter a few threads of saffron (and a little paprika if liked) over the rice.

Cold Spiced Chicken

Vyaund de Ciprysse Ryalle

This dish was served at the coronation feast of Henry IV at Westminster on 13 October 1399. It is a delicious relish, rather like a chutney, and should be eaten as a garnish for roast chicken rather than as a dish by itself.
(*Two Fifteenth-century Cookery Books*)

Serves 4
½ PT (1 CUP) WHITE WINE
4 OZ (½ CUP) SUGAR
6 OZ (½ CUP) HONEY
1 TSP GROUND CLOVES
1 OZ (¼ CUP) RAISINS
1 TSP GRATED LEMON PEEL
3 EGG YOLKS
1¼ LB (2½ CUPS) COOKED CHICKEN, FINELY CHOPPED
2 EGG WHITES (OPTIONAL)

Make a syrup of the wine and sugar and boil for 10 minutes, until thickened. Reserve 4 tablespoons (¼ cup). Add the honey, cloves, raisins and lemon peel, then bring to the boil and simmer for 2 minutes. Beat the egg yolks in a bowl and stir in the syrup. Pour back into the saucepan and cook, stirring over low heat, without boiling, until thickened. Stir in the chicken. Pour into a 3-pint dish and pour the reserved syrup over the top. Chill thoroughly.

If you prefer a fluffier texture, fold in 2 whipped egg whites at the end, before pouring into the dish.

Galantine of Capon

Capon Galantine :
To make two capons of one, take a capon and scald him clean, and keme off the skin by the back. Then flay off the skin but keep it whole. Then grind figs and fresh pork with powder of ginger and cinnamon, and stuff the skin and sew it fast and rost it sokingly and serve it.
(*Two Fifteenth-century Cookery Books*)

Serves 4–6
A 5-LB CAPON
¼ LB (½ CUP) MINCED (GROUND) PORK
1 OZ (2 TBS) BUTTER
¼ LB (1 CUP) DRIED FIGS, CHOPPED
1 TSP GROUND GINGER
2 TSP CINNAMON
1 TSP SALT
⅛ TSP PEPPER

Gently loosen the skin at the breast of the capon, using your fingers. Cut out the breasts and chop. Sauté the pork in butter until tender. Combine the chicken, pork, chopped figs, ginger, cinnamon, salt and pepper. Stuff the breast cavities with the mixture, on each side, under the skin. Sew down, or secure the skin with a small skewer. Rub the outside of the chicken with butter and sprinkle with salt and pepper. Put in the oven at 350° (Mark 4) with butter and roast for 2½ hours, basting frequently.
Serve hot or cold.

Stuffed Neck of Capon

Poddinge of CapounNecke
Take Percely, gysour & the lever of the herte, and perboyle in fayre water ; than choppe hem smal, and put raw yolkyes of Eyroun. .ij. or .iij. ther-to, and choppe fro-with. Take Maces and

*Clowes, and put ther-to, and Safroun, and a
lytil pouder Pepir, and Salt; and fill him uppe,
and sew him, and lay him a-long on the Capon
Bakke, and prykke him ther-on, and roste hym,
and serue forth.*
(*Two Fifteenth-century Cookery Books*)

Serves 2
GIZZARD, LIVER AND HEART OF THE CAPON
3 OR 4 SPRIGS (1 TBS) PARSLEY
½ OZ (1 TBS) SUET OR LARD, FINELY MINCED
   (GROUND)
1 EGG YOLK
1 OZ (½ CUP) BREADCRUMBS
½ TSP MACE
¼ TSP GROUND CLOVES
GOOD PINCH SAFFRON
½ TSP PEPPER
½ TSP SALT
NECK SKIN OF CAPON

Cook the hearts, gizzard and parsley in water
until tender, for about 1 hour. Add the liver
and simmer for 10 minutes. Chop. Add the
suet, egg yolk, breadcrumbs and seasonings.
Stuff the neck with the mixture. Roast in pan
with the bird or skewer onto under-side of
birds for barbecueing. If you are making a dish
of stuffed necks alone, cook in a baking tin for
45 minutes at 375° (Mark 5).

Small Birds in a Pie

Tartes of Flesh:
*Take pork sodden and grind it small, take eggs
boiled hard and ground and put thereto with
cheese ground, take good powd^r and whole
spice sugar, safron, and salt and do thereto make
a coffin as to hold the same and do this therein
and poant it with small birds and conyngs and
hew them in small pieces and bake it as tofore
and serve it forth. (The Forme of Cury, 1378)*

Serves 4–6
1 LB (2 CUPS) MINCED (GROUND) PORK
2 HARD-BOILED EGGS, CHOPPED
1 OZ (½ CUP) GRATED CHEESE
1 TSP ALLSPICE
1 TBS SUGAR
⅛ TSP SAFFRON

1 TSP SALT
1 LB PASTRY
2–3 SMALL BIRDS (E.G. QUAIL), CUT IN HALF (OR
   CHICKEN PIECES)
1 OZ (2 TBS) BUTTER
¼ PT (½ CUP) STOCK

Mix together the pork, eggs, cheese, sugar
and seasonings. Line a 9-inch pie dish with
half the pastry. Spread with the mixture.
Brown the pieces of fowl in butter and lay
them on top. Pour in the stock. Cover with a
pastry lid and bake at 375° (Mark 5) for 35–40
minutes.

Great Pies

Grete Pyes:
*Take faire yonge beef, And suet of a fatte
beste, or of Motton, and hak all this on a borde
small; And caste thereto powder of peper and
salt; And whan it is small hewen, put hit in a
bolle, and medle hem well; then make a faire
large Cofyn, and couche som of this stuffur in.
Then take Capons, Hennes, Mallardes,
Connynges, and parboile hem clene; take
wodekokkes, teles, grete briddes, and plom hem in
a boiling potte; And then couche al this fowle in
the Cofyn, And put in euerych of hem a quantite
of pouder and salt. Then take mary, harde
yolkes of egges, Dates cutte in ij peces, reisons of
coraunce, prunes, hole clowes, hole maces, Canell,
and saffron. But first, whan thou hast couched
all thi foule, ley the remenaunt of thyne other
stuffur of beef a-bought hem, as thou thenkest
goode; and then strawe on hem this: dates, mary,
and reysons, &c., And then close thi Coffyn
with a lydde of the same paast, And putte hit
in the oven, And late hit bake ynogh; but be
ware, or thou close hit, that there come no
saffron nygh the brinkes there-of, for then hit
will neuer close.*
(*Two Fifteenth-century Cookery Books*)

Serves 10–12
1½ LB PASTRY
1½ LB (3 CUPS) MINCED (GROUND) BEEF
2 OZ (½ CUP) SHREDDED OR GRATED SUET

2 TSP SALT
¼ TSP PEPPER
I LARGE ROASTING CHICKEN, CUT IN SERVING
   PIECES
I DUCK, CUT IN SERVING PIECES
2 SMALL GAME BIRDS (WOODCOCK, SNIPE OR
   PARTRIDGE) CUT IN PIECES
I TSP SALT
¼ TSP PEPPER
I–2 OZ (2–4 TBS) RAW BEEF MARROW, CHOPPED
4 HARD-BOILED EGG YOLKS, CHOPPED
4 DATES, HALVED
2 OZ (½ CUP) PRUNES, CHOPPED
2 OZ (½ CUP) RAISINS
4 CLOVES
½ TSP MACE
I TSP CINNAMON
¼ TSP SAFFRON
¾ PT (I–I½ CUPS) STOCK

Roll out half the pastry and line a 12-inch pie or casserole dish with it. Mix the minced beef and suet together and season with salt and pepper. Spread some of this forcemeat over the pastry.

Parboil the birds for 15–20 minutes in the stock. Arrange them on top of the forcemeat and season with salt and pepper. Pack the remaining forcemeat between the birds. Chop the marrow, egg yolks, dates and prunes and spoon over the birds with the raisins. Sprinkle with the spices and pour over the stock. Cover with a pastry lid and bake at 350° (Mark 4) for 1–1½ hours.

To Boil Pheasants, Partridges, Capons and Curlews

Take good broth and do thereto Fowle and do thereto whole pepper and flower of canel a gude quantity and let them seeth therewith and mix it forth and then cast thereon sweet aromatic powder. (*The Forme of Cury, 1378*)

Serves 3–4
A 4–5 LB PHEASANT OR CAPON
2 PT (5 CUPS) CHICKEN OR GAME STOCK
I TSP SALT
6 WHOLE PEPPERCORNS
I–3 CINNAMON STICKS (TO TASTE)
⅛ TSP POWDERED GINGER
½ TSP CINNAMON
¼ TSP NUTMEG

Poach the bird in the game or chicken stock, seasoned with the salt, pepper and cinnamon sticks. When the bird is tender, remove it, carve and skin it, returning the skin to the broth. Keep the bird warm while the broth reduces and thickens slightly. Sprinkle the 'aromatic powder' – a mixture of powdered ginger, cinnamon and nutmeg – over the bird and pour the broth over the top.

Serve with boiled vegetables.

Roast Goose with Sauce Madame

Take sage, parsley, hyssop and savoury, quinces and pears, garlic and grapes and fill the geese therewith and sew the hole that no grease come out and roast them well and keep the grease that falleth thereof – take gallantyne and grease and do in a possynet when the geese be roasted enough : take and smite them in pieces and that that is within and do it in a possynet and put therein wine if it be too thick, do thereto powder of galingale, sweet aromatic powder and salt and boil the sauce and dress the geese in dishes and lay the liquor thereon. (*The Forme of Cury, 1378*)

Serves 4–6
A 5–6 LB GOOSE
½ TSP SAGE
I TSP PARSLEY
I TSP HYSSOP
½ TSP SAVOURY
4 TBS QUINCE JELLY
2–3 (I CUP) PEARS, PEELED, CORED AND CHOPPED
I CLOVE GARLIC, CRUSHED
3 OZ (½ CUP) GRAPES, PEELED AND SEEDED
¼ PT (½ CUP) JELLIED CHICKEN OR VEAL STOCK
¼ PT (½ CUP) RED WINE
¼ TSP GINGER
½ TSP CINNAMON
½ TSP NUTMEG
½ TSP GALINGALE (OPTIONAL, *see* glossary)

Stuff the goose with the herbs, quince jelly, pears, garlic, grapes and seasoning to taste. Roast the goose.

Carve it and put the pieces and the stuffing in a sauté pan with the gravies and stock. Cook until reduced a little and add the wine and spices, with salt to taste. Simmer for a few minutes, until the wine has been absorbed, and serve.

Poached Partridge

Pertrych Stewyde :
Take fayre mary, brothe of Beef or of Motoun, an whan it is wyl sothyn, take the brothe owt of the potte, an strayne it throw a straynoure, an put it on an erthen potte ; than take a gode quantyte of wyne, as thow it were half, an put ther-to ; than take the pertrych, an stuffe him wyth whole pepir, an merw, an than swew the ventys of the pertryche, an take clowys and maces, and hole pepir, an caste it in-to the potte, an let it boyle to-gederys ; an when the pertryche is boylid y-now, take the potte of the fyre, an whan thou schalt serue hym forth, caste in-to the potte powder gyngere, salt, safron, an serue forth.
(Two Fifteenth-century Cookery Books)

Serves 2–4
4 MARROW BONES
A 2–2½ LB PARTRIDGE
6 PEPPERCORNS
A LITTLE FLOUR
OIL FOR FRYING
I PT (2½ CUPS) BEEF STOCK
I PT (2½ CUPS) RED WINE
¼ TSP GROUND CLOVES
½ TSP MACE
⅛ TSP SAFFRON
½ TSP GINGER
I TBS FRESHLY CHOPPED PARSLEY

Secure the cavities of the bird. Dust it with flour and brown it in oil. Add the stock, wine, cloves and mace. Simmer for 1½ hours, or until tender. Remove the bird, carve and keep warm. Add the saffron and ginger, simmer the sauce, letting it reduce somewhat, until it is well coloured by the saffron. Check the seasoning.

Pour the sauce over the bird and sprinkle with freshly chopped parsley.

Serve with boiled rice.

Spicy Game Casserole

Smale byrdys y-stwde :
Take smale byrdys, an pulle hem an drawe hem clene, an washe hem fayre, an schoppe of the leggys, and frye hem in a panne of freysshe grece ryght wyl ; than lay hem on a fayre lynen clothe, an lette the grece renne owt ; than take oynonys, an mynce hem smale, an frye hem on fayre frysshe grece, an caste hem on an erthen potte ; than take a gode porcyon of canel, an wyne, and draw thorw a straynoure, an caste in-to the potte with the oynonys ; than caste the byrdys ther-to, an clowys, an maces, an a lytil quantyte of powder pepir ther-to, an lete hem boyle to-gederys y-now ; than caste ther-to whyte sugre, an powder gyngere, salt, safron, an serue it forth.
(Two Fifteenth-century Cookery Books)

Serves 2–4
3 OZ (I CUP) CHOPPED ONION
I OZ (2 TBS) BUTTER
A 2-LB GAME BIRD (OR 2 SMALLER ONES)
2 TBS FLOUR
¼ PT (½ CUP) WINE
¼ PT (½ CUP) GAME OR CHICKEN STOCK
2 STICKS CINNAMON (OR I TSP GROUND
   CINNAMON)
3 CLOVES
½ TSP FRESHLY GROUND WHITE PEPPER
½ TSP SALT
⅛ TSP SAFFRON
I TSP SUGAR
I TSP GROUND GINGER

Toss the onion in the butter in a saucepan until soft but not brown. Dust the bird or birds with flour and fry them with the onions, until they have taken colour on all sides. Remove and drain on kitchen paper. Meanwhile simmer the wine, broth and spices (except the sugar and ginger) together. Put the onions in the bottom of a narrow, deep earthenware casserole with a lid. Lay the bird on top; it should be a tight fit. Pour in the wine, broth and spice mixture and simmer, covered, very gently until the bird is cooked (1–1½ hours approximately). Add the sugar and ginger about 10 minutes before the end of the cooking time.

Remove the bird to a warmed serving dish and keep warm. Reduce the sauce by rapid boiling until it has thickened somewhat and become syrupy. Carve the bird and strain the sauce over it. Remove the cloves and cinnamon sticks and rub the onions through a sieve, along with the sauce.

Roast Peacock

The skin and feathers were pulled forwards from the back of the bird to the front, in one whole piece, but left attached to the neck and head. The bird was then trussed and roasted on a spit, care being taken to keep the feathery portion away from the heat. When it was done it was allowed to cool, and the skin and feathers were then pulled back over the breast and the tail feathers spread open. The meat was probably very tough, but guests would be used to that, as under the sway of Galen's system of medicine young game and fowl were considered indigestible and therefore dangerous.

Spicy Creamed Rabbit

This is an early, spicy version of creamed rabbit, for which leftovers can be used.

Conyngys in graveye :
Take Conyngys, and make hem clene, and hakke
hem in gobettys and sethe hem, other larde hem
and rost hem ; and thanne hakke hem, and take
Almaundys, and grynde hem, and temper hem
vope with gode Freysshe brothe of Flesshe, and
coloure it with Safroun, and do ther-to a porcyon
of flowre of Rys, and do ther-to then pouder
Gyngere, Galyngale, Canel, Sugre, Clowys,
Maces, and boyle it onys and sethe it ; then take
the Conyngys, and putte ther-on, and dresse it
and serue it forth.
(*Two Fifteenth-century Cookery Books*)

Serves 2
1 OZ (2 TBS) BUTTER
2 TBS FLOUR OR RICE FLOUR
½ PT (1 CUP) STOCK (CHICKEN, RABBIT OR VEAL)
1 OZ (¼ CUP) GROUND ALMONDS
¼ TSP SAFFRON
1 TSP GINGER
½ TSP GALINGALE (OPTIONAL, *see* glossary)

½ TSP CINNAMON
¼ TSP GROUND CLOVES
I TBS SUGAR
I LB (2 CUPS) CHOPPED COOKED RABBIT (OR
    SADDLE OF HARE, CHICKEN OR TURKEY)
2 SLICES FRESH TOAST (OPTIONAL)

Melt the butter, add the flour and cook for
1 minute. Add the stock, almonds, spices and
sugar, and cook until thickened. Stir in the
chopped rabbit and heat thoroughly. Add
pepper and salt to taste. Serve on a bed of
toast triangles or fingers.

Hare in Ale with Saffron

Hares in Cinee :
Should be parboyled and larded and rosted &
nym onions and mince them right small & fry
them in white grease and grind pepper bread &
ale and the onions thereto and colour it with
safron & salt and serve it forth.
(The Forme of Cury, 1378)

Serves 6–8
A 4–5 LB HARE OR RABBIT
I OZ (¼ CUP) FLOUR
4 TBS OIL
1¼ PT (3 CUPS) ALE
I TSP SALT
¼ TSP PEPPER
I MEDIUM ONION, SLICED
I OZ (2 TBS) BUTTER
½ OZ (¼ CUP) BREADCRUMBS
⅛ TSP SAFFRON

Cut the hare into joints and toss them in the
flour; brown in a saucepan in the oil; cover
with the ale, season with the salt and pepper
and simmer gently for 3 hours.
  Brown the onions in the butter in a frying-
pan. Add the breadcrumbs and saffron and
season. Serve the hare with the onion dressing
and some of the cooking broth reduced until it
has become rather syrupy.

Venison in Broth

Roe broth :
Take the flesh of the deer or of the roe-buck ;
parboil it in small pieces. Seethe it well, half in
water and half in wine. Take bread and bray it
with the self broth, and draw blood thereto, and
let it seethe together with powder-forte of
ginger or of cinnamon and mace, with a great
portion of vinegar and currants.
(The Forme of Cury, 1378)

Serves 4–6
2 LB VENISON
I OZ (¼ CUP) FLOUR
2 TBS OIL
½ TSP GINGER
½ TSP CINNAMON
½ TSP PEPPER
¼ TSP MACE
½ PT (I CUP) GAME OR CHICKEN STOCK
½ PT (I CUP) RED WINE
2 TBS WINE VINEGAR
2 OZ (½ CUP) CURRANTS

Cut the meat into chunks and dust them in the
flour; brown in a saucepan in the oil and add
the spices. Cover with the stock and wine and
simmer until the meat is tender. Add the
vinegar and currants at the end. If any blood
from the venison is available, this must be
added right at the end and heated without
boiling, as otherwise it will curdle.

Meat

Beaf Steaks

Alows de Beef or de Mouton :
Take fayre Bef of the quyschons, & mouton of
the bottes, & kytte in the maner of Stekys ;

*than take raw Percely, and Oynyonys smal
y-scredee, and yolkys of Eyroun sothe hard, and
Marow or swette, and hew alle thes to-geder
smal; than caste ther-on poudere of Gyngere and
Saffroun tolle hem to-gederys with thin hond,
and lay hem on the Stekys al a-brode; and caste
Salt ther-to; then rolle to-gederys, and put hem
on a round spete, and roste hem til they ben
y-now; than lay hem in a dysshe, and pore
ther-on Vynegre and a lityl verious, and pouder
Pepir ther-on y-now, and Gyngere, and Canelle,
and a fewe yolkys of hard Eyroun.*
(*Two Fifteenth-century Cookery Books*)

Serves 4
1 OZ (½ CUP) PARSLEY, FINELY CHOPPED
1½ OZ (½ CUP) ONION, FINELY MINCED
4 HARD-BOILED EGG YOLKS
2 OZ (4 TBS) RAW BEEF MARROW, MINCED (OR
  SHREDDED SUET)
½ TSP POWDERED GINGER
½ TSP POWDERED CINNAMON
1 TSP PEPPER
1 TSP SALT
4 STEAKS, THINLY SLICED
BUTTER FOR BASTING

Sauce
2 OZ (4 TBS) BUTTER
1 TBS WINE VINEGAR
1 TBS VERJUICE (*see p. 53*) OR CIDER
½ TSP POWDERED GINGER
½ TSP POWDERED CINNAMON
2 HARD-BOILED EGG YOLKS, MASHED

Mash together the parsley, onion, egg yolks,
marrow, ginger, cinnamon and seasoning
and spread on one side of the steaks, pressing
it down firmly. Roll the steaks like pancakes and
secure with skewers. Put them in an oiled pan
under the grill and grill on both sides, basting
with the butter. When they are done arrange
them on a serving dish and keep warm while
you prepare the sauce.

Pour the butter and drippings from the grill
pan into a small saucepan and add the butter,
the vinegar and the verjuice or cider. Stir in
the spices and thicken the sauce with the
mashed egg yolks. Bring to the boil and simmer
for a few seconds. Add pepper and salt to
taste and pour the sauce over the steaks through
a strainer. Serve very hot.

Stewed Beef

Beef y-stewyd:
*Take fayre beef of the rybbys of the fore-
quarterys, an smyte in fayre pecys, and wasche
the beef in-to a fayre potte; than take the water
that the beef was sothin yn an strayne it thorw a
straynowr, an sette the same water and beef in a
potte, an let hem boyle to-gerderys; than take
canel, clowes, maces, graynys of parise, quibibes,
an oynons y-mynced, perceli, an sawge, an caste
ther-to an let hem boyle to-gederys; an than take
a lof of brede, an stepe it with brothe an
venegre, an than draw it thorw a straynoure,
and let it be stylle; an whan it is nere y-now,
caste the lycour ther-to, but nowt to moche, an
than let boyle onys, an cast safroun ther-to a
quantyte; than take salt an venegre, and caste
ther-to, an loke that it be poynant y-now, a
serue forth.*
(*Two Fifteenth-century Cookery Books*)

Serves 4–5
2–3 LB SHORT RIBS OF BEEF, CUT INTO RIBS
1 OZ (¼ CUP) FLOUR
4 TBS (¼ CUP) OIL
2 PT (5 CUPS) BEEF STOCK
½ TSP CINNAMON
½ TSP GROUND CLOVES
½ TSP GROUND MACE
1 TBS CARDAMOM, CRUSHED
4 PEPPERCORNS (OR 1 TSP FRESH GREEN
  PEPPERCORNS)
1 LARGE ONION, FINELY CHOPPED
6 SPRIGS PARSLEY, CHOPPED
1 TSP SAGE
2 SLICES WHOLEWHEAT BREAD, CRUSTS REMOVED,
  OR HOME-MADE SAFFRON BREAD (*see p. 56*)
4 TBS (¼ CUP) TARRAGON VINEGAR
A GOOD PINCH (¼ TSP) SAFFRON

Dust the ribs with the flour and brown in the
oil; add the stock, lightly salted, and then the
spices and herbs, except for the saffron. Simmer
for about 2 hours. Leave the bread to soak in
the vinegar, with the saffron, while the stew is

simmering. Then purée it in the blender and
stir into the stew. Check seasoning. Simmer
for another 15 minutes.

Meat Loaf with Almonds

For To Make a Bruet of Sarcynesse :
Take the flesh of the fresh beef and cut it all in
pieces and bread and fry it in fresh grease take it
up and dry it and do it in a vessel with wine and
sugar and powder of cloves, boil it together till
the flesh have drunk the liquor and take the
almond milk and quibibs maces and cloves and
boyl them together, take the flesh and do thereto
and mix it forth. (*Ancient Cookery, 1381*)

The Saracen brew shows the influence the
Saracens exerted on Europe during their long
occupation of Spain.

Serves 4–6
2 LBS (4 CUPS) MINCED (GROUND) BEEF
2 OZ (1 CUP) FRESH BREADCRUMBS
4 TBS ($\frac{1}{4}$ CUP) RED WINE
1 TSP SUGAR
$\frac{1}{4}$ PT ($\frac{1}{2}$ CUP) ALMOND MILK (*see p. 53*)
$\frac{1}{4}$ TSP BLACK PEPPER
$\frac{1}{8}$ TSP GROUND MACE
$\frac{1}{8}$ TSP GROUND CLOVES

Combine all the ingredients in a bowl and
shape into a loaf. Put into a deep, covered
casserole and bake at 350° (Mark 4) for 1 hour.
Drain off the fat and turn out onto a serving
platter.

Veal Quiche

Vele, kede, or henne in Bokenade :
Take Vale, Kyde, or Henne, an boyle hem in
fayre water, or ellys in freysshe brothe, an smyte
hem in an pecys, an pyke hem clene ; an than
draw the same brothe thorwe a straynoure, an
caste ther-to Percely, Sawge, Ysope, Maces,
Clowys, an let boyle tyl the flesshe be y-now ;
than sette it from the fyre, & a-lye it vp with
raw yolkys of eyroun, & caste ther-to pouder

Gyngere, Veriows, Safroun, & Salt, & thanne
serue it forth for a gode mete.
(*Two Fifteenth-century Cookery Books*)

Serves 4
1$\frac{1}{2}$ LB PASTRY
6 OZ ($\frac{3}{4}$ CUP) MINCED (GROUND) VEAL
$\frac{1}{2}$ TSP HYSSOP
$\frac{1}{4}$ TSP SAGE
$\frac{1}{4}$ TSP SAVORY
$\frac{1}{8}$ TSP SAFFRON
2 TBS CHOPPED PARSLEY
$\frac{1}{4}$ TSP CINNAMON
$\frac{1}{4}$ TSP MACE
4 CLOVES (OR $\frac{1}{8}$ TSP GROUND CLOVES)
$\frac{1}{2}$ PT (1 CUP) WATER
$\frac{1}{2}$ PT (1 CUP) WHITE WINE
$\frac{1}{4}$ PT ($\frac{1}{2}$ CUP) VERJUICE (*see p. 53*) OR CIDER
4 EGGS PLUS 2 EXTRA YOLKS
GINGER
DATES

Roll out half the pastry and line a 9-inch pie
dish with it, reserving the rest for the lid.

Combine the veal, herbs, spices, water and
wine and simmer, covered, for 45 minutes.
Remove the meat and measure the liquid.
There should be about $\frac{3}{4}$ pint (1$\frac{1}{2}$ cups). If
there is not enough, add more wine. Now
pour in the verjuice, heat the liquid and beat
into the eggs. Return the meat to the sauce
and pour into the pastry shell. Sprinkle the
ginger and dates over the top. Put a pie funnel
in the centre. Place the reserved pastry on top
and flute the edges. Bake at 400° (Mark 6) for
10 minutes. Reduce the heat to 350° (Mark 4)
and bake for another 30 minutes. Pour some
extra cooking liquid into the pie through the
funnel before serving. This can be made in a
pie dish with a top lid of pastry only. Decorate
with pastry leaves and wash with egg yolk
before baking.

Tartlet of Veal

The filling for this tart tastes like mincemeat.
It used to be served as a hot or cold relish
with a stew of beef or pork.

Tartlet :
Take veal sodden and grind it small, take eggs
hardboiled & ground and do thereto with prunes
whole, dates, cut in pieces, pynes, and raisins
currants whole spices and powder, sugar, salt and
make a little coffin and do this farce therein
and bake it and serve it forth.
(The Forme of Cury, 1378)

Serves 6
1½ LB PASTRY
I LB (2 CUPS) MINCED (GROUND) LEAN VEAL
4 HARD-BOILED EGGS, CHOPPED
6 PRUNES, STONED, SOFTENED IN WATER AND
    CHOPPED
6 DATES, STONED AND CHOPPED
2 TBS PINE-NUTS
I OZ (¼ CUP) CURRANTS, PLUMPED IN HOT WATER
    AND DRAINED
2 CLOVES
¼ TSP MIXED GINGER, CINNAMON AND NUTMEG
    (ALL POWDERED)
4 OZ (½ CUP) SUGAR
I TSP SALT
A LITTLE VEAL STOCK
I TBS BRANDY (OPTIONAL)
I EGG, BEATEN

Roll out half the pastry and line a 9-inch pie
dish with it, reserving the rest for the lid.
Mix all the other ingredients in a bowl,
except the egg, moistening with the veal stock
and brandy. Spoon into the pastry shell and
cover with a lid. Crimp the edges and glaze with
beaten egg. Bake at 375° (Mark 5) for 35–40
minutes.

Jellied Calves' Feet

Vyaund leche :
Take calfes fete an hepe, & lat stepe in cold
watere ; then boyle hem smal ; then take the
brothe & gode Milke of Almaundys, & choppe
the Syneys in-to the same milk rythte smal ; than
boyle it ouer the fyre, & coloure it with
Saunderys, & put Sugre y-now in-to the potte ;
& if thou wolt haue hym of ij colour, than take
an coloure but half with Saunderys, & caste
that othere half in a dysshe, & lat it kele ; &
whan it is cold, then that is y-colouryd with

Saunderys, het it, & euene melle it hote ; caste
hem a-bouyn the other, & lat kele, an than
serue forth. Than take Sugre, a quantyte of
swete Wyne, & Blaunche pouder ther-on, &
make Sawce ther-of ; And so colde, ley it in the
dysshis, be-helyd, and serue forth. And so lay it
cold in the dysshis, an that but a lytil, that
vnnethe the bottumys be holuyd.
(Two Fifteenth-century Cookery Books)

2 CALVES' FEET
2 PT (5 CUPS) STOCK OR WATER
¼ PT (½ CUP) ALMOND MILK (*see p.* 53)
A FEW DROPS COCHINEAL
2 OZ (¼ CUP) SUGAR

Sauce
I PT (2½ CUPS) SWEETISH WHITE WINE
½ LB (I CUP) SUGAR
I TSP GINGER
I TSP CINNAMON
½ TSP NUTMEG

Simmer the calves' feet in the stock or water
for 2½ hours. Leave to cool. Remove the meat
from the bone and chop finely. Strain the stock.
Measure ½ pint (I cup) of the strained stock
and boil it with the almond milk, the colouring
and the sugar for 10 minutes. Pour over the
meat and chill until set.

Boil together the ingredients for the sauce
for about 10 minutes, until it has thickened
and reduced by almost half. Chill. Turn out
the meat, place in a concave dish and pour
the sauce over it.

Jellied Veal Hocks

Storioun leche :
Take a howe of vele, & let boyle, butte fyrste
late hym be stepid ij. or iij. owrys in clene
Water to soke out the blode, & whan it is
tender y-sothe, take hym vppe as fast as you may ;
than take harde yolkys of Eyroun redy sothe, &
caste also ther-to, & pouder Pepir y-now, & also
choppe among the yines of the fete clene y-pikyd,
& a lytil salt, nowt to moche, & presse hem on a
clowte tyl a-morwe ; than leche it, & lay hem in
dysshis, an pore ther-on a quantyte of Venegre,

*& Pepir, & Percely, & Oynonys smal mencyd,
& serue forth.*
(*Two Fifteenth-century Cookery Books*)

2 VEAL HOCKS (SHANKS)
2 PT (5 CUPS) WATER
I TSP SALT
I BAY LEAF
3 SPRIGS PARSLEY
6 PEPPERCORNS
I CARROT, SLICED
I ONION, QUARTERED
I STALK CELERY, SLICED
4 HARD-BOILED EGG YOLKS

Cook the veal hocks for 2 hours in salted water
with the herbs, peppercorns and vegetables.
Take out the meat and cool slightly. Remove
the bones, cut the meat into pieces and mix
them with the egg yolks. Wrap them in a cloth
and press under a weight for 12 hours. Slice
and serve with a vinaigrette sauce.

Lamb Steak

Allowes de Mutton :
*Take faire Mutton of the Buttes, and kutte hit
in the maner of stekes; an than take faire rawe
parcely, and oynons shred smale, yolkes of eron
sodden hard, and mary or suet; hewe all thes
smale togidre, and then caste thereto pouder of
ginger, and saffron, and sterr hem togidre, with
thi honde, and ley hem vppe-on the steke al
abrode; and caste there-to salt, and rolle hem
togidre, and put hem on a spitte, and roste hem
till thei be ynough.*
(*Two Fifteenth-century Cookery Books*)

Serves 4
I LB LAMB STEAKS, SLICED ¼ INCH THICK*
I½ OZ (½ CUP) PARSLEY, CHOPPED
I½ OZ (½ CUP) ONION, MINCED
2 HARD-BOILED EGG YOLKS
I OZ (4 TBS) BEEF MARROW OR SUET
½ TSP GINGER
⅛ TSP SAFFRON

Season the meat with salt and pepper. Mix
all the other ingredients together and spoon
some of the resulting mixture onto each steak.
Roll up the steaks and secure them. Grill
(broil) on a spit or skewers.

Mutton Stewed with Mustard

Stwed Mutton
*Take faire Mutton that hath ben roste, and
mynce it faire; put hit into a possenet, or
elles bitwen ij (2) siluer disshes; caste thereto
faire parcely, And onynons mynced; then caste
there-to wyn, and a littull vynegre or vergeous,
ouder of peper, Canel, salt and saffron, and lete
it stue on the faire coles, And then serue hit
forthe; if he have no wyne ne vynegre, take Ale,
Mustard, and a quantyte or vergeous, and do
this in the stede of vyne or vinegre.*
(*Two Fifteenth-century Cookery Books*)

Serves 3–4
I½ LB (3 CUPS) COLD ROAST MUTTON, MINCED
4 TBS PARSLEY, MINCED
I MEDIUM ONION, SLICED
I¼–I½ PT (3–4 CUPS) WINE (OR ALE)
2 TBS VERJUICE (*see p. 53*)
¼ TSP PEPPER
I TSP SALT
½ TSP CINNAMON
⅛ TSP SAFFRON
I TBS MUSTARD ⎫
2 SLICES BREAD ⎭ (OPTIONAL)

Make a fine mince of cold roast mutton; put
into a fireproof earthenware casserole and add
the parsley and onion. Pour in the wine and
verjuice. Bring to the boil, add the pepper and
salt, cinnamon and saffron and then simmer
gently for 30 minutes.

The wine should be replaced by ale when
using mustard. Mustard may be liberally
spread on to slices of crustless bread which are
then laid over the meat and stirred in, when
softened, to thicken the stew.

*If your butcher looks blank, ask him to bone half a leg of lamb and cut it into thin slices.

Savoury Meat Custard

Soupes of salomere :
Take boylid Porke, & hew yt an grynd it ;
then take cowe Mylke, & Eyroun y-swonge, &
Safroun, & mynce Percely bladys, & caste
ther-to & let boyle alle y-fere ; & dresse vppe-on
a clothe, & kerue ther-of smal lechys, & do hem
in a dysshe ; then take almaunde mylke &
flowre of Rys, and Sugre an Safroun, & boyle it
alle y-fere ; then caste thin sewe of thin lechys,
& serue forth alle hote.
(Two Fifteenth-century Cookery Books)

The reference to 'salomere' or Salomon, shows
the Near-Eastern influence in food during
those centuries.

1 LB (2 CUPS) MINCED (GROUND) PORK, COOKED
¾ PT (2 CUPS) MILK
4 EGGS, BEATEN
⅛ TSP SAFFRON
2 TBS PARSLEY, CHOPPED

Sauce
½ PT (1 CUP) ALMOND MILK (*see p.* 53)
1 TBS RICE FLOUR
⅛ TSP SAFFRON

Mix together the meat, milk, eggs, saffron and
parsley. Put in a dish and bake in the oven at
350° (Mark 4) for about 25 minutes until the
custard is very firm. Cut into slices and serve
with a sauce made of almond milk thickened,
over low heat, with rice flour, and seasoned with
pepper, salt and the saffron.

Casserole of Pork

Brawn in peuerade :
Take Wyne an powder Canel, and draw it thorw
a straynour, an sette it on the fyre, and lette it
boyle, an caste ther-to Clowes, Maces, an powder
Pepyr ; than take smale Oynonys al hole, an
par-boyle hem in hot watere, an caste ther-to, an
let hem boyle to-gederys ; than take Brawn, an
lesshe it, but nowt to thinne. An if it sowsyd be,
lete it stepe a whyle in hot water tyl it be
tendere, than caste it to the Sirip ; then take
Sawnderys, an Vynegre, an caste ther-to, an

lete it boyle alle to-gederys tyl it be y-now ; then
take Gyngere, an caste ther-to, and so serue forth ;
but late it be nowt to thikke ne to thinne, but as
potage shulde be.
(Two Fifteenth-century Cookery Books)

Serves 6–8

2LB BONELESS PORK, CUBED
4 OZ (½ CUP) SMOKED HAM, DICED
4 TBS FLOUR
1 OZ (2 TBS) BUTTER
¾ PT (2 CUPS) CHICKEN STOCK
¾ PT (2 CUPS) RED WINE
12 WHITE ONIONS
1 TSP JUNIPER BERRIES, CHOPPED (OPTIONAL)
½ TSP CINNAMON
¼ TSP GROUND CLOVES
½ TSP GROUND MACE
¼ TSP PEPPER
⅛ TSP SAFFRON
1 TSP SALT
1 SLICE BREAD
1 TBS VINEGAR

Toss the pork and ham in the flour and brown
in the butter. Add them to the stock and wine,
with the onions and seasonings, and simmer
for 1½ hours. Remove the onions and purée
them. Return them to the pot and cook for
another half hour. Soak the bread in the
vinegar, purée it and add it to the stew, to
thicken it. Cook for another 10 minutes and
serve.

Hedgehogs

Yrchouns :
Take Piggis mawys, & skalde hem wel ; take
groundyn Porke, & knede it with Spicerye, with
pouder Gyngere, & Salt & Sugre ; do it on the
mawe, but fille it nowt to fulle ; then sewe hem
with a fayre threde, & putte hem in a Spete as
men don piggys ; take blaunchid Almaundys, &
kerf hem long, smal, & scharpe, & frye hem in
grece & sugre ; take a litel prycke, & prykke
the yrchouns, An putte in the holes the
Almaundys, every hole half, & eche fro other ;
ley hem then to the fyre ; when they ben rostid,
dore hem sum whyth Whete Flowre, & mylke of
Almaundys, sum grene, sum blake with Blode,

& lat hem nowt brone to moche, & serue forth.
(*Two Fifteenth-century Cookery Books*)

Serves 6–8
2 LB (4 CUPS) MINCED (GROUND) PORK
2 TBS BREADCRUMBS
½ TSP GINGER
½ TSP MACE
2 TSP SALT
¼ TSP PEPPER
2 TBS SUGAR
½ OZ (1 TBS) SOFTENED BUTTER
2 EGG YOLKS
2 OZ (4 TBS) BUTTER
4 TBS VEGETABLE STOCK OR WATER
2 OZ SLIVERED ALMONDS
VEGETABLE COLOURINGS

Mix the pork, breadcrumbs, spices, seasonings
and softened butter. Bind with the beaten egg
yolks and form in a ball. Place in a buttered
pan. Cook, covered, for 1 hour, basting at
intervals with the rest of the butter melted in
the vegetable stock or water. Stick the slivered
almonds, dyed with vegetable colourings, all
over the pudding, so that they look like the
quills of a hedgehog or sea urchin.

Liver Pasties

Chewettes

(*Two Fifteenth-century Cookery Books*)

For 4–6 pasties
1 PIG'S LIVER
4 CHICKEN LIVERS
1½ OZ (3 TBS) COOKING FAT
4 HARD-BOILED EGGS
¼ TSP GROUND GINGER
1½ LB PASTRY

Chop the livers together and fry in the fat.
Add the chopped eggs and the ginger, seasoning
with salt and pepper. Roll out the pastry and
cut it into 4-inch circles. Spoon tablespoons of
the liver mixture on one half of each circle,
then fold the other half over and pinch the
edges together. Fry: or bake at 375° (Mark 5)
for 15–20 minutes.

For a modern version, replace the ginger

with fried onions, or chopped herbs, and
perhaps a drop of sherry. Calves' instead of
pig's liver, or chicken livers alone, or chicken
livers plus minced chicken are also excellent.

Pies of Paris

Pyez de Parez:
Take and smyte fayre buttys of Porke, &
buttys of Vele, to-gederys, & put it on a fayre
potte, & do ther-to Freyssche brothe, a quantyte
of wyne, & lat boyle alle to-gederys tyl yt be
y-now; than take it fro the fyre, & lat kele a
lytelle; than caste ther-to yolkys of Eyroun,
& pouder of Gyngere, Sugre, & Salt, &
mynced Datys, & Roysonys of Coraunce; then
make fayre past, and coffynnys, & do, ther-on;
kyuer it, & let bake, and serue forth.
(*Two Fifteenth-century Cookery Books*)

½ LB BONELESS PORK BUTTS
½ LB BONELESS VEAL BUTTS
1 PT (2½ CUPS) STOCK
½ PT (1 CUP) WINE
4 EGG YOLKS
¼ TSP GINGER
2 TBS SUGAR
½ TSP SALT
1 OZ (¼ CUP) MINCED DATES
1 OZ (¼ CUP) RAISINS
¾ LB PASTRY

Chop up the pork and veal butts together.
Boil in the stock and wine for about 45 minutes
or until cooked. Remove, leave to cool a little
and add the egg yolks, ginger, sugar, salt,
dates and raisins.

Line a pie dish with the pastry. Fill with
the meat mixture and stock to cover and bake
at 350° (Mark 4) for 30–40 minutes.
Serve with reduced stock in a sauceboat.

Pickled Pigs' Trotters

Sauoge:
Take Pigis fete and much sage clene y-pekkyd;
then take Freysshe brothe of Beff, & draw
mylke of Almaundys, & the Piggys ther-in;

*then mence Sawge ; then grynd hym smal,
& draw owt the Ius thorw a straynoure ; then
take clowys y-now, & do ther-in pouder Gyngere,
& Canelle, Galyngale, Vynegre, & Sugre y-now ;
Salt it than, and thanne serue it forth.*
(*Two Fifteenth-century Cookery Books*)

Serves 3–4
4 PIG'S TROTTERS (FEET)
I PT (2½ CUPS) BEEF STOCK
½ PT (I CUP) ALMOND MILK (*see p. 53*)
8 SPRIGS FRESH SAGE
¼ TSP GROUND CLOVES
I TSP POWDERED GINGER
I TSP GALINGALE (OPTIONAL, *see* glossary)
½ PT (I CUP) EXTRA BEEF STOCK
2 TBS VINEGAR
2 TBS SUGAR
2 TSP SALT

Boil the pig's trotters in the beef stock and
almond milk with half the sage until tender.
Remove the trotters and allow to cool. Cut the
meat off the bones; slice and arrange in a
shallow dish. Sprinkle with the ground spices.
Pour some fresh beef stock into the blender,
add the rest of the sage, the vinegar and sugar,
and blend. Strain over the pig's trotters and
leave them to marinate in the refrigerator until
needed. Serve cold with salad.

Vegetables

Onion Tart

Tart in Ember Day :
*Take and parboil onions pass out the water and
hew them small, take bread and bray it in a
mortar and temper it up with eggs. Do thereto
butter, saffron and salt and raisons corants and a
little sugar with powd^r douce and bake it in a
trap and serve it forth.*
(*The Forme of Cury, 1378*)

Serves 4
¾ LB PASTRY
6 OZ (2 CUPS) ONIONS, SLICED
I OZ (2 TBS) BUTTER

2 EGGS PLUS 2 EXTRA YOLKS
⅛ TSP SAFFRON
½ PT (I CUP) THICK CREAM
I OZ (¼ CUP) RAISINS, PLUMPED IN HOT WATER
   AND DRAINED
I OZ (¼ CUP) CURRANTS
¼ TSP EACH GINGER, CINNAMON AND NUTMEG
I OZ (2 TBS) SUGAR
½ TSP SALT
⅛ TSP PEPPER

Roll out the pastry and line a 9-inch pie ring
with it. Crimp the edges and bake blind (unfilled) for 10 minutes at 400° (Mark 6).

Fry the onions in butter until golden ;
reserve. Beat the eggs and extra yolks in a
bowl. Leave the saffron to infuse in the warm
cream, then heat it until bubbles appear round
the edges. Beat into the eggs. Stir in the fried
onions, raisins, currants, spices, ginger and
seasonings and pour into the cooled pie shell.
Bake at 350° (Mark 4) for 25–30 minutes or
until the mixture has set.

Beans Fried with Onions

Beans fried :
*Take beans and seethe them almost till they
burst, take and wring out the water clean, do
thereto onions sodden and minced and garlick
therewith fry them in oil or in grease and do
thereto powder douce and serve it forth.*
(*The Forme of Cury, 1378*)

Serves 2
I ONION, CHOPPED
I CLOVE GARLIC, FINELY CHOPPED
4 TBS OIL
¼ TSP GINGER
½ TSP CINNAMON
¼ TSP NUTMEG
6 OZ (I CUP) KIDNEY BEANS, COOKED

Fry the onions in the oil with the garlic, spices
and seasoning. Stir in the cooked beans and
mix thoroughly. Reheat and serve.

Desserts

An Early Apple Tart

For to make Tartys in Apples :
Take good apples and good spices & Figs and
raisins and Pears and when they are well braid
colour with safron well and do it in a coffin and
do it forth to bake well.
(Ancient Cookery, 1381)

Serves 4–6
4 APPLES
4 PEARS
½ PT (I CUP) WATER
I TBS SUGAR
2 TBS FLOUR
2 OZ (⅓ CUP) CHOPPED DRIED FIGS*
2 OZ (⅓ CUP) RAISINS
I TSP CINNAMON
6 OZ (¾ CUP) SUGAR
I TBS LEMON JUICE
½ TSP NUTMEG
½ TSP GINGER
¼ TSP SAFFRON
A LITTLE RED WINE OR RUM
1½ LB FLAKY PASTRY

Peel and core the apples and pears and slice
them thinly. Put the cores and skins in a
saucepan with the water and a little sugar.
Leave to boil until reduced by about a third.
Meanwhile, make the pastry.

Toss the fresh fruit in a bowl with the flour,
then add the sugar and the dried fruits and
dates, steeped with the lemon juice and spices
in a little red wine or rum. Roll out the pastry
and line a 9-inch pie dish with it, reserving
enough for the lid. Fill the pie with the mixed
fruit and strain over the juice from the cores
and skins. Cover with the pastry lid and bake
at 350° (Mark 4) for about 30 minutes.

Apples and Rice

Serves 6
2½ LB APPLES, PEELED, CORED AND SLICED
¼ PT (½ CUP) WATER
⅛ TSP SAFFRON
I TSP 'POUDER DOUCE' (MIXED POWDERED GINGER,
   CINNAMON AND NUTMEG)
3 OZ (½ CUP) RICE
I PT (2½ CUPS) ALMOND MILK (*see p.* 53)
¼ PT (½ CUP) THICK CREAM
(*Two Fifteenth-century Cookery Books*)

Serves 6
Stew the apples and spices in the water for
20–30 minutes.

Stir the rice into the almond milk (do not
strain out the almonds) and simmer gently,
stirring occasionally, for 20–30 minutes, or
until the rice is tender and the liquid has been
absorbed. Add a little more milk during the
cooking time if necessary. At the last minute
add the cream, warmed, and combine well.

Arrange a mound of rice at each end of a
serving dish and pile the golden apple compote
into the centre. Serve piping hot.

Spiced Pears

The warden pears referred to in this recipe
grew in England in medieval times. Shaped
somewhat like acorn squash, they are bright
green with black skin bruises. After picking
they taste like winter pears and quince. Like
so many fruits and spices grown or imported
into England at this date, they originated in the
Mediterranean region. I have found them on
the Greek island of Patmos, in the Dodecanese.
Hard winter pears, any rather unripe pears or,
in autumn, quinces can be used instead.

Chare de Wardoun leche :
Take Perys, and sethe ham, and Pike ham and
stampe ham and draw hem thorw a straynoure,
and lye it with Bastard ; then caste hem into a
potte, and Safroun with-al, and boyle with Maces,
Clowes, pouder Canel, Quibibes, and a litel
pouder Pepir, and Rolle hem vppe with Brede,
the cromes with the hondys, and serue forth.
(Two Fifteenth-century Cookery Books)

*Almost all the figs mentioned in English recipes of this period would have been dried and imported, as would the
spices and raisins.

Serves 3–4

2 LB PEARS, PEELED, CORED AND SLICED
¼ PT (½ CUP) SWEET WHITE WINE*
A PINCH OF SAFFRON
¼ TSP POWDERED MACE
¼ TSP ALLSPICE
4 CLOVES, CRUSHED
4 OZ (½ CUP) SUGAR
2 OZ (1 CUP) BREADCRUMBS
2 OZ (¼ CUP) SUGAR

Cook all the ingredients together over low heat until thickened (about 20–30 minutes). Push through a food mill or purée in blender. Instead of rolling the resulting purée into balls and breading them, as in the original recipe, I prefer to put the crumbs on top. Brown the crumbs in the oven, or in a pan, with the sugar. Put the pear purée in a shallow dish and sprinkle the crumbs on top. Bake at 375° (Mark 5) for 15–20 minutes. Serve hot or cold.

Pears in Syrup

Peris in Syrippe :
Take Wardons, and cast hem in a faire potte, and boile hem till thei ben tendre ; and take hem vppe, and pare hem in ij or iij. And take powder of Canell, a good quantite, and cast hit in good red wyne, And cast sugur thereto, and put hit in an erthen potte, And lete boile ; And then cast the peris thereto, and late hem boile togidre awhile ; take powder of ginger, and a littel saffron to colloure hit with and loke that hit be poynante, and also Doucet.
(*Two Fifteenth-century Cookery Books*)

Serves 4–6

8 PEARS
1 PT (2½ CUPS) RED WINE
½ LB (1 CUP) SUGAR
1 TSP POWDERED CINNAMON
4 TBS QUINCE JAM
4 OZ (1 CUP) DATES, FINELY CHOPPED

Peel the pears leaving on the stalks. Poach them in the wine, basting frequently, when tender (test with the point of a knife, close to the stalk), remove. Add the sugar, cinnamon and quince jam. Bring to the boil, when the sugar will dissolve. Continue boiling until the syrup has thickened, which will be in about 15 minutes. Stir in the dates and arrange in a bowl. Put back the pears. Cool and then chill in the refrigerator.

Serve with whipped cream to which a little pear brandy has been added.

Pureed Quinces

Quynade :
Take Quinces, & pare hem clene, cast hem on a potte, & caste ther-to water of Rosys ; do it over the fyre, & hele it faste, & let it boyle a gode whyle tyl they ben neysshe ; & if they wol not ben neysshe, bray hem in a Morter smal, draw hem thorw a straynoure ; take gode Mylke of Almandys, & caste in a potte & boyle it ; take whyte Wyne & Vynegre, an caste ther-to the Mylke, & let it stonde a whyle ; take than a clene canvas, & caste it on the potte ; gedyr vppe the quynces, & caste to the creme, & do it over the fyre, & lat boyle ; take a porcyon of Pouder of Clowys, of Gyngere, of Graynys of Perys, of Euery a porcyon ; take Sugre y-now, with Salt, & a party of Safroun, & alle menge to-gederys ; & when thou dressyst forth, plante it with foyle of Syluer.
(*Two Fifteenth-century Cookery Books*)

Serves 4

4 QUINCES
¼ PT (½ CUP) WHITE WINE
½ LB (1 CUP) SUGAR
½ TSP GROUND CLOVES
½ TSP GINGER
1 TSP SALT
⅛ TSP SAFFRON
1 TBS VINEGAR

Poach the quinces in the water until tender. Purée. Combine in a saucepan with the remaining ingredients. Simmer until the purée has thickened and holds its shape on a spoon.

*I think that Greek resinated wines come closest to the flavours used in the fifteenth century.

Apple Fritters

For to make fritters :
Nym flour and eyerin and grind pepper and
saffron and make thereto a batter & pare apples
and cut them to broad pieces and cast them therein
and fry them in the batter with fresh grease and
serve it forth.
(*Ancient Cookery, 1381*)

Serves 2–3
3 OZ (¾ CUP) FLOUR
4 EGGS, BEATEN
A PINCH OF PEPPER
⅛ TSP SAFFRON
2–3 APPLES
CASTER (CONFECTIONER'S) SUGAR, FOR GARNISH

Sift the flour and mix with the beaten eggs to
make a smooth batter. Add the pepper and
saffron.

Peel, core and slice the apples, put them into
the batter and leave for 1 hour. This will allow
the saffron to colour and flavour the batter.
Drop by large spoonfuls into deep fat heated
to 375° and fry for 3–4 minutes; the fritters
will rise to the surface when cooked and should
be a golden brown. Drain, sprinkle with the
sugar and serve hot.

Apple Blossom Fritters

The flowers of the vegetable marrow used to
be a favourite alternative for these flower-
fritters, as they still are in Italy today.

For to make Fritters :
Take croms of white bread and the flowers of the
sweet appletree and yolkes of Eggis and bray
them together in a mortar and temper it up with
white wine and make it to seeth and when it is
thick do thereto good spices of ginger, galyngal,
canel, and cloves and serve it forth.
(*Ancient Cookery, 1381*)

Serves 4–6
2 EGG YOLKS
¼ PT (½ CUP) WHITE WINE
1 TBS MELTED BUTTER
2 OZ (½ CUP) FLOUR

2 OZ (½ CUP) VERY FINE DRY BREADCRUMBS
¼ TSP SALT
¼ TSP POWDERED GALINGALE (OPTIONAL, *see*
glossary)
¼ TSP GROUND CINNAMON
⅛ TSP GROUND GINGER
⅛ TSP GROUND CLOVES
2 EGG WHITES, BEATEN FAIRLY STIFF
2 CUPS APPLE BLOSSOM, TIGHTLY PACKED

Beat together the egg yolks, wine and butter.
Sift together the flour, breadcrumbs, seasonings
and spices and blend into the egg mixture.
Chill, covered, for as long as possible, then fold
in the egg whites just before using the batter.

Pick the blossoms in the early morning,
when they are still fresh and dewy. Dip them
in the batter and deep-fry them in fat
heated to 350°.

Almond Fritters

Cyuele :
Nym almandes, Sugur and salt, & payn de
mayn, & bray hem in a morter. Do thereto
eyren, frie hit in oylle or in grese, cast theron
sugur, & serue hit forth.
(*Two Fifteenth-century Cookery Books*)

Serves 4
2 EGGS
4 OZ (½ CUP) SUGAR
2½ OZ (1¼ CUPS) VERY FINE, DRY WHITE
BREADCRUMBS
5 OZ (1¼ CUPS) GROUND ALMONDS
1 TSP BAKING-POWDER
1 PT (2½ CUPS) MILK OR WHITE WINE
ICING SUGAR FOR DUSTING

Beat together the eggs and the sugar until the
mixture is light and creamy; then mix together
the breadcrumbs, ground almonds and baking-
powder and blend well. Beat the milk or wine
into the egg mixture and gradually add the dry
ingredients until you have a rich, creamy
batter. Leave to rest for 2 hours and then
deep-fry in hot fat, like fritters, a spoonful at a
time. Sprinkle with icing sugar before serving.

Brown Fries

'Pain perdu', which is prepared in the same way, but with white bread instead of brown, still exists.
(*Two Fifteenth century Cookery Books*)

Serves 2–3
6 EGG YOLKS PLUS 2 WHITES
2 TBS FLOUR
4 OZ ($\frac{1}{2}$ CUP) SUGAR
$\frac{1}{8}$ TSP SAFFRON
$\frac{1}{2}$ TSP SALT
6 THIN SLICES BROWN BREAD
BUTTER OR LARD FOR FRYING
CASTER (CONFECTIONER'S) SUGAR FOR GARNISH

Beat together the eggs, flour, sugar, saffron and salt; strain the mixture into a dish. Dip the slices of bread into this batter, making sure they are well coated. Fry in the hot fat until lightly browned. Remove, drain and serve sprinkled with fine sugar.

Medieval Bread and Butter Pudding

Soupes dorye :
Take gode almaunde mylke y-draw wyth wyn, an let hem boyle to-gederys, an caste ther-to Safroun & Salt; an than take Paynemayn, an kytte it an toste it, an wete it in wyne, an ley it on a dysshe, an caste the syrip ther-on. An than make a dragge of powder Gyngere, Sugre, canel, Clowes, Maces, an caste ther-on. When it is y-dressid, an serue thanne forth for a pottage gode. (*Two Fifteenth-century Cookery Books*)

Serves 6
10 SLICES OF BREAD, TOASTED
4 OZ ($\frac{1}{2}$ CUP) BUTTER
$\frac{1}{2}$ PT (1 CUP) WHITE WINE
4 EGGS
1 PT (2$\frac{1}{2}$ CUPS) ALMOND MILK (*see p.* 53)
$\frac{1}{4}$ TSP SAFFRON
$\frac{1}{8}$ TSP SALT
3 TBS SUGAR
$\frac{1}{4}$ TSP GINGER
$\frac{1}{4}$ TSP CINNAMON
$\frac{1}{4}$ TSP GROUND CLOVES
$\frac{1}{4}$ TSP MACE

Cut the crusts off the slices of toast and butter them. Lay them in a 10-inch shallow ovenproof earthenware dish and sprinkle a little of the wine over them. Beat the eggs, almond milk, the remaining wine, saffron, salt and sugar together and pour over the bread. Mix the spices and sprinkle half the mixture over the top. Stand the dish in a tin half filled with boiling water, bake at 350° (Mark 4) for 25 minutes or until set.

Sprinkle with the remaining spices and serve hot, warm or chilled.

Honey and Saffron Quiche

This is one of the many dishes served to Henry IV at his coronation feast at Westminster on 13 October 1399. It is very rich, and will serve eight guests if cut into thin slices.

Doucetye :
Take Creme a gode cupfulle, & put it on a straynoure; thanne take yolkys of Eyroun & put ther-to, & a lytel mylke; then strayne it thorw a straynoure in-to a bolle; then take Sugre y-now, & put ther-to, or ellys hony forde faute of Sugre, than coloure it with Saffroun; than take thin cofyns, & put in the ovynne lere, & lat hem ben hardyd, than take a dysshe y-fastenyd on the pelys ende; & pore thin comade in-to the dyssche, & fro the dyssche in-to the cofyns; & when they don a-ryse wel, take them out, & serue hem forth.

Serves 8
$\frac{3}{4}$ PT (2 CUPS) THICK CREAM
$\frac{1}{8}$ TSP SAFFRON
$\frac{1}{4}$ PT ($\frac{1}{2}$ CUP) MILK
3 EGGS PLUS 2 EXTRA YOLKS
$\frac{1}{4}$ PT ($\frac{1}{2}$ CUP) HONEY
A 9-INCH PASTRY SHELL, BAKED BLIND
    (UNFILLED)

Heat the cream, saffron and milk together in a saucepan until cooked. Beat the eggs and yolks with honey in a bowl. Slowly add the hot liquid, beating constantly with a wire whisk.

Pour into the cooled shell. Bake at 350° for 25–30 minutes until set.

=====

Spiced Wine Custard

Cawdelle ferry :
Take yolkys of eyroun Raw, y-tryid fro the
whyte ; than take gode wyne, and warme it on
the potte on a fayre Fyre, an caste ther-on
yolkys, and stere it wyl, but let it nowt boyle
tylle it be thikke ; and caste ther-to Sugre,
Safroun, & Salt, Maces, Gelofres, an Galyngale
y-grounde smal, & flowre of Canelle : & whan
thou dressyst yn, caste blanke pouder ther-on.
(Two Fifteenth-century Cookery Books)

Serves 4
4 EGGS PLUS 2 YOLKS
1 PT (2½ CUPS) RED WINE
2 OZ (¼ CUP) SUGAR
½ TSP EACH CINNAMON AND GROUND CLOVES
⅛ TSP SAFFRON
½ TSP MACE
¼ TSP GALINGALE, *see* glossary, (OPTIONAL)
A PINCH EACH OF GINGER, CINNAMON AND
 NUTMEG

Beat the eggs. Heat the wine and whisk it into the eggs; stir in the sugar and add the cinnamon, cloves, saffron, mace and galingale if available. Stir over low heat, or in the top of a double boiler, until thickened. Pour into a serving dish. Chill. Sprinkle the ginger, cinnamon and nutmeg very lightly on top.

The mixture can also be very slightly thickened by longer cooking and taken as an egg-nog, served as a hot custard with baked apples, or chilled and poured over vanilla ice-cream.

=====

Rice Mould

Rys
Take a porcyoun of Rys & pyke hem clene,
& sethe hem welle & late hem kele ; then
take gode Mylke of Almaundys & do ther-to,
& sethe & stere hem wyle ; & do ther-to sugne
an hony, & serue forth.
(Two Fifteenth-century Cookery Books)

Serves 4
3 OZ (½ CUP) RICE
1 PT (2½ CUPS) WATER
1 PT (2½ CUPS) ALMOND MILK (*see p.* 53)
2 OZ (¼ CUP) SUGAR
4 TBS HONEY

Pour the rice into the boiling water, stir and then simmer until tender. Drain. Return the rice to a smaller saucepan, add the almond milk, sugar and honey and stir well. Bring to the boil and then simmer gently, stirring continually, for 10–12 minutes, or until thick. Allow to cool. Pour into an oiled mould and chill. Turn out and serve surrounded with a ring of cold baked apples or stewed pears.

Fruit Pudding

Gaylede :
Take Almaunde Mylke & Flowre of Rys, & do
ther-to Sugre or Hoy, & Powder Gyngere &
Galyngale ; then take figys, an kerue hem a-to, or
Roysons y-hole, or harf Wastel y-dicyd and
coloure it with Saunderys, & sethe it & dresse
hem yn.
(Two Fifteenth-century Cookery Books)

Serves 4
1 PT (2½ CUPS) ALMOND MILK (*see p.* 53)
1½ TBS RICE FLOUR
2 OZ (¼ CUP) SUGAR
4 TBS HONEY
1 TSP POWDERED GINGER
1 TSP POWDERED GALINGALE (OPTIONAL), (*see*
 p. 236)
4 OZ (1 CUP) EACH, CHOPPED FIGS AND RAISINS
2 OZ (1 CUP) ANY PLAIN CAKE, SLIGHTLY STALE,
 DICED SMALL

Garnish
1 OZ (2 TBS) BUTTER
1 OZ (½ CUP) CAKE CRUMBS
2 TBS SUGAR

Put the almond milk, rice flour, sugar, honey, ginger and galingale into a saucepan and mix well. Bring to the boil, then simmer, stirring until the mixture has thickened. Stir in all the other ingredients and pour into a pudding dish.

Melt the butter in a saucepan. Stir in the

cake crumbs and the sugar and cook over low heat until crisp and crumbly. Scatter the resulting mixture over the pudding and transfer to a hot oven until brown and crisp on top. Serve with cream.

Sauces

Almond Milk

Almond milk and verjuice are the two basic sauces without which you cannot hope to recapture the flavour of English medieval cooking. Whether you use milk or cream depends on the consistency of the dish you are preparing. For instance, cream is too sticky with rice, but is good with puddings where a little thickening is needed.

¾ PT (2 CUPS) MILK OR CREAM
2 OZ (½ CUP) COARSELY GROUND ALMONDS
¼ TSP BITTER ALMOND ESSENCE
2 TBS ORGEAT SYRUP (MADE BY COMBIER OF
   SAUMUR IN FRANCE)

Simmer all the ingredients together for 10 minutes and allow to cool, covered. It can be strained or not, as desired.

Verjuice

Although it was a most important basic ingredient in medieval English cookery, it is hard to define verjuice, as each family apparently had its own method. It was the juice (sometimes fermented) of various unripe fruits such as grapes, crab-apples or goose-berries. In some cases the fruits were kept separate, while at other times they were mixed together. The leaves of Damask roses were often added.

Verjuice was closer to a very sharp cider than to vinegar, although the mild cider apple vinegars now available in health-food shops are an acceptable substitute. It can also be replaced by cider mixed with a little rose-hip syrup or juice. The practice of distilling verjuice for pickles explains the apparent mildness of some pickles.

I have made my own verjuice by crushing some crab-apples and unripe grapes in a mortar. I put it all in a jar with a little cider and leave it on the window-sill to ferment for a day or two. I then strain it into a bottle and keep it in the refrigerator. An American lady from the South tells me that this fermented fruit juice is still made and used by most of her neighbours.

Melted Butter Sauce

5 OZ (⅔ CUP) BUTTER
2 OZ (½ CUP) FLOUR
1 PT (2½ CUPS) COLD WATER
½ TSP SALT
¼ TSP PEPPER

Melt 2 oz (4 tbs) of the butter in a saucepan over a low flame. Stir in the flour and cook gently for 2–3 minutes. Add the water gradually, raise the heat and stir continually until the mixture simmers. Lower the heat immediately. Beat in the remaining butter in small pieces, continuing to beat until it is all melted. The spoon should eventually remain coated when you remove it from the sauce. Do not allow it to boil after adding the butter as this will thin the sauce. Season.

Sorrel Sauce
Sauce Sorell

Take Sorell, grynde hem small, And drawe hem thorgh a Streynoure, and caste there-to Salt, and serue hit-forth.
(*Two Fifteenth-century Cookery Books*)

Serves 2
½ LB SORREL (CALLED SCHAV OR SOUR-GRASS
   IN THE USA)
¼ CUP WATER
SALT AND PEPPER TO TASTE

Wash the sorrel, put into a saucepan with the

water, and cook gently until wilted. Puree in blender and season to taste. (Modern palates may require the addition of a little butter and/or cream.)
or
The well-washed sorrel leaves left raw can be very finely chopped and sprinkled over the fish before serving.

Sauce for Salt Fish (1)

Stokfish in Sauce
(*Two Fifteenth-century Cookery Books*)

¾ PT (2 CUPS) STRAINED FISH STOCK
2 OZ (¾ CUP) FINELY CHOPPED PARSLEY
3 TBS VERJUICE (*see p.* 53) OR CIDER VINEGAR
½ TSP GINGER

Combine all the ingredients in a saucepan. Bring to the boil and simmer for 5 minutes. Serve over the fish, which you have soaked sufficiently to desalt it and then poached. I like to add pepper and salt, but if the fish is still quite salty, omit the salt.

This sauce can also be used for smoked fish, haddock or cod.

Sauce for Salt Fish (2)

Sauce for Stokfysshe in an-other maner
(*Two Fifteenth-century Cookery Books*)

This sauce reminds me a little of the walnut sauce served with spaghetti in northern Italy. The names of so many medieval dishes came from Lombardy that it is possible that this too originally came from there.

4 OZ (1 CUP) WALNUTS
2 CLOVES GARLIC, CRUSHED
¾ OZ (⅓ CUP) BREADCRUMBS
½ TSP PEPPER
¼ TSP SALT
½ PT (1 CUP) FISH STOCK

Put all the ingredients into a blender and purée.

Pour into a saucepan, heat and serve with boiled salt cod or poached smoked haddock.

Sauce for a Goose (or Chicken)

Sauce for a Gos
(*Two Fifteenth-century Cookery Books*)

Stuff the goose with parsley, peeled and seeded grapes, garlic; season the stuffing with salt and pepper. When the goose is done, take out the stuffing, put it in a bowl and mix it with riced hard-boiled egg yolk (1 egg yolk to 1 cup of stuffing.) Mix well and add a little verjuice or cider vinegar. Reheat in a pan and serve with the goose, and its gravy.

Garlic Sauce (for Goose or Chicken)

Sauce Gauncile
(*Two Fifteenth-century Cookery Books*)

¾ PT (2 CUPS) MILK
2 TBS FLOUR
1 OZ (2 TBS) BUTTER
1–2 CLOVES GARLIC

Thicken the milk with the flour and butter and cook, stirring, until creamy. Squeeze the garlic into the milk through a garlic-press and season with salt and pepper. Simmer for 5 minutes and spoon over the carved pieces of bird.

The addition of a pinch of saffron transforms this into another medieval sauce called 'gauncile', which was served with boiled or roast pork.

Poivrade or Pepper Sauce

Sauce Piper for Veel and for Venysoun
(*Two Fifteenth-century Cookery Books*)

8 SLICES FRIED BREAD
4 TBS MEAT STOCK
2 TBS VINEGAR
¼ TSP PEPPER
½ TSP SALT

Take the fried bread, which you have soaked in the meat stock and vinegar, and add the pepper and salt. Purée in a blender and then put into a saucepan; bring to the boil and simmer until the sauce is thick and smooth. Serve with venison.

Apple Sauce with a Medieval Flavour

(Adapted from two Fifteenth-century Cookery Books)

¼ PT (½ CUP) WATER
⅛ TSP SAFFRON
4 OZ (1 CUP) APPLES, PEELED AND SLICED
1 OZ (¼ CUP) COARSELY GROUND DATES

Boil the water with the saffron until it is bright yellow. Add the remaining ingredients, season and cook until the apples are soft. Serve with roast pork.

Sage Sauce (for Pork or Ham)

(Two Fifteenth-century Cookery Books)

4 HARD-BOILED EGG YOLKS
4 TBS FRESH SAGE, CHOPPED
1–2 TBS VINEGAR
¼ PT (½ CUP) STOCK
¼ PT (½ CUP) CREAM

Mash the egg yolks, the chopped sage and half the vinegar to a smooth paste in a mortar. Put in a small pan and beat in the stock and cream gradually, using a whisk. When the sauce is smooth and perfectly blended, taste and add a little more vinegar if necessary. Heat and pour over sliced pork or ham.

This is also excellent cold, but it must be allowed to cool after being poured over the meat, as it becomes semi-jellied if the stock is concentrated.

Almond Caramel Sauce

Froyde Almoundys

(Two Fifteenth-century Cookery Books)

5 OZ (1 CUP) BROWN SUGAR
½ PT (1 CUP) WATER, LIGHTLY SALTED
2 OZ (½ CUP) GROUND ALMONDS

Boil the sugar and water together until you have a thick syrup. Add the almonds when it has cooled a little. Serve hot, especially over ice-cream. Excellent also with fried chicken or pork.

Bread, Biscuits and Cakes

Manchet Bread

In the fourteenth century the following method was used. Bolted meal (sifted white whole wheat flour) was put into a clean tub. Ale barme (yeast) and salt were added. Enough warm water was put in to make the dough, which was kneaded with a 'break' (like a machine for cutting paper), or with the feet. The dough was then wrapped in a cloth and left to rise for an hour. Finally it was formed into round flat loaves which were slashed, pricked and then baked.

½ OZ (1 PACKAGE) YEAST
½ PT (1 CUP) WARM WATER
10 OZ (2–2½ CUPS) WHITE WHOLE-WHEAT FLOUR
5 OZ (1 CUP) ALL-PURPOSE FLOUR
1 TSP SALT
2 OZ (4 TBS) SOFTENED BUTTER

Dissolve the yeast in half the warm water. Put the two types of flour and the salt into a bowl; make a well in the flour and add all the water and butter. Mix well. Add more flour if the mixture is too sticky to knead. Knead for 10 minutes until smooth and elastic and then put into a greased bowl, covered with a cloth. Let the dough rise for 1–1½ hours, or until it has doubled in bulk.

Punch it down and shape it into rather flat,

round loaves. Put these on to a greased baking sheet, cover with a cloth and leave to rise for 45 minutes (or until twice the size). The loaves can be brushed with egg wash, to 'endore' them, before baking, and the tops can be slashed and pricked with a fork. Bake at 375° (Mark 5) for 35–40 minutes.

Rastons

The original recipe (in *Two Fifteenth-century Cookery Books*) tells you to make a round loaf as in the recipe for manchet bread (*p.* 55). The loaf should be crisp and hot from the oven. Cut off the crust, making a serrated division as for a radish, 'in the manner of a crown'. Lift off the top, reserve it and scoop out the crumb. Grind this very finely in a blender and sauté it in butter, but do not crisp. Pack back into the loaf, replace the 'lid' and return to the oven for about 10–15 minutes.

Here is my modernized version: buy 2 large round loaves or follow the preceding recipe for manchet bread. Warm them in the oven. Slice the top off one and scoop out nearly all the crumb. Cut all the crust off the other loaf, cut into neat serving pieces and butter them (adding garlic if you wish). Pack these crusty pieces upright into the loaf, replace the lid and reheat for 5–10 minutes in the oven.

Saffron Bread

This is the English pre-Reformation Lenten bread, probably made in the late fifteenth or early sixteenth century. It used to be made sweet, and you can still do this by adding ¼ lb (½ cup) sugar and 3 oz (½ cup) raisins and currants. This sweet version makes a delicious tea bread, and is very good toasted. The crust is shiny and golden and the crumb a delicious yellow.

The bread keeps for a long time and makes attractive crumbs for breading veal and fish fillets, while stale slices baked very slowly in the oven can be turned into excellent rusks. Rub these with garlic and use them as a garnish for fish soup.

Makes 1 loaf
¼–⅓ PT (¾ CUP) MILK
¼ TSP SAFFRON
½ OZ (1 PACKAGE) YEAST
4 TBS LUKEWARM WATER
1 LB (3½ CUPS) FLOUR
2 TSP SALT
2 EGGS

Scald the milk with the saffron. Let it cool. Dissolve the yeast in the lukewarm water. Sift together ¾ lb (3 cups) of the flour and the salt. Make a well in the flour, spoon in the eggs, milk and yeast mixture and blend. Add enough flour to prevent it becoming sticky. Knead, adding more flour as needed, until the dough is smooth and elastic. Put in a greased bowl in a warmish place and leave to rise until it is double in bulk (about 45 minutes). Punch down and shape into a round loaf. Place this on a greased baking sheet and leave to rise until it has again doubled in size.

Bake at 375° (Mark 5) for 25–30 minutes, then cool on a rack.

If you decide to use raisins, knead them in after punching the dough down the first time. The sugar should be mixed in with the flour at the beginning.

Gingerbread

In the Middle Ages this gingerbread would sometimes be covered with gold leaf.

Gyngerbrede :
Take quart of hony, & sethe it, & skeme it clene ; take Safroun, pouder Pepir, & throw ther-on ; take gratyd Brede, & make it so chargeaunt that it wol be y-lechyd ; then take pouder Canelle, & straw ther-on y-now ; then make yt square, lyke as thou wolt leche yt ; take when thou lechyst hyt, an caste Box leves a-bouyn, y-stykyd ther-on, on clowys. And if thou wolt haue it Red, coloure it with

Saunderys y-now.
(*Two Fifteenth-century Cookery Books*)

1½ LB (2 CUPS) HONEY
¼ TSP EACH SAFFRON AND GROUND PEPPER
2½ OZ (5 CUPS) BREADCRUMBS
½ TSP GROUND CINNAMON
18 SMALL BAY LEAVES
6 CLOVES

Bring the honey to the boil in a pan with the saffron and pepper. Remove from the heat and stir in the breadcrumbs so as to make a very thick paste. Simmer on an asbestos mat over low heat for 15–20 minutes until the paste has dried out. Place in a 9–inch by 5–inch loaf tin. Smooth over the top and sprinkle with cinnamon. Make 6 trefoils on the top by sticking groups of three bay leaves together at the stalk end with a clove pierced through each group into the surface of the ginger bread. Chill for several days in the refrigerator. Serve in small slices.

Pickles and Preserves

Mixed Fruit and Vegetable Pickle
(*The Forme of Cury, 1378*)

A 2-INCH PIECE OF PARSLEY ROOT
1 MEDIUM TURNIP
¼ HEAD CABBAGE
4 PEARS, PEELED AND CORED
¼ PT (½ CUP) VINEGAR
¼ TSP ALLSPICE
⅛ TSP SAFFRON
¼ PT (½ CUP) RESINATED OR DRY WHITE WINE
¾ LB (1 CUP) HONEY
2 TBS MUSTARD
2 OZ (½ CUP) EACH RAISINS AND CURRANTS
¼ TSP EACH ANISEED, FENNEL SEED, GINGER AND
  CINNAMON
½ TSP NUTMEG

Peel the parsley root and turnip and grate. Shred the cabbage finely. Put all these in enough water to cover and boil until almost tender. Add the pears and cook until tender. Drain and cool. Combine the vinegar, allspice, saffron, wine, honey and mustard and bring to the boil. Add the remaining ingredients and simmer for 15 minutes. Add the vegetables and fruit and leave overnight, or pour into sterilized jars and seal.

Forcemeats and Garnishes

Stuffing for a Roast Chicken
The chicken would be scalded with boiling water, then the skin at the neck was pierced and the chicken was 'blown'. I have seen much later French recipes for *canard a l'orange* which refer to this ballooning process. Hard-boiled egg yolks were used instead of bread-crumbs in the fifteenth century for stuffings, while breadcrumbs were used instead of flour for thickening soups, stews and sauces.
(*Two Fifteenth-century Cookery Books*)

For a 2½-lb chicken or double the quantity for a
  5-lb capon:
5–6 HARD-BOILED EGG YOLKS
4 OZ (½ CUP) PARSLEY, BLANCHED AND FINELY
  CHOPPED
2 OZ (¼ CUP) BUTTER
⅛ TSP GROUND GINGER (OR FRESH GINGER, FINELY
  CHOPPED)
¼ TSP PEPPER
½ TSP SALT
⅛ TSP SAFFRON

Combine all the ingredients and stuff the chicken with the resulting mixture.

Stuffing for a Capon (or Goose)

(*Two Fifteenth-century Cookery Books*)

For a 4-lb bird:
2 SLICES BACON, FINELY CHOPPED
4 TBS PARSLEY, FINELY CHOPPED
4 HARD-BOILED EGG YOLKS, RICED
¼ TSP GROUND GINGER
½ TSP GROUND CINNAMON
⅛ TSP SAFFRON
2 CLOVES, CRUSHED
¼ LB (¾ CUP) PEELED SEEDLESS GRAPES (IN SUMMER) *or* 2 OZ. (¾ CUP) ONION, FINELY CHOPPED AND PARBOILED (IN WINTER)
4 TBS DICED PORK SCRAPS

Melt the chopped bacon in a saucepan, stir in the parsley and cook for a few minutes. Add all the other ingredients and mix thoroughly. Stuff the bird and roast it in the usual way.

Raisin Stuffing for Small Birds

This stuffing, which was intended as a raisin soup in the fifteenth century, is about the right quantity for squab, pigeons and cornish or game hen; for quail two-thirds would be ample. (*Two Fifteenth-century Cookery Books*)

For each bird:
1 OZ (¼ CUP) SEEDLESS RAISINS
4 TBS APPLE SAUCE OR PUREE
2 TBS GROUND ALMONDS, MIXED WITH THICK CREAM
⅛ TSP GROUND GINGER
¼ TSP GALINGALE (OPTIONAL, *see* glossary)
¼ TSP PEPPER
¼ TSP SALT

Combine all the ingredients and stuff the bird with the mixture.

Stuffing for a Pig

(*Two Fifteenth-century Cookery Books*)

For a 9-lb sucking-pig:
3 EGGS, LIGHTLY BEATEN
2 OZ (1 CUP) BREADCRUMBS
2 OZ (½ CUP) GRATED SUET

⅛ TSP SAFFRON
½ TSP SALT
¼ TSP POWDERED GINGER *or* FINELY CHOPPED FRESH GINGER
¼ TSP PEPPER

Combine all the ingredients and stuff the pig with the mixture, or slip it into pockets slit in a piece of pork for roasting.

Sage as a Garnish

(*Two Fifteenth-century Cookery Books*)

¼ TSP GROUND GINGER
¼ TSP POWDERED GALINGALE (OPTIONAL, *see p.* 000)
⅛ TSP GROUND CLOVES
4 HARD-BOILED EGGS
1 TSP CHOPPED SAGE
2 TBS WINE VINEGAR

Mix together the ginger, galingale and cloves. Mash the egg yolks with the sage and vinegar and mix with the powdered spices. Add the chopped egg whites. Spoon the mixture into a buttered grill pan and lay pieces of chicken or fish fillets on top. Grill (broil) until done.

Alternatively, bake in a shallow covered dish in the oven at 370–75° (Mark 4–5). This is perhaps preferable for fish fillets, which dry out easily.

Medieval Endoring

This process was used to give a roast bird an 'endored' or gilded appearance.
(*Two Fifteenth-century Cookery Books*)

1 OZ (2 TBS) BUTTER
¼ TSP SAFFRON
1 OZ (2 TBS) SUGAR
2 TBS VINEGAR
1 EGG YOLK

Cook the butter with the saffron very gently, in a small saucepan, until the butter has turned bright yellow. Then add the sugar and vinegar and cook until syrupy. Draw off the heat and stir in the egg yolk. Return to low heat and continue cooking, without boiling, until the mixture has become very thick.

10 minutes before serving remove the bird from the oven and paint it with the endoring mixture. Return to the oven and leave for a few minutes to set.

THE SEVENTEENTH CENTURY

THE SEVENTEENTH CENTURY embraced the reigns of James I and Charles I, the Commonwealth and the Protectorate and three more Stuart reigns – those of Charles II, James II and William and Mary. It was the rise of a new class in England. Those who had made their fortunes in such great trading ventures as the wildly renumerative East India Company, founded in 1600, spent their funds on country estates, often buying old houses from ruined nobles – impoverished by the imbalance that had developed between the production of wool and corn in Tudor times. These *nouveaux riches* filled the countryside with the spacious houses, but the raftered hall that had been the focus of the country house from Saxon times until Elizabeth I had been replaced by single-storey drawing rooms and dining rooms, where the family ate in greater privacy.

These proud new landowners spent recklessly on their new lands: kitchen gardens flourished, and on the big estates glasshouses were used to grow peaches, nectarines, even oranges and lemons. A gardening book written in 1629 by John Parkinson, apothecary to James I, tells how to grow and use beetroots, endive, spinach, asparagus, cabbages, carrots, turnips, parsnips, radishes, potatoes, beans, peas, artichokes, cucumbers, melons and pumpkins.

Market gardening was another new seventeenth-century idea; growing vegetables, especially lettuce and other salad plants, had become a thriving industry in Holland in the fifteenth century. Now produce was beginning to be brought into London from gardens to the north and north-west, and sold in the vicinity of St Paul's.

In 1673 the Lord Mayor had to restrict the sale of garden produce to certain streets in order to prevent stalls being set up in the churchyard itself. The structure at Covent Garden was erected in 1630 by Inigo Jones for the fourth Earl of Bedford and became the main centre for selling produce. One of the surviving records dealing with purchases of fresh produce concerns fruit and vegetables bought by the fifth Earl's kitchen clerk for the week of 21 June 1663. It is not clear whether any came from Covent Garden, but the list is impressive: pippins, Duke cherries, half-heart cherries, gooseberries, strawberries, white and red currants, raspberries, cherries, oranges and lemons; peas, artichokes, cucumbers, carrots, turnips, asparagus, lettuce, sorrel, parsley, onions and potherbs. The July account showed the addition of pears, white plums, red plums, Morocco plums, Newington peaches, great apricots and carnation cherries, as well as a number of candied fruits and other delicacies such as stoned dried currants in bunches, dried cherries with raspberries, dried apricots, currant paste, orange pills, marchpane (now called marzipan), candied cherries, candied currants, white apricots and white cherries.

Agriculture did not change much during the seventeenth century. In 1664 an effort was made to encourage the growing of potatoes, which had become the staple food of the peasantry in Ireland and might take the place of expensive grains on the tables of the English poor as well. John Forster wrote a lyrical volume called *England's Happiness Increased, or a Pure and Easie Remedy against all succeeding Dear Years; by A Plantation of the Roots called Potatoes*. The educated landowners and farmers were anxious to learn and to experiment, and books on agriculture proliferated, the most important historically being those of Gervase Markham.

The most intriguing cookery book of the seventeenth century is a posthumous work, published anonymously, in its eighth edition by 1675, written by Sir Kenelme Digbie who was an English eccentric, a Royalist, philosopher, gentleman and writer on cookery, a friend of Bacon, Galileo, Descartes, Harvey, Ben Jonson and Cromwell, a favourite of kings, and especially of queens, including Marie de Medici of France and Henrietta Maria of England.

Digbie went to Montpellier in 1658 for medical treatment, and it was there that he developed a 'magic powder' that made him famous. He came back to England at the Restoration as Chancellor to the Queen. In 1664, the king banished him from court again. He died in 1665, and four years later his son allowed the publication of *The Closet of the Eminently Learned Sir Kenelme Digbie, Knight, Opened: Whereby is discovered several ways for making of Metheglin, Sider, Cherrie Wine, Etc. Together with Excellent Direction for COOKERY – also for Preserving, conserving, Candying, etc.*, dedicated to the Countess Dowager of Exeter.

Unlike Sir Kenelme, Robert May, who published *The Accomplisht Cook* in 1660, was a professional cook and the son of a professional cook. His life spanned the reigns of Elizabeth I, James I, Charles I, Cromwell and Charles II, perhaps even James II.

Here are May's directions for one of the set pieces – called subtleties – that had been the Elizabethan idea of a good time at dinner:

Make the likeness of a ship in paste-board and cover it with paste, with Flags and Streamers, the guns belonging to it of Kickses [Kickshaws, generally almond paste or marzipan, but could be of any sweet materials; derived from French *quelque chose*], with such holes and trains of powder that they may all take Fire; place your ship firm in a great Charger; then make a salt round about it, and stick therein egg shells filled with rose-water.

Then in another Charger have the proportion of a stag made of course [sic] paste, with a broad arrow in the side of him and his body filled with claret wine.

In another Charger have the proportion of a Castle with Battlements, Percullises, Gates and Drawbridges made of paste-board, the guns of Kickses, and covered with course paste as the former; place it at a distance from the Ship, to fire at each other, the Stage being placed between them . . . At each end of the Charger, wherein is the Stag, place a Pie made of course paste in one of which let there be live Frogs, in the other live Birds. Make these Pies of course paste filled with Bran, and yellowed over with Saffron or Yolks of Eggs, gild them over in spots, as also the Stag, the Ship and the Castle; bake them and place them with gilt bay-leaves on the turrets and tunnels of the Castle and Pies; being baked make a hole in the bottom, take out the bran, put in your Frogs and Birds and close up with course paste.

Fire the trains of powder, order it so that some of the Ladies may be persuaded to pluck the Arrow out of the Stag, then will the claret follow as blood running from a wound. This being done with admiration to the beholders, after some short pause, fire the train of the Castle, that the pieces all of one side may go off; then fire the trains of one side of the Ship, as in a battle, and by degrees fire the trains of each other side, as before. This done, to sweeten the stink of the powder, let the Ladies take the eggshells full of sweet waters, and throw them at each other. All dangers being over, by this time you may suppose they will desire to see what is in the Pies; where, lifting off the lid of one pie, out skips some Frogs, which makes the Ladies to skip and shreek; next after the other Pie, whence comes out the Birds, who by a natural instinct flying at the light, will put out the Candles, so that what with the flying Birds, and skipping Frogs, the one above, the other beneath, will cause much delight and pleasure to the company: at length the candles are lighted and a banquet brought in, the music sounds, and everyone with much delight and content rehearses their actions in the former passages. These were formerly the delights of the Nobility, before good-housekeeping had left England, and the sword really acted that which was only counterfeited in such honest and laudable Exercises as these.

And here is May's advice on sauces: 'Mustard is good with brawn, beef etc. . . verjuice good to boiled chickens; swan with chaldrons, Ribs of beef with Garlick . . . sparrows and thrushes with salt and cinnamon . . .' and his menu for a Christmas dinner:

1st Course	2nd Course
Oysters	Oranges and lemons
A coller of brawn	Two couple of rabbits, one
Stewed Broth of mutton	larded
marrow bones	A pig sauced with tongues
A grand sallet	Three ducks, one larded
A Pottage of capons	Three pheasants, one larded
A breast of veal in stassado	Made dish with puff paste
A boiled Partridge	Bolonia sausages, and
A chine of beef, or sirloin	anchovies, mushrooms and
roast	caviare and pickled oysters
Mince Pies	in a dish
A jegote of mutton with	Six teels, three larded
anchove sauce	A gammon of Westphalia
A made dish of sweetbreads	Bacon

A swan roast
A pasty of venison
A kid with a pudding in
his belly
A steak pie
A haunch of venison roasted
A turkey roast and stuffed
with cloves
A made dish of chickens with
puff paste
Two brangeese, one roasted
one larded
Two large capons, one larded
A custard

Ten plovers, five larded
A quince pie, or Warden pie
Six woodcocks, three larded
A standing tart in puff paste
preserved fruits, pippins,
etc.
A dish of larks
Six dried neat's tongues
Sturgeon
Powdered geese
Jellies

The rapid growth of the big farming estates in the seventeenth century and the winter feeding of cattle with turnips brought more meat to the town dwellers. Much of this still went to the cook shops near the river in London. A French visitor, M. Misson, wrote this description of their operation:

Generally, four Spits, one over another, carry round each five or six Pieces of Butchers' Meat, Beef, Mutton, Veal, Pork and Lamb; you have what Quantity you please cut off, fat, lean, much or little done; with this, a little Salt and Mustard upon the Side of a Plate, a Bottle of Beer and a Roll; there is your whole Feast.

Thomas Muffet, writing in 1655, quoted this popular saying of the day: 'The Spaniard eats, the German drinks, and the English exceed in both'. Breakfast, still taken at 6 or 7, was made up of cold meats, fish, cheese, and ale or beer. Herrings, salted and dried, were often served. Pepys offered his New Year's guests a 'barrel of oysters, a dish of neats' (calves') tongues, and a dish of anchovies, wine of all sorts and Northdown ale'.

One source of details about what the king and his household were eating in the seventeenth century came from the pen of Patrick Lambe, who called his book – published in 1710, three years after his death – *Royal Cookery, or The Compleat Court-Book*, with a subtitle that is a book in itself: 'Containing the Choicest Receipts in all the Several Branches of Cookery, viz., for the making of Soups, Bisques, Olios, Terrines, Surtouts, Puptons, Ragoos, Forc'd Meats, Sauces, Pattys, Pies, Tarts, Tansies, Cakes, Puddings, Jellies, etc. By Patrick Lambe, Esq. Near Fifty years Master-Cook to their late Majesties, King Charles II, King James II, King William and Queen Mary, and Queen Anne'.

That Lambe was superbly qualified to write about royal cookery there is no doubt; he, and apparently his father before him, served in one capacity or another in the royal kitchens through his entire adult life. His book, though not really useful in the kitchen, gives a picture of the changing food habits of his day and the French manners and dishes introduced by Charles II's court – and later taken up by other Englishmen. Privacy was the big change: great public feasts lost favour, and hours of labour and quantities of ingredients were lavished on one small dish for the private table of a king.

Toward the end of the seventeenth century, the dinner hour began its slide from noon to the evening hours. The introduction, in mid-century, of tea, coffee, and chocolate provided for those who could afford them a new kind of social entertainment that both sexes could enjoy. A late breakfast, about 9 or 10, of coffee or chocolate and rolls became fashionable; and that meant a later dinner hour. The dinner itself was still a formidable meal. Our French friend, Misson, described the situation this way: The English eat a great deal at Dinner; they rest a while, and to it again, till they have quite stuff'd their Paunch. Their Supper is moderate: Gluttons at Noon, and abstinent at Night'.

A reel of dishes of meat and fish was still served; and poultry – once a poor man's dish – was now regarded as a delicacy. Chickens and geese were expensive and became status foods. It is at this time that the order of the courses was switched, with the fish coming before the meat instead of after, as it did in Tudor times. Vegetables still appeared chiefly in soups, but toward the end of the century they began to join the meat in the modern way. Orchards were developing even faster than kitchen gardens, and fruits were the luxuries of those with money to spend. As more trade with the East opened up, the price of sugar fell. Now to the traditional English beef, bread, and beer was added the incomparable English pudding, a descendent of the Saxon one, now made with milk, eggs, flour, butter, sugar, suet, marrow, raisins and other fruits. M. Misson wrote: 'Blessed be he that invented pudding, for it is manna that hits the Palates of all Sortes of People'.

During the seventeenth century, the cheaper wines disappeared; and the man in the street drank ale or beer, except in the West Country where cider was the thing. Cromwell's Navigation Act of 1651, designed to replace the Dutch trading ships with English ones, had the unfortunate effect of cutting off the importing of French and German wines – which had been coming in on Dutch ships. The 1688 tax on imported wines was another blow. At the time, all wines were still stored in their wooden casks, to be drawn off in bottles with wooden stoppers just before serving at table. The custom of bottling and laying down special wines came with the introduction of the cork stopper at the end of the century.

Beer was still brewed at home in the country, but more often it was provided by innkeepers in a range of strengths. It has been calculated that 'small beer' had about 150–200 calories to the pint, provided by the alcohol and sugar content, and even a modest amount of calcium and various vitamins. Three pints of good home-brewed beer a day were a worthwhile part of a youngster's diet. It was the loss of this food value that caused a furore among the nutrition-conscious when tea, drunk without milk and thus without any calories, replaced beer and ale in the daily lives of working people a century later. No one has yet come forward to defend another favourite seventeenth-century drink as a health food, *Aquavitae*, a crude gin probably first imported from Holland, a rapid success already being distilled by two hundred different firms in London and Westminster. Hard spirits got another boost when an Irish drink called Usquebagh began to catch on, and was later known as Whiskey.

Coffee, a newer drink, was imported in turn from Arabia, Jamaica, Brazil, and Africa. In 1652, a Turkish merchant opened the first coffee house in London in St Michael's Alley. It was a smash success, and imitators sprang up all over town. One in Queen's Head Alley has been credited with first serving chocolate, which had become fashionable as a breakfast drink with the rich. Chocolate came from Mexico, where the Aztecs had mixed it with honey. It remained a luxury drink as long as the price of sugar was high and never did reach the popularity of the more stimulating drinks – coffee and tea. From the time of Charles II to the late eighteenth century, the London coffee house was the centre of social life. By Queen Anne's time the list of coffee houses ran to nearly five hundred. The coffee houses were nearly as important as business centres as they were as social spas. The newspapers of the day carried no shipping or business news, so news from mouth to ear was essential and the coffee house a good place to hear it.

Tea, at first expensive and drunk in the Chinese fashion, without milk, did not become a popular cheap drink until the eighteenth century. Whey was well thought of as a beverage; for some reason it was considered to be more wholesome than milk, as skimmed milk is today.

The seventeenth century was a good one for London taverns, too. They were happy meeting places for all sorts of people and offered in a convivial atmosphere – and also in private rooms – ale and beer, sack from Jerez, Rhenish wine from Germany, cider from Kent. A tavern dinner might begin with anchovies, scallops, neat's tongue and gherkins, followed by mutton chops, pigeons, ham, puddings and pies. There were the 'ordinaries', such as Hercules Pillars and Fleet Street, where diners sat at a long table and shared the food and the bill. And

grander establishments like the Mitre in Wood Street, marked for fame in Pepys's *Diary*. Perhaps the greatest was the Mermaid in Bread Street, which early on was the haunt of the 'Noble Band of Sirenaicans': Ben Jonson, Francis Beaumont, John Fletcher, Will Shakespeare, and their cronies. Jonson fixed its place against any claims of rivals by the same name when he wrote:

> At Bread Street's Mermaid having dined and merry,
> Proposed to go to Holborn in a wherry . . .

and mentioned

> . . . A pure cup of rich canary wine
> Which is the Mermaid's now but shall be mine.

Soups

Summer Soup with Meatballs

Serves 4

1 LB (2 CUPS) MINCED (GROUND) BEEF
¼ TSP GROUND CLOVES
1 TSP SALT
¼ TSP PEPPER
⅛ TSP SAFFRON
1 EGG
2 PT (5 CUPS) BEEF STOCK
½ PT (1 CUP) ALMOND MILK (*see p.* 53)
2 OZ (½ CUP) CURRANTS, SOAKED IN 4 TBS
    (¼ CUP) SHERRY
½ TSP GROUND GINGER
(*Andrew Boorde, 1542*)

Combine the beef, cloves, salt, pepper, saffron and egg in a bowl and blend together. Shape into small meatba ls. Heat the stock and almond milk in a saucepan; add the currants and ginger. Simmer for 10 minutes. Then poach the meatballs in the stock for 5–8 minutes and serve in the liquid.

Portugal Broth

This was the favourite broth of Katharine, daughter of Don John IV, King of Portugal, who married Charles II of England.

Make very good broth with some lean of veal, beef and mutton, and with a scrawny hen or young cock. After it is scummed, put in an onion quartered (and, if you like it, a clove of garlic), a little parsley, a sprig of thyme, as much mint, a little balm; some coriander seeds bruised, and a very little saffron; a little salt, pepper, and a clove. When all the substance is boiled out of the meat, and the broth very good, you may drink it so, or, pour a little of it upon toasted sliced bread, and stew it, till the bread have drunk up all that broth, then add a little more, and stew;

so adding by little and little, that the bread may imbibe it and swell: whereas if you drown it at once, the bread will not swell, and grow like jelly; and thus you will have a good potage. You may add parsley roots or leeks, cabbage or endive in the due time before the broth is ended boiling, and time enough for them to become tender. In the summer you may put in lettuce, sorrel, purslane, borage and bugloss, or what other pot-herbs you like.
(Sir Kenelme Digbie, 1669)

Serves 8

4 OZ BONELESS LAMB
4 OZ BONELESS VEAL
4 OZ BONELESS BEEF
1½ LB CHICKEN BACKS
1 LARGE ONION
1 CLOVE GARLIC
3 SPRIGS PARSLEY
½ TSP THYME
1 TSP BALM
1 TSP PENNYROYAL (WHEN AVAILABLE), OR MINT
½ TSP CORIANDER SEEDS, CRUSHED
½ TSP SAFFRON
2 TSP SALT
10 PEPPERCORNS
5 CLOVES
1 PARSLEY ROOT, SLICED
1 TSP BORAGE
2 LEEKS
3 PT (7½ CUPS) WATER

Combine all the ingredients in a large soup pan and boil for 2–3 hours. Strain.

The Queen's Soup

The Queen's ordinary Bouillon de sante in a morning was thus. A hen, a handful of parsley, a sprig of thyme, three of spear-mint, a little balm, half a great onion, a little pepper and salt, and a clove, as much water as would cover the hen; and this boiled to less than a pint, for one good porrenger full.
(Sir Kenelme Digbie, 1669)

Serves 1

A CHICKEN
A HANDFUL OF PARSLEY

I SPRIG THYME
3 SPRIGS MINT OR SPEARMINT
I SPRIG BALM
½ AN ONION
I CLOVE

Put all the ingredients in a pot with water to cover, bring to the boil, and simmer until the liquid is reduced to ¾ pint (2 cups). Strain and serve.

AVAILABLE), ALL BOILED FOR 5 MINUTES IN A LITTLE STOCK

Optional extras
A LITTLE MEAT GRAVY
A FEW DARK SCRAPS OF ROASTED MEAT

Combine all the ingredients in a large soup pan and boil gently for 2–3 hours. Strain and remove all fat from the surface before serving.

An English Potage

Another potage :
A good potage for dinner is thus made : boil beef, mutton, veal, volaille, and a little piece of the lean of a gammon of the best bacon, with some quartered onions, (and a little garlic, if you like it) you need no salt, if you have bacon, but put in a little pepper and cloves. If it be in the winter, put in a bouquet of sweet herbs, or whole onions, or roots, or cabbage. If season of herbs, boil in a little of the broth apart, some lettuce, sorrel, borage, and bugloss, etc. till they be only well mortified. If you put in any gravy, let it boil or stew a while with the broth ; put it in due time upon the toasted bread to mittoner, etc. If you boil some half-roasted meat with your broth it will be the better. (Sir Kenelme Digbie, 1669)

Serves 8–10
4 OZ BONELESS BEEF
4 OZ BONELESS MUTTON OR LAMB
4 OZ BONELESS VEAL
1½ LB CHICKEN PIECES (LEGS, BACKS, FEET ETC.)
4 OZ GAMMON
2 ONIONS, QUARTERED
I CLOVE GARLIC (OPTIONAL)
IO PEPPERCORNS
5 CLOVES
3–4 PT (8–10 CUPS) WATER

In winter add
2 TBS DRIED, MIXED HERBS
ANY ROOT VEGETABLES, SLICED
SOME CABBAGE, SLICED OR SHREDDED

In summer add
LETTUCE, SORREL, BORAGE AND BUGLOSS (IF

Nourishing Broth

Make a very good gelly-broth of Mutton, Veal, joynt-bones of each, a Hen, and some bones (with a little meat upon them) of rosted Veal or Mutton, breaking the bones that the marrow may boil out. Put to boil with these some barley (first boiled in water, that you throw away) some Hartshorn rasped, and some stoned raisins of the Sun. When the broth is thoroughly well boiled, pour it from the Ingredients, and let it cool and harden into a gelly ; then take from it the fat on the top, and the dregs in the bottom. To a porrenger full of this melted, put the yolk of a new-laid egg beaten with the juyce of an Orange (or less if you like it not so sharp) and a little Sugar ; and let this stew gently a little while altogether, and so drink it. Some flesh of rosted Veal or Mutton, or Capon, besides the rosted-bones, that have marrow in them, doth much amend the broth.
(Sir Kenelme Digbie, 1669)

Serves 6–8
4 OZ BONELESS MUTTON OR LAMB
1½ LB CHICKEN BACKS, LEGS, ETC.
2 ONIONS, QUARTERED
I CLOVE GARLIC (OPTIONAL)
IO PEPPERCORNS
5 CLOVES
3–4 PT (8–10 CUPS) WATER
I VEAL HOCK OR KNUCKLE OR BONES OF VEAL
A HANDFUL OF PEARL BARLEY, BLANCHED AND DRAINED
A HANDFUL OF STONED RAISINS
1–2 EGG YOLKS
JUICE OF 1–3 ORANGES (OR I ORANGE AND I LEMON)

Garnish (for cold version)
A FEW SLIVERS OF CHICKEN BREAST
FRESH MINT

Boil the meat and bones in the water with the onions, garlic, peppercorns, cloves, barley and raisins. Cook gently for 2–3 hours, then strain and leave to cool. When the broth has set to a jelly, remove all fat from the top and the sediment from the bottom. Beat up 1 egg yolk per person with the juice of 1 orange (or orange and lemon juice mixed) and heat gently in the melted broth without allowing it to boil.

For a delicious cold jellied consommé, allow the soup to cool again and chill until it has set to a jelly, adding some tiny slivers of cooked breast of chicken as a garnish. Sprinkle some freshly chopped mint on top. Cold jellied consommés should always be chopped, as they then refract the light in a delectable way.

Pease Porridge

Take a Leg of Beef, or other fresh Meat, and make of it strong Broth; take two or three Quarts of hull'd Pease, and boil them by themselves to a Pulp with a little piece of Bacon; then take Sorrel, Spear Mint and Parsley chopt, put it into the strong Broth, and stew it over some Coals, with a quarter of a pound of Butter; thicken it with the Pulp of the Pease, and stir it; when you put them together, put in some French *bread with a little Salt, Pepper and Butter when you eat it.* (The Family Dictionary, *1695*)

Serves 6–8

2 LB SHIN OF BEEF (BEEF SHANK)
1 LARGE ONION
4 STALKS (STICKS) CELERY
2 CARROTS
1 TBS SALT
10 PEPPERCORNS
1 BAY LEAF
2 PT (5 CUPS) BROAD BEANS OR LIMA BEANS
¼ LB BACON
1 LB SORREL, CHOPPED
4 TBS EACH SPEARMINT AND PARSLEY, CHOPPED
1 OZ (2 TBS) BUTTER
6–8 SLICES OF FRENCH BREAD, TOASTED

Make some stock by boiling together the beef, onion, celery, carrots, salt, pepper and bay leaf with water to cover. Cook 3–4 hours and strain. Boil the beans with the bacon in water until they are soft enough to mash against the side of the pan. Drain and sieve. Put the sorrel, spearmint, parsley and butter into the beef broth and simmer for 10–15 minutes. Stir in the sieved beans to thicken and cook for 10 minutes longer. Serve with French bread.

Eggs

A Fricassee of Eggs

Eggs to frigacy:
Take 12 Eggs, boil them hard, cut them into Quarters; to which put a Pint of Strong Gravy, and half a pint of White Port Wine; season with a Blade or two of Mace, bruised Pepper, and a little Salt. Scald a little Spinage to make them look green, with a Pint of large Oisters to lay around the Dish. Put the Eggs into the Stewpan, with a few Mushrooms and Oisters, and rowl up a piece of Butter in the Yolk of an Egg and Flower, and shake it up thick for Sauce, Garnish with crisp Sippets, Limon and Parsly. A side Dish. (The Family Dictionary, *1695*)

Serves 6

½ LB MUSHROOMS, WASHED AND TRIMMED
1 OZ (2 TBS) BUTTER
1½ TBS FLOUR
1 PT (2½ CUPS) BEEF STOCK
½ PT (1 CUP) WHITE PORT (FRENCH *porto blanc*) OR
    WHITE WINE
1 TSP MACE
1 EGG YOLK
1 LB. (2 CUPS) SPINACH, COOKED AND CHOPPED
12 OYSTERS, SHUCKED, WITH THEIR LIQUOR
12 EGGS, HARD-BOILED, PEELED AND QUARTERED

Garnish
FRIED BREAD, CUT IN TRIANGLES

A FEW LEMON SLICES
CHOPPED PARSLEY

Cook the mushrooms in butter until softened. Sprinkle in the flour to thicken slightly and stir well. Add the stock, port and mace, and season. Blend well and simmer for 10 minutes. If the sauce is too thin, beat the egg yolk with a little of the sauce and stir it in, cooking gently without boiling.

Heat the spinach. Heat the oysters in their own liquid, barely cooking them, or they will toughen.

Arrange the eggs in the centre of a serving dish and cover with the sauce. Spoon the spinach in a ring round the edge with the oysters on top. Sprinkle with parsley, and garnish with lemon slices and fried bread. Reheat for a few seconds in a hot oven before serving.

Apples and Eggs in Pastry

A made dish of butter and eggs:
Take the yolks of twenty-four eggs, and strain them with cinnamon, sugar and salt, then put melted butter to them, some fine minced pippins, and minced citron, put it on your dish of paste, and put the slices of citron round about it, bar it with puff paste, and the bottom also, or short paste in the bottom.
(*Robert May, 1660*)

Serves 3–4
2 LARGE APPLES, PEELED, CORED AND SLICED
2 OZ (4 TBS) UNSALTED BUTTER
¼ TSP CINNAMON
4 EGGS
2 TBS SUGAR
I TSP SALT
I TSP GRATED LEMON PEEL
I TBS LEMON JUICE
I BAKED PUFF-PASTRY PIE SHELL, WARMED IN THE
    OVEN

Cook the apple slices lightly in butter with the cinnamon until tender. Scramble the eggs with a generous amount of butter and add the sugar,

salt, lemon peel and juice. Pour half the eggs into the pie shell, arrange the apple slices on top, then pour the butter from the pan in which the apples were cooked into the rest of the eggs. Stir and add them to the pie.

Serve hot as a luncheon dish. If the pie has to wait a little in a warm oven, undercook the eggs a little to prevent them hardening.

Very good with cold, sliced pork.

Eggs with Anchovies

Break twenty eggs into your Butter in a Dish and set them on Coals, take six Anchovies, and dissolve them in six spoonfuls of White-wine, and pour them into your Eggs, and having one handful of Pistaches beaten small in a Mortar, put them into your Eggs with a quarter of a Pint of Mutton Gravy: If you please, you may leave out your White-wine, and dissolve your Anchovies in Mutton-Gravy: let not your eggs be too stiff; then having a Dish full of Toasts, cut into large Sippets, lay your eggs by spoonfuls on the Toasts, or else dish them otherways, with the Toasts about them, on the Brims of the Dish.
(*The Family Dictionary, 1695*)

Serves 6
12 EGGS
3 OZ (6 TBS) BUTTER
I OZ (⅓ CUP) PISTACHIO NUTS, SHELLED AND
    CRUSHED
4 ANCHOVIES, CRUSHED
3–4 TBS WHITE WINE, BEEF STOCK OR LAMB
    DRIPPINGS
6 SLICES TOAST, BUTTERED

Start scrambling the eggs in the butter over very low heat or in the top of a double boiler. Stir in the nuts. Purée the anchovies in the wine or stock and stir into the eggs as they begin to thicken. Season with pepper. Keep the eggs rather light and runny. Serve on toast.

To make the best Tansy

This is a seventeenth-century version of *omelette fines herbes*, using 3 yolks for every 2 whites, and moistening the beaten eggs with a little cream. 'Succory' is chicory and the 'walnut-tree buds' could also be hawthorn buds, picked just before they open.

First then, for making the best Tansie, you shall take a certain number of Eggs, according to the bigness of your Frying-pan; and break them into a dish, abating ever the white of every third Egg: then with a spoon you shall cleanse away the little white Chicken knots, which stick into the Yolks; then with a little Cream, beat them exceedingly together; then take of green Wheat-blades, Violet leaves, Strawberry leaves, Spinage, Sucory, of each a like quantity, and a few Walnut-tree buds; chop and beat all very well, and then strain out the Juice, and mixing it with a little more Cream, put it to the Eggs, and stir all well together, then put in a few Crums of bread, fine grated bread, cinamon, Nutmeg and Salt, then put some sweet butter into the Frying-pan, and so soon as it is dissolved or melted, put in the Tansey, and fry it brown without burning. (Gervase Markham, 1660)

Quelquechose or Kikshaw

To make any quelquechose:
Take eggs, and half the quantities of white to yolks. Beat them. Add some cream, currants, cinnamon, cloves, mace, salt, a little ground ginger, spinach, endive and marigold flowers – coarsely chopped. Add well-chopped Pigg's Pettitoes; stir well. Melt butter in a frying pan and cook this mixture well on one side, turn and brown on the other and serve. This can be done with other mixtures of herbs and meats in the eggs . . . flesh, small Birds, sweet Roots, Oysters, Mussels, Cockles, Giblets, Lemons, Oranges, or any Fruits, Pulse or any Sallet herbs whatsoever . . . (Gervase Markham, 1660)

Serves 6
8 EGG YOLKS PLUS 4 WHITES
3 OZ (6 TBS) BUTTER

Filling
3 OZ ($\frac{1}{2}$ CUP) EACH SPINACH AND ENDIVE, FINELY CHOPPED
1 TBS MARIGOLD FLOWERS (*see* glossary), FINELY CHOPPED
2 OZ ($\frac{1}{2}$ CUP) CURRANTS
$\frac{1}{2}$ TSP CINNAMON
$\frac{1}{8}$ TSP GROUND CLOVES
$\frac{1}{4}$ TSP EACH POWDERED MACE AND GINGER
$\frac{1}{2}$ TSP SALT
2 TBS CREAM
2 OZ ($\frac{1}{4}$ CUP) MEAT FROM PIG'S TROTTERS, CHOPPED

Beat the eggs lightly and season to taste. Toss the combined filling ingredients in the butter in a saucepan until they are thoroughly warmed through. Season. Combine both mixtures and fry in the remainder of the butter in a large frying-pan. Brown on one side, then turn and repeat.

This early Western omelette is excellent cold.

Tea with Eggs

This nourishing brew seems to be a Europeanized version of Tibetan buttered tea, which is however made with salt, not sugar.

The Jusuite that came from China, Ann. 1664. told Mr. Waller, that they used tea sometimes in this manner. To near a pint of the infusion, take two yolks of new-laid eggs, and beat them very well with as much fine sugar as is sufficient for this quantity of Liquor; when they are very well incorporated, pour your Tea upon the Eggs and Sugar, and stir them well together. So drink it hot. This for when you come home from attending business abroad, and are very hungry, and yet have not conveniency to eat, presently a competent meal. (Sir Kenelme Digbie, 1669)

Serves 2
1 TSP CHINA TEA
1 PT (2$\frac{1}{2}$ CUPS) WATER

2–3 TSP SUGAR
2 EGG YOLKS

Pour the boiling water on to the tea and infuse lightly. Pour into a blender, add the sugar and eggs and blend for a few seconds. Drink while still very hot.

Fish

Poached Salmon Steaks

To seeth fresh salmon:
Take a little water, and as much Beere and
Salte, and put thereto Parsley, and Time, and
Rosemarie, and let all these boyle togethere. Then
put in your Salmon, and make your broth sharp
with some Vinegar.
(*The Good Huswife's Handmaid, 1594*)

Serves 4
½ PT (1 CUP) WATER
½ PT (1 CUP) BEER
I TSP SALT
4 TBS CHOPPED PARSLEY
I TSP THYME
I TSP ROSEMARY
2 LB SALMON STEAKS
2 TBS VINEGAR

Mix the water, beer and seasonings together and simmer for 10 minutes. Sharpen with the vinegar to taste. Poach the fish for 10–15 minutes, or until it flakes.

Baked Stuffed Salmon

(*Robert May, 1660*)

Serves 4–6
A 3–4 LB SALMON, CLEANED
I OZ (½ CUP) THYME, CHOPPED
I OZ (½ CUP) ROSEMARY, CHOPPED
I OZ (½ CUP) SAVORY, CHOPPED
I OZ (½ CUP) MARJORAM, CHOPPED
4 TBS FINELY CHOPPED ONION
I CLOVE GARLIC, FINELY CHOPPED
¼ TSP GROUND NUTMEG
½ PT (1 CUP) WINE
I BAY LEAF
½ TSP EACH SALT AND PEPPER
2 ANCHOVIES
3 OZ (6 TBS) BUTTER

Stuff the salmon with the herbs, onion, garlic and nutmeg. Put in a baking dish. Pour in the wine, add the bay leaf, salt and pepper, and put the anchovies in the bottom of the pan. Baste with half the butter and bake at 375° (Mark 5) for 20–25 minutes or until the fish flakes. Remove the fish onto the serving dish and keep warm. Reduce the sauce in the pan and beat in the remaining butter. Pour over the fish and serve.

Poached Fish with Fruit

Thicken sauce with a little cornstarch, fish stock,
verjuice, onions, barberries and currants, salt and
pepper. May layer the fish with dates and prunes
with sauce over top. (*Gervase Markham, 1660*)

Serves 3–4
I LB RIVER FISH, FILLETED
I PT (2½ CUPS) WATER
2 TBS VERJUICE (*see p. 53*) OR CIDER VINEGAR
I TSP SALT
4 OZ (1 CUP) SLICED ONION
2 OZ (½ CUP) CURRANTS
I OZ (¼ CUP) RED CURRANTS OR CRANBERRIES,
    LIGHTLY SWEETENED

73

1 TBS CORNFLOUR (OR CORNSTARCH)
1 TBS WATER
2 OZ (½ CUP) EACH DATES AND PRUNES, CHOPPED

Poach the fish in the water and verjuice, with the salt and onion. Remove and keep hot. Add the currants and berries to the pan and simmer for 5 minutes. Thicken with cornflour dissolved in the cold water.

Arrange the fish in layers with the chopped prunes and dates and pour the sauce over. Reheat and serve.

Rolled Fish Fillets

(*Robert May, 1660*)

Serves 4
1 LB FISH FILLETS (E.G. SOLE OR PLAICE)

Stuffing
2 OZ (4 TBS) BUTTER
1 OZ (½ CUP) BREADCRUMBS
2 OZ (1 CUP) SPINACH, WASHED AND CHOPPED
2 TBS CHOPPED SAGE
4 TBS CHOPPED PARSLEY
1 TSP CHOPPED THYME
1 TSP CHOPPED ROSEMARY
1 TSP CHOPPED MARJORAM
1 TSP CHOPPED SAVORY
½ TSP GROUND CINNAMON
½ TSP GROUND MACE
½ TSP GROUND NUTMEG
2 HARD-BOILED EGG YOLKS, CHOPPED
2 OZ (½ CUP) CURRANTS

Basting fluid
½ PT (1 CUP) WINE
2 TBS VINEGAR
2 TBS SUGAR
1 OZ (2 TBS) BUTTER

Melt the butter in a frying-pan. Toss in the breadcrumbs, spinach, herbs and seasonings, plus the egg yolks and currants. Mix all together and place about 4 tablespoons of the stuffing mixture on each fillet and roll it up, securing it with a toothpick. Place in a baking dish. Pour the wine, vinegar, sugar and butter into the bottom of the pan. Bake at 350°

(Mark 4) for 15–20 minutes or until the fish flakes, basting occasionally.

Buttered Whitings with Eggs

Boil whitings as if you would eat them in the ordinary way with thick butter sauce. Pick them clean from skin and bones, and mingle them well with butter, and break them very small, and season them pretty high with salt. In the mean time butter some eggs in the best manner, and mingle them with the buttered whitings, and mash them well together. The eggs must not be so many by a good deal as the fish. It is a most savoury dish. (Sir Kenelme Digbie, 1669)

Serves 4
1 LB WHITING, CLEANED (or POMPANOS IN USA)
2 OZ (¼ CUP) BUTTER, MELTED
2 EGGS
1 OZ (2 TBS) BUTTER
1 TSP SALT
¼ TSP PEPPER

Poach the whiting in salted water until it flakes. Remove the skin and bones and flake the fish into small pieces. Mix with the melted butter.

Scramble the eggs in butter until set. Toss with the fish. Season with salt and pepper.

Herring Pie

Take white pickled herrings, boil them a little, remove the skin, keep the backs only and remove the bones. Put them in a pastry casing with some raisins, some sliced winter pears or quince sliced very fine, sugar, cinnamon, sliced dates, sweet butter. Cover (with a pastry hole) and leave a vent at the top. Bake. Take claret, a little verjuice, sugar, cinnamon, and sweet butter. Boil them together and then pour them through the vent-hole; shake the pie a little and put it back into the oven a few minutes. Candy the pastry lid with sugar and water and glaze it in the oven. Serve hot. (Gervase Markham, 1660)

Serves 4

1½ LB PASTRY
1 LB PICKLED HERRINGS, FILLETED AND CHOPPED
2 PEARS, PEELED, CORED AND SLICED
2 OZ (½ CUP) RAISINS
2 OZ (½ CUP) DATES, STONED AND SLICED
2 TBS SUGAR
2 TBS FLOUR
1 TSP CINNAMON
1 OZ (2 TBS) BUTTER
4 TBS (¼ CUP) CLARET
4 TBS (¼ CUP) VERJUICE (*see p. 53*) OR CIDER
    VINEGAR
½ OZ (1 TBS) BUTTER
¼ TSP SUGAR
⅛ TSP CINNAMON

Roll out half the pastry and line a 9-inch pie dish with it. Arrange on the pastry alternate layers of herring, pear slices, raisins and dates. Sprinkle each layer with sugar, flour and cinnamon. Dot the top layer with butter. Cover with the pastry lid and make a vent in the top. Bake at 375° (Mark 5) for 20–25 minutes. Bring the wine, verjuice, butter, sugar and cinnamon to the boil and pour through the vent. Return to the oven and bake for another 10 minutes.

Salt Fish Pie with Sweet Spices

This pie is typical of the seventeenth century, with its high proportion of sweet ingredients, a tradition developed from the oriental sweet and sour combinations of the Middle Ages.

A Salt-Fish Pie, Sweet :
Take the best barrel cod, and water it very well; boil it, but not too much; take it out, and drain it; then pick all the white fish from the skin and bones, and mince it very fine; put to it a dozen of yolks of hard eggs minced; put to it a good handful of spinach and parsley minced; put in grated bread; season it with cloves, mace, ginger and cinnamon, some sack and orange-flower, or rose-water; put in currants and
raisins, according to the quantity of your meat, as you do for minced pies; put in citron, orange, and lemon candied, and work it up with the yolks of eggs, thick butter, and some cream; make your coffin, and fill it; lay some eringo roots over, and suckets, and close it, and bake it; when baked, put over a sweet leer, as for other sweet pies; dish it, and put round chewets of the same. (Robert May, 1660)

Serves 4–6

1½ LB PASTRY
1 LB SALT COD OR HADDOCK, POACHED OR FLAKED
4 HARD-BOILED EGG YOLKS, CHOPPED
½ LB SPINACH, COOKED, DRAINED AND CHOPPED
    (1½ LB BEFORE COOKING)
1 OZ (½ CUP) PARSLEY, MINCED
1 OZ (½ CUP) BREADCRUMBS
2 OZ (¼ CUP) CURRANTS
2 OZ (¼ CUP) CANDIED ORANGE AND LEMON PEEL,
    MIXED
1 TSP GRATED LEMON PEEL
¼ TSP GROUND CLOVES
1 TSP EACH GROUND CINNAMON AND GROUND MACE
½ TSP GROUND GINGER
1 TBS SHERRY
1 TBS ORANGE-FLOWER WATER OR ROSE WATER

Sauce
2 OZ (4 TBS) BUTTER
1 OZ (4 TBS) FLOUR
¾ PT (2 CUPS) CREAM

Line a 9-inch pie dish with half the pastry. Arrange layers of fish, egg, spinach, parsley, breadcrumbs, currants and candied peel in the shell. Season each layer with spices, sherry and the orange or rose water.

Make a white sauce with the butter, flour, cream and salt and pepper. (A little white wine or sherry can be used instead of the cream, if preferred). Pour the sauce over the pie filling. Leave to cool. Cover with a lid made from the remaining pastry and bake at 375° (Mark 5) for 35–40 minutes.

Serve with extra 'chewets' or fingers of pastry.

Fish Pie

(Robert May, 1660)

Serves 4

1½ LB SHORT PASTRY
I LB CARP FILLETS, CHOPPED
½ LB BONELESS EEL, CHOPPED
4 ARTICHOKE BOTTOMS, CHOPPED
4 TBS (¼ CUP) GOOSEBERRIES
I TSP SALT
¼ TSP PEPPER
I TSP NUTMEG
¼ PT (½ CUP) WINE
¼ PT (½ CUP) FISH STOCK
3 EGG YOLKS
2 TBS ORANGE JUICE
I TBS VERJUICE (*see p.* 53) OR CIDER VINEGAR
I OZ (2 TBS) BUTTER

Line a 9-inch pan with half the pastry. Arrange on top alternate layers of fish, artichoke bottoms and gooseberries. Season each layer with salt, pepper and nutmeg. Heat the wine and stock. Beat the egg yolks and beat in the hot stock. Pour over the fish. Sprinkle the orange juice and verjuice over the fish, dot with butter, then leave to cool. Cover with the remaining pastry. Bake at 375° (Mark 5) for 30–35 minutes.

Crab Pie

(Robert May, 1660)

Serves 4

1½ LB SHORT PASTRY
I LB CRABMEAT
¼ EEL, SKINNED AND CHOPPED, OR ½ LB SALMON, FILLETED
I MEDIUM ONION, FINELY CHOPPED
2 OZ (½ CUP) CURRANTS
2 TBS PEELED GRAPES OR GOOSEBERRIES, SLICED
½ OZ (¼ CUP) BREADCRUMBS
4 TBS SWEET HERBS (E.G. TARRAGON, DILL OR CHERVIL), CHOPPED
¼ TSP GROUND NUTMEG
I OZ (2 TBS) BUTTER
¼ PT (½ CUP) WHITE WINE

Line two small 4-inch (or one 8-inch) soufflé or pie dishes with half the pastry. Arrange layers of crab, eel, onion, currants, grapes or gooseberries, breadcrumbs and herbs, seasoning the layers with salt, pepper and nutmeg. Dot with the butter and pour the wine over the top of each dish. Cover each with a pastry lid and bake at 375° (Mark 5) for 15–20 minutes. Serve hot or cold.

Soused Oysters

Remove oysters from shells. Save the liquor of the oysters, strain it and put it into an earthen pipkin, add half a pint of white wine and half a pint of wine vinegar; add some whole pepper, and sliced ginger, boil together with some cloves. Simmer awhile and add the oysters, boil gently but not too much, and then remove them. Let the syrup cool and then put in your oysters and you may keep them all year. (John Murrel, 1617)

Serves 6 (as hors d'oeuvre)

½ PT (I CUP) WHITE WINE
½ PT (I CUP) VINEGAR
6 WHOLE PEPPERCORNS
I TSP GROUND GINGER
4 CLOVES
I PT (2½ CUPS) OYSTERS

Simmer the wine and vinegar with the spices

for 10 minutes. Add the oysters and cook until they curl. Remove them. Cool the liquid. Put back the oysters and marinate in the liquor.

Poultry and Game

To Boil a Capon with Cauliflower
(*Robert May, 1660*)

Serves 4–6
1 CAULIFLOWER
1 PT (2½ CUPS) MILK
1 BLADE MACE
4 EGG YOLKS
4 TBS SHERRY
1 OZ (2 TBS) BUTTER
1 TBS FLOUR
1 TBS VINEGAR
½ LEMON, PEELED AND SLICED
1 CAPON OR 4–5 LB CHICKEN, BOILED AND CARVED INTO PIECES
1 'SIPPET' FOR EACH GUEST (FINGER OF TOAST OR FRIED BREAD)

Divide the cauliflower into flowerets and cook them in the milk, flavoured with the mace, until just tender. Strain, reserving the milk. Put the raw egg yolks and the sherry into a mixing bowl and beat in the hot milk. Put the butter into a saucepan over low heat; stir in the flour, vinegar and lemon and cook gently until the butter darkens. Add the milk mixture and stir until the sauce thickens and becomes creamy. Season with pepper and salt to taste. Put in the cauliflower and the pieces of chicken, skinned. Warm through thoroughly, without boiling.

Put the sippets on a warmed serving dish and arrange the chicken pieces on them; pour over the sauce and serve.

Chicken with Gooseberries or Grapes
(*Hannah Wolley, 1664*)

In the old days bread was the main thickener for soups and sauces. It is still used in the English and French countryside today and I prefer the taste it gives, which is much nuttier than flour. It also saves wasting bread, which to even the most sophisticated of us has remained one of the original sins.

Serves 4
1 PT (2½ CUPS) CHICKEN STOCK
½ PT (1 CUP) WHITE WINE
1 BLADE MACE
A 3–4 LB CHICKEN
2–3 EGG YOLKS
1–2 SLICES BREAD (ACCORDING TO SIZE OF BIRD)
3 TBS VERJUICE (*see p.* 53) OR CIDER VINEGAR
A PINCH OF SUGAR
1 OZ (2 TBS) BUTTER
6 OZ (1 CUP) GOOSEBERRIES OR SEEDLESS GRAPES

Put the stock, wine and mace into a pan that is just large enough for the chicken. Season the cavity of the chicken, bring to the boil in the stock and then simmer over lower heat until tender (about 45 minutes). Remove the chicken and carve it. Put the pieces in a concave dish in a warm oven until the sauce is ready.

Beat the egg yolks in a bowl. Beat in ½ pint (1 cup) of the hot broth and return to the pot. Crumble the bread into the broth, still over low heat, and stir until it has dissolved and thickened the broth. Do not allow to boil. Add the verjuice, sugar and butter, and the gooseberries or grapes (the gooseberries should be stewed, the grapes peeled and uncooked). Simmer very gently until everything is well heated. Pour the sauce over the chicken and serve.

To Boil a Capon with Oranges after Mistres Duffeld's Way

(*The Good Huswife's Handmaid*, *1594*)

Serves 4–6

1 PT (2½ CUPS) CHICKEN STOCK
A 5-LB CAPON
1 TSP POWDERED MACE
½ LB (1 CUP) SUGAR
2 ORANGES, PEELED, SLICED AND POUNDED IN A
   MORTAR
½ PT (1 CUP) WINE
4 EGG YOLKS
½ TSP SALT
½ TSP PEPPER

Garnish
1–2 EXTRA ORANGES, PEELED AND SLICED

Put the stock into a stewpan, season and
poach the capon in this, until it is tender.
Remove the capon and reserve in a covered
dish in a warm oven.

Spoon about ½ pint (1 cup) of the broth into
a saucepan and add the mace, sugar and the
sliced and pounded oranges. Simmer
10 minutes, then add the wine, simmer
10 minutes longer and remove from the heat.
Beat the egg yolks in a bowl and stir in the
broth. Return to a low heat and cook gently,
without boiling, stirring until thickened. Add
more sugar, if necessary, and the salt and
pepper. The sauce should be sweet and syrupy,
yet tart from the wine and oranges.

Carve and skin the capon, put the pieces into
the sauce and heat them through. Serve in a
casserole dish, garnished with slices of fresh
peeled oranges.

Sweet and Sour Chicken
To Boil Chickens with a Cawdle

(*The Good Huswife's Handmaid*, *1594*)

Serves 4

A 3-LB CHICKEN
2 SPRIGS PARSLEY
1 PT (2½ CUPS) STOCK OR WATER
1 TSP SALT

½ TSP PEPPER
12 STONED PRUNES
2 OZ (⅓ CUP) CURRANTS
1 OZ (¼ CUP) RAISINS
3 EGG YOLKS
4 TBS (¼ CUP) VINEGAR
3–4 OZ (⅓–½ CUP) SUGAR
4 SIPPETS (FINGERS OF TOAST)

Stuff the chicken with the parsley. Place it in a
braising-pan with the stock (or water), seasoned,
and cook covered for 1 hour or until tender.
Add the prunes, currants and raisins, bring to
the boil and cook for 10 minutes. Remove the
chicken, and dried fruit, drain in a colander,
and keep warm in a covered dish in a low oven.

Beat the egg yolks lightly, gradually adding
the vinegar, with a little of the broth, and the
sugar. Add the mixture to the broth and cook
over low heat, without boiling, until the broth
thickens and becomes the consistency of light
cream.

Carve the chicken into serving pieces, return
them to the sauce and reheat carefully. Arrange
the chicken and dried fruit on top of the
sippets in a deep warmed serving dish. Pour
over the sauce and serve.

Chicken Fricassee

(*The Family Dictionary*, *1695*)

Serves 3–4

A 3½–4 LB CHICKEN
½ PT (1 CUP) STRONG CHICKEN STOCK
1 PT (2½ CUPS) WHITE WINE
4 OZ (1 CUP) DATES, SLICED
2 OZ (¼ CUP) FINE SUGAR
4–5 BLADES MACE
MARROW FROM 3 BONES
1–2 ENDIVES, SHREDDED
½ LB BOILED PARSNIPS OR TINNED WATER
   CHESTNUTS
4 EGG YOLKS
3–4 TBS PRESERVED BARBERRIES, LOGANBERRIES
   OR BLACKCURRANT JAM etc.

Truss the chicken, put it into the stock and
wine, seasoned with salt and pepper, and bring
to the boil. Reduce the heat and simmer for

30 minutes. Now add the dates, sugar, mace, marrow and shredded endives. When the chicken is tender, remove it to a serving dish and keep it warm in the oven while you prepare the sauce.

Strain the cooking broth. Arrange the vegetables on a serving dish and put them in the oven with the chicken. Whip the egg yolks lightly and stir in ½ pint (1 cup) of the broth. Return this to the pan and cook over low heat, stirring, until the sauce thickens; it must not curdle. Take off the heat.

Carve the chicken. Arrange the pieces on the dish with the vegetables. Heat up the sauce, adjust the seasoning if necessary and pour it over the chicken. Heat the preserves or jam and put a little at each end of the dish.

Bride Pie

This 'extraordinary pie' was probably served at wedding feasts in the seventeenth century. It is a direct descendant of the medieval Grete Pyes and Pyes of Paris. Unless you have a huge oven, or live in the country and can borrow your baker's oven, you will have to adapt the recipe. The pie-shells were arranged one inside the other, like a giant rose, with a different filling for each one. The central pie contains the custard, the custom of serving savoury custards with meat being common in the Middle Ages. The design of the pie is strangely similar to garden plans of the same period.

To make an extraordinary Pie, or a Bride Pye, of severall Compounds, being several different Pies on one bottom : Provide cocks-stones and combs, or lamb-stones and sweetbreads of veal, a little set in hot water and cut to pieces ; also two or three ox-pallets blanched and slic't ; a pint of oysters, sliced dates, a handful of pine kernels, a little quantity of broom-buds pickled, some fine interlarded bacon sliced, nine or ten chesnuts roasted and blanched, season them with salt, nutmeg, and some large mace, and close it up

with some butter. For the caudle, beat up some butter, with three yolks of eggs, some white or claret wine, the juyce of a lemon or two ; cut up the lid, pour on the lear, shaking it well together ; then lay the meat, slic't lemon, and pickled barberries, and cov again, let these ingredients be put into the moddle or the lops of the Pie Several other Pies belong to the first form, but you be sure to make the three fashions proportionably answering one the other, you may set them on one bottom paste, which will be more convenient ; or if you set several you may bake the middle one full of flour, it be baked and cold, take out the flour in the bottom, and in live birds, or a snake, which will seem strange to the beholders, which cut up the pie at the Table. This is for a Wedding to pass away time.

Now for the other Pies you may fill them with several ingredients, as in one you may put oysters, being parboiled and bearded, season them with large mace, pepper, beaten ginger, and salt, season them lightly and fill Pie, then lay on marrow and some good butter, close and bake it. Then make a lear of it with white-wine, oister liquor, three of four oisters bruised in pieces to it stronger, but take out the pieces, and an onion, on the bottom of the dish with a clove of garlick ; it boild, put in a piece of butter, with a lemon, sweet will be good boild in it, bound up, fast together, cutt lid, or make a hole to let the lear in, &c.

Another you may make of prawns and cockles, seasoned as the first, but no marrow : a few pickled mushrooms, (if you have them) it being baked, heat piece of butter, a little vinegar, a slic't nutmeg, and juyce of two or three oranges thick, an pour it into the Pie.
(Robert May, 1660).

Serves 16
1 SWEETBREAD
1 LB PASTRY
A ¾-OZ TIN TRUFFLES
16 QUAILS
4 OZ (2 TBS) BUTTER

Sauce
ABOUT 4 OZ (½ CUP) BUTTER (*see recipe*)

2 ONIONS, CHOPPED
½ LB MUSHROOMS, SLICED
6 TBS FLOUR
1¼ PT (3 CUPS) STOCK
RESERVED LIQUOR FROM 1 PT (2¼ CUPS) OYSTERS
1 TBS LEMON JUICE
3 TBS MANGO CHUTNEY
½ TSP GROUND MACE
1½ TSP CUMIN

12 OZ (2 CUPS) CHICKEN OR VEAL MINCEMEAT
14–16 MEATBALLS
1 PT (2¼ CUPS) OYSTERS
4 TBS RAW BEEF MARROW
GRATED PEEL OF 2 LEMONS
1 TSP GELATINE, DISSOLVED IN 2 TBS WATER

Soak the sweetbread for 1 hour in cold water; pull off the membranes and poach in acidulated water for about 20 minutes. Drain, cool, dice, and reserve. Roll out the pastry and use to line a tin measuring about 14 by 12 inches. Bake for 10–15 minutes at 400° (Mark 6). Cut 16 decorative shapes out of the truffles (hearts, stars etc.) and reserve the scraps. Brown the quails in butter and reserve, leaving the butter in the pan. For the sauce, measure the butter and make it up to 8 tablespoons; cook the onions in the same pan until they are lightly browned. Add the sliced mushrooms and cook for another 5 minutes. Blend in the flour, then the chicken stock and oyster liquor. Bring to the boil, then simmer, stirring until the mixture is smooth and thick. Stir in the lemon juice, chutney, truffle scraps, mace and cumin. Season to taste, and stir in the diced sweetbread.

Cover the bottom of the pastry case with the mincemeat. Arrange 15 quails round the edge and 1 in the centre. Pour the sauce with the diced sweetbread into the pie, round and between the quail. Arrange the meatballs, oysters and marrow on top of the sauce. Sprinkle with grated lemon peel. Paint the quails and truffles lightly with melted aspic and stick a truffle shape on each one. Cover with greaseproof paper until ready, and then bake, still covered, at 350° (Mark 4) for 30 minutes.

Serve with Bride Pie Custard (see below), which was originally served in the centre of the Bride Pie, though we must serve it separately.

Bride Pie Custard

(*Robert May*, 1660).

¾ LB PASTRY
6 SLICES BACON
1 PT (2½ CUPS) CREAM
4 EGGS PLUS 2 EXTRA YOLKS
16 CHESTNUTS, COOKED AND PEELED
1–2 TBS RAW BEEF MARROW, CHOPPED

Line a 10-inch pie dish with the pastry, and bake blind (pre-bake) at 400° (Mark 6) for 10 minutes. Fry the bacon until crisp and crumbly and sprinkle in the bottom of the pie-shell. Heat the cream; beat the eggs, then beat the cream into them. Season to taste. Pour this mixture into the pie-shell. Arrange the halved chestnuts and scraps of marrow in the pie. Bake at 350° (Mark 4) for 25 minutes.

A Mallard, Smothered

A Mallard, smoared:
When trussed, parboil the duck in salted water. Fill the pipkin and put in the duck head down and tail uppermost. Half fill the pipkin with the broth from parboiling the duck and the other half with white wine, add some sliced onions, herbs in season. Shred currants and dates and add. Cover the pipkin tightly and stew very gently until the onions are tender and soft and the Mallard tender. Remove the Mallard and carve it. To the broth add a good lump of butter, sugar, cinnamon, (in summer) as many gooseberries as will give it a sharp taste (in winter) or wine vinegar instead. Simmer on the fire and stir well. Lay the bird in a dish with sippets and trim the edge of the dish with sugar. Arrange the duck in the centre and pour the broth over it.
(*Gervase Markham, 1660*)

Serves 2–3

A 3-LB MALLARD OR WILD DUCK
2 TBS FLOUR
2 TBS OIL
1–2 OZ ($\frac{1}{2}$ CUP) ONIONS, CHOPPED
$\frac{1}{2}$ PT (1 CUP) STOCK
$\frac{1}{2}$ PT (1 CUP) WHITE WINE
8 TBS ($\frac{1}{2}$ CUP) MIXED HERBS, CHOPPED
2 OZ ($\frac{1}{2}$ CUP) CURRANTS
2 OZ ($\frac{1}{2}$ CUP) DATES, CHOPPED
1 OZ (2 TBS) BUTTER
2 TBS SUGAR
1 TSP POWDERED CINNAMON
2 TBS WINE VINEGAR OR $\frac{1}{4}$ LB ($\frac{1}{2}$ CUP) GOOSEBERRIES
2 SLICES TOAST, CUT IN SIPPETS

Dust the duck with the flour and brown it in oil; brown the onions in the same oil. Braise the duck in the same pan and add the stock, wine and herbs. Simmer for about 1 hour; then add the currants and dates and simmer for another 30 minutes or until the duck is tender. Remove the bird and keep it warm. Add the butter, sugar, cinnamon, wine vinegar or gooseberries, reduce the sauce and pour over the bird in a dish garnished with sippets.

Quails

(The Good Huswife's Handmaid, 1594)

Serves 4

4 QUAILS
3 TBS FLOUR
$\frac{1}{2}$ OZ (1 TBS) BUTTER
1 TBS OIL
1 PT (2$\frac{1}{2}$ CUPS) CHICKEN STOCK
2 CARROTS, SLICED
2 SPRIGS PARSLEY
1 TSP EACH BASIL, TARRAGON, CINNAMON
$\frac{1}{2}$ TSP EACH THYME, NUTMEG
1 TSP SALT
$\frac{1}{4}$ TSP PEPPER
2 TBS VERJUICE *(see p. 53)* OR CIDER VINEGAR

Garnish
SIPPETS
FIGS OR APRICOTS

Dust the birds with flour and brown in the butter and oil. Put the stock into a braising-pan

with all the other ingredients. Bring to the boil, put in the quails, bring to the boil again, then reduce the heat and simmer, very gently, for about 30 minutes partially covered. Serve the quail on 'sippets' (slices of toast) with some of the broth; garnish with fresh, peeled figs or apricots, warmed in the oven.

Hare Pie

To bake four hares in a pye :
Bone them and lard them with great lard, being first seasoned with nutmeg and pepper, then take four ounces of pepper, four of nutmegs, and eight ounces of salt, mix them together, season them, and make a round or square pye of course boulted rye and meal; then the pie being made, put some butter in the bottom of it, and lay on the hares one upon another, then put upon it a few whole cloves, a sheet of lard over it, and good store of butter, close it up and bake it, being first basted over with eggs beaten together, or saffron; when it is baked liquor them with clarified butter.

Or bake them in white paste or pasty, if to be eaten hot, leave out half the seasoning.
(Robert May, 1660)

Serves 3–4

2 OZ (4 TBS) GAME DRIPPING
4 TBS FLOUR
1 PT (2$\frac{1}{2}$ CUPS) GAME OR CHICKEN STOCK
2 LB (4 CUPS) COOKED SADDLE OF HARE, CUBED
$\frac{1}{4}$ TSP PEPPER
1 TSP GRATED NUTMEG
$\frac{1}{4}$ TSP GROUND CLOVES
1$\frac{1}{2}$ LB PASTRY MADE WITH WHOLE WHEAT
    OR RYE FLOUR
1 OZ (2 TBS) LARD OR BACON FAT

Make the gravy by melting the dripping in a pan, stirring in the flour and gradually adding the stock until it is creamy and smooth.

Combine the gravy with the cubes of hare and the seasonings and spices. Line a 9-inch pie dish with half the pastry and spoon in the cooled mixture. Top with bits of lard or bacon. Cover with the remainder of the pastry and crimp the edges. Make a vent or slit in the pastry lid. Glaze with beaten egg. Bake at 375° (Mark 5) for 35–40 minutes.

Venison Roasted with Cloves

(*Gervase Markham, 1660*)

Serves 8
4 LB VENISON
CLOVES (*see recipe*)
6 OZ ($\frac{3}{4}$ CUP) BUTTER

For the sauce
4 TBS VENISON DRIPPINGS (*see recipe*)
4 TBS FLOUR
I PT (2$\frac{1}{2}$ CUPS) GAME, CHICKEN OR VEAL STOCK
2 TBS SUGAR
2 TBS VINEGAR
I TSP SALT
$\frac{1}{2}$ TSP PEPPER
$\frac{1}{2}$ TSP POWDERED GINGER
$\frac{1}{2}$ TSP POWDERED CINNAMON
I OZ ($\frac{1}{2}$ CUP) BREADCRUMBS

Stud the venison with cloves, as for a ham. Roast it in the oven at 350° (Mark 4) for 20–30 minutes per pound, depending on the age and cut of the meat. Baste frequently with a lot of butter. Keep the meat warm while you make the sauce.

Melt 4 tablespoons of the drippings from the roasting pan in a saucepan; add the flour and cook for I minute. Pour in the stock, then scrape up the particles from the roasting pan and stir them in. Cook until thickened. Now add the sugar, vinegar, salt and pepper, ginger and cinnamon. Thicken by stirirng in the breadcrumbs. Cook for 5 minutes.

Slice the venison and serve it with the sauce poured over it.

Meat •

Barthelmas Beef

To make barthelmas beef:
Take a fat brisket of beef and bone it and put it into so much water as will cover it, shifting it three times a day for three days together, then put it into as much white wine and vinegar as will cover it; and when it hath lyen twenty-four hours, take it out and drye it in a clothe, then take nutmeg, ginger, cinnamon, cloves and mace of each a like quantity, beaten small and mingled with a good handfull of salt. Strew both sides of the beef with this, and roul it up as you do Brawn; tye it as close as you can, then put it into an earthen pot, and cover it with some paste, set it into the oven when household bread and when it is cold, eat it with mustard and sugar.
(*Hannah Wolley, 1664*)

Mix the spices by putting I part of mixed ground nutmeg, ginger, cinnamon, cloves and mace and I part of salt into a flour sifter; shake it well and sprinkle the meat with the mixture. Place the meat in a dutch oven or earthenware pot, cover it with water and bake at 350° (Mark 4) for 20–30 minutes per pound, or until very tender. Cover with aluminium foil under a very tight lid, or seal with a flour and water paste. The spices rubbed into the meat will flavour the broth.

Serve hot, with root vegetables and dumplings, or cold, sliced, with a sauce made of 4 parts mustard to I part sugar, moistened to a paste with vinegar.

To Roast a Fillet of Beef

(*Robert May, 1660*)

Fresh green peppercorns, bottled or tinned, are delicious in this sauce. They can be bought at Robert Jackson's, Harrods and Elizabeth

David in London, Hédiard in Paris and food speciality shops in New York.

Serves 6–8

4–5 LB FILLET OF BEEF
BUTTER FOR BASTING
¾ PT (2 CUPS) BEEF STOCK
2 TBS BASIL, CHOPPED
2 TBS TARRAGON, CHOPPED
2 TBS PARSLEY, CHOPPED
3 EGG YOLKS, BEATEN
1 TSP FRESHLY GROUND PEPPER

Roast the fillet, basting it with butter. When it is done, remove the meat and keep it warm. Pour the stock into the roasting pan, scraping all the residue back into the stock as it begins to boil. Add the herbs and simmer, covered, for 15 minutes; then strain the stock into a saucepan, beat some hot stock into the egg yolks, return to the saucepan, and cook over very low heat, until it has thickened. Add pepper and salt if needed. Carve the fillet and pour the sauce over the slices.

To Stew Beef

(*Sir Kenelme Digbie, 1669*)

Serves 3–4

2 LB BONELESS TOPSIDE (ROUND OF BEEF)
4 TBS FLOUR
2 OZ (4 TBS) BUTTER
¾ PT (2 CUPS) RED WINE
¾ PT (2 CUPS) BEEF STOCK OR WATER
1 ONION, SLICED
1 ANCHOVY, CRUSHED
2 OR 3 DRIED MARIGOLD FLOWERS (IF AVAILABLE)
½ TSP ALLSPICE
¼ TSP GROUND NUTMEG

Garnish
FINGERS OF TOAST

Cut the meat into cubes, dust them in the flour and brown them in the butter. Put them into a 'pipkin' (a stewing-jar or earthenware vessel, with a lid, of the kind used for cooking tripe in France). Cover with the wine and water, add the onion and the anchovy. Bring to the boil, then lower the heat and simmer for 2 hours. Then 15–20 minutes before serving add the marigold flowers and the spices. Serve on 'sippets' of toast.

Serve with blackcurrant, sloe or boysenberry jam, heated in a saucepan, and poured into a sauceboat.

Hotchpot

(*Sir Kenelme Digbie, 1669*)

Serves 8

2 LB BRISKET OF BEEF
2 LB BONELESS MUTTON
2 LB STEWING VEAL
3–4 PT (8–10 CUPS) STOCK
3 OZ (1 CUP) PARSLEY, CHOPPED
1½ OZ (½ CUP) BASIL, CHOPPED
¾ OZ (¼ CUP) TARRAGON, CHOPPED
1 BAY LEAF
½ LB CABBAGE, SLICED
6–8 SMALL ONIONS
6 CARROTS, SLICED
2–3 LARGE HARD APPLES, CORED, PEELED AND
   QUARTERED

Put all the meat into a deep braising-pan and pour over the cold stock, which should come about 6 inches above the meat. Bring to the boil and skim. Add the herbs and vegetables, or steam them over the meat, covered. Simmer for 1–1½ hours and then add the apples. The cooked meat should shred easily. Stir frequently to prevent it sticking to the bottom and burning.

To Roast a Chine, Rib, Loin, Brisket or Fillet of Beef

(*Robert May, 1660*)

Serves 4

4 RIBS BEEF, IN ONE PIECE
BUTTER FOR BASTING
¼ TSP ROSEMARY
½ TSP SAGE
½ TSP THYME
½ TSP SWEET MARJORAM
1 TBS WINE VINEGAR
½ PT (1 CUP) BEEF STOCK OR GRAVY OR ORANGE
   AND LEMON JUICE
½ TSP SALT
½ TSP PEPPER

The meat can be grilled (broiled), barbecued on a spit or roasted, depending on the nature of the piece and on the facilities available. It must be well and frequently basted with plenty of butter. When it is done, remove the meat and keep it warm. Pour the basting butter and the drippings into a frying-pan and toss the chopped herbs in this fat. Add the vinegar, cook for a few seconds and then add the stock or seasoned gravy or orange and lemon juice. (A mixture of fruit juice and gravy is delicious). Heat and pour the sauce over the meat, which should be sliced into serving portions.

Olives of Veal

Take some veal scallops. Chop some herbs and scallions, bind with egg yolk, season, and roll up inside the veal. Roast them on skewers, or skewer them closed and braise in oven or on top of stove in butter. Cook together some butter, verjuice, sugar, cinnamon and currants, add herbs and season with salt. Serve the veal olives in this sauce. (Gervase Markham, 1660)

Serves 4

1 LB VEAL ESCALOPES (SCALLOPS)
1 OZ (½ CUP) CHOPPED MIXED HERBS, AS AVAILABLE
   (BASIL, TARRAGON, CHERVIL, ETC.)
4 TBS SPRING ONIONS (SCALLIONS), CHOPPED
1 EGG YOLK

2 TBS FLOUR
I TBS OIL
½ OZ (I TBS) BUTTER
½ PT (I CUP) STOCK
I TBS VERJUICE (*see p.* 53) OR CIDER VINEGAR
I TBS SUGAR
½ TSP POWDERED CINNAMON
I TSP SALT
¼ TSP PEPPER
I OZ (¼ CUP) CURRANTS

Pound the escalopes and then season them. Make a stuffing by combining the herbs, spring onions and egg yolk. Divide equally between the escalopes, roll them up and secure them. Dust each with flour and brown in the oil and butter. Remove the 'olives' from the pan and keep them warm while you add the stock and deglaze the pan. Stir in the remaining ingredients (except the currants), replace the olives and simmer for I hour. Stir in the currants and simmer for 15 minutes longer.

Roast Calves' Feet

First boil them tender and blanch them, and being cold lard them thick with small lard, then spit them on a small spit and roast them. Serve them with a sauce made of vinegar, cinnamon, sugar and butter. (*Robert May, 1660*)

2 CALVES' FEET
I ONION, SLICED
2 CARROTS, SLICED
2 CLOVES
I BAY LEAF
½ TSP THYME
I SPRIG PARSLEY
4 SLICES BACON

Sauce
¼ PT (½ CUP) VINEGAR
2 OZ (¼ CUP) SUGAR
½ TSP GROUND CINNAMON
I OZ (2 TBS) BUTTER

Boil the calves' feet gently in water, adding salt and pepper, onion, carrots and herbs. Cook for 2–2½ hours, or until tender. Remove

the feet, drain and keep warm. Wrap them in the bacon and put under the grill, turning on all sides to cook evenly until the bacon is very crisp.

Meanwhile make the sauce. Bring all the ingredients to the boil, simmer for I minute and serve with the grilled feet, accompanied by a watercress salad.

Poached Meat Balls

This is an excellent recipe for meat balls made from leftover roast lamb.
How to make fystes of portingale:
Take a piece of a leg of mutton, mince it smal and season it with cloves, mace, pepper and salt, and Dates minced with Currans, then roll it into round rolles, and so into little balles, and so boyle them in a little beefe broth and so serve them foorth.
(*The Good Huswife's Handmaid, 1594*)

I LB (2 CUPS) ROAST LAMB, MINCED (GROUND)
¼ TSP GROUND CLOVES
½ TSP EACH GROUND MACE, SALT AND PEPPER
½ OZ (¼ CUP) BREADCRUMBS
I OZ (¼ CUP) CHOPPED DATES
I OZ (¼ CUP) CHOPPED CURRANTS
I EGG, BEATEN
1½ PT (4 CUPS) BEEF STOCK

Mix all the dry ingredients, binding them with the lightly beaten egg. Use an extra yolk if the egg is small. Form the mixture into round balls and poach in the beef stock for 5–7 minutes. The meat balls can also be fried in butter instead of being poached.

To Boil a Leg of Mutton

This recipe is much too complicated for modern cooks, but the taste can be captured by flavouring the gravy from roast lamb in the same way.

To boyl a leg of mutton:
Parboil the meat a little and then put in on a

spit (or in the oven on a rack) and give it five or six turns before the fire (seize it in a sharp oven, turning it so that it browns on all sides). Take it off the spit (or out of the oven) and put it between two dishes (with a weight on top) and save all the gravy which comes out. Slash it with a knife and stick it back in the oven for about 10 minutes. Press it again between the dishes, pressing and weighing it down. Again collect and save the gravy. Repeat the slashing, roasting and pressing and collecting of gravy as many times as you have patience for. Mix some mutton-broth (not the gravy pressed out of the meat) with white wine and verjuice and finish cooking the joint by poaching it gently in this until tender. Keep stewing the pressed gravy over a low flame, adding to it salt, sugar, cinnamon, ginger, some lemon slices, a little orange peel and a few white breadcrumbs. Remove the joint, reduce the cooking broth and add it to the gravy, serve the mutton with bread sippets on which are the poached lemon slices and 'trim about with sugar'.
(*Gervase Markham, 1660*)

Serves 6–8

5–6 LB LEG OF LAMB
FAT FOR ROASTING
½ PT (1 CUP) WHITE WINE
4 TBS (¼ CUP) VERJUICE (*see p.* 53) OR CIDER
   VINEGAR
4 OZ (½ CUP) SUGAR
1 TSP GROUND CINNAMON
1 TSP GROUND GINGER
1 TBS GRATED ORANGE PEEL
½ OZ (¼ CUP) BREADCRUMBS
1 PEELED LEMON, THINLY SLICED

Roast the leg of lamb in the usual way, counting 15 to 20 minutes to the pound, for rare or medium cooked meat. Remove the joint and keep warm. Skim off all the fat from the gravy in the roasting pan, set the pan over sharp heat and add about ¼ pint (half a cup) of boiling water. Boil up, stirring in all the glaze that has stuck to the pan. Strain this into a clean saucepan and add the remainder of the ingredients, except the lemon.

Season and simmer sauce until it has refined

somewhat. Spoon over the slices of the lamb and arrange the poached lemon slices on top.

Boiled Mutton with Lemons

To boyle a leg of mutton with lemons:
When your mutton is halfe-boyled, take it up, cut it in small pieces; put it into a pipkin, and cover it close, and put thereto the best of the broth, as much as shall cover your mutton, your Lemmons being sliced verie thin, and quartered, and Currans, put in pepper grosse beaten, and so let them boyle together, and when they bee well boyled, season it with a little Vergious, sugar, pepper grosse beaten, and a little saunders, so lay it in fine dishes upon Soppes. It will make three messe for the table.
(*The Good Huswife's Handmaid, 1594*)

Serves 6–8

3 LB BONELESS LAMB, CUT INTO 1-INCH CUBES
1 OZ (¼ CUP) FLOUR
2 TBS OIL
2 PT (5 CUPS) STOCK
2 LEMONS, PEELED AND THINLY SLICED
2 TBS SUGAR
1 TSP SALT
¼ TSP COARSE PEPPER
2 TBS VERJUICE (*see p.* 53) OR CIDER VINEGAR
A FEW SLICES OF DRY BREAD

Toss the cubed lamb in the flour. Brown in the oil in a dutch oven. Add the stock scraping in the glaze, lemon slices, sugar, salt and pepper and simmer for 1–2 hours, or until tender. Stir in the currants and verjuice and cook for 10–15 minutes. Put the bread slices into bowls, spoon over the meat mixture and serve.

Roast Sucking Pig (1)

To dress pig:
Mince some sweet Herbs, as sage, and Penniroyal, rowl them up in Balls, with some Butter, and put them in the Pig's Belly, roast him, and being roasted, make Sawce with some Butter, Vinegar, the Brains, and some Barberries, and serve it up.
(*The Family Dictionary, 1695*)

Serves 8–10

4 OZ (8 TBS) BUTTER
6 OZ (2 CUPS) CHOPPED, SWEET HERBS (SAGE,
    PENNYROYAL, MINT)
2 TSP SALT
½ TSP PEPPER
I SUCKING PIG (ABOUT 9 LB)
½ LB (I CUP) BUTTER
4 TBS VINEGAR
4 TBS BARBERRIES OR REDCURRANTS OR COOKED
    CRANBERRIES, SEPARATELY OR MIXED

Melt the butter in a frying-pan. Sauté the herbs
for 2–3 minutes. Season the inside of the pig
with salt and pepper. Stuff with herbs and
secure opening. Roast at 375° (Mark 5) for
2½–3 hours or until done. Melt the butter,
vinegar and berries together and pour over
the pig.

Roast Sucking Pig (2)

To dress pigs :
Scald, draw, and wash it clean, put a Crust of
Bread and some Sage in the belly, prick it up
and Spit it, Roast it, and Baste it with Butter ;
Salt it, and being roasted fine and crisp, make
Sawce with chopt Sage, Currants, a little grated
Nutmeg, boil'd in fair Water and Vinegar,
adding a little grated Bread, the Brains, some
Barberries, and Sugar ; give them a Walm or
two with a good stirring, and adding a little
beaten Butter, divide the Pig's Body, and Head,
take off the Ears, place them on the Shoulder,
and so serve it up. (Family Dictionary, 1695)

Serves 8–10

2 OZ (2 CUPS) STALE BREAD, DICED
6 TBS SAGE, CHOPPED
2 OZ (4 TBS) BUTTER
A SUCKING PIG (ABOUT I 2 LB)
I OZ (¼ CUP) CURRANTS
2 TBS SUGAR
½ TSP NUTMEG
2 TBS VINEGAR
I PT (2½ CUPS) CHICKEN OR VEAL STOCK
I OZ (½ CUP) BREADCRUMBS
2 TBS BARBERRIES OR REDCURRANTS, OR
    BLUEBERRIES AND COOKED, UNSWEETENED
    CRANBERRIES, OR A FEW GREEN GOOSEBERRIES
    MIXED WITH REDCURRANTS

Sauté the bread cubes and 4 tablespoons of
the sage in the butter. Stuff the pig with the
mixture. Secure and roast for 4–5 hours at
325° (Mark 3) or 2½–3 hours at 375° (Mark 5).
Add the rest of the sage, currants, sugar,
nutmeg, vinegar and stock to 2 tablespoons of
the pan drippings. Stir in the breadcrumbs and
berries and cook until thickened.

Vegetables

A Dish of Artichokes

(The Good Huswife's Handmaid, 1559)

Serves 4

4 TINNED ARTICHOKE BOTTOMS
¼ TSP SALT
⅛ TSP PEPPER
½ TSP GROUND CINNAMON
½ TSP GROUND GINGER
4 BEEF MARROW BONES
I TBS VINEGAR
½ OZ (¼ CUP) BREADCRUMBS (OPTIONAL)
I OZ (2 TBS) MELTED BUTTER

Arrange the artichoke bottoms in a buttered
casserole dish. Sprinkle them with the salt,
pepper, cinnamon and ginger. Chop up the
raw beef marrow from the bones, season it and
sprinkle it with the vinegar. Pile some of this
on each artichoke bottom.
Breadcrumbs mixed with the marrow add
texture and 'stretch' the filling. Brush with a
little melted butter and bake until the marrow
is cooked and golden, or put under a slow
grill. The original recipe adds: '. . . stick three
or four leaves of the Artechoks in the Dish
when you serve them up, and scrape sugar in
the dish'. Bake at 350° (Mark 4) for 15–20
minutes.

Bean Tarts

Take green Garden beans boil'd and hull'd, put them into Puff Paste in Patty Pans; a layer of Beans, and a layer of wet Sweet Meats, as of Apples, Apricocks, Peaches, Pears, Plums. Strew in a little Sugar between each layer, cover your Tarts; making a hole therin, into which put a quarter of a pint, more or less, of Limon Juice, or Lime Juice, Marrow seasoned with salt, Cloves, Mace, Nutmeg, Candid Limon and Orange Peel. When they come out of the Oven, put into every Tart white wine thickened with the Yolk of an Egg and a bit of Butter, and so let them be eaten hot. (The Family Dictionary, 1695)

Serves 4–6

1½ LB PUFF PASTRY
¼ LB (1 CUP) BROAD (OR LIMA) BEANS, COOKED
2 OZ (½ CUP) WALNUTS, COARSELY CHOPPED
1 APPLE, PEELED, CORED AND THINLY SLICED
2 APRICOTS, PEELED AND SLICED
1 PEACH, SKINNED AND SLICED
1 PEAR, PEELED AND SLICED
2 PLUMS, SKINNED AND SLICED
6 OZ (¾ CUP) SUGAR
2 TBS LEMON JUICE
4 TBS RAW BEEF MARROW, CHOPPED
2 OZ (½ CUP) CANDIED ORANGE AND LEMON PEEL, CHOPPED
½ PT (1 CUP) WHITE WINE
1 EGG YOLK
1 TSP SALT
¼ TSP GROUND CLOVES
½ TSP GROUND MACE

Egg wash
1 EGG YOLK, BEATEN WITH 1 TBS MILK

Line a 9-inch pie dish with the pastry, reserving enough for the lid. Arrange in it layers of beans, nuts, apple, apricot, peach, pear and plum, dusting each layer with a little sugar. Sprinkle the lemon juice, marrow and candied peel over the top.
Heat the wine. Beat the egg yolk in a bowl and beat in the wine. Stir in the spices. Pour over the pie. Cover the pie with pastry and flute the edges, cutting a vent in the top. Brush with egg wash. Bake at 375° (Mark 5) for 35–45 minutes.

Cauliflower with Orange and Lemon Juice

(Robert May, 1660)

Serves 4

1 CAULIFLOWER
4 OZ (½ CUP) BUTTER, MELTED
JUICE OF ½ ORANGE
JUICE OF ½ LEMON

Trim the cauliflower of leaves and stalk, put into boiling salted water and then boil gently for 15 minutes or until tender. Remove, drain and separate into flowerets. Place in a serving dish. Pour over the melted butter, seasoned with salt and pepper, into which half an orange and half a lemon have been squeezed.

Peas in Oil

(Andrew Boorde, 1542)

6 OZ (1 CUP) COOKED SPLIT PEAS
1 TBS CHOPPED BASIL
1 TBS CHOPPED TARRAGON
1 TSP CHOPPED WINTER SAVORY
1 TSP CHOPPED PARSLEY
1 TSP CHOPPED THYME
4 TBS OIL

Heat all the ingredients through in the hot oil, season with salt and pepper and serve. This dish is particularly good with roast or grilled lamb.

Split Peas with Saffron

(Robert May, 1660)

Serves 6

1 LB (2½ CUPS) GREEN SPLIT PEAS
½ TSP SAFFRON
2 OZ (4 TBS) BUTTER
1 TSP SALT
3 OZ (6 TBS) SUGAR
1 TBS VERJUICE (see p. 53) OR CIDER VINEGAR
⅛ TSP PEPPER
2 TBS SUGAR FOR GLAZING

Boil the dried split peas in lightly salted water until tender, for about 1 hour; about 20 minutes before the end of the boiling period add ¼ teaspoon saffron for flavour. Drain. Put the butter and the rest of the saffron into a pan and place over low heat, on asbestos, to allow the butter to infuse until it is bright orange. Add the salt, 2 oz (4 tablespoons) of the sugar, the verjuice and pepper. When the sugar has dissolved add the peas and stir over low heat until all is well blended. Put the mixture into an earthenware dish or shallow pot, strew the remaining sugar over the top and set it under the grill for about 1 minute until the surface is glazed, or 'iced', with a crust of sugar.

Spinach Garnished with Eggs

(*John Murrel, 1617*)

Serves 4

2 LB SPINACH
2 OZ (4 TBS) BUTTER
2 TBS VINEGAR
1 TSP GROUND CINNAMON
½ TSP GROUND GINGER
1 OZ (2 TBS) SUGAR
2 OZ (½ CUP) CURRANTS, PLUMPED IN HOT WATER
4 HARD-BOILED EGGS
4 SLICES STALE BREAD
4 TBS (¼ CUP) CREAM
1 OZ (2 TBS) BUTTER

Cook the spinach with the water in a covered pan for 5 minutes or until slightly wilted. Remove, drain and chop. Put into a frying-pan with the butter and vinegar and add the cinnamon, ginger, sugar and currants.

Have ready the peeled hard-boiled eggs, cut into quarters. Dip the stale bread in the cream and then fry the slices in the butter until crisp.

Put the spinach in the centre of a warm serving dish and arrange the egg slices and 'sippets' round the edge. This dish is very good with braised or roast veal.

Forcemeat and Garnishes

Poached Forcemeat Balls

(*The Good Huswife's Handmaid, 1594*).

These are rather like gnocchi, if gnocchi tasted like mince-meat! Try them with roast pork, goose or turkey.

4 EGG YOLKS
2 TBS SUGAR
½ PT (1 CUP) SWEET WINE OR SHERRY
1 OZ (¼ CUP) SUET, MINCED
1 OZ (½ CUP) BREADCRUMBS, GRATED IN A BLENDER
¼ TSP SAFFRON
1 TSP CINNAMON
¼ TSP GINGER
1 TSP SALT
2 OZ (½ CUP) CURRANTS

Beat the egg yolks and sugar together in a saucepan. Pour in the wine or sherry gradually to blend. Add the suet, breadcrumbs, spices and salt and cook over low heat until very thick. Do not boil. Stir in the currants. Chill for 2–3 hours. Drop a spoonful at a time into lightly salted, boiling water and poach for 2–3 minutes.

Oatmeal Puddings (called Isings) for Stuffing Birds

(*Robert May, 1660*)

3 OZ (½ CUP) OATMEAL
1 PT (2½ CUPS) WARM MILK
1 PT (2½ CUPS) SINGLE CREAM
3 EGGS
¼ TSP MACE
¼ TSP SAFFRON
½ TSP PEPPER
2 TBS GRATED SUET
1 OZ (¼ CUP) DATES, PITTED AND SLICED

1 OZ (¼ CUP) CURRANTS
¼ TSP SALT
2 OZ (¼ CUP) SUGAR

Put the oatmeal into the warm milk and
steep for 8 hours, then drain and cook the
oatmeal in the cream. Cool. Separate the eggs
and lightly whip the whites. Add all the other
ingredients, but fold in the whipped egg whites
last. The result should be a rather thick paste
which you can then spoon into the cavities of
chickens, quails, game hens, pigeons or
pheasants. It is particularly useful for rather
dry birds. The birds can be roasted, braised or
boiled; if boiled, the cavities should be sewn
up with strong thread.

Desserts

A Phrase of Apples

To make a phrase of apples:
Take two pippins, pare them and cut them in
thin slices, then take three eggs, yolks and
whites, beat them very well, then put to it some
nutmeg grated, some rose-water, currans and
sugar, with some grated bread, as much as will
make it thick as batter, then fry your apples
very well with sweet butter, and pour it away;
then fry them in more butter till they are tender,
then lay them in order in the pan, and pour all
your batter on them, and when it is fried a little
turn it: and when it is enough, dish it with the
apples downwards, strew sugar on it and serve
it in. (Hannah Wolley, 1664)

Serves 3–4

2 HARD APPLES, PEELED, CORED AND THINLY
   SLICED
2 OZ (4 TBS) BUTTER
3 EGGS
1 TSP GROUND NUTMEG
1 TBS ROSEWATER
1 OZ (¼ CUP) CURRANTS
2 TBS SUGAR
2 TBS BREADCRUMBS
1 TBS CASTER SUGAR FOR GARNISH

Sauté the apple slices in butter until tender.
Beat the eggs, nutmeg, rosewater, currants,
sugar and crumbs together in a bowl. Pour over
the apples, which you have arranged in a
circular pattern in the bottom of the pan.
Cook until the eggs are set, then turn over and
brown on the other side (or place under a hot
grill if it is too difficult to turn it). Turn out
on to a dish. Sprinkle with sugar and serve.

Apple and Orange Tart

(*The Good Huswife's Handmaid, 1594*)

Serves 4

2 ORANGES
5 MEDIUM APPLES
2 TBS FLOUR
6 OZ (¾ CUP) SUGAR
1 TSP CINNAMON
½ TSP GINGER
½ OZ (1 TBS) BUTTER
1½ LB SHORT PASTRY

Peel the oranges and divide into segments.
Peel and core the apples and slice thinly.
Combine in a bowl and toss with the flour,
sugar, cinnamon and ginger. Pile in a pie dish
lined with half the pastry. Dot with butter.

Cover with the rest of the pastry and flute. Sprinkle sugar on top. Bake at 375° (Mark 5) for 40–45 minutes.

A Tart of Cherries

To make a tart of cherries when the stones be out : Seeth them in white wine or in Claret, strain them thick ; when they are sodden ; then take two yolks of eggs and thicken it withall. Then season it with Sinamon, Ginger and Sugar, and bake it and so serve it.
(*The Good Huswife's Handmaid, 1594*)

½ LB PASTRY
2 PT (5 CUPS) SOUR CHERRIES, STONED
¾ PT (2 CUPS) WHITE WINE OR CLARET
3 EGG YOLKS
½ LB (1 CUP) SUGAR
¼ TSP SALT
½ TSP GROUND CINNAMON
¼ TSP GROUND GINGER

Roll out the pastry and line a 9-inch pie dish with it. Bake blind (unfilled) for 10 minutes at 400° (Mark 6). Cook the cherries in the wine until tender. Drain, reserving the wine. Beat the egg yolks, sugar, salt, cinnamon, ginger and add the wine. Pour into the pie shell and arrange the cherries on top. Bake at 350° (Mark 4) for 25–30 minutes, or until set.

A Tart of Damsons

To make a tart of damsons :
Seeth the Damsons in Wine, and straine them with a little Creame, them boile your fruits over the fire till it be very thicke, put thereto sugar, Sinamon and Ginger so spread them on your paste, but set it not in the oven after, but let the paste be baked before.
(*The Good Huswife's Handmaid, 1594*)

2 LB DAMSONS
¼ PT (½ CUP) RED WINE
½ LB (1 CUP) SUGAR

MORE SUGAR TO TASTE (*see recipe*)
1½ TSP GROUND CINNAMON
¾ TSP GROUND GINGER
¼ PT (½ CUP) THICK CREAM
A 9-INCH PASTRY SHELL, BAKED BLIND

Simmer the damsons with the sugar in a little red wine until tender. Remove and rub them through a sieve, discarding stones and skins. Add enough sugar to sweeten to your taste, plus the cinnamon and ginger. Chill. Whip the cream until stiff and fold into the purée. Spoon into the pie shell and chill before serving.

This tart can also be made with plums or greengages, but as they are sweeter they will require less sugar.

A Tart of Gooseberries

How to make a tart of gooseberries :
Take gooseberries and perboile them in white or claret wine ; or strong ale and withal boil a little white bread ; then take them up and draw them through a strainer as thick as you can with the yolkes of five eggs, then season it with sugar, and half a dishe of butter, and so bake it.
(*The Good Huswife's Handmaid, 1594*)

1 LB (3 CUPS) GOOSEBERRIES
¼ PT (½ CUP) WHITE WINE
1 SLICE BREAD, CRUMBLED
12 OZ (1½ CUPS) SUGAR
5 EGG YOLKS
A 9-INCH UNBAKED PIE-SHELL
½ OZ (1 TBS) BUTTER

Cook the gooseberries with the wine, bread and sugar until the fruit is tender. Force through a food-mill. Stir in the egg yolks and pour the filling into the pie shell. Dot with butter. Bake at 350° (Mark 4) for 25 minutes.

Pears, to Stew

Take the greatest Wardens, bake them in an Oven with Household Bread, putting in a Pint of Strong Ale or Beer ; when Baked, take them from the Liquor; take half a pint of it, half a pint of Red Port, and four ounces of Sugar; put them into the Stew-pan, with two Cloves slit, and a little Cream; cover them close, and let them stew till they are very Red; turn them now and then; when they are enough, put them into a Dish you intend to serve them in at Table and strew D.L.S. [Double-refined Loaf Sugar] on them. (The Family Dictionary, 1695)

Serves 4
4 PEARS, PEELED
½ PT (1 CUP) BEER OR ALE
¼ PT (½ CUP) PORT
2 OZ (¼ CUP) SUGAR
2 CLOVES, CRUSHED
4 TBS (¼ CUP) CREAM
SUGAR FOR SPRINKLING

Bake the pears in a dish for 20–30 minutes at 350° (Mark 4), with the beer in the bottom. Combine ¼ pint (half a cup) of the beer the pears were cooked in, port, sugar, cloves and cream in a saucepan. Add the pears and cook, covered, until tender, turning them in the mixture to colour them. Serve with sugar sprinkled over them.

Quince Pies

*To bake quince pies:
Pare them and cut out the core; then perboyle them in water till they be tender; then take them foorth, and let the water run from them till they be drie. Then put into everie Quince sugar, sinamon and ginger and fill everie pie therewith, and then you may let them bake the space of an houre, and so serve them.
(The Good Huswife's Handmaid, 1594)*

Serves 4
4 QUINCES OR WINTER PEARS
ABOUT 2 OZ (4 TBS) SUGAR
1 TSP GROUND CINNAMON
1 TSP GROUND GINGER
4 INDIVIDUAL SOUFFLÉ DISHES
¾ LB FLAKY PASTRY

Peel and core the quinces, but leave them whole. Put them into a deep, narrow saucepan, cover them with water, add the sugar to taste, bring to the boil and simmer until they are tender. Put a quince upright in each soufflé dish, sprinkling with sugar, cinnamon and ginger. Reduce the cooking juice by fast boiling, until it is rather thick and syrupy. (A little honey can be added, for thickening). Pour some of this over the quinces and cover each with a pastry lid. Seal the pastry firmly with cold water to the lip of the soufflé dish. Bake at 350° (Mark 4) for 30 minutes, or until the pastry is crisp and golden.

Barley Cream

*French barley cream:
Take a porringer full of French perle barley, boil it in eight or nine several waters very tender, then put it in a quart of cream, with some large mace, and whole cinnamon, boil it about a quarter of an hour; then have two pound of almonds blanched and beaten fine with rose-water, put to them some sugar, and strain the almonds with some cold cream, then put all over the fire, and stir it till it be ready to boil, take it off the fire, still stirring it till it be half cold, then put to it two spoonfuls of sack or white wine, and a little salt, and serve it in a dish cold.
(Robert May, 1660)*

3 OZ (½ CUP) PEARL BARLEY
1 PT (2½ CUPS) ALMOND MILK (see p. 53)
½ TSP GROUND MACE
1 TSP GROUND CINNAMON
1 TBS ROSEWATER
2 OZ (¼ CUP) SUGAR
1 OZ (¼ CUP) GROUND ALMONDS
4 EGG YOLKS
1 TBS SHERRY OR DESSERT WINE

Put the barley into a saucepan, cover with boiling water, parboil for 10–15 minutes and then drain. Put the barley back into a saucepan with the almond milk, the spices, the rosewater, sugar and ground almonds; bring to the boil and simmer gently until the barley is tender.

Beat the egg yolks and pour the almond milk mixture into them in a thin stream, beating with a whisk. Put this mixture into the top of a double boiler, over simmering water, and add the sherry. Cook, stirring, until the mixture has thickened and will coat the spoon. Pour into a serving bowl and chill.

A Cheese Tart

This is not like a quiche or a cheesecake, but more like a cheese fondu encased in pastry if eaten hot. A little kirsch sprinkled in with the rosewater will make the resemblance even closer. If allowed to cool before serving it makes a smooth cheese filling and is an attractive way of serving cheese with a salad.

How to make a tart of cheese :
Make your Tart, then take some Banbury
Cheese, and pare away the outside of it and cut
the cleane cheese into small pieces and put them
into the Tart, and when your Tart is full of
Cheese ; then put two handfuls of sugar, and cast
into it five or sixe spoonfuls of Rosewater, and
close it up with a cover, and with a feather,
lat sweet molten butter upon it, and fine sugar
and bake it in a soft oven.
(The Good Huswife's Handmaid, 1594)

Serves 4–5
I LB PASTRY
8 OZ (2 CUPS) MILD CHEESE, GRATED
4 OZ (½ CUP) SUGAR
6 TBS ROSEWATER
½ OZ (I TBS) BUTTER
2 TBS SUGAR

Line a 9–10-inch pie-dish with the pastry. Mix the cheese and sugar, and spoon into the pastry shell. Sprinkle over the rosewater and

cover with the pastry lid. Melt the butter and sugar together and paint on to the lid. Bake at 375° (Mark 5) for 30–40 minutes.

Try giving this tart a savoury filling by replacing the sugar with a little butter, pepper, salt and chopped fresh herbs. Do not glaze the top with sugar in this case.

Cheesecake

To make cheesecakes :
Set some Cream over the Fire, and turn it with
Sack and Eggs then drain it well and season it
well with Rose-water and Sugar and Eggs, Spice,
Currants and a few spoonfuls of Cream and put
it into your Crust, adding a little Salt and so
bake them. (Hannah Wolley, 1664)

Serves 6
½ PT (I CUP) CREAM
4 TBS SHERRY
3 EGGS PLUS 2 YOLKS
2 OZ (½ CUP) SUGAR
2 TBS ROSEWATER
¼ TSP EACH GROUND MACE, CINNAMON AND
   NUTMEG
½ TSP SALT
4 OZ (½ CUP) COTTAGE CHEESE
2 TBS CURRANTS
A 9-INCH PASTRY SHELL, BAKED BLIND

Heat the cream and sherry in a saucepan. Beat the eggs, sugar, rosewater, spices and salt in a bowl until the mixture is creamy and light. Beat in the cottage cheese and then add the hot cream and sherry in a thin stream, beating with a whisk. Stir in the currants and pour into the shell. Bake at 350° (Mark 4) for 20–25 minutes. Cool before serving.

'Mon Ami'

This lovely dessert can be served in champagne flutes for a wedding breakfast. The top can be made to resemble a nosegay with a ring of angelica leaves round the rim followed by smaller and smaller concentric circles of crystallized flowers, and a marshmallow in the centre, carved into the shape of a magnolia and surrounded by a few more angelica leaves.

Mon amy :

To mak mon amy, tak and boile cows creme and when it is bolid set it asid and let it kele then take cow cruddes and press out the whey, then bray them in a mortair and cast them in a potte to the creme and boile all togedure put therto to sugur hony and may butter colour it up with saffron and in the settynge doun put in yolks of eggs, well bett and do away the streyne and let the potage be stonding and then put it in dyshes and plant ther in floures of violettes and serve it.
(Andrew Boorde, 1542)

Serves 4-6
1 PT (2½ CUPS) THICK CREAM
4 OZ (1 CUP) COTTAGE CHEESE
2 OZ (¼ CUP) SUGAR
4 TBS HONEY
⅛ TSP SAFFRON
1 OZ (2 TBSP) BUTTER, SOFTENED
4 EGG YOLKS
CRYSTALLIZED OR FRESH VIOLETS

Boil the cream and set it aside. Beat up the cottage cheese and mix it with the sugar, honey, saffron and cream. Blend well. Beat in the softened butter, in small pieces, and the egg yolks. Pour into a saucepan, heat and cook over low heat, stirring until thickened. Do not boil. Pour into a custard bowl and chill. Decorate with fresh or crystallized violets.

Rice Pudding

Boil your rice with cream, strain it, and put to it 2 penny loaves grated, eight yolks of eggs, and three whites, beef-suet, one pound of sugar, salt, rose water, nutmeg, coriander beaten.
(Robert May, 1660)

Serves 4
3 OZ (½ CUP) RICE
4 OZ (½ CUP) SUGAR
½ TSP GROUND NUTMEG
¼ TSP CORIANDER

½ TSP SALT
2 TBS GRATED SUET
1 PT (2½ CUPS) MILK
4 EGG YOLKS PLUS 1 EGG WHITE
½ OZ (4 TBS) BREADCRUMBS
2 TBS ROSEWATER

Combine the rice, sugar, spices, seasoning, suet and milk in a saucepan. Cook over low heat, stirring occasionally, for about 30 minutes, or until the mixture is thick and creamy. Beat in the egg yolks and white, the breadcrumbs and rosewater. Serve warm.

Trifle

To make a trifle :

Take a pinte of thicke Creame, and season it with Sugar and Ginger and Rosewater, so stirre it as you would then have it and make it luke warm in a dish on a chafing dishe and coales, and after put it into a Silver piece or a Bowle, and so serve it to the board.
(The Good Huswife's Handmaid, 1594)

Serves 3-4
¾ PT (2 CUPS) THICK CREAM
¼ PT (½ CUP) ROSEWATER
1 TSP GROUND GINGER
4 EGG YOLKS
4 OZ (½ CUP) SUGAR

Heat the cream, rosewater and ginger together. Beat the egg yolks and sugar until creamy. Pour in the hot cream mixture, beating constantly. Cook in the top half of a double boiler, over simmering water, until it has thickened enough to coat a spoon. Pour into a silver bowl and chill.

Syllabub

(Traditional, adapted from contemporary sources).

Serves 6–8

1 PT (2½ CUPS) THICK CREAM
½ PT (1 CUP) SHERRY
JUICE AND GRATED RIND OF 1 LEMON
2 OZ (¼ CUP) SUGAR

Chill a large mixing bowl and put all the ingredients into it. Beat lightly and continuously with a wire whisk, skimming off the foam as it rises. Continue until all the mixture has turned into foam. Put the foam in a bowl and chill in the refrigerator. Serve in individual glass bowls or champagne glasses.

For a solid version, whip the cream alone until it is stiff, then fold in the other ingredients and chill.

Little Puddings

Take a handful of grated Bread, a spoonful of Flower, Yolks of two Eggs, a spoonful of Orange Flower Water, a handful of Beef-suet shred, a little grated Nutmeg, a spoonful of Cheese-Curds, and a little Salt; work all well together, wet it as little as you can, and make it up with Cream; lay it in round Balls in the bottom of your Dish, which must be well butter'd, and so bake them, but not too much. When baked, put them in another dish, with a little Canary, melted butter and sugar, beaten together.
(The Family Dictionary, 1695)

Serves 4

2 OZ (1 CUP) BREADCRUMBS
2 TBS FLOUR
2 OZ (½ CUP) GRATED SUET
¼ TSP GROUND NUTMEG
½ TSP SALT
2 TBS COTTAGE CHEESE
1 TBS ORANGE-FLOWER WATER
2 EGG YOLKS
2–4 TBS CREAM

Hard sauce
2 OZ (4 TBS) BUTTER
2 TBS SUGAR
2 TBS WINE

Combine the breadcrumbs, flour, suet, nutmeg, salt and cheese in a bowl. Add the orange-flower water, egg yolks and enough cream to moisten the mixture. Shape into 1-inch balls. Arrange these in a buttered baking dish and bake at 350° (Mark 4) for 10–15 minutes.

Make the sauce by creaming the butter and sugar together. Gradually add the wine, and serve with the little puddings.

Sauces

Sauce for Land-fowl

(Robert May, 1660)

10 OZ (1 CUP) BOILED PRUNES, DRAINED AND
    STONED
½ PT (1 CUP) PAN GRAVY FROM ROASTING CHICKEN
½ TSP GROUND CINNAMON
¼ TSP GROUND GINGER
1 OZ (2 TBS) SUGAR

Purée all the ingredients in a blender with salt to taste and serve, very hot, with roast chicken.

Horseradish Sauce

(Sir Kenelme Digbie, 1669)

1½ OZ (½ CUP) GRATED HORSERADISH
2 TBS VINEGAR
2 TSP SUGAR

Mix the ingredients together and serve with cold roast beef.

Sauce for Loin of Veal

(Gervase Markham, 1660)

4 TBS MIXED HERBS
½ PT (1 CUP) WINE OR CIDER VINEGAR
1 OZ (2 TBS) BUTTER

½ OZ (¼ CUP) BREADCRUMBS
4 OZ (½ CUP) SUGAR
I TSP GROUND CINNAMON
½ TSP GROUND CLOVES
2 HARD-BOILED EGG YOLKS, SIEVED

Garnish
ORANGE AND LEMON SLICES

Chop the herbs finely. Boil the vinegar and butter together, then add the breadcrumbs, sugar, cinnamon, cloves, herbs and sieved egg yolks. Stir and heat without boiling. Serve poured over a small piece of roast loin of veal, with slices of orange and lemon arranged round the edge of the dish. Double the quantities for a large piece of meat.

Sauce for Boiled Mutton

(*The Family Dictionary, 1695*)

¼–½ PT (¾ CUP) WHITE WINE OR CLARET
6 OZ (I CUP) UNCOOKED PRUNES
6 ALLSPICE BERRIES
I OZ (½ CUP) BREADCRUMBS
JUICE OF I LEMON
¼ TSP SALT

Stew the prunes in the wine with the spices until soft. Purée the contents of the pan in the blender with the breadcrumbs. Add the lemon juice and salt. Reheat and pour the sauce over a carved leg or shoulder of mutton which has been boiled, not roasted.

Bread, Biscuits and Cakes

Almond Cake

This makes a big, light cake bread, which seems to have been typical of this period. One senses an influence from Italian bakery in these *panetonne*-like creations.

Take one and a half Pounds of fine Flour, twelve Ounces of Sugar, half a Pound of Almonds, blanched and beaten with Rosewater. Mingle all these together with as much Sack as will work it into a Paste, add some Spice, some Yeast and plumped Currants with a Pound of Butter. So make it into a Cake and bake it.
(*Hannah Wolley, 1664*)

¾ LB (2½ CUPS) FLOUR
2 OZ (¼ CUP) SUGAR
I TSP GROUND CINNAMON
½ TSP GROUND NUTMEG
I TSP SALT
½ OZ (I PACKAGE) YEAST
4 TBS TEPID WATER
2 EGGS
I OZ (2 TBS) BUTTER
½ TSP ROSE WATER
4 TBS MILK
4 TBS SHERRY
2 OZ (½ CUP) ALMONDS
2 OZ (½ CUP) CURRANTS

Egg glaze
I EGG YOLK, BEATEN WITH 2 TBS MILK OR CREAM

Mix 2½ cups of the flour, the sugar spices and salt in a bowl. Dissolve the yeast in the warm water. Make a well in the flour, and put in the yeast, eggs, butter, rosewater, milk and sherry. Mix to blend thoroughly. Add more flour if it is too sticky to knead. Knead for 8–10 minutes. Put the dough in a greased bowl, covered in a warm place and let rise for about I hour until double in bulk. Punch down. Work in the nuts and currants. Form into a round ball. Put onto a greased baking sheet and let rise for another hour until double in bulk. Brush with egg glaze and bake at 350° for 35–45 minutes.

This makes a big, light cake bread, which seems to have been rather typical of this period. One feels an influence from Italian bakery in these panettone-like creations.

Barnet Sugar-Cakes

(*The Family Dictionary, 1695*)

Makes 12 small cakes

¾ LB (1½ CUPS) BUTTER
8 OZ (1 CUP) SUGAR
2 EGGS
4 OZ (1 CUP) FLOUR
4 TBS CREAM
4 TBS SHERRY
4 OZ (1 CUP) CURRANTS
1 TSP GROUND NUTMEG
2 OZ (½ CUP) ICING (CONFECTIONER'S) SUGAR
1 EGG WHITE

Beat the butter and sugar until light and fluffy; then add the eggs, one at a time. Add the flour, cream and sherry. Stir in the currants and the nutmeg. Shape into 4–5-inch rounds about ¼ inch thick. Prick on the top with a fork and bake at 350° (Mark 4) for 10–15 minutes. Glaze with icing (confectioner's) sugar mixed with egg white and return to the oven for a few minutes until the icing is crisp.

Cakes with Currants

(*The Family Dictionary, 1695*)

½ OZ (1 PACKAGE) YEAST
4 TBS TEPID ROSEWATER
1 TSP SUGAR
1¼ LB (4½ CUPS) FLOUR
1 TBS SALT
2 TBS CARAWAY SEEDS
¼ TSP GROUND CLOVES
¼ TSP MACE
½ TSP GROUND NUTMEG
½ TSP CINNAMON

2 EGGS PLUS 1 EXTRA YOLK
4 TBS MARMALADE
¼ LB (½ CUP) BUTTER, SOFTENED
¼ PT (½ CUP) SHERRY
¼ PT (½ CUP) CREAM
½ LB (2 CUPS) CURRANTS
3 OZ (¾ CUP) CANDIED ORANGE AND LEMON PEEL, MIXED

Icing
9 OZ (2 CUPS) ICING (CONFECTIONER'S) SUGAR
2 EGG WHITES, BEATEN

Prove the yeast in the lukewarm rosewater and sugar; if it bubbles it is active: this is the proof! In a bowl mix ¾ lb (3 cups) of the flour, the salt, seeds and spices. Make a well in the centre and put in the eggs, marmalade, butter, sherry and cream and blend well. Add sprinklings of flour until the dough is no longer sticky. Knead for 10 minutes or until smooth and elastic, adding flour as needed. Put into a greased bowl and leave to rise for about 1 hour, until the dough has doubled in size. Punch down and knead in the currants and candied peel. Put into a round 10-inch spring-form cake tin, buttered and lined with buttered wax-paper. Leave to rise until it has again doubled and bake at 350° (Mark 4) for 35–40 minutes, until golden.

Trickle the icing on or lightly brush over the top with a pastry brush. The original recipe from which I have adapted this suggests using a 'tiny sprig of rosemary'! It should look as though snow had lightly fallen on it and spread a little down the sides. As this is a light cake rather resembling the Italian *panettoni* the icing should not be so heavy that it weighs down the cake.

Spice Cake

Take a half peck of flour, a scant pound of sweet butter, some milk and cream mixed. Set the milk on the fire, add the butter, a good deal of sugar, and allow to dissolve. Strain a good deal of saffron into the milk, and add seven to eight spoonfuls of ale-barm. Stir in eight eggs,

*with two extra egg yolks, one at a time and mix
together. Cool the milk and add it. Into the flour
put crushed anisseeds, cloves, mace and a good
deal of cinnamon. Work all the above ingredients
together until good and stiff, then add a little
cold rosewater, and knead well. If the dough is
not sweet enough, knead in a little more sugar.
Pull it all in pieces, and hurl in a good quantity
of currants. Knead again, and bake your cakes
in a warm oven.*
(*Gervase Markham, 1660, abridged*)

Makes 36 small cakes
14 OZ (3 CUPS) SIFTED FLOUR
1 TSP BAKING SODA
1 TSP SALT
1 TSP CINNAMON
½ TSP GROUND CLOVES
½ TSP GROUND MACE
½ LB (1 CUP) BUTTER, SOFTENED
12 OZ (1½ CUPS) SUGAR
3 EGGS
1 TSP ROSEWATER
½ LB (2 CUPS) CURRANTS

Sift together the flour, baking soda, salt and
spices. Cream the butter and sugar in a bowl
until light and fluffy. Add the eggs and rosewater; beat them into the creamed butter. Add
the flour mixture, beating well. Stir in the
currants. Chill for 30 minutes. Drop on to a
greased baking sheet in rounded teaspoonfuls.
Bake at 375° (Mark 5) for 10–12 minutes.

To Make a Marchpane

*Take two pound of almonds blanched and beaten
in a stone mortar, till they begin to come to a
fine paste, and then take a pound of sifted sugar,
put it in the mortar with the almonds, and make
it into a perfect paste, putting to it now and then
in the beating of it a spoonful of rose-water to
keep it from oiling; when you have beaten it to a
puffpaste, drive it out big as a charger, and set an
edge about it as you do upon a quodling tart, and
a bottom of wafers under it, thus bake it in an
oven or baking-pan; when you see it is white,*

*hard, and dry, take it out, and ice it with
rose-water and sugar, being made as thick as
butter for fritters, so spread it on with a wing
feather, and put it into the oven again; when you
see it rise high, then take it out and garnish it
with some pretty conceits made of the same stuff,
stick long comfets upright on it, and so serve it.*
(*Robert May, 1660*)

2 LB (8 CUPS) GROUND ALMONDS
1 LB (4 CUPS) ICING (CONFECTIONER'S) SUGAR
1–2 EGG WHITES
2–4 TBS ROSEWATER

Icing
4½ OZ (1 CUP) ICING (CONFECTIONER'S) SUGAR
1–2 TSP ROSEWATER

Combine the ground almonds and sugar in a
bowl; work with your hands to form a stiff
paste by adding the egg whites and rosewater,
a little at a time.

To make a tart; roll half of this paste out in a
circle on a floured board. Put on a baking
sheet, cover with a piece of brown paper of the
same size and lift up the edges, as for a very
shallow tart, and crimp them to form a fancy
edging. Bake at 300° (Mark 2) until dry and
hard, (about 15–20 minutes). Ice the top with
the icing sugar mixed with rosewater. Return to
the oven for a few minutes until set.

Garnish with the remaining mixture and
cut into designs. An inner serrated quatrefoil
pattern can be made with strips of paste,
crimped like the border and put into the
marchpane shell before it goes into the oven.
This will give an edible dish for sweet,
chocolates, sugared nuts and any pretty
sweetmeats you would like to serve. Small
pieces of the paste can be shaped in any way
you wish. They do not need to be baked – at
the very most they can be dried out in a low
oven.

Pickles and Preserves

Sweetmeats of My Lady Windebanks

(*Sir Kenelme Digbie, 1669*)

4 LB FRESH APRICOTS, PEELED AND STONED
¼ PT (½ CUP) WATER
SUGAR

Put the apricots into a saucepan with the water, bring to the boil and simmer until tender (about 15 minutes). Purée the fruit in a blender and measure the quantity. Add ½ lb (1 cup) sugar for each cup of fruit purée. Put back in the saucepan and simmer very gently for 1–2 hours or until the mixture is thick enough to stick to a plate when it is turned upside-down. Stir frequently so that the bottom does not burn. Spoon into sterilized jars.

To Make an Excellent Syrup of Apples

As above, but use apples instead of apricots

Sweetmeat of Apples

As above, but add some apple rings, lightly stewed. A little orange and lemon juice, to taste, is cooked with the jelly.

Preserved Cherries

Cherries, to preserve:
Take a pound of Cherries, put them into a pint of red Wine, take a quarter of a pound of green Pipins, pare and slice them into it; then put in two ounces of Sugar, boil them very fast till they be the Colour of Claret, take half a Pint of that Syrup to a pound of Cherries stoned, and three-quarters of a pound of Sugar, divide your Sugar into three parts, melt one part in your Syrup, then put in your Cherries, boil them very fast, strew in the rest of the Sugar in the boiling; when your Syrup gellies, and the Cherries look clear, they be enough, then Lade them with a
Spoon till they be cold, and put them into Glasses, and cover them two or three days after.
(*The Family Dictionary, 1695*)

2 PT (5 CUPS) CHERRIES, STONED
2 APPLES, PEELED, CORED AND SLICED
1½ LB (3½ CUPS) SUGAR
½ PT (1 CUP) RED WINE

Combine all the ingredients in a 10-qt (50 cup) pan; bring to the boil to dissolve the sugar. Cook, allowing to boil down until the jelly registers 220° on a sugar thermometer. Spoon into sterilized jars. The cherries should remain whole and will have a beautiful translucent appearance.

Redcurrant Jelly

Gelly of red currants:
Take them clean picked, and fresh gathered in the morning, in a bason, set them over the fire, that their juyce may sweat out, pressing them all the while with the back of your preserving spoon, to squeese out of them all that is good. When you see all is out, strain the Liquor from them, and let it stand to settle four or five hours, that the gross matter may sink to the bottom. Then take the pure clear, (the thick settling will serve to add in making of Marmulate of Cherries, or the like) and to every pint or pound of it, put three quarters of a pound of the purest refined Sugar, and boil them up with a quick fire, till they come to a gelly height (which will be done immediately in less then a quarter of an hour) which you may try with a drop upon a plate. Then take it off, and when it is cold enough, put it into Glasses. You must be careful to skim it well in due time, and with thin brown Paper to take off the froth, if you will be so curious.
(*Sir Kenelme Digbie, 1669*)

Makes 1¼ pints (3 cups)

3 LB (10 CUPS) REDCURRANTS
1½ PT (3½ CUPS) WATER
1–1½ LB (2–3 CUPS) SUGAR

Mash the currants, having stripped them from their stalks with the prongs of a fork. Put them into a 10-quart pan, cover with the water and bring to the boil. Simmer for 30 minutes. Line a colander with a triple thickness of cheese-cloth; pour the berries and juice in and let the juice drain through, but do not squeeze the berries. Measure the juice and for each half-pint (1 cup) of juice allow half a pound (1 cup) of sugar. Transfer to a saucepan and bring to the boil, stirring until the sugar dissolves. Boil until the jelly reaches 220° on a sugar thermometer. Skim off the foam and spoon into sterilized jars.

Candied Roots, Fruits and Flowers

Tiny baby carrots are delicious treated this way, and so are kernels of sweet-corn. The flower petals should be prepared a few at a time so that they do not stick together.

Dissolve sugar or sugar-candy in rose-water, boyle it to an height, put in your roots, fruits or flowers, the sirrup being cold, then rest a little; after take them out and boyle the sirrop again, then put in more roots, etc., then boyle the sirrop a third time to a hardness, putting in more sugar, but not more rosewater, put in the roots, etc. the sirrop being cold, and let them stand till they candy.
(*Sir Kenelme Digbie, 1669*)

½ LB (1 CUP) SUGAR
½ PT (1 CUP) ROSEWATER
ROOTS, FRUITS OR FLOWERS

Combine the sugar and rosewater in a saucepan and bring to the boil to dissolve the sugar. Add the roots or flowers and simmer for 10–15 minutes, or until tender. Remove with a perforated spoon and boil the syrup until it registers 234° on a sugar thermometer. Dip the roots or flowers into the syrup to coat them, remove with the perforated spoon and put on racks to dry.

Marmalade of Cherries and Raspberries

Marmulate of cherries with juyce of raspes and currants: Mingle juyce of Raspes and red Currants with the stoned Cherries, and boil this mixture into Marmulate, with a quarter, or at most, a third part of Sugar. The juyces must be so much as to make Gelly of them to mingle handsomely with the Cherries, to appear among and between them.

Madam Plancy (who maketh this sweet-meat for the Queen) useth this proportion. Take three pounds of Cherries stoned; half a pound of clear juyce of raspes, and one pound of the juyce of red currants, and one pound of fine Sugar. Put them all together into the preserving pan; boil them with a quick fire, especially at the first, skimming them all the while, as any scum riseth. When you find them of a fit consistence, with a fine clear gelly, mingled with the Cherries, take the preserving pan from the fire, and braise the Cherries with the back of your preserving spoon; and when they are of a fit temper of coolness, pot them up.
(*Sir Kenelme Digbie, 1669*)

1¼ LB OR (4 CUPS) DARK CHERRIES, STONED
2½ LB (5 CUPS) SUGAR
A 10-OZ (½ CUP) JAR REDCURRANT JELLY
1¼ LB OR (4 CUPS) RASPBERRIES
1 BOTTLE CERTO (PECTIN)

Combine the cherries, sugar, currant jelly and raspberries in a pan. Bring to the boil and continue to boil briskly for 2–3 minutes. Remove from the heat and stir in the Certo immediately. Pour into sterilized jars.

I have tried making this with 1¼ lb frozen cherries and two 10-oz packets of frozen raspberries. It did not set into a jelly, despite the pectin, but turned into a delicious thick fruit sauce for serving over ice-cream. Nowadays this seems almost more useful than a preserve proper.

Quince Marmalade

Marmulate of quince :
Take six pounds of Quince-flesh ; six pounds of
pure Sugar ; and eight pints of juyce ; boil this up
with quick fire, till you have scummed it, then
pull away all the Coals, and let it but simper,
for four or five hours, remaining covered,
renewing from time to time so little fire, as to
cause it so to continue simpring. But as soon as it
is scummed, put into it a handful of Quince
kernels, two races of Ginger sliced, and fourteen
or fifteen Cloves whole ; all these put into a
Tyffany-bag tyed fast ; when you finde that the
colour is almost to your minde, make a quick fire,
and boil it up a pace, then throw away your bag
of kernels, Ginger and Cloves, and pot up your
Marmulate, when it is cool enough.
(Sir Kenelme Digbie, 1669)

3 LB (12 CUPS) QUINCE, PEELED AND SLICED
3 LB (7 CUPS) SUGAR
2 PT (5 CUPS) APPLE JUICE
2 OZ ($\frac{1}{2}$ CUP) QUINCE KERNELS
2 SLICES GINGER
10 CLOVES

Combine the quince, sugar and apple juice in a
large preserving pan. Tie the kernels, ginger
and cloves in a cheesecloth bag and put in the
pan. Bring to the boil, stirring to dissolve the
sugar, and cook without stirring until the
mixture registers 220° on a sugar thermometer.
Remove the bag and pour into sterilized jars.

Mincemeat

(Sir Kenelme Digbie, 1669)

1 LB MINCED (GROUND) BEEF
1 LB GRATED (GROUND) SUET
$\frac{1}{2}$ LB (2 CUPS) CURRANTS
1 LEMON, PEELED AND CHOPPED
4 PIPPINS (HARD APPLES), MINCED (3 CUPS)
2 TSP GROUND NUTMEG
1 TSP GROUND MACE
1 TBS GROUND CINNAMON
1 TSP GROUND CLOVES
14 OZ (2 CUPS) SUGAR

3 TBS ROSEWATER
2 OZ ($\frac{1}{2}$ CUP) CANDIED LEMON PEEL, CHOPPED
2 OZ ($\frac{1}{2}$ CUP) CANDIED ORANGE PEEL, CHOPPED
4 TBS CARAWAY SEEDS
4 OZ (1 CUP) DATES, CHOPPED

Mix all the ingredients together and keep
for 2 weeks, at least, in the refrigerator or in a
cool larder, then use for making mincepies.

Tongue Mincemeat

This delicious mincemeat is used for making
the basic forcemeat for the Bride Pie (p. 79)
and in general gives an interesting flavour
when mixed with beef or chicken forcemeat.
As it keeps for months under refrigeration, you
can give a flavour of the seventeenth century
to your own cooking by adding a little of it to a
meat loaf, savoury pie or rissole.
(Sir Kenelme Digbie, 1669)

1 COOKED FRESH (NOT SALTED) CALF'S TONGUE,
   FINELY CHOPPED
$\frac{1}{2}$ LB GRATED (GROUND) SUET
4 OZ (1 CUP) RAISINS
$\frac{1}{2}$ LB (2 CUPS) PEELED APPLES, FINELY CHOPPED
2 OZ ($\frac{1}{2}$ CUP) CANDIED ORANGE-PEEL
2 OZ ($\frac{1}{2}$ CUP) CANDIED CITRON
4 TBS SHERRY
PEEL OF 1 LEMON, GRATED
1 TSP NUTMEG
1 TSP MACE
$\frac{1}{2}$ TSP CLOVES
2 TSP CINNAMON
4 OZ ($\frac{1}{2}$ CUP) SUGAR

Mix all the ingredients together in a bowl.
Keep refrigerated for as long as possible and
then use for making mincepies.

RONE
(from Dublin)
Living near
St Georges Church
Southwark.

Has a large Quantity of fine
Genuine Green, & Saffron Colour'd
Usquebaugh,
Citron Water, Ratafia
& several other fine Cordials
Sold here.

THE EIGHTEENTH CENTURY

WHEN QUEEN ANNE was crowned, in 1702, Britannia did rule the waves: Portugal and Spain were vanquished; the French, crippled; the Dutch, outdone. Industry was booming. Good weather brought good harvests; corn was cheap. Townsmen could afford good rations of meat; and villagers again had their cows, pigs, chickens or ducks, and 'white meats' – dairy products – for their tables. But all this changed by 1760 when George III took the throne. Wet weather had ruined crops and prices soared. Only the big farmers and landowners prospered. The simple economic structure of English village life had been shattered by the spread of enclosed lands, and the agricultural revolution was as drastic as the industrial one.

Agricultural methods, not much different from those in the Middle Ages had to change, and change they did – almost to modern standards. All sorts of farm machinery came into being. The annual crop of wheat rose enormously; Thomas Coke made Norfolk the 'Granery of England'. Jethro Tull devised the first practical field drill and further advanced the raising of turnips as food for cattle and sheep. So prejudiced were the English against the potato that it took seven years of experiments by Coke to prove that this was good winter feed for cattle. Clover and cabbages were raised as fodder, too. The fact the cattle could now be kept alive through the winter meant that it was worthwhile to spend money on improving the breeds. Pedigree animals brought enormous prices.

Heavy drinking turned out to be the real menace to the social structure in the reigns of Queen Anne and the Georges. Since Edward VI, the sale of ale and beer had been controlled; but there was no restriction of the sale of spirits – and they were absurdly cheap. Gin shops abounded, and a government attempt to raise the tax on spirits led to rioting. Hogarth's *Gin Lane* was far from exaggerated. Large quantities of wine were imported, a number of them unknown in England today: the Portugese Bucellas, Colares, and Calcevella; Sheraaz, Lunel, Zante, and Lissa. French brandy, first used in the seventeenth century, became in the eighteenth a favourite of the middle and upper classes, and West Indian rum was popular also.

The wane of the eighteenth century saw the English country squire dubbed a 'four-bottle' man, and because magistrates were known to appear on the bench after considerable wine, the Mutiny Act specified that courts martial must be held *before* dinner. Queen Anne herself was thought by some of her subjects to console herself in a life shut in by ill health and a dull husband by sipping 'cold tea' – brandy in a tea cup. She seldom kept court, and her one real pleasure in life may well have been her dinner. When she was young, this rhyme made the rounds:

> King William thinks all,
> Queen Mary talks all
> Prince George drinks all,
> And Princess Anne eats all

Though many of the most famous English breweries date from the eighteenth century, the rise of tea drinking gave the brewers alarm. Tea had been brought in by Jesuit priests from China, and by mid-eighteenth century was being imported at the rate of five million pounds a year. An early recipe for this restorative drink is on page 72.

So popular did this cheap and warming drink become, that it was attacked as a pernicious drug by some, on the very sound grounds that it did not provide the poor with the nourishment found in ale or beer. Jonas Hanway, writing in 1757, scolded: 'When will this evil stop?... Your very *Chambermaids* have lost their bloom, I suppose by *sipping tea*'. Toward

the end of the century, tea had replaced both coffee and chocolate, and many of the famous coffee houses had already disappeared.

The eighteenth-century landowners not only drank well, they ate well too. This excerpt from *The Expedition of Humphrey Clinker* by T. Smollett (1771), sets the tone:

At Brambleton Hall . . . I drink the virgin lymph, pure and crystalline as it gushes from the rock, or the sparkling beverage home-brewed from malt of my own making; or I indulge with cider, which my own orchard affords; or with claret of the best growth, imported for my own use, by a correspondent on whose integrity I can depend: my bread is sweet and nourishing, made from my own wheat, ground in my own mill, and baked in my own oven; my table is, in a great measure, furnished from my own ground; my five-year-old mutton, fed on the fragrant herbage of the mountains, that might vie with venison in juice and flavour; my delicious veal, fattened with nothing but the mother's milk, that fills the dish with gravy; my poultry from the barn door, that never knew confinement but when they were at roost; my rabbits panting from the warren; my game fresh from the moors; my trout and salmon struggling from the stream; oysters from their native banks; and herrings, with other sea-fish, I can eat in four hours after they are taken. My salads, roots, and pot-herbs, my own garden yields in plenty and perfection; the produce of the natural soil, prepared by moderate cultivation. The same soil affords all the different fruits which England may call her own so that my dessert is every day fresh-gathered from the tree; my dairy flows with nectareous tides of milk and cream, from whence we derive abundance of excellent butter, curds, and cheese; and the refuse fattens my pigs, that are destined for hams and bacon.

Breakfast in the country house of coffee, tea, or chocolate with rusks or cakes now came at 9 or 10 am, followed at 11 by a glass of sherry and a biscuit. This postponed the dinner to about 2 pm early in the century; by 1780 the squire's chief meal came at 3 or even 4 pm. An ordinary dinner consisted of: '. . . three boiled chickens at top, a very fine haunch of venison at bottom; ham on one side, a flour pudding on the other, and beans in the middle. After the cloth was removed, we had gooseberries, and a remarkably fine dish of apricots'. Another dinner, described by the host as 'elegant' included: 'part of a large Cod, a Chine of Mutton, some Soup, a Chicken Pye, Puddings and Roots, etc. Second course, Pidgeons and Asparagus. A Fillet of Veal with Mushrooms and high Sauce with it, rosted Sweetbreads, hot Lobster, Apricot Tart and in the Middle a Pyramid of Syllabubs and Jellies. We had a Dessert of Fruit after Dinner, and Madeira, White Port and red to drink as Wine'. Supper, made up of a variety of cold meats, followed about 10 pm.

As meals got later, so did they take on more French and Italian overtones. The rise of French food on the English menu became as alarming to some as the replacement of ale by tea had been earlier. A 'depraved Taste of spoiling wholesome Dyet, by costly and pernicious Sauces, and absurd mixtures' was the way Robert Campbell, author of *The London Tradesman* (1747) described this trend. The French influence was felt in table manners, too; and books on the subject became popular.

In time, the leisured classes took their light breakfast at 10 or 11, met their friends at a coffee house an hour later, and dined at 5 or 6. Supper was then so late that it merged with

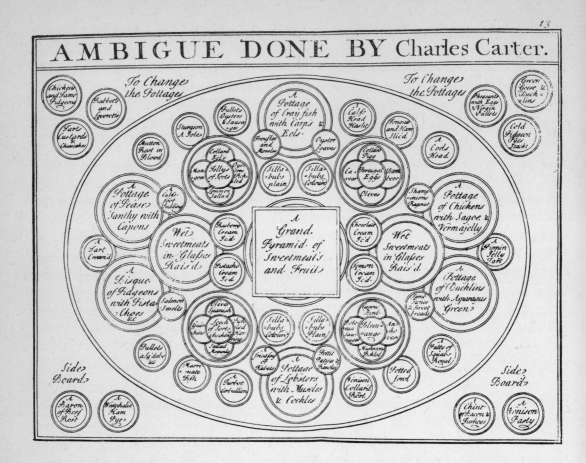

AMBIGUE DONE BY Charles Carter.

breakfast. Finally, toward the turn of the century, dinner drifted back to 2 or 3 pm, with supper at 7 or 8. This was the time that 'afternoon tea' at 5 pm came into being. The thin bread and butter served with this tea is still a symbol of English drawing-rooms.

The eighteenth century produced three remarkable cookbooks written by women. This was due in part to an invention attributed to Count Rumford: the cookstove. In earlier ages men took charge of the huge central fires with their spits of roasting mutton and beef; side fire-places with chimneys made this work a little less arduous, but still a man's job. It was the development of the enclosed brick stove, with flues, iron plates on top, and a grate that could be cleaned from below that changed cooking into a job that women could manage. Whether he actually invented the first range or not, Count Rumford did produce the cast-iron version and gave his name (like Benjamin Franklin in America) to a fireplace form as well.

These woman-sized stoves brought about a new cuisine suitable to smaller houses, and the women of the rising middle class, who had learned to read, were an eager market for the cookbooks written by those 'liberated' women Hannah Glasse, Elizabeth Raffald, and Maria Rundell.

The Art of Cookery made Plain and Easy, 'which far exceeds any Thing of the Kind yet published' was the claim of a book by Hannah Glasse, published first in 1747 (and reproduced in facsimile by S. R. Publishers in 1971), and the claim was fully justified. The book was a best-seller for almost one hundred years. The prejudice against enterprising women was so strong at that time, however, that many people claimed that the book must have been written by a man, and her name did not appear on the volume until after her death.

Mrs Glasse had married very young; she bore eight children and seems to have worked as a dressmaker: in 1731 she described herself as 'Habit Maker to Her Royal Highness, the Princess of Wales, in Tavistock Street, Covent Garden'. Mrs Glasse's book is organised with clarity and gives us recipes for the most popular dishes of the eighteenth century. Her chapter on the high cost of French cooking adds its further spark to the flaming controversy over the complications of French cuisine, especially as they were distilled in the elaborate recipes for the 'infamous' French broth – cullis. Many an Englishman felt that simple pan juices were superior to stock brewed from several different kinds of meat and game and seasoned with numbers of vegetables and herbs. She included a chapter on preserving food; but this was directed to 'Captains of Ships'. A quote from this energetic lady is as follows: 'Stick your pig just above the breast bone and run your knife to the heart.' Her first edition fetched £31.10 in 1901.

Elizabeth Raffald was an even more impressive example of a woman liberated two centuries before the Women's Lib Movement. The wife of a florist and mother of thirteen daughters, she had been a housekeeper; and in 1764, she opened a confectioner's shop in Fennel Street in Manchester. She also established a Register Office there, probably one of the first employment agencies for servants. This brought her considerable notice, and in time she expanded her shop to sell all sorts of food and to offer a fairly complete catering service. Eight hundred of her original recipes went into her book *The Experienced English Housekeeper*, published in 1769. The book went through thirteen editions and was pirated in twenty-three more. It is available now in a facsimile edition published by E & W Books Ltd in 1970. The book is a thoroughly professional one and contains many excellent recipes – though not quite all of Mrs Raffald's trade secrets.

Our third lady-author living in the eighteenth century was Maria Rundell. Her husband was one of an eminent firm of jewellers in London; after her retirement, they moved to Bath, which had by then become the resort of the middle classes; but it also had been for a century and a half the site of aristocratic and regal gambollings, a gourmet's haven where Cheddar cheese, fresh sole, turbot, sturgeon and Welsh mountain mutton were sold. Dukes and dukes' cooks elbowed each other, vying for bargains at the stalls. A Bath physician, Dr Oliver, there invented the first biscuit – still stamped with his name and face – as an antidote to all the rich food; and it was there that Sally Lunn invented her famous bun. Mrs Rundell may have started making notes for her cooking book while living at Bath; the book was completed after her husband's death when she went to live with a married daughter in Swansea.

Mrs Rundell's intimate and charming style made her book, *A New System of Domestic*

Cookery . . . 'by a Lady', finally published in 1808, a super-seller that surprised both her and her publisher. Mrs Rundell's chapter on carving suggested that the hostess would do this job, a departure from the previous custom of having the host ceremoniously serve his guests, or, in earlier times, giving this job to the most trusted retainer. Mrs Rundell's book contains many more exotic recipes than those previously published; the influence of England's expanding Empire was beginning to be felt on the tables at home.

Two other eighteenth-century cookbooks represent the masculine point of view. One was written by John Farley, head cook at the London Tavern. His book *The London Art of Cookery, and Housekeeper's Complete Assistant* was first published in 1783.

The London Tavern was built on a site in Bishopsgate street where it replaced the White Lion Tavern, destroyed by fire in 1765, together with a tavern called the Black Lion and fifty other buildings. Begun in 1767, the London Tavern was opened the following year with an impressive facade and an elaborately decorated forty-by-thirty-three-foot dining room, the 'Pillar-room', which could seat three hundred 'banqueters' along with one hundred and fifty ladies as spectators in galleries at each end. Every delicacy was provided there. Live turtles were kept at the ready; two tons are said to have swum in one tank. The cellars (the whole basement storey) were stocked with porter, port, sherry, Johannisberg, Tokay, Burgundy, champagne and claret. The wines represented, according to an 1852 estimate, a capital investment that was worth five or six hundred pounds a year at simple interest.

The London Tavern was famous not only for its mighty wines and luxurious food, but also as an excellent spot for public meetings. But in 1877, The Royal Bank of Scotland, Bishopsgate, close to Cornhill, replaced the London Tavern. It was then that its name was bequeathed to the former Queen's Head in Fenchurch Street, where Elizabeth I ate her pork and peas.

John Farley reigned in the kitchen at the London Tavern in its golden days, and his book is a wonderful record of the dishes served at those impressive banquets.

The other book is by Charles Carter who was cook to the Duke of Argyll, the Earl of Pontefract and Lord Cornwallis.

Soups

Chestnut Soup

Pick half a hundred of chestnuts, put them in an earthen pan, and put them in the oven for half an hour, or roast them gently over a slow fire ; but take care they do not burn. Then peel them, and set them to stew in a quart of good beef, veal, or mutton broth, till they be quite tender. In the mean time, take a piece or slice of ham or bacon, a pound of veal, a pigeon beat to pieces, an onion, a bundle of sweet herbs, a piece of carrot, and a little pepper and mace. Lay the bacon at the bottom of a stewpan, and lay the meat and ingredients on it. Set it over a slow fire till it begins to stick to the pan, and then put in a crust of bread, and pour in two quarts of broth. Let it boil softly till one third be wasted, then strain it off, and put in the chestnuts. Season it

with salt, and let it boil till it be well tasted. Then stew two pigeons in it, and a French roll fried crisp. Lay the roll in the middle of the dish, and the pigeons on each side ; pour in the soup, and send it up hot. (John Farley, 1783)

Serves 6

4 SLICES BACON, CHOPPED
$\frac{1}{4}$ LB (1 CUP) HAM, CHOPPED
1 SMALL CHICKEN OR PIGEON, JOINTED
1 ONION, CHOPPED
1 CARROT, SLICED
A HANDFUL ($\frac{1}{2}$ CUP) SWEET HERBS
$\frac{1}{2}$ TSP PEPPER
1 TSP GROUND MACE
3 PT ($7\frac{1}{2}$ CUPS) BEEF STOCK
2 LB CHESTNUTS, ROASTED AND SKINNED
6 ROUND FRENCH ROLLS

Fry the bacon in the bottom of the soup pan and add the ham and chicken or pigeon pieces. Brown them lightly. Add the vegetables, herbs, seasonings and stock, bring to the boil and simmer for 1 hour. Add the chestnuts and

simmer for 20 minutes. Taste and add seasoning if needed. Crisp the rolls well in the oven; put a roll and a piece of bird in each warmed serving bowl and pour the soup with the chestnuts on top.

Chicken Soup with Vermicelli

Potage of vermajelly with capon:
Take celery, and endive, and lettuce, and an onion; chop them pretty small, and so pass them in brown butter thickened; put in half broth half gravy, as much as will fill your dish; put in an ounce and half of vermajelly of two sorts, and stove it up in your soup till tender; stove some of another sort in broth till thick, and tincture it with a little saffron; lay a capon boiled white in the middle of your dish, put in manchet, fill your dish, and lay the yellow in heaps on it and garnish with resoles fried, and lemon, and yellow vermajelly. (John Farley, 1783)

Serves 4 to 6
Stage 1
A 4–5 LB CAPON
STOCK OR WATER TO COVER
I SPRIG THYME
I BAY LEAF
2 CLOVES
I STALK CELERY
I LEEK, WHITE PART ONLY

Stage 2
2 STALKS CELERY, CHOPPED
I ENDIVE, SLICED
I HEAD LETTUCE, COARSELY SHREDDED
I ONION, SLICED
2 OZ (4 TBS) BUTTER
2 PTS (5 CUPS) WATER
1½ OZ (⅓ CUP) VERMICELLI

Stage 3
4 PT (10 CUPS) WATER
¼ LB (1 CUP) MACARONI
¼ TSP SAFFRON

Stage 1: place the capon, stock, herbs, celery and leek in a braising-pan and bring to the boil. Simmer until the bird is tender, for about 1 hour.

Stage 2: brown the celery, endive, lettuce and onion in the butter in a soup pan. Add the water, season, bring to the boil and simmer for about 15–20 minutes until the vegetables are just tender. Add the vermicelli 10 minutes before they are done.

Stage 3: bring the water to the boil in a saucepan, add the saffron and the macaroni, season and cook until tender. Drain well.

Carve the chicken, removing the skin. Lay the pieces in a warm soup tureen, add the saffron-coloured macaroni and pour the soup and vegetables on top.

It seems unnecessary to bother with the rissoles of the original recipe, but they could be made with the dark meat of the chicken, chopped fine, mixed with breadcrumbs, herbs and seasonings, bound with egg yolk, dipped in egg and breadcrumbs and sautéd in butter.

Duck Soup with Onions

Potage of onions santhy:
First boil off a good Quantity of old Onions tender; then pulp them through a Strainer; then make a Ragoust of Onions, with a little Sellery amongst them, and likewise force that, and strain it into your other; then take a Quarter of a Pound of Jordan Almonds, blanch them, and beat them in a Mortar very fine; mince a Sweetbread very small, and stove all this together in good Gravy, and put in a little scalded Parsly minc'd; stove it with a Duck or two half-roasted, till enough; stove French Manchet dry'd in Gravy, and put in the Bottom of your dish; fill up your Dish, put in your Ducks, and garnish your Dish with whole Onions, boil'd down and stov'd in Gravy; put up and down in your Pottage after dish'd, some whole Onions; put sliced Lemon round and serve it. (Charles Carter, 1730)

Serves 6
¾ LB (2 CUPS) SLICED ONIONS
2 STALKS CELERY, CHOPPED
2 OZ (4 TBS) BUTTER

4 PTS (10 CUPS) STOCK
I OZ (¼ CUP) GROUND ALMONDS
2 TBS CHOPPED PARSLEY
I DUCK, HALF-ROASTED
6 ONIONS, PARBOILED
2 OZ (1 CUP) DRY BREADCRUMBS
¼ PT (½ CUP) DUCK GRAVY
I SWEETBREAD, COOKED AND FINELY CHOPPED
I LEMON, SLICED, FOR GARNISH

Sauté the onions and celery in the butter until tender. Purée. Stir in the stock. Add the almonds, parsley, duck and onions and simmer until the duck is tender. Stir the breadcrumbs and gravy together and stir into the soup to thicken it. Add the sweetbreads.

Garnish with lemon slices and serve with sliced duck meat and one onion for each person.

White Soup with Poached Eggs

This is a very good one-dish meal rather than a soup. It is perfect before going to the theatre or opera when supper is planned for later.

Your stock must be with Veal and Chicken, then beat half a Pound of Almonds in a Mortar very fine, with the Breast of a Fowl; then put in some white Broth, and strain it off; then stóve it gently, and poach eight Eggs and lay in your Soop, with a French Roll in the middle, fill'd with minc'd Chicken or Veal; so serve it hot. (Charles Carter, 1732)

Serves 6

2 PT (5 CUPS) VEAL OR CHICKEN STOCK
I–½ LB (1–2 CUPS) GROUND ALMONDS
6 CHICKEN BREASTS, FINELY CHOPPED
6 EGGS

Bring the stock to the boil, simmer for a few minutes, then add the almonds and chicken breasts and simmer very gently for 15 minutes.

Meanwhile crisp the rolls in the oven. Cut a hole in the top of each and scoop out most of the crumb before you put them in the oven. Strain the soup into a bowl and fill the rolls with the minced chicken, well seasoned, reserving the equivalent of about 2 breasts.

Put this and the soup into the blender and purée. Return to the saucepan and reheat, seasoning with salt and pepper. Keep the rolls warm in the oven and poach the eggs. Place a filled roll in each warmed soup bowl, slide an egg on top of each and pour the hot soup over. Serve at once.

Sorrel Soup with Eggs

Your stock must be made with a Knuckle of Veal and a Neck of Mutton, well Skim'd and clean; put in a Faggot of Herbs; season with Pepper, Salt, Cloves and Mace, and when it is well boiled and tender strain all off, then let it settle a little, and skim all the Fat off; then take your Sorrel and chop it, but not small, and put it in brown Butter; put in your Broth and Slices of French Bread; stove in the middle a Fowl, or a Piece of a Neck of Mutton; then garnish your Dish with Slices of Fry'd Bread and some stewed Sorrel and poach six Eggs, and lay them round the Dish, or in your Soop, so serve away hot. (Charles Carter, 1732)

Serves 6–8

I KNUCKLE OF VEAL
I LB NECK OF LAMB
4 PT (10 CUPS) WATER
I FAGGOT, MADE OF 3–4 SPRIGS OF PARSLEY OR
   CHERVIL, OR BOTH, I BAY LEAF, A LARGE SPRIG
   OF THYME, I LEEK, WHITE PART ONLY, STUCK
   WITH 2 CLOVES, I STICK CELERY, THE WHOLE
   TIED WITH THREAD
I TBS SALT
¼ TSP PEPPER
I TSP MACE
I·LB SORREL, CHOPPED
¼ LB (½ CUP) BUTTER
½ MEDIUM CHICKEN
6–8 SLICES FRENCH BREAD
6–8 EGGS

Put the veal knuckle and the lamb in a soup pan and add the water, the faggot of herbs, salt, pepper and mace. Bring to the boil, skim thoroughly and simmer for 2 hours.

Sauté the sorrel in butter, allowing the butter to darken, then add this and the bread to the reheated stock. Add the chicken and simmer for 45 minutes. Remove the meat and chicken. Purée the remaining soup in the blender and keep warm in a saucepan. Cut the chicken meat into strips and add to the soup. Taste and add salt and pepper if necessary.

Poach the eggs and place one in each warmed soup plate. Pour the hot soup over the top and serve at once.

Sweet Melon Soup

This soup looks very pretty served in a scooped-out melon shell. It is delicious flavoured with curry plus a tablespoon of apricot jam or chutney, well blended.

Melon Soop Sweet :
You must have two good Melons, cut the Inside into small Dice, then pass them off in Butter of Gold Colour, put in half a Handful of Flour, then put in two Quarts of Cream, season with Sugar, and stir it about gently, and when it is as thick as Cream, garnish with Savoy Biskets and Melon slic'd. (Charles Carter, 1732)

Serves 4
2 SMALL MELONS, THE FLESH CUT INTO DICE
2 OZ (4 TBS) BUTTER
4 TBS FLOUR
2 PT (5 CUPS) CREAM
2 TBS SUGAR

Sauté the melon cubes in butter until golden; stir in the flour and cook for 1 minute. Add the cream and cook until slightly thickened. Season with sugar. Garnish with savoy biscuits (*see p.* 147) and slices of fresh melon.

A Vegetable Broth

A broth for all sorts of soops in maigre :
In the evening set a Kettle on the Fire, with what quantity you please of Peas, Cabbages, Carrots, Celery, Onions, Parsnips, Turnips, and Cloves; and let them boil till the next Morning; and when they are well boil'd, take off the Kettle, set it by for the Liquor to settle.

Then having cut some Carrots in two, put them in a Stew-pan, with some Parsnips and whole Onions, with some Butter; set it over the Fire, cover it and let it stand, stirring it now and then; and when the Roots have gotten a good colour, moisten them with your Pea-Soop; put all the roots, with their Liquor into a Kettle or Pot, and fill it up with the Pea-Soop, and let them stew gently, then season it, putting in a branch of Celery, another of Leeks, and another of Parsley-Roots, a Mignonette; and if you have any Carcasses of Fish, put them to it; for all sorts of Fish are good for this purpose, if they have no scent of muddy Water.
(Charles Carter, 1732)

Serves 6–8

Stage 1
1 LB (2½ CUPS) SPLIT PEAS
½ MEDIUM CABBAGE, SHREDDED
4 CARROTS, SLICED
2 STICKS (1 CUP) CELERY, CHOPPED
2 ONIONS, QUARTERED
2 PARSNIPS, SLICED
4 CLOVES
8 CUPS WATER

Stage 2
2 OZ (4 TBS) BUTTER
6 WHITE ONIONS
4 CARROTS, QUARTERED
1 STICK CELERY
1 LEEK, SPLIT
1 PARSLEY ROOT
4 WHITE PEPPERCORNS
THE CARCASES AND HEADS OF A FEW FISH (OPTIONAL)

Stage 1: combine all the first group of ingredients in a stewpan with water, bring to the boil and then simmer, half-covered, for about 30 minutes. Strain.

Stage 2: combine all the remaining ingredients in a pan with the strained broth, adding salt to taste. Bring to the boil and simmer for 30 minutes. Strain and serve.

Carp Soup

Pottage of carps:

Take a brace of good carps, male if you can; scale them and flay them; save the milts whole; take the fish off the bones, and make a hash of it; pass it in brown butter thickened; take it from the fat, and save it; put to it some of your fish gravy, and the milts of your carps; put in some forced fish balls; save the heads of your carps to stove in your broth, to put in the dish at last; take a little celery, a little spinach and sorrel, and some green onions, mince these, and a little parsley, and pass them in brown butter thickened till tender; then put in your fish stock, as much as will fill your dish; stove it up with the heads of your carps, and an anchovy or two; stone French bread dried for the bottom of your dish, fill up your dish with the soup, put in your carps' heads, and head it with a coolio made with your hash; let it be pretty thick, and garnish with scalded spinach, forced fish, and sliced lemon. (Charles Carter, 1730)

Serves 6

2 SMALL CARP
2 OZ (4 TBS) BUTTER
3 PT (7½ CUPS) FISH STOCK
    (1 CUP) SLICED CELERY
½ LB SPINACH
½ LB SORREL
1 BUNCH SPRING ONIONS (SCALLIONS), FINELY
    CHOPPED
1 ANCHOVY, CRUSHED
6 SLICES FRENCH BREAD, TOASTED

Garnish
FORCEMEAT FISH BALLS OR SLICES OF TINNED
    GEFILTE FISH
6 LEMON WEDGES

Sauté the carp in butter, then remove the skin and bones and flake the fish. In a large pot combine the fish stock, celery, spinach, sorrel and spring onions and simmer for 20 minutes. Add the fish, the anchovy and the forcemeat balls and heat through. Season to taste and serve over the slices of toast, with wedges of lemon.

Oyster Stew

Pottage of oysters:

Take your oysters, about a gallon of the largest, set them, and wash and beard them only for to fry; leave some of the largest with the beards on; take some of the smallest, and all the beards, and beat them in a mortar with the spawn of a lobster; put to them some fish gravy, and strain them, and force them through your strainer; save this for your coolio: mince some of your bearded oysters and put in, and the rest whole; put in some scalded parsley minced, and a faggot of thyme, an anchovy or two, and a little red wine; you may likewise put in the body of your lobster minced, and stove it up; stove French manchet dried, and put in your dish; put in some fish broth, and stove it, and head your potage with the coolio; put in the middle of your dish an oyster loaf open, with a ragout of oysters in it, and lay round it a dozen of yolks of eggs poached in fish gravy; garnish with oysters fried in batter, and sliced lemon, and serve it away hot.
(Charles Carter, 1730)

Serves 4–6

2 PT (5 CUPS) FISH STOCK
4 TBS PARSLEY, FINELY CHOPPED
1 TSP THYME
1 ANCHOVY, FINELY CHOPPED
½ PT (1 CUP) RED WINE
2 PT (5 CUPS) OYSTERS, SHELLED, WITH THEIR
    LIQUID
½ LB LOBSTER MEAT
SPAWN AND CORAL OF 1 LOBSTER
6–8 SLICES FRENCH BREAD, TOASTED

Garnish
4–6 POACHED EGGS
12 FRIED OYSTERS
4–6 LEMON WEDGES

Put the stock into a saucepan with the herbs, anchovy and wine; season, bring to the boil and then simmer for 15–20 minutes. Mince 1 pint of the oysters. Add all the oysters (whole and minced) with their liquor, the lobster meat and the coral and simmer for 10 minutes. Taste, adding pepper and salt if necessary.

Serve over the slices of toast. Garnish with poached eggs and fried oysters. Serve with lemon wedges.

Eggs

Broccoli and Eggs

Boil the broccoli tender, saving a large bunch for the middle, and six or eight little thick sprigs to go around; take a toast half an inch thick, toast it brown, as big as you would have it for your dish or butter-plate; butter some eggs thus:

Take six eggs, (more or less as you have occasion), beat them well put them into a saucepan with a good piece of butter, a little salt, keep beating them with a spoon till they are thick enough, then pour them on the toast; set the highest bunch of broccoli in the middle, and the other little pieces round about; and garnish the dish with little sprigs of broccoli; this is a pretty side-dish or corner-plate. (John Farley, 1783)

Serves 3–4
2 LARGE HEADS BROCCOLI
6 EGGS
3 SLICES BREAD, CUT ½-INCH THICK
1½ OZ (3 TBS) BUTTER
I SPRIG RAW BROCCOLI, FINELY CHOPPED

Boil the heads of broccoli in salted water until tender but still crisp. Leave one head whole and divide the other into sprigs. Keep warm. Beat the eggs lightly and scramble in the butter until barely set, seasoning them as you do so. Toast the bread and lay it in the centre of a warm buttered casserole. Pour the eggs on to the toast, arrange the whole head of broccoli in the centre and the sprigs all round. Sprinkle the eggs with the chopped, raw broccoli.

Cucumbers with Eggs

Pare, quarter, and cut six large cucumbers into squares, about the size of a dice. Put them into boiling water, and give them a boil. Then take them out of the water, and put them into a stewpan, with an onion stuck with cloves, a

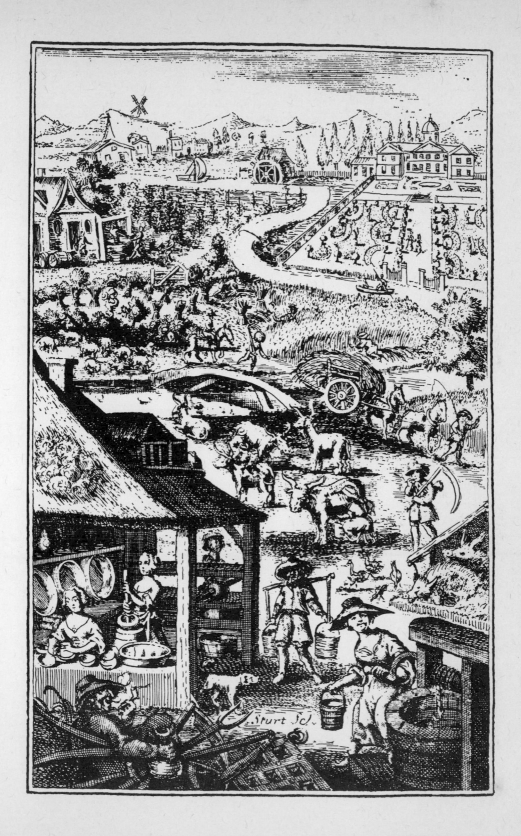

J. Sturt Sc.

*slice of ham, a quarter of a pound of butter, and
a little salt. Set it over the fire a quarter of an
hour, keep it close covered, skim it well, and
shake it often, for it is apt to burn. Then dredge
in a little flour, and put in as much veal gravy as
will just cover the cucumbers. Stir it well together,
and keep a gentle fire under it till no scum will
rise. Then take out the ham and onion, and put
in the yolks of two eggs beat up with a tea-cupful
of good cream. Stir it well for a minute, then
take it off the fire, and just before you put it
into the dish, squeeze in a little lemon juice.
Lay on the top of it five or six poached eggs.*
(*John Farley, 1783*)

Serves 6

3 CUCUMBERS, PEELED AND CUT INTO CUBES
¼ LB (½ CUP) BUTTER
I ONION, STUCK WITH 2 CLOVES
I SLICE HAM
½ TSP SALT
2 TBS FLOUR
½ PT (I CUP) VEAL STOCK
2 EGG YOLKS
¼ PT (¾ CUP) THICK CREAM
2 TBS LEMON JUICE
6 POACHED EGGS
DILL OR SALAD BURNET, CHOPPED

Parboil the cucumber cubes for about
5 minutes; drain. Melt the butter in a saucepan,
add the cucumber, onion, ham and salt, and
stew gently, stirring and shaking the pan,
to dry out the cucumber without burning it.
After about 15 minutes dredge in the flour and
add the veal stock. Simmer quite briskly,
uncovered, for another 15 minutes, to let the
stock reduce and thicken.

Remove the onion and ham and stir in the
cream, beaten with the egg yolks, off the heat.
Return to low heat and stir until thickened.
Add the lemon juice. Put in a warmed casserole
and lay the drained, trimmed poached eggs on
top. Sprinkle with finely chopped dill or burnet.

Eggs with Gravy

*Poach new laid eggs in boiling water in which is a
little vinegar, lay them handsomely in a dish,
and having warmed either veal or plain gravy,
and seasoned it with salt, pepper, a whole
onion, pass it through a sieve, and pour it over
the eggs, and serve them up hot.*
(*Charles Carter, 1732*)

I–2 EGGS PER PERSON
I TBS VINEGAR
I–2 ONIONS PER PERSON
I OZ (2 TBS) BUTTER PER PERSON
A LITTLE GOOD GRAVY, PREFERABLY VEAL

Poach the eggs, adding a little vinegar to the
water. Drain.

Soften the onions in the butter and sieve, or
purée in the blender. Mix with the heated
gravy, season with salt and pepper, pour over
the eggs and serve very hot.

Gratin of Eggs with Herbs

(*Hannah Glasse, 1747*)

Serves 4–6

2 COS OR ICEBERG LETTUCES
2 OZ (I CUP) MUSHROOMS
4 TBS PARSLEY, FINELY CHOPPED
¼ LB (½ CUP) SORREL, COOKED AND CHOPPED
2 TBS CHERVIL, CHOPPED
8 HARD-BOILED EGGS, YOLKS AND WHITES
    CHOPPED SEPARATELY
I TSP GRATED NUTMEG
1½–2 OZ (3–4 TBS) BUTTER
¼ PT (½ CUP) CREAM

Garnish
2 TBS PARSLEY, FINELY CHOPPED
¼ TSP GRATED NUTMEG

Poach the lettuces and mushrooms together in
lightly salted water until tender; drain. Chop
the lettuce and slice the mushrooms. Mix with
the chopped sorrel, chervil and egg yolks.

Season with salt and nutmeg. Melt the butter
in a saucepan and toss the mixture in it until

it is well coated and hot. Add the cream, cook for a few minutes and pour into a buttered casserole dish. Sprinkle the chopped egg whites, parsley and nutmeg round the edge of the dish. Put under the grill for a few minutes and serve.

Eggs in French Rolls

Hannah Glasse used Seville oranges, the bitter ones that are used for Seville orange marmalade. You can use lemon and orange juice combined if the available oranges are too sweet, or lemon juice by itself.
(*Hannah Glasse, 1747*)

Serves 4

4 FRENCH ROLLS
BUTTER FOR SPREADING
8 EGGS
JUICE OF 1–2 BITTER ORANGES

Cut the rolls in half and scoop out some of the crumb. Toast the crumb side and spread with butter. Break an egg into each half roll and season with salt and pepper. Bake in the oven until the eggs are set. Sprinkle the orange juice over the eggs and serve very hot.

Fish

Mackerel with Fennel and Mint

The common Way for Mackerel is, after boil'd, to make Sauce with thick Butter, Mint, Fennel and Parsly boil'd and minc'd, and drawn up with the Butter; If you broil them whole, hack them, and season them with Pepper, Salt and Nutmeg, some Mint and Fennel minc'd, and grated Bread, and wash them over with Butter, and dredge them over, and fill the Hacks full of that Seasoning, and broil them over a gentle Fire, and sauce them with thick Butter drawn up with an Anchovy, and garnish with Lemon.
(*Charles Carter, 1730*)

Serves 2

2 MACKEREL
¼ TSP PEPPER
1 TSP SALT
1 BUNCH MINT, CHOPPED
8 STALKS FENNEL, CHOPPED
1 TSP GROUND NUTMEG
2 OZ (1 CUP) BREADCRUMBS, BROWNED
BUTTER FOR BASTING
2 OZ (4 TBS) MELTED BUTTER
2 FILLETS ANCHOVIES, MASHED

Stuff the mackerel with the pepper, salt, mint, fennel, nutmeg, and breadcrumbs. Baste with the butter and grill (broil). Serve with melted butter in which the anchovies have been cooked.

Salmon Steaks, Poached

To calver salmon:
Cut it in round thin slices as you do cod to crimp; then boil your water with salt, two Onions, a Faggot of Thyme and Parsley, and a lemon slic'd and half a pint of white wine Vinegar. Then boil all this and skim it; then put in your salmon, and in four Minutes it is enough; Lay it on a Pye-Plate, and send it away dry.
(*Charles Carter, 1730*)

Serves 4
1¼ PT (3 CUPS) WATER
I TBS SALT
I LARGE ONION, SLICED
I TSP THYME
4 SPRIGS PARSLEY
I LEMON, SLICED
¼ PT (½ CUP) WINE VINEGAR
4 SALMON STEAKS

Bring all the ingredients, except for the fish, to
the boil and simmer for 10 minutes. Put in the
salmon steaks and poach for 10–15 minutes.
Drain and serve.

A Salmon Pie

*Take a good sole, or a side of salmon, scale it,
and cut it into pieces two inches broad, and
wash them over with the yolk of an egg, and
season with pepper, salt, nutmeg and ginger,
and thyme and parsley minced; lay it in a
raised coffin; lay in some fish force-meat, and
some oysters set, and some shrimps picked and
washed; lay over butter, and close it; but first lay
over two or three blades of mace, and some
slices of lemon; bake it, and then have a leer
made with a litte red wine and a lobster minced,
and what is in the body; put in two or three
anchovies, and a little beaten ginger; draw it up
with thick butter, and take off the fat of the pie,
and put in this leer, and shake it well together,
and serve it away. (Charles Carter, 1732)*

Serves 4–6
1½ LB PASTRY
I LB SALMON
½ PT (I CUP) OYSTERS, SHELLED
6–8 PICKLED SHRIMPS (OPTIONAL)
½ LB LOBSTER MEAT, DICED
I TSP SALT
¼ TSP PEPPER
¼ TSP NUTMEG
I TSP THYME
¼ TSP GINGER
¼ TSP MACE
¼ PT (½ CUP) FISH STOCK
¼ PT (½ CUP) RED WINE
I TBS ANCHOVY ESSENCE
I OZ (2 TBS) BUTTER
I TSP LEMON JUICE

Line a pie dish with half the pastry. Arrange
alternate layers of salmon, oysters, shrimps and
lobster in the pie, ending with a salmon layer.
Season with the seasonings, herbs and spices.
Pour over the stock, wine and anchovy
essence. Dot with butter and lemon juice.
Cover with the rest of the pastry. Bake at
375° (Mark 5) for 30–40 minutes.

Soles with Spinach

*Marinate soles:
Boil your soles in salt and water, bone and
drain them, and lay them on a dish with their
belly upwards. Boil some spinach, and pound it in
a mortar; then boil four eggs hard, chop the
yolks and whites separate, and lay green, white,
yellow, among the soles, and serve them up with
melted butter in a boat. (John Farley, 1783)*

Serves 4
I LB SOLE, FILLETED
3 LB (RAW) SPINACH, COOKED, DRAINED AND
   CHOPPED
4 HARD-BOILED EGGS, WHITES AND YOLKS
   CHOPPED SEPARATELY
¼ LB (½ CUP) MELTED BUTTER

Poach the fillets in enough water to cover
them. Drain. Arrange in a serving dish,
alternating the spinach, egg whites, yolks and
fish. Reheat at 350° (Mark 4) for 15 minutes.
Serve with melted butter.

A Trout Pie

*Take your trouts, and scale them; cut off their
fins and tails; force their bellies with forced
fish; hack the trouts on the sides, and season
them with pepper, salt and nutmeg, thyme and
parsley minced; lay them in a raised coffin, and
before you season them, wash them over with an
egg; lay some forced fish over between; cover it
over with butter, and bake it open; make a leer
with some wine, ginger, anchovies, horse-radish,
an onion stuck with cloves, and a lemon diced;
draw it up thick with thick butter; put in some*

oysters and shrimps; take out the fat, and head
the pie with this, so serve it away.
(*Charles Carter, 1730*)

Serves 3
I OZ (2 TBS) BUTTER
¾ OZ (¼ CUP) ONION, CHOPPED
I OZ (½ CUP) BREADCRUMBS
½ LB WHITE FISH FILLETS
½ TSP SALT
⅛ TSP PEPPER
½ TSP THYME
3 SMALL TROUT
A 9–10 INCH PASTRY CASE, ROUND OR SQUARE
I OZ (2 TBS) BUTTER
6 OYSTERS, SHELLED
6 SHRIMPS, SHELLED
I SMALL ONION, SLICED
½ TSP GRATED HORSERADISH
¼ PT (½ CUP) WINE
I TSP LEMON JUICE

Forcemeat
I OZ (2 TBS) BUTTER
I SMALL ONION, CHOPPED
I OZ (½ CUP) BREADCRUMBS
½ LB FISH FILLETS
½ TSP SALT
⅛ TSP PEPPER
½ TSP THYME

Seasoning
½ TSP SALT
⅛ TSP PEPPER
½ TSP THYME
2 TBS PARSLEY, FINELY CHOPPED
¼ TSP GROUND NUTMEG

Melt the butter in a frying-pan and sauté the
onion and breadcrumbs. Add the fish fillets and
cook until they flake. Draw off the heat and
toss with the seasonings. Stuff the trout with
some of the forcemeat. Lay them in the pastry
case and sprinkle with more of the seasonings.
Spoon the remaining forcemeat round the trout.
Dot with the butter, cut into small pieces. Add
the oysters and shrimps, the sliced onion and
the grated horseradish, and pour over the wine.
Bake at 350° (Mark 4) for 40–45 minutes.

Trout with Sorrel

*Take your fish and draw them, wash them and
boil them off in a courbouillon; then take sorrel
and scald it, and mince it very well; then draw it
up with thick butter and anchovies; dish your
fish upon some sippets of French bread and pour
the sauce all over it, and garnish with horse-radish
and lemon. Mackerel and flounders may be
dressed the same way.* (*Charles Carter, 1730*)

Serves 2
2 TROUT
¾ LB (2 CUPS) SORREL, COOKED
2 OZ (4 TBS) BUTTER
2 ANCHOVIES, CRUSHED

Garnish
TOAST SIPPETS
I LEMON, SLICED

Poach the trout until the flesh flakes, but take
care not to overcook them. Toss the sorrel in
the butter with the anchovies, seasoning to
taste. Serve the trout on a bed of sorrel,
surrounded by the sippets and slices of lemon.

Salt Cod in Cream Sauce

Salt-fish, with cream:
*Take good barrel-cod, and boil it; then take it all
into flakes, and put it in a sauce-pan with cream,
and season it with a little pepper; put in a
handful of parsley scalded, and minced, and
stove it gently till tender, and then skake it
together with some thick butter and the yolks of
two or three eggs, and dish it; and garnish with
poached eggs and lemon sliced.*
(*Charles Carter, 1730*)

Serves 4
I LB SALT COD, POACHED AND FLAKED
  (OR SMOKED HADDOCK)
2 EGG YOLKS
½ PT (I CUP) CREAM
4 TBS CHOPPED PARSLEY
I OZ (2 TBS) BUTTER
I TSP SALT
¼ TSP PEPPER

4 POACHED EGGS
LEMON SLICES

Keep the cooked, flaked fish hot while you make the sauce.

Beat the egg yolks in a bowl. Heat the cream and beat it in. Cook until thickened, without boiling; stir in the chopped parsley, butter and seasonings. Pour the sauce over the poached fish. Serve garnished with poached eggs and lemon slices.

Poultry and Game

Chicken Couscous

Cuscasooee of Capons, or Pullets:
Let your fowl be clean drawn, and singed, and trussed to boil; put a forcing in the bellies made with lumps of marrow, some chestnuts and pistachio nuts blanched, some raisins, currants and citron cut in pieces, and some dates sliced; work this up with some grated bread, a little cream, and a little sack, and the yolks of some eggs; season with sugar, cinnamon and ginger, a little salt, and a little pepper; fill up the bellies of your fowls with this; take a pound of rice, and brown half a pound of butter, of a golden colour; put your rice into it, and stir it well together; put in about a pint of thin broth to it; lay in your fowls, put in some sugar and a pound or two of raisins picked, some dates sliced, and season with a little pepper, salt, cinnamon and ginger; so cover it, and stove very gently till tender; then put your rice into the bottom of your dish, and your fowl on that; mingle a little saffron with some of the rice, and garnish with that and sliced orange or lemon.
(Charles Carter, 1732)

Serves 6

A 5–6 LB CHICKEN

Stuffing
¼ LB (1 CUP) RAW BEEF MARROW
8 CHESTNUTS, PEELED AND HALVED
2 OZ (½ CUP) PISTACHIO NUTS
2 OZ (½ CUP) RAISINS
1 OZ (¼ CUP) CITRON, CUT INTO PIECES
2 OZ (½ CUP) CHOPPED DATES
1 OZ (½ CUP) BREADCRUMBS
2 TBS SHERRY
2 TBS CREAM
2 TBS SUGAR
½ TSP CINNAMON
½ TSP GINGER
2 TBS SALT
½ TSP PEPPER

Couscous
12 OZ (2 CUPS) RICE
2 OZ (4 TBS) BUTTER
2 PT (5 CUPS) STOCK
2 OZ (½ CUP) RAISINS
2 OZ (½ CUP) CHOPPED DATES
2 TSP SALT
¼ TSP PEPPER
I TSP CINNAMON
½ TSP GINGER
⅛ TSP SAFFRON

Combine all the stuffing ingredients and stuff the chicken with the mixture.

Sauté the rice in the butter until golden. Add the stock, raisins, dates and seasonings. Bring to the boil. Place the stuffed chicken on top and simmer for 1½ hours or until golden.

Pullets with Chestnuts

Truss them to boil and singe them, and soak them in warm Water; then take them out and dry them with a Cloth, and fill the Bellies with Chestnuts, Oysres and Lumps of Marrow rolled in Yolks of Eggs; season with Nutmeg and Salt and put one in a Bladder and tie it up close and boil it, two will make a Dish, then sauce them with melted Butter and Gravy, and the juice of an Orange. (Charles Carter, 1732)

Serves 4
A 4-LB CHICKEN
½ LB COOKED CHESTNUTS, CHOPPED
  (FRESH OR TINNED)
¼ LB (¾ CUP) SHELLED OYSTERS, CHOPPED (FRESH
  OR TINNED)
2 TBS RAW BEEF MARROW, CHOPPED
I EGG YOLK
2 TBS FLOUR
2 TBS OIL
I PT (2½ CUPS) CHICKEN STOCK
¼ TSP GRATED NUTMEG
I TSP SALT
I OZ (2 TBS) BUTTER
4 TBS ORANGE JUICE

Season the inside of the bird with pepper and salt. Combine the chestnuts, oysters and marrow in a bowl with enough egg yolk to bind them, and stuff the bird with this mixture; secure the cavities. Dust the pullet with flour and brown it in oil in a casserole. Add the stock, nutmeg and salt and cook in a 350° (Mark 4) oven for 1½ hours, or until tender. Remove the bird to a serving dish. Add a little butter to the cooking broth, then the orange juice; reduce until syrupy and pour over the carved bird.

Pullets with Endives

Serve this dish in coloured soup-plates. It will keep for hours in a warm oven and is useful for serving to guests who remain after a cocktail party, to card-players, dilatory lovers and motoring guests who always take the wrong turn to one's house. It must have been useful when the post-chaise was delayed by highwaymen!
(Charles Carter, 1732)

Serves 4
4 ENDIVES, TIED WITH THREAD
2 OZ (4 TBS) BUTTER
A 3½-4-LB PULLET OR CHICKEN
I PT (2½ CUPS) CHICKEN STOCK
PINCH OF SUGAR (OPTIONAL)
2 EGG YOLKS
¼ PINT (½ CUP) CREAM
2 TBS PARSLEY, FINELY CHOPPED

Toss the endives in butter in the bottom of a braising-pan; put the chicken on top and cover with the stock. Taste and season. (A pinch of sugar may be needed if the endives are at all bitter.) Cover and cook gently for 1 hour.

When the chicken is tender, remove it and carve it ainto serving pieces. Put the egg yolks in a bowl; add the cream and stir in a little of the broth. Put this back into the pan with the parsley and cook over low heat, without boiling, until slightly thickened. Put the chicken pieces into a warmed soup-tureen, pour the soupy sauce over them and add the endives, whole, with the threads carefully removed.

Chicken on Toast

(*Hannah Glasse, 1747*)

Serves 6–8

2 PT (5 CUPS) CHICKEN STOCK
2 3-LB CHICKENS CUT INTO SERVING PIECES
¾ LB LEAN BACON OR HAM
2 LARGE ONIONS, SLICED
4 SHALLOTS, MINCED (¼ CUP)
⅛ TSP EACH GROUND CLOVES, MACE AND SAFFRON
1 TSP SALT
2 TBS FLOUR
2 TBS VINEGAR
6–8 FINGERS RATHER STALE BREAD OR TOAST

Combine in a braising-pan the stock, chicken, bacon or ham, onions, shallots, spices, salt and a little pepper. Stew gently for about 1 hour, until the chicken is tender. Mix the flour and vinegar and stir until smooth, adding a little of the broth. Add this mixture to the broth and boil gently for 10 minutes. Put the fingers of bread or toast into a rather shallow warmed soup-tureen, arrange the chicken on the bread and pour the soup over the top.

Chicken forcemeat balls can be served with this soup, in which case they should be poached in the soup before serving.

Hot Chicken Mousse

(*Charles Carter, 1732*)

I tried out this recipe with leftover chicken and to my great surprise it turned out to be a soufflé of sorts; it rose in the oven and was light and flavoursome, and the remains next day made an excellent snack with mustard and a salad.

Serves 4

½ LB (1 CUP) COOKED CHICKEN, MINCED
½ OZ (¼ CUP) GRATED PARMESAN OR GOOD
  CHESHIRE CHEESE
2 TBS HOMEMADE BREADCRUMBS
3 EGGS
½ PT (1 CUP) RICH CREAM
⅛ TSP PEPPER

¼ TSP NUTMEG
4 SLICES TOAST

Pound the chicken with the cheese and breadcrumbs in a mortar until it becomes a paste. Arrange the toast in the bottom of a 4-pint soufflé dish. Beat the eggs in a bowl and add the cream, pepper and nutmeg while beating. Stir in the chicken mixture. Pour this over the toast. Bake at 350° (Mark 4) for 20–25 minutes.

Attlets of Fat Livers

Take fat livers of Turkeys, or Capons, or Pullets, Take the Livers, cut them in two, or double them; you must have handsome Skures of a pretty Length, and you must have large Oysters set; then take your Livers and Oysters, and roll them in Eggs, and then dredge them with Pepper, Salt, Nutmeg, Thyme and Parsley minc'd, and Bread grated, so braoch them on the Skures; first two or three Oysters, and then a Liver; then two or three Oysters more, and that will serve for one Skure; six is enough for a Plate. Broil them on a butter's Paper, and sauce with good Gravy, the juice of an Orange, and some thick Butter, and garnish with Orange and Lemon.
(*Charles Carter, 1730*)

Serves 2

4 CHICKEN LIVERS, HALVED
12 OYSTERS
½ TSP SALT
¼ TSP PEPPER
¼ TSP NUTMEG
¼ TSP THYME
2 TBS PARSLEY
1 CUP BREADCRUMBS
1 CUP GRAVY
2 TBS ORANGE JUICE
2 TBS BUTTER
LEMON AND ORANGE SLICES

Mix together the breadcrumbs and seasonings in a bowl; roll the livers and oysters in the eggs, then in the breadcrumbs. Thread onto skewers. Meanwhile heat the gravy, orange juice and butter in a saucepan and serve with the skewers. Garnish with lemon and orange slices.

Duck with Horseradish

(*Charles Carter, 1732*)

Serves 3–4
A 4–4½ LB DUCK
2 TBS FLOUR
I OZ (2 TBS) BUTTER
I PT (2½ CUPS) CHICKEN STOCK
3 OZ (I CUP) GRATED HORSERADISH

Garnish
FRESHLY GRATED HORSERADISH
I LEMON, SLICED

Dust the duck with flour and brown it in the butter on all sides. Add the chicken stock and grated horseradish and simmer gently until the duck is tender. Remove the duck and carve it. Arrange the pieces on a warm serving dish, then skim the fat from the surface of the sauce and pour the sauce over the bird. Arrange the fresh horseradish at each end of the dish and the sliced lemon around the edges.

Pigeons Fricando

(*John Farley, 1783*)

The morels referred to in this recipe are an edible fungus that used to be picked by gypsies in the New Forest. They are known in France as *morilles* and can be bought in tins under that name.

Serves 4–6

2 OR 3 YOUNG PIGEONS
I OZ (¼ CUP) FLOUR
2 TBS OIL
I¼ PT (3 CUPS) GRAVY OR STRONG CHICKEN STOCK
I–2 TSP LEMON PICKLE
I TBS WALNUT KETCHUP
I TBS BROWNING (OPTIONAL)
PINCH OF SALT
PINCH OF CAYENNE PEPPER

½ OZ (¼ CUP) MORELS
4 HARD-BOILED EGG YOLKS, SIEVED

Garnish
LEMON PEEL
BARBERRIES OR CLOUD-BERRIES OR RED OR BLACK
  CURRANTS

Stuffing
I OZ (2 CUPS) BREADCRUMBS
½ ONION, CHOPPED
2½ OZ (½ CUP) CELERY, CHOPPED
I OZ (2 TBS) BUTTER
4 TBS HERBS, CHOPPED

Brown the onions and celery in butter, then toss in the remainder of the stuffing ingredients. Stuff the craw of the birds and truss them. Dust with some of the flour and brown in the oil. Add the gravy or stock, the pickle, ketchup, browning, salt and cayenne pepper, and cook for 1–1¼ hours or until tender. Remove the birds and skim the fat off the stock. Add some flour through a sprinkler or sifter, a little at a time, and stir it in, to thicken the sauce slightly. Add the whole morels and the sieved egg yolks. Cut the pigeons in half and put them in a casserole dish. Strain the sauce over them, keeping the morels whole. Arrange the lemon slices round the edge of the dish and serve fresh barberries or currants on a separate dish.

A Pupton of Pigeons

For a little Dish you may take six pigeons, or more according to the Bigness of your Dish, truss them, singe and blanch them; then fry them in a little Butter or Hog's Lard, being first larded with small Lardons; then put them in stewing with a little Broth or Gravy; when they are almost tender, put to them two sweet breads cut in large bits and fry'd, a handful of Morils and Mushrooms well pick'd and wash'd and twelve chestnuts blanched; Put all this together then take a Sauce-pan with a quarter of a pound of Butter, a small handful of Flower, and two whole Onions; brown it over the Fire with a pint of Gravy, put in your ingredients aforesaid having first seasoned them with Pepper, Salt and Nutmeg.

    Let it stew so that most of your ragoo sticks to your Meat, then set it off the Fire a-cooling. Take a Patty-pan or Sauce Pan and butter the Bottom and Sides; then cut four or five Slices of Bacon as long as your Hand and as thin as a Shilling; place them at the Bottom and sides of your Pan at an equal Distance, then place over it a Quantity of the forc'd Meat, for which you have a Receipt under Letter F, half an Inch thick, as high on the Sides of your Pan as you think will hold your Pigeons and Ragoo. Then pour in your cold Ragoo and Pigeons, placing them with the Breasts to the Bottom of the Pan, because the Bottom side is turned up when it goes to Table; then take out your whole Onion, Bacon and Cloves that was in your Brown, and squeeze in a whole lemon, place your pigeons with the Breasts to the middle of the Pan, and your Ragoo betwixt your Pigeons at an equal Distance. Cover it all over with the same forc'd Meat an Inch thick, and close it well round the Sides, smooth it well with your Hands and with Egg, strew on it a little grated Bread, bake it an Hour before you have Occasion to use it; then loose it from the Sides of your Patty-pan or Sauce-pan, with your Knife, put it on your Mazarine or little Dish, wherein you intend to serve it, and turn it upside down clearly; if it is well baked it will stand upright, like a brown Loaf. Squeeze over it an Orange, lay round it fry'd Parsley; the Sauce in the middle. So serve it for First Course. (Charles Carter, 1730)

Serves 4–6

2 PIGEONS
I OZ (2 TBS) LARD
I ONION, SLICED
I OZ ($\frac{1}{4}$ CUP) FLOUR
I TSP SALT
$\frac{1}{4}$ TSP PEPPER
I TSP GRATED NUTMEG
2 PT (5 CUPS) STOCK
I SWEETBREAD, CLEANED AND DICED
6 MUSHROOMS, SLICED
12 CHESTNUTS, PEELED
4 SLICES BACON
2 CUPS FORCEMEAT WITH CREAM (*see p. 136*)

JUICE OF I LEMON
JUICE OF I ORANGE

Brown the pigeons in the lard and remove. Brown the onion in the same fat and cook until soft. Add the flour, salt, pepper and nutmeg and cook for I minute. Replace the pigeons in the pan, add the heated stock and simmer until the birds are tender (I hour for young birds). Add the diced sweetbread, mushrooms and chestnuts. Cook for 10 minutes longer. Line the bottom of a well-buttered ovenproof dish with the bacon and spread with half the forcemeat. Arrange the pigeons on top and moisten with some of the stock and the lemon juice. Cover with the remaining forcemeat and cook in a moderate oven (350°, Mark 4) for 45–60 minutes, or until done. Turn out onto a dish, squeeze the orange juice over it and serve garnished with parsley.

Jugged Hare

Cut your hare into little pieces, and lard them here and there with little flips of bacon. Season them with a little pepper and salt and put them into an earthen jug, with a blade or two of mace, an onion stuck with cloves and a bundle of sweet herbs. Cover the jug close, that nothing may get in, and set it in a pot of boiling water and three hours will do it. Then turn it out into the dish, take out the onion and sweet herbs and send it hot to table. As to the larding, you may omit it if you wish. (John Farley, 1783)

Serves 6

A 4–5-LB HARE, JOINTED
3 TBS FLOUR
I$\frac{1}{2}$ OZ (3 TBS) BACON DRIPPING
2 ONIONS, SLICED
$\frac{1}{4}$ LB ($\frac{1}{2}$ CUP) DICED BACON
I PT (2$\frac{1}{2}$ CUPS) LIGHT GAME STOCK
$\frac{1}{4}$ TSP GROUND CLOVES
4 TBS ($\frac{1}{4}$ CUP) MIXED SWEET HERBS
$\frac{1}{2}$ TSP MACE

Flour the pieces of hare and brown them in the bottom of a dutch oven or deep fireproof jug, in the bacon dripping; remove the pieces when browned, add the onions and brown them, and then add the bacon. Replace the hare and add the stock, cloves, mixed herbs and mace. Bring to the boil, then reduce the heat and simmer gently for 2–3 hours, or until tender.

Boiled Haunch of Venison

Having let it lie in salt a week, boil it in a cloth weel floured; and allow a quarter of an hour's boiling for every pound it weighs. For sauce, you may boil some cauliflowers, pulled into little sprigs, in milk and water, with some fine white cabbage, and some turnips cut in dice; add some beetroot, cut into narrow pieces, about an inch thick. Lay a sprig of cauliflower, and some of the turnips, masked with some cream and a little butter. Let your cabbage be boiled, and then beat in a saucepan with a piece of butter and salt. Lay that next the cauliflower, then the turnips, then the cabbage, and so on, till the dish be full. Place the beetroot here and there, according to your taste. Have a little melted butter in a cup, if wanted. This is a very fine dish, and looks very prettily.

The haunch, or neck, thus dressed, eats well the next day, hashed with gravy and sweet sauce. (*John Farley, 1783*)

Serves 10–15

The haunch would probably weigh from 18 to 20 lb, depending on whether it came from a doe or buck. This takes from 3 to 4 hours' slow boiling or simmering, depending on the age of the deer, in a light venison broth made from the bones of the deer. This can be done quite fast in a pressure cooker, or from melted and diluted glaze. A good way is to wrap the haunch in cheesecloth, with a large amount of herbs, any spices that are available (cloves, bay leaves, blades of mace or cinnamon, and even the very early galingale which comes in root form); they all remain inside the muslin, adding a delicious flavour to the meat, and can easily be removed before serving.

All the vegetables can be boiled with the venison, in the same pot, also in their own muslin bags, which means that you can remove them one at a time when they are done.

This glorious feast, normally only possible for those who can procure their own game, can easily be made from frozen venison, all in one pot. It can even be cooked over a well-tended open fire, indoors or out, in an old fashioned black-iron three-legged cauldron.

Farley's 'sweet sauce' could be a currant sauce or Cumberland sauce.

Meat

Beef Chops

(*John Farley, 1783*)

Serves 4

4 RUMP STEAKS, SCORED WITH A KNIFE
1¼ OZ (5 TBS) FLOUR
2½ OZ (5 TBS) BUTTER, SOFTENED
1 PT (2½ CUPS) GOOD BEEF GRAVY OR STOCK
2–3 OZ (½ CUP) CUCUMBER, CHOPPED
2½ OZ (½ CUP) ONION, VERY FINELY CHOPPED
½ PICKLED WALNUT, CRUSHED
1 TBS CAPERS
½ TSP SALT
½ TSP PEPPER

Dust the steaks with some of the flour and fry them in 1 oz (2 tbs) butter in a very hot frying-pan for about 1 minute on each side. Remove them and keep warm in a low oven. Add the remaining butter, mixed to a paste with the rest of the flour, to the drippings in the pan, then add the gravy, cucumber, onion, walnut and capers. Season. Cook for about 5 minutes and pour the mixture over the steaks. Serve piping hot.

As the raw onion has only five minutes in which to cook it must be chopped very fine. It should remain a little under-cooked and add a crunchy texture to the gravy.

Epigram of Beef

(*John Farley, 1783*)

Serves 8–10

5–6 LB ROAST SIRLOIN OF BEEF, FRESH FROM THE
    OVEN
½ PT (1 CUP) RICH BEEF STOCK
1 SMALL ONION, FINELY CHOPPED (¼ CUP)
2 TBS MUSHROOM KETCHUP
6 SMALL PICKLED CUCUMBERS, THINLY SLICED
    (½ CUP)
½ OZ (1 TBS) BUTTER
1 TBS FLOUR

Slip a knife under the top skin of the roast sirloin and lift it up carefully, leaving it attached to the meat on one side. Cut a 'well' into the meat and lift out the resulting chunk, but do not cut too near the ends or sides. Keep the shell of beef warm while you prepare the filling.

Cut the piece of meat into generous-sized dice and put these into a chafing dish or thick iron frying-pan with all the other ingredients, except for the butter and flour. Toss for 5 5 minutes, mixing well, then remove the meat and keep it warm while you thicken the gravy. Mix the butter and flour to a paste and add to the gravy, stirring until blended. Put back the diced beef, mix well and pack into the hole in the meat, covering with the skin. Replace the joint in the oven for 15 minutes to reheat thoroughly, then serve.

Beef Tremblant

(*Hannah Glasse, 1747*)

Serves 6–8

FAT END OF A BRISKET OF BEEF, 3–4 LB
2 TBS ALLSPICE BERRIES
2 ONIONS
2 PEELED TURNIPS
1 CARROT

Sauce I
2 OZ (4 TBS) BUTTER
4 TBS FLOUR
2 PTS (5 CUPS) GRAVY OR STRONG BEEF STOCK
1 TBS MUSHROOM KETCHUP
1 TBS BROWNING (OPTIONAL)
¼ PT (½ CUP) WHITE WINE
A FEW CARROTS AND TURNIPS, SLICED THINLY

Sauce II (alternative)
3–4 TBS CHOPPED PARSLEY
1 ONION, FINELY CHOPPED
4 PICKLED CUCUMBERS OR DILL PICKLES, FINELY
    CHOPPED
1 PT (2½ CUPS) GOOD GRAVY OR BEEF STOCK (FROM
    COOKING THE BRISKET)
¼ TSP PEPPER
1 TSP SALT
1 TSP BUTTER ROLLED IN 1 TSP FLOUR

1 PICKLED WALNUT, CRUSHED
1 TBS CAPERS

Tie up the brisket with strong thread or string. Cover it well with cold water in a braising-pan and bring to the boil. Skim. Salt the water and add the spice and vegetables. Simmer until tender, for about 3 hours. Remove the meat.

To make the sauce (I), first melt the butter in a saucepan, then add the flour, cook a little and stir until smooth. Slowly stir in the gravy, ketchup, browning, wine and sliced vegetables; bring to the boil and simmer until the vegetables are tender. Season with pepper and salt. Skim the fat from the surface and serve the brisket in the sauce. Serve with pickles.

For a sharper sauce (II), put the parsley, onion and cucumbers into the gravy, season, bring to the boil and then simmer. Add the butter rolled in flour to thicken the sauce, then the pickled walnut and the capers. Simmer for 10 minutes and then pour over the beef.

Beef a la Royale

(*John Farley, 1783*)

Serves 6–8

4 LB BONED BRISKET OF BEEF
$\frac{1}{4}$ LB ($\frac{1}{2}$ CUP) FAT BACON, FRIED AND CRUMBLED
4 TBS CHOPPED PARSLEY
6 OZ (1 CUP) CHOPPED OYSTERS (TINNED OR FRESH)
$\frac{1}{4}$ TSP EACH PEPPER AND SALT
$\frac{1}{2}$ TSP NUTMEG
2 TBS OIL
1 OZ ($\frac{1}{4}$ CUP) FLOUR
1 PINT ($2\frac{1}{2}$ CUPS) RED WINE
PICKLES FOR GARNISH

Make holes about an inch apart all over the brisket. Stuff these, in turn, with the bacon, parsley and chopped oyster. Each stuffing should be seasoned with salt, pepper and nutmeg. When the meat is completely stuffed, dredge it well with flour, put it in a dutch oven, brown it in oil and cover it with the red wine. Season with pepper and salt. Bring the wine to the boil, then put the pot into a moderate

oven, preheated to 300–325° (Mark 2–3). Let it remain in the oven for a little more than 3 hours, or until quite tender. Then strain off the fat, pour the gravy over the meat and garnish with pickles.

Vegetables can be added to the pot while the meat is cooking in the oven. Put them in only just long enough to cook them, for they should remain crisp and firm. The classic choice of vegetables would include: onions, turnips, parsnips, swedes, Jerusalem artichokes, artichoke bottoms, celery hearts, potatoes.

Veal in Sharp Sauce

(*John Farley, 1783*)

Serves 6–8

2–3 LB FILLET (ROUND) OF VEAL
3 OZ BACON, CUT INTO STRIPS ABOUT THE SIZE OF FRENCH FRIED POTATOES
3 OZ SMOKED HAM, CUT AS ABOVE
4 TBS MIXED SWEET HERBS, COARSELY CHOPPED (OPTIONAL)
6 SLICES STREAKY BACON, PARTLY COOKED
6 OZ STEWING VEAL, CUT IN THIN SLICES
4 TBS MIXED SWEET HERBS, COARSELY CHOPPED
2–3 CLOVES
$\frac{1}{2}$ TSP GROUND MACE
1 MEDIUM ONION, FINELY CHOPPED
$\frac{1}{4}$ TSP PEPPER
$\frac{1}{2}$ TSP SALT
VEAL STOCK, TO COVER

Sauce
$\frac{1}{4}$ PT ($\frac{1}{2}$ CUP) WHITE WINE
4 TBS TARRAGON VINEGAR
$\frac{1}{2}$ LEMON, PEELED AND SLICED

Lard the fillet of veal with pieces of bacon and smoked ham by punching holes all over it with a skewer and inserting the lardoons. The lardoons can be rolled in herbs before insertion. Dust with pepper and salt. Line the bottom of a thick braising-pan or dutch oven with the slices of bacon and stewing veal. Sprinkle them with herbs, spices, onion, pepper and salt and cook over low heat until this layer is lightly browned on the underside. Place the fillet on top and cover with the boiling stock. Bring to the boil and simmer very gently for 1–1½ hrs or until the meat is done.

For the sauce, pour off 6 fluid ounces (¾ cup) of the broth into a saucepan. Add the white wine, tarragon vinegar and lemon; taste and season generously with pepper and salt. The sauce should be quite sharp, to offset the bland taste of the veal. Reduce the sauce until it is quite syrupy or thicken it with a little butter rolled in flour. Strain and serve over the sliced veal.

Strips of Veal, Fried

(*John Farley, 1783*)

Serves 3–6

2 LB COLD COOKED VEAL, CUT INTO 6 THIN STRIPS
2 EGG YOLKS
4 TBS CHOPPED HERBS (INCLUDING TARRAGON)
1 TSP GRATED LEMON PEEL
½ TSP GRATED NUTMEG
2 OZ (1 CUP) BREADCRUMBS
2–3 OZ (4–6 TBS) BUTTER
1 TSP FLOUR
¼ PT (½ CUP) HIGHLY CONCENTRATED VEAL STOCK
JUICE OF ½ LEMON

Dip the veal slices into the egg yolk, into which you have stirred the herbs, lemon peel and seasonings; coat evenly with the breadcrumbs and fry in the butter until golden. Place the meat on a paper towel in a warmed dish and keep warm in the oven. Stir the flour into the butter in the pan, cook for 1 minute and then stir in the veal glaze and the lemon juice. Cook for a few minutes, until syrupy, and pour into a heated sauceboat.

Serve the meat on a separate dish, garnished with mashed potatoes and sprigs of parsley.

Escalopes and Oysters

Cut your collops very large, and not too thin; hack them well, and wash over the inside with the yolk of an egg; then take large oysters set and bearded, and roll them in the yolks of eggs; season them with pepper, salt and nutmeg; thyme and parsley minced; lay them thick half over your collops, and turn over the other half, and skure it at the side and each end, washing them over with thick butter and the yolk of an egg, and broil them on a buttered paper; sauce them with good gravy, thick butter, and the juice of an orange, and then garnish with either orange or lemon sliced. (*Charles Carter, 1732*)

Serves 4

4 VEAL ESCALOPES (SCALLOPS)
4 OYSTERS
1 EGG
½ TSP SALT
⅛ TSP PEPPER
½ TSP NUTMEG
½ TSP THYME
1 TBS PARSLEY
¼ PT (½ CUP) VEAL GRAVY
1 TBS ORANGE JUICE

Pound the escalopes thin, Roll the oysters in the beaten egg, season with salt, pepper and nutmeg, and roll in thyme and parsley. Roll the oysters in the escalopes and secure each little package. Brush with butter and grill (broil). Serve with the gravy flavoured with a little orange juice.

Veal Patties

Petit patties:
These are a very pretty garnish, and give a handsome appearance to a large dish. Make a short crust, roll it thick, and make them as big as the bowl of a spoon, and about an inch deep. Take a piece of veal big enough to fill the patty, and as much bacon and beef suet. Shred them all very fine, season them with pepper and salt, and a little sweet herbs. Put them into a little stew-pan, keep turning them about, with a few mushrooms chopped small, for eight or ten minutes.

Then fill your patties, and cover them with crust. Colour them with the yolk of an egg, and bake them. (John Farley, 1783)

Serves 2–3

1½ LB PASTRY
¼ LB VEAL ESCALOPES (SCALLOPS), CHOPPED
1 OZ (2 TBS) BUTTER
A FEW MUSHROOMS, CHOPPED
¼ TSP SALT
⅛ TSP PEPPER
½ TSP THYME
½ TSP TARRAGON
½ OZ (2 TBS) GRATED SUET
2 SLICES BACON, CHOPPED
4–6 TBS BEEF STOCK

Roll out the pastry. Cut into rounds with a biscuit cutter. Press half of the circles into muffin pans. Sauté the veal in the butter with the chopped mushrooms. Stir in the salt, pepper and herbs. Arrange in the tart shells alternate layers of the veal mixture, suet and bacon. Moisten each with 1 tablespoon stock. Cover with the remaining circles of pastry and seal. Bake at 400° (Mark 6) for 15 minutes.

Veal Galantine

First take out all the Bones, stretch it, and beat it as flat as you can; season it with Salt, Pepper, and Nutmeg, Marjoram, Marygolds, Parsly, Thyme and Winter Savoury, all well minced, then roll it up well, and tie it very close and afterwards tie it up in a Cloth, and boil it in good, well-season'd Wine, Broth and a little Thyme, when it is enough, let it lie in the Liquor till it is cold; serve it up either whole or in Slices, upon a Napkin, garnish it according to your Mind. (Charles Carter, 1732)

Serves 4

1½ LB BREAST OF VEAL, BONED
½ TSP SALT
¼ TSP PEPPER
½ TSP NUTMEG
1 TSP MARJORAM
1 TSP MARIGOLD FLOWERS (*see* glossary)
2 TBS CHOPPED PARSLEY

1 TSP THYME
1 TSP SAVORY
1 TBS FLOUR
2 TBS OIL
4 SLICES LEMON
½ PT (1 CUP) WINE
½ PT (1 CUP) LIGHT VEAL STOCK

Flatten the meat; season and sprinkle with the herbs (but reserving half the thyme). Roll and tie securely. Sprinkle the outside of the meat with flour and brown it in oil on all sides. Add the rest of the thyme, the lemon slices, wine and stock. Bring to the boil and then simmer for 2 hours. Cool. Serve sliced, with mayonnaise.

Veal Cutlets from Pontack's

(The Family Cook, 1738)

Serves 6

6 STEAKS, CUT FROM A PIECE OF NECK OF VEAL
3 OZ (6 TBS) BUTTER
½ PT (1 CUP) STRONG VEAL STOCK
2 ANCHOVIES, MASHED
½ TSP NUTMEG
½ TSP GRATED LEMON PEEL
½ TSP PENNY-ROYAL OR MINT, CHOPPED OR DRIED
1 TBS PARSLEY, FINELY CHOPPED
¼ PT (½ CUP) WHITE WINE
1 OZ (2 TBS) BUTTER
1 TBS FLOUR
JUICE OF 1 ORANGE OR ORANGE AND LEMON
    WEDGES

Fry the seasoned steaks in butter; when they are done, remove and keep warm. Combine the seasoned stock, anchovies, nutmeg, lemon peel and herbs with the wine and simmer until the sauce has reduced and become syrupy. If it is not thick enough burn the flour in a dry iron pan, roll the butter in it and add to the sauce a little at a time, stirring until it is the right consistency.

Add the veal steaks to the sauce and heat them through. Put the veal and sauce into a serving dish and squeeze juice over the top, or serve orange wedges, to be squeezed individually. They can also be interspersed with lemon wedges.

Lamb Cutlets a la Maintenon

Take a neck of mutton, cut it into chops, with a bone in each, and take the fat off the bone, and scrape it clean. Take some crumbs of bread, parsley, marjoram, thyme, and winter savory, and chop all fine; grate some nutmeg in it, and season with pepper and salt. Having mixed these all together, melt a little butter in a stewpan, and dip the chops into the butter. Then roll them in the herbs, and put them in half sheets of buttered paper. Leave the end of the bone bare, and broil them on a clear fire for twenty minutes. Send them up in the paper, with the following sauce in a boat; Chop four shallots fine, put them in half a gill of gravy, a little pepper and salt, and a spoonful of vinegar, and boil them for a minute. (John Farley, 1783)

Serves 4

4 LAMB CUTLETS, WELL TRIMMED
I EGG, LIGHTLY BEATEN
2 OZ (I CUP) BREADCRUMBS
4 TBS CHOPPED PARSLEY
I TSP MARJORAM
I TSP THYME
I TSP WINTER SAVORY
½ TSP NUTMEG
¼ TSP PEPPER
I TSP SALT
2 OZ (4 TBS) BUTTER
4 SHALLOTS, FINELY CHOPPED
½ PT (I CUP) GRAVY OR RICH STOCK
I TBS VINEGAR

Farley's method is perfectly clear to the modern reader. His buttered paper can be replaced by buttered wax paper or one of the new roasting wraps that are now available.

Leg of Mutton with Cauliflowers and Spinach

Cut a leg of mutton venison fashion, and boil it in a cloth; boil three or four cauliflowers in milk and water, pull them into sprigs, and stew them with butter, pepper, salt and a little milk; stew some spinach in a saucepan; put to the spinach a quarter of a pint of gravy, a piece of butter and flour. When it is enough, put the mutton in the middle, the spinach round it, and the cauliflower over all. The butter the cauliflower has stewed in must be poured over it, and it must be melted, like a smooth cream. (John Farley, 1783)

Serves 6–8

A 4-LB LEG OF MUTTON OR LAMB, BONED, ROLLED
    AND TIED
2 TBS OIL
4 SPRIGS BURNET (when available)
4 SPRIGS PARSLEY
4 SPRIGS THYME
4 SPRIGS TARRAGON
2 PT (5 CUPS) STOCK
I ONION, STUCK WITH A CLOVE
I BAY LEAF
I CAULIFLOWER, CUT INTO FLOWERETS
4 TBS MELTED BUTTER
I LB SPINACH
2 OZ (4 TBS) BUTTER
4 TBS FLOUR

Brown the meat in the oil. Press the herb sprigs into the cavity from which the bone was removed, sprinkle with salt and pepper and tie the meat up in a piece of cheesecloth. Simmer in the stock with the onion and bay leaf for 2 hours, or until tender. Meanwhile cook the cauliflower in water until tender (15–20 minutes). Drain and season with salt and pepper; add the melted butter and keep warm. Cook the spinach, then drain and chop. Melt the butter in a pan, add the flour and cook for I minute. Add ¾ pint (2 cups) of liquid from the meat and beat until thickened. Stir in the chopped spinach. Arrange the meat in the centre of a dish, with the spinach round it, and pour the buttered cauliflower over the top.

Roast Welsh Leg of Lamb, Minted, in a Crust

(*from an unsigned document, late eighteenth century*)

Serves 8–10

A 5–6 LB LEG OF LAMB
I LARGE BUNCH FRESH MINT, STEMS REMOVED
2 OZ (4 TBS) BUTTER OR DRIPPING
$\frac{1}{2}$–$\frac{3}{4}$ PT (1$\frac{1}{2}$ CUPS) WATER
I OZ (2 TBS) BUTTER
2 TBS BROWN SUGAR
I TBS VINEGAR
2 TBS CHOPPED MINT
1$\frac{1}{2}$ LB (5 CUPS) FLOUR
I OZ (2 TBS) BUTTER, SOFTENED

Insert a pointed knife between the meat and the skin and loosen the skin until pockets are formed. Sprinkle the fresh mint leaves with pepper and salt and insert into the pockets until the largest possible area of flesh is covered with mint. Put the lamb in a roasting pan with the butter or dripping and roast at 400° (Mark 6) for 15 minutes, then reduce the heat to 350° (Mark 4) and roast for another 30 minutes.

Remove from the oven, wipe off the fat and trim the meat of any charred pieces. Cool. Mix 1 oz (2 tbs) butter, brown sugar, vinegar and chopped mint to make a thick cream. Rub this all over the leg of lamb. Make a stiff paste by mixing the flour with water, roll it out on a floured board and wrap the meat in it until it is completely covered. Seal the edges with cold water. Put this in an ungreased roasting pan, bake at 350° (Mark 4) for 25 minutes per pound, or 20 minutes per pound if you prefer rarer meat. If the crust browns too fast, cover with aluminium foil.

When the meat is done the shell can be discarded, or half of it can be used as a bowl in which to serve the carved meat. As soon as the crust has been removed the meat should be put back into the roasting pan with the softened butter and basted until nicely browned.

Braised Mutton with Chestnuts

A leg of mutton larded a la braise, with a ragoo of chestnuts :
First skin the Mutton, and lard it with Bacon and Ham through and through ; but let the Ham and Bacon be well seasoned, tie it up and stew it a la Braise : then having roasted Chestnuts, and taken off the Shells and Skins very clean, put them into some good Cullis of Veal and Ham, setting them over a gentle Fire, and when they begin to be soft, if they are well relished, put them over the Mutton, and serve them up hot. (*Charles Carter, 1732*)

Serves 6–8

A 4-LB LEG OF LAMB
2 OZ (4 TBS) HAM, CUT IN JULIENNE STRIPS
6 SLICES BACON, CUT IN STRIPS
2 TSP SALT
$\frac{1}{4}$ TSP PEPPER
2 TBS OIL
I PT (2 CUPS) STOCK
$\frac{1}{2}$ LB (2 CUPS) CHESTNUTS, PEELED

Lard the leg of lamb by using a larding needle or by sticking a heavy knitting needle through the meat and inserting the seasoned ham and bacon. Brown in oil. Pour over the stock and simmer, covered, for 2 hours. Add the chestnuts and simmer for 20–30 minutes longer, or until the lamb is tender and the chestnuts are soft.

Mutton like Venison

To dress a haunch of mutton, venison fashion, take a fat hind quarter of mutton, and cut the leg like a haunch. Lay it in a pan, with the backside of it down, and pour a bottle of red wine over it, in which let it lie twenty-four hours. Spit it and roast it at a good quick fire, and keep basting it all the time with the same liquor and butter. It will require an hour and a half roasting ; when it is done, send it up with a little good gravy in one boat, and sweet sauce in in another. (*John Farley, 1783*)

Serves 6–8

A 6-LB LEG OF MUTTON OR LAMB
MARINADE
2 OZ (4 TBS) BUTTER

Sauce
½ LB (½ CUP) REDCURRANT JELLY
½ PT (1 CUP) RED WINE
½ PT (1 CUP) VINEGAR
½ LB (1 CUP) SUGAR

Pour the marinade over the lamb and leave for 24 hours.

Remove the lamb from the marinade and brown it in butter. Put it on a rack in a roasting pan. Bring the marinade to the boil with a good piece of butter and use this to baste the mutton frequently. Cook on a spit or roast at 350° (Mark 4) for 20–25 minutes per lb.

Meanwhile make the sauce. Warm the currant jelly. Add the wine and vinegar and half the quantity of sugar. Simmer for 5–6 minutes, add the remaining sugar and cook to a light syrup.

When the joint is tender, remove it and carve it in a concave dish, or on a board with a gravy well. Keep warm. Pour the collected juices back into the pan; degrease. Set the pan on top of the stove over strong heat, add a little boiling water and stir to melt the glaze and make the gravy. Strain into a smaller pan, stir in a lump of butter and pour the gravy into a hot sauceboat. Serve the sweet sauce in a separate sauce-boat.

Saddle of Mutton

Take a saddle and remove the skin very neatly, without taking it quite off, or breaking it. Take some lean ham, truffles, morells, green onions, parsley, thyme, sweet herbs, all chopped small, with some spice, pepper and salt. Strew it over the mutton where the skin is taken off; put the skin over it neatly, and tie over it some white paper, well buttered, and roast it. When it is nearly enough, take off the paper, strew over some grated bread, and when it is of a fine brown, take it up. Have ready some good gravy for sauce. (John Farley, 1783)

Serves 6–8

A 6-LB SADDLE OF MUTTON

Stuffing
4 OZ (½ CUP) CHOPPED HAM
2 TRUFFLES OR PICKLED WALNUTS, CHOPPED
2 MORELLES OR DRIED ITALIAN MUSHROOMS, CHOPPED
4 TBS SPRING ONIONS (SCALLIONS), CHOPPED
4 TBS PARSLEY, CHOPPED
1 TSP THYME
4 TBS SWEET HERBS, CHOPPED
1 TSP ALLSPICE
2 TSP SALT
¼ TSP PEPPER
2 OZ (4 TBS) BUTTER
1 OZ (½ CUP) BREADCRUMBS

Gravy
1 PT (2½ CUPS) STOCK
2 OZ (4 TBS) FLOUR
4 TBS DRIPPINGS FROM MUTTON

Remove the skin from the saddle of mutton and proceed exactly as in the original recipe.

Stir the flour into the drippings. Gradually add the stock and cook, stirring, until thickened.

A Cheshire Pork Pie

Skin a loin of pork, cut it into steaks, and season it with salt, nutmeg and pepper. Make a good crust, put a layer of pork, then a layer of pippins pared and cored, and a little sugar, enough to sweeten the pie, and then a layer of pork. Put in half a pint of white wine, lay some butter on the top, and close your pie. It will take a pint of wine, if your pie be a large one. (The Universal Cook, 1797)

6 SLICES RAW PORK CUT FROM THE LOIN, LIKE VEAL ESCALOPES (SCALLOPS)
2 APPLES, PEELED, CORED AND SLICED
2 TBS SUGAR
NUTMEG, SALT AND PEPPER
¾ PT (2 CUPS) WHITE WINE
1 OZ (2 TBS) BUTTER
½ LB PASTRY

Arrange alternate layers of pork and apples in

a pie dish, sprinkling the layers with sugar, salt, pepper and nutmeg. Add the wine. Dot the top of the dish with butter and cover with a pastry crust. Bake at 375° (Mark 5) for 45–50 minutes.

Roast Gammon in Oatmeal

Ham or gammon of bacon roasted :
Take off the skin of your ham or gammon as soon as it be half boiled, and dredge it with oatmeal sifted very fine. Baste it with butter, which will make a stronger froth than either crumbs of bread or flour. Then roast it, and when it be enough, dish it up, and pour brown gravy into your dish. Send it up garnished with green parsley. (John Farley, 1783)

Serves 4–6

2 LB HAM OR GAMMON
1 ONION, STUCK WITH 2 CLOVES
1 BAY LEAF
2 CARROTS
1 STALK CELERY
4 PEPPERCORNS
$\frac{1}{4}$ LB ($\frac{1}{2}$ CUP) BUTTER
1$\frac{1}{2}$ OZ ($\frac{1}{2}$–1 CUP) FINE OATMEAL
A FEW SPRIGS FRESH PARSLEY FOR GARNISH

Put the ham in a pan with enough cold water to cover. Bring to the boil and then skim the surface of the broth. Add the onion, bay leaf, carrots and celery and simmer for 45 minutes. Lift out, drain, remove the skin and pat dry. Dip in melted butter and roll in the oatmeal, until it is well coated. Place in a roasting pan on a rack with a little of the cooking broth. Bake for 45 minutes at 350° (Mark 4), basting frequently with the remaining butter.

Gammon Steaks on Toast

Cut slices of Ham of a moderate Thickness, and sharp-pointed at both Ends, lay them in a Stew-pan with a little melted Bacon, cover the Pan, set it on a stove over a gentle Fire, and let it soak. When one side of the Ham is coloured turn the Slices, and when they are enough, take them out, and put into the Pan thin Slices of Bread, like those of the Ham. When they are fry'd, take them out, and put in half a spoonful of Flour, which moisten with Gravy or Broth and a little of the ordinary Cullis, seasoning it with a Clove of Garlick, whole Chibbols, and Mushrooms, adding a Glass of White-Wine, and some slices of Lemon.

When it has stewed a little, skim off the Fat and strain it, then put it into the Stew-pan again with the fry'd Slices of Ham, and keep them warm.

When you are ready to serve up, lay the Slices of fry'd Bread on the Bottom of the Dish, laying a Slice of fry'd Ham on each Slice of Bread, and pour the Sauce over it, and serve it up hot for a Dainty Dish. (Charles Carter, 1732)

Serves 4–6

2 HAM OR GAMMON STEAKS, EACH WEIGHING
    1–1$\frac{1}{2}$ LB
1 OZ (2 TBS) BACON FAT
4 SLICES BREAD
1 CLOVE GARLIC, FINELY CHOPPED
2–4 SPRING ONIONS (SCALLIONS), FINELY CHOPPED
4 MUSHROOMS, SLICED
2 TBS FLOUR
$\frac{1}{2}$ PT (1 CUP) STOCK
$\frac{1}{4}$ PT ($\frac{1}{2}$ CUP) WHITE WINE
4 LEMON WEDGES, FOR GARNISH

Sauté the steaks until golden on both sides. Remove and keep warm. Brown the bread in the same fat. Reserve. Cook the garlic, onions and mushrooms in the remaining fat, adding more if necessary, until tender. Stir in the flour. Add the stock and wine and cook until thickened. Cut the steaks in half, reheat, and serve on fried bread covered with the sauce. Garnish with lemon wedges.

Bacon Fraise

Take a piece of middling Bacon, cut it in thin Pieces of about an Inch long, and then make a a Batter, with Milk, Eggs, and Flour; beat the Eggs very well, mix them together, then put some

*Lard, or good Beef Dripping, and when it is
very hot pour in your Mixture, and put a Dish
over it, but now and then trow on some of the
Fat upon the Fraise, till you think the lower
Part is enough; then turn it, and in a little
Time the whole will be ready for the Table. In
this Mixture put what Spices you think proper,
for in the Taste 'tis to every one what they like.*
(*The Housekeeper's Pocket Book, 1738*)

Makes 10–12 pancakes
2 EGGS
$\frac{1}{2}$ PT (1 CUP) MILK
$4\frac{1}{2}$ OZ (1 CUP) FLOUR
$\frac{1}{8}$ TSP PEPPER
1 TSP SALT
$\frac{1}{4}$ TSP NUTMEG
$\frac{1}{4}$ TSP MACE
15 SLICES STREAKY BACON, CUT IN HALF

Beat the eggs very well, then beat into the
milk and flour. Season with pepper, salt,
nutmeg and mace. Fry the bacon gently until
very crisp. Drain and keep hot. Pour some of
the batter into a little of the bacon fat. When it
is set, arrange some of the bacon pieces over it
in an even layer. Cover with more batter, and
as soon as it sets turn over and brown the
other side. Remove and keep warm, continuing
to make the pancakes until the batter is
finished. They can also be served as a
breakfast dish with a fried egg on top.

A simpler version of this dish can be made
by crumbling the cooked bacon into the
batter and frying in the same way as ordinary
pancakes.

Pig's Pettitoes

*Let the feet boil till they are pretty tender; but
take up the heart, liver and lights, when they
have boiled ten minutes, and shred them pretty
small. Take out the feet, and split them;
thicken your gravy with flour and butter, and
put in your mince-meat a spoonful of white wine,
a slice of lemon, a little salt, and give it a
gentle boil. Beat the yolk of an egg: put to it two
spoonfuls of cream, and a little grated nutmeg.
Then put in the pettitoes, and shake it over the
fire, without letting it boil. Lay sippets round the
dish, and pour in your mince-meat.*
(*John Farley, 1783*)

4 PIG'S TROTTERS (FEET)
1 PIG'S HEART
1 PIG'S LIVER
1 SET PIG'S LIGHTS
$1\frac{1}{2}$ PT (3–4 CUPS) WATER
4 TBS FLOUR
2 OZ (4 TBS) BUTTER
2 TBS WHITE WINE
A SLICE OF LEMON
$\frac{1}{2}$ TSP SALT
1 EGG YOLK
2 TBS CREAM
$\frac{1}{4}$ TSP NUTMEG
8 SLICES BREAD, CUT IN FINGERS AND TOASTED
  (SIPPETS)

Proceed exactly as in Farley's recipe.

Forcemeats and Stuffing

Forcemeat Balls

Take half a pound of veal, and half a pound of suet, cut fine, and beat them in a marble mortar or wooden bowl. Shred a few sweet herbs fine, a little mace dried and beat fine, a small nutmeg grated, a little lemon-peel cut very fine, some pepper and salt, and the yolks of two eggs. Mix all these well together, then roll them in little round balls, and some in long pieces. Roll them in flour and fry them brown. If they be for the use of white sauce, put a little water in a saucepan, and put them in when the water boils. Let them boil a few minutes; but when they be used for white sauce, be sure not to fry them.
(*John Farley, 1783*)

½ LB (1 CUP) MINCED (GROUND) VEAL
½ LB (2 CUPS) SHREDDED SUET
2 TBS CHOPPED MIXED HERBS
½ TSP GROUND MACE
1 TSP GRATED LEMON PEEL
2 EGG YOLKS
A LITTLE FLOUR

Farley's recipe can be followed exactly.

Forcemeat with Cream

Cut some Veal in pieces with a piece of Bacon and a piece of Beef-suet; set it all on the Fire in a Stew-pan; give it some Tosses; then season it with Salt, Pepper, fine Spices, sweet Herbs and a little Garlic; then put them on a Table and mince them together; add some crumbl'd Bread the largeness of your Fish, first boil'd in Milk; and eight or ten Yolks of Eggs; beat up half of the Whites to Snow, put them all into a Mortar and Pound them well.
This minc'd Meat is to be used for stuffing fish or Fowls in Cawl.
(*Charles Carter, 1732*)

4 SLICES BACON, DICED
1½ LB (3 CUPS) MINCED (GROUND) VEAL
5 OZ (1¼ CUPS) GRATED SUET
1 TSP SALT
½ TSP PEPPER
2 TBS BASIL
1 TBS THYME
1 TBS TARRAGON
1 CLOVE GARLIC, MINCED
1 OZ (½ CUP) BREADCRUMBS, SOAKED IN MILK
2 EGG YOLKS PLUS 1 WHITE

Melt the bacon in a frying-pan over medium heat. Fry the minced veal and suet in this fat. Add the seasonings and herbs. Put into a mixing bowl and add the breadcrumbs and the egg yolks. Finally, fold in the egg white, whipped. Use for stuffing fish or poultry.

Forcemeat of Game

(*Charles Carter, 1732*)

This forcemeat is used as a lining and as a cover for pies 'poupetons' containing small birds. A layer of it was used on top of pies in the seventeenth and eighteenth centuries to keep the contents moist, instead of a pastry lid.

1 OZ (½ CUP) BREADCRUMBS
4 TBS (¼ CUP) CREAM
1 LB (2 CUPS) RAW VEAL, MINCED (GROUND)
1 LB (2 CUPS) RAW CHICKEN OR PHEASANT, MINCED (GROUND)
2 OZ (½ CUP) GRATED SUET
1 OZ (½ CUP) CHOPPED MUSHROOMS
1½ OZ TRUFFLES OR PICKLED WALNUTS
4 TBS PARSLEY, CHOPPED
4 TBS SPRING ONIONS (SCALLIONS), CHOPPED
2 EGG YOLKS
1 EGG WHITE, BEATEN

Boil the breadcrumbs and cream together until they form a smooth paste. Leave to cool and then combine with all the other ingredients in a mixing bowl, folding in the beaten egg white last.

Fish Forcemeat

(Charles Carter, 1730)

Makes 20 small balls

¼ LB (½ CUP) FRESH COD, FILLETED
¼ LB (½ CUP) EEL, SKINNED AND BONED
¼ LB (½ CUP) OYSTERS, CHOPPED
4 TBS MUSHROOMS, CHOPPED
2 ANCHOVIES, CRUSHED
½ TSP PEPPER
½ TSP SALT
¼ TSP NUTMEG
⅛ TSP GINGER
4 TBS ONIONS, CHOPPED
I SHALLOT, CHOPPED
½ TSP THYME
2 TBS PARSLEY, CHOPPED
2–4 TBS CREAM
4 TBS BREADCRUMBS
2 EGG YOLKS
I EGG WHITE

Skin the fish and pound it to a purée. Mix in a bowl with all the other ingredients, moistening the mixture with the eggs and cream until it holds together as a ball.

Use as a stuffing for baked fish or roll into little balls with floured hands and poach in fish soup a few minutes before serving.

Vegetables

Stuffed Artichokes

To force artichokes :
They must first be boil'd and the Bottoms taken out whole, and thrown into cold Water ; then take them out and wash them with Yolks of Eggs, and making a Forcing of two Bottoms, boil'd Yolks of Eggs, Pepper, Salt, Nutmeg, and a little Marrow ; beat them in a Mortar very fine, and fill up your Bottoms pointed like a Sugar Loaf, bake them gently and serve with a cup of Butter. (Charles Carter, 1732)

Serves 4

6 ARTICHOKES (OR TINNED ARTICHOKE BOTTOMS)
3 TBS RAW BEEF MARROW, CHOPPED
I TBS LEMON JUICE
½ TSP SALT
¼ TSP PEPPER
½ TSP GROUND NUTMEG
3 HARD-BOILED EGG YOLKS
A LITTLE MELTED BUTTER

Boil the artichokes and remove the bottoms (or use tinned artichoke bottoms). Chop 2 of the bottoms finely. Combine together in a bowl the chopped artichokes, marrow, lemon juice, salt, pepper, nutmeg and egg yolks. Beat to a paste, using a pestle and mortar, a fork or a blender. Pile this mixture on to the remaining 4 bottoms and shape it to form a point. Brush with melted butter and bake at 350° (Mark 4) for 20 minutes.

Artichoke Pie

Boil twelve bottoms very tender, then force six and at the Bottom of your Crust, put in some lumps of Marrow and dic'd Sweetbreads, and then put in half a Pint of Cream, season with Nutmeg and Salt, so bake it.
(Charles Carter, 1732)

E.Kirkall fc

Serves 4–6

6 ARTICHOKES OR TINNED ARTICHOKE BOTTOMS
3 TBS BEEF MARROW, CHOPPED
2 TBS LEMON JUICE
A 9-INCH BAKED PASTRY SHELL
2 SWEETBREADS, SOAKED, CLEANED AND CHOPPED
½ TBS TARRAGON, CHOPPED
I TBS LEMON JUICE
¾ PT (1½ CUPS) THICK CREAM
½ TSP SALT
½ TSP NUTMEG
3 EGGS PLUS 2 EXTRA YOLKS

Boil the artichokes until they are well done (or use tinned artichoke bottoms). Remove the bottoms and finely chop them. Place in a bowl with the marrow and lemon juice and pound with a pestle to make a paste, or purée in a blender. Spread the paste over the bottom of the pie-shell. Scatter over the diced sweetbreads and sprinkle with the tarragon and a little more lemon juice. Season well with pepper and salt. Heat the cream, salt and nutmeg; beat the eggs and extra yolks in a bowl; pour the hot cream over them, beating with a whisk. Pour over the mixture in the pastry crust and then bake at 350° (Mark 4) for 25 minutes, or until set.

Asparagus in Cream

Take your large asparagus, and cut them in pieces, half an inch long, as far as they are green; then stove them in clear strong broth till crisp and tender; season them with pepper, salt, and nutmeg and a little onion; then toss them up thick with the yolks of eggs beat up in a little white wine and cream, and some thick butter, and so serve them, and garnish with lemon. (*John Farley, 1783*)

Serves 3–4

4 TBS ONION, FINELY CHOPPED
I OZ (2 TBS) BUTTER
¼ PT (½ CUP) THICK CREAM
¼ PT (½ CUP) WHITE WINE
½ TSP SALT

¼ TSP PEPPER
½ TSP GROUND NUTMEG
4 EGG YOLKS
½ LB (2 CUPS) ASPARAGUS TIPS, COOKED AND KEPT WARM
A SQUEEZE OF LEMON JUICE
4 LEMON SLICES

Cook the onions in the butter until soft, then add the cream, wine, seasoning and nutmeg and reheat. Beat up the egg yolks and stir the hot mixture into them. Cook gently, without boiling, until thickened. Toss the sauce and the asparagus tips together, squeeze over a little lemon juice, and serve with slices of lemon.

Asparagus in French Rolls

This is a pretty dish to serve with roast veal, or with any meat or fish dish that is not itself made with a sauce. It makes a good treat for children.

Asparagus forced in French rolls:
Cut a piece out of the crust of the tops of three French rolls, and take out all their crumb; but be careful that the crusts fit again in the places from whence they were taken. Fry the rolls brown in fresh butter. Then take a pint of cream, the yolks of six eggs beat fine, and a little salt and nutmeg. Stir them well together over a slow fire till it begin to be thick. Have ready an hundred of small grass boiled, and have tops enough to stick the rolls with. Cut the rest of the tops small, put them into the cream, and fill the loaves with them. Before you fry the rolls, make holes thick in the top crusts, to stick the grass in. Then lay on the pieces of crust, and stick the grass in, that it may look as if it were growing. At a second course, this makes a pretty side dish. (*John Farley, 1783*)

Serves 6

6 EGG YOLKS
¾ PT (2 CUPS) THICK CREAM
I TSP SALT
¼ TSP PEPPER
½ TSP NUTMEG

½ LB (2 CUPS) COOKED ASPARAGUS, CHOPPED, OR
   ASPARAGUS TIPS
6 FRENCH ROLLS
2 OZ (4 TBS) BUTTER
6 THIN ASPARAGUS SPEARS, COOKED UNTIL BARELY
   TENDER

Beat the egg yolks and then beat the hot cream into them. Cook, stirring, until well thickened, but do not boil. Season with salt, pepper and nutmeg and stir in the chopped asparagus. Cook for a few minutes.

    Meanwhile, cut an oval piece out of the top of each roll, pull out most of the inside crumb and fry the rolls in the butter until golden and crisp on the outside. Fill each roll with some of the cream sauce and asparagus mixture and stick an extra spear upright in each, so that it looks as if it were growing out of the roll. Warm in the oven until ready to serve.

Celery with Cream

Tye up four bunches and boil them tender; cut them three Inches long, the best and white Heart of it; then take half a Pint of Cream and four Yolks of Eggs; season with Salt and put in a small Piece of Butter, and shake it together and serve away hot. (Charles Carter, 1732)

Serves 3–4
3–4 CELERY HEARTS
½ PT (1 CUP) CREAM
2 EGG YOLKS
¼ TSP SALT
⅛ TSP PEPPER
½ OZ (1 TBS) BUTTER

Take the celery hearts (the white part) and cut them into 3-inch pieces. Simmer in enough water to cover until tender. Drain. Heat the cream; beat the egg yolks and stir the cream into them. Season with salt, pepper and a scant tablespoon of butter. Toss with the celery and serve.

To Make an Onion Pie

Wash and pare some potatoes and cut them in slices, peel some onions, cut them in slices, pare some apples and slice them, make a good crust, cover your dish, Lay a quarter of a pound of butter all over, take a quarter of an ounce of mace beat fine, a nutmeg grated, a tea-spoonful of beaten pepper, three teaspoonfuls of salt; mix all together, strew some over the butter, lay a layer of potatoes, a layer of onions, a layer of apples, and a layer of eggs, and so on till you have filled your pie, strewing a little of the seasoning between each layer, and a quarter of a pound of butter in bits, and six spoonfuls of water; close your pie, and bake it an hour and a half. (Hannah Glasse, 1747)

1½ LB PASTRY
2 OZ (4 TBS) BUTTER
½ TSP MACE
½ TSP NUTMEG
¼ TSP PEPPER
1 TSP SALT
2 POTATOES, PEELED AND THINLY SLICED
2 ONIONS, PEELED AND THINLY SLICED
2 APPLES, PEELED, CORED AND SLICED
4 HARD-BOILED EGGS, SLICED
4 TBS WATER

Line a 9-inch pie dish with half the pastry. Spread half the butter over the pastry. Mix together the spices, salt and pepper. Arrange alternate layers of potatoes, onions, apples and eggs, sprinkling each layer with the spice mixture. Dot with the remaining butter. Pour in the water. Cover with the remaining pastry and bake at 350° (Mark 4) for 1 hour or until the potatoes are tender.

Stewed Peas and Lettuce

(John Farley, 1783)

Serves 4
1 PT (2½ CUPS) FRESH GREEN PEAS, SHELLED
1 HEAD LETTUCE, SLICED
4 TBS (¼ CUP) VEGETABLE STOCK

2 EGG YOLKS
1 OZ (2 TBS) BUTTER (OPTIONAL)

Garnish (*optional*)
8 SLICES HAM
1 OZ (2 TBS) BUTTER
or
2 SLICES HAM, OR PROSCIUTTO, CUT IN JULIENNE
   STRIPS

Simmer the peas and lettuce, covered, in a thick braising-pan for about 20 minutes, or until tender. Add a little vegetable stock if necessary. Beat the egg yolks in a bowl, stir into them a little of the hot cooking liquid and return to the pan with the vegetables. Season with pepper and salt. The butter may prove unnecessary; it merely makes the dish richer. Cook until thickened, but do not boil.

   For the ham garnish, cook the ham very gently in the butter, or put the slices in a dish with a little butter, covered, in a warm oven to heat and cook slightly while you prepare the vegetables. Pile the vegetables on top of them in the serving dish to make a pleasent lunch dish. Alternatively, cut the ham or prosciutto into thin julienne strips and stir them into the vegetables, leaving them just long enough to warm, but not to cook.

1 TSP SALT
$\frac{1}{2}$ TSP NUTMEG
$\frac{1}{4}$ TSP GINGER
$\frac{1}{2}$ TSP CINNAMON
2 TBS SHERRY
1 TSP ORANGE-FLOWER WATER
2 TSP GRATED LEMON PEEL
1 EGG YOLK
2 NAPLES BISCUITS OR SPONGE FINGERS (*see p.* 147),
   GRATED OR CRUMBLED
2 OZ ($\frac{1}{4}$ CUP) SUGAR
1 OZ (2 TBS) BUTTER OR MARGARINE FOR FRYING

Combine all the ingredients except the butter, make stiff patties and fry them in the butter on both sides until golden.

   Serve with turkey, fried chicken, duck or spare ribs.

Sweet Potato Rissoles

For resoles of potatoes, sweet :
Take artichoke bottoms boiled, or potatoes boiled, either Spanish or English, and beat them in a mortar, with as much marrow as stuff; season them with salt, nutmeg, ginger, cinnamon and sugar, some sack, orange-flower water, or rosewater; put in some grated citron, and orangado; work it up with Naples biscuit grated, and the yolks of eggs, and put it in sugar paste, and either bake it, or fry it. (Charles Carter, 1730)

Serves 2 (4 patties)
$\frac{1}{2}$ LB (1 CUP) MASHED SWEET POTATOES
4 OZ (1 CUP) RAW BEEF MARROW

Desserts

A Pupton of Apples

Pare some apples. Take out the cores and put them into a skillet; to a quart mugful heaped put in a quarter of a pound of sugar, and two spoonfuls of water; do them over a slow fire, keep them stirring, add a little cinnamon; when it is quite thick and like a marmalade, let it stand till cool; beat up the yolks of four or five eggs, and stir in a handful of grated bread and a quarter of a pound of fresh butter, then form it into what shape you please, and bake it in a slow oven, and then turn it upside down on a plate for a second course. (Hannah Glasse, 1747)

Serves 4–6
6 APPLES, PEELED, CORED AND CHOPPED
¼ LB (½ CUP) SUGAR
1 TSP CINNAMON
2 TBS WATER
4–5 EGG YOLKS, BEATEN
1 OZ (½ CUP) BREADCRUMBS
¼ LB (½ CUP) BUTTER

Place the apples in a saucepan with the sugar, cinnamon and water and cook until soft. Beat in the egg yolks, breadcrumbs and butter. Spoon the mixture into a buttered dish and bake at 300° (Mark 2) for 20–30 minutes. Turn out onto a serving dish.

A Florendine of Oranges and Apples

Lay a puff paste all over the dish, spread marmalade over the bottom. Boil pippins, pared, quartered and cored, in a little water and sugar, and slice two of the oranges and mix with the pippins in the dish; sprinkle with orange juice. Bake it in a slow oven for 30–40 minutes, with a crust as above; or just bake the crust and lay in the ingredients. (Hannah Glasse, 1747)

Serves 4
½–¾ LB (1 CUP) MARMALADE
2–4 TBS ORANGE JUICE
2 ORANGES, SLICED
4 APPLES, CORED, PEELED AND QUARTERED
4 TBS SUGAR
½ LB PUFF PASTRY

Prepare as above and bake at 350° (Mark 4).

Lemon Pudding Pie

Take two clear Lemons, grate off the outside Rind, also grate a couple of Naples Biskets, and mix them into your grated Peel, and add to it the Yolks of twelve and the whites of six Eggs well beaten, three Quarters of a Pound of Sugar, and three Quarters of a Pound of Butter and half a Pint of thick Cream. Lay a Sheet of Paste at the Bottom of the Dish, put in the Batter, set it into the Oven immediately, having first sifted a little refined Sugar over it. Let it stand an Hour. (Charles Carter, 1732)

Serves 6
¾ LB PASTRY
½–¾ PT (1½ CUPS) THICK CREAM
3 EGGS PLUS 2 EXTRA YOLKS
2 OZ (½ CUP) SUGAR
2 TBS GRATED LEMON PEEL
¼ PT (½ CUP) LEMON JUICE
1 OZ (¼ CUP) NAPLES BISCUITS (*see* glossary)
A FEW DROPS OF ALMOND ESSENCE AND ROSE
    WATER
2 OZ (¼ CUP) BUTTER
2 TBS ICING (CONFECTIONER'S) SUGAR

Line a 9-inch pie dish with the pastry and bake blind (pre-bake) for 10 minutes at 400° (Mark 6). Heat the cream. Beat together the remainder of the ingredients, except for the icing sugar, and beat the mixture into the hot cream. Pour into the pre-baked pastry shell. Sprinkle with icing sugar and bake for 25 minutes at 350° (Mark 4).

This very rich pudding can also be made with oranges. Simply replace the lemon peel and juice with 4 tablespoons grated orange peel and ¼ pint (½ cup) orange juice, then peel 2 oranges, divide them into segments and stir these into the cream just before pouring the mixture into the pastry shell.

―――――――――

Buttered Oranges

Take eight Eggs, and the Whites of four; beat them well together, then squeeze into them the Juice of seven good Oranges, and three or four Spoonfuls of Rose-water, and let them run through a hair Sieve into a silver Bason; put to it half a Pound of Sugar beat, then set it over a gentle Fire, and when it begins to thicken put in a bit of Butter, about the bigness of a large nutmeg, and when it is somewhat thicker pour it into a broad, flat China dish, and eat it cold. It will not keep very well above two Days, but is very wholesome and pleasant to the taste.
(The Housekeeper's Pocket Book, 1738)

Serves 3–4

4 EGG YOLKS PLUS 2 WHITES
2 OZ (½ CUP) SUGAR
¾ PT (1½ CUPS) ORANGE JUICE
2 TBS ROSEWATER
I OZ (2 TBS) BUTTER

Beat the eggs and sugar together. Beat in the orange juice and rosewater. Cook in the top of a double saucepan until the mixture starts to thicken. Add the butter, in small pieces, and cook gently until it is thick enough to coat a silver spoon. Pour into a custard bowl and chill.

―――――――――

Preserved Peaches in Cream

Sweetmeat cream:
Take some good Cream, and slice some preserv'd Peaches into it; or Apricocks, or Plumbs; sweeten the Cream with fine Sugar, or with Syrup the Fruit was preserv'd in; mix these well together, and serve it cold in China Basons.
(The Housekeeper's Pocket Book, 1738)

Serves 2–3

½ LB (I CUP) SLICED PRESERVED PEACHES
  (see page 154)

¼ PT (½ CUP) OF THE SYRUP FROM THE PEACHES
I PT (2 CUPS) THICK CREAM

Drain the peaches from their syrup. Measure ¼ pint (½ cup) of the syrup and mix it with the cream. Fold in the sliced peaches. Serve in glass bowls.

―――――――――

Gooseberry Cream

Take two quarts of gooseberries, put to them as much water as will cover them, scald them, and then run them through a sieve with a spoon; to a quart of the pulp you must have six eggs well beaten; and when the pulp is hot, put in an ounce of fresh butter, sweeten it to your taste, put in your eggs, and stir them over a gentle fire till they grow thick, then set it by; and when it is almost cold, put into it two spoonfuls of juice of spinach, and a spoonful of orange flower water or sack; stir it well together, and put it into your basin; when it is cold, serve it to table.
(Hannah Glasse, 1747)

Serves 8

2 LB (8 CUPS) GOOSEBERRIES
6 EGGS
I OZ (2 TBS) BUTTER
ABOUT ½–¾ LB (I–2 CUPS) SUGAR
2 TBS SPINACH JUICE OR GREEN FOOD COLOURING
  (A FEW DROPS)
I TBS ORANGE-FLOWER WATER OR WHITE WINE

Cook the gooseberries in a little water until soft. Drain them and push through a sieve. For 2 pints (5 cups) of the purée, take 6 eggs and beat them well. Reheat the purée in a pan and stir in the butter, sugar to taste and the beaten eggs. Stir over very low heat until thickened, but do not let it boil. When cool, stir in the spinach juice, made in a juice extractor, or in the blender with a little water. Add orange-flower water or wine. Mix well and chill.

―――――――――

Raspberry Cream

Take half a pound of preserved raspberries, wet, and bruise them, and boil them gently up in a

quart of cream; put in a blade of mace; season them with fine sugar, orange-flower or rose water; strain it, and force it through your strainer, and then draw it up with the yolks of three eggs, and put it in basins or glasses.
(*Charles Carter, 1730*)

Serves 4

½ LB (1½ CUPS) FRESH (OR 10–OZ PACKET) FROZEN
    RASPBERRIES
SINGLE CREAM (*see recipe*)
4 EGG YOLKS
4 OZ (½ CUP) SUGAR
½ TSP GROUND MACE
4 TBS ORANGE-FLOWER WATER OR ROSEWATER

Rub the raspberries through a fine sieve and add enough cream to make 1 pint (2½ cups). Heat the cream and raspberry purée to just below boiling point. Beat together the egg yolks, sugar, mace and orange-flower water. Pour the cream and raspberry mixture into the egg mixture in a thin stream and beat until smooth. Cook in the top of a double boiler, over simmering water, until it is thick enough to coat a spoon. Pour into a serving bowl and chill.

Scottish Burnt Cream

(*Traditional, adapted by the author*)

Serves 4–6

1 PT (2½ CUPS) DOUBLE (HEAVY) CREAM
½ TSP CINNAMON
1 TBS GRATED ORANGE PEEL
8 EGG YOLKS
2 OZ (¼ CUP) SUGAR
ABOUT 1½ OZ (¼ CUP) BROWN SUGAR

Heat the cream to boiling point with the cinnamon and orange peel. Beat the egg yolks and sugar in a bowl. Pour the hot cream into the egg mixture and beat with a whisk to keep it smooth. Put this mixture into the top half of a double-boiler over simmering water and cook, stirring, until the custard is thick enough to coat a silver spoon. Pour into an 'ashet' or enamel dish that can be transferred from the refrigerator to the grill without breaking. Chill thoroughly.

Sprinkle brown sugar on top, being very careful to make an even layer, since any lumps and bumps will burn easily. Put under the grill broiler for a minute or two until the sugar has melted, watching it like a hawk to prevent the sugar burning.

Pistachio Cream

To a quart of good cream, take three quarters of a pound of pistachio nut kernels blanched: beat half a pound very fine, and boil up in your cream, and season it with fine sugar, and orange-flower water; grate in a little lemon peel, and thicken it with two or three yolks of eggs, or some Naples, or Savoy biscuits dried, beat, sifted, and strained, and force it through your strainer, and dish it in basins of china ware.
(*Charles Carter, 1730*)

Serves 4

1 PT (2½ CUPS) CREAM
2 OZ (½ CUP) PISTACHIO NUTS, GROUND IN THE
    BLENDER
4 OZ (½ CUP) SUGAR
4 TBS ORANGE-FLOWER WATER
1 TSP GRATED LEMON PEEL
4 EGG YOLKS
2–3 NAPLES OR SAVOY BISCUITS (*see p. 147*), GRATED
    (OPTIONAL) OR SWEET BISCUITS

Heat the cream, add the nuts and bring to the boil. Draw off the heat and stir in the sugar, the orange-flower water and the grated lemon peel. Beat the egg yolks in a bowl and pour in a little of the almost boiling cream. Return to the pan and stir gently until the mixture is slightly thickened, without allowing it to boil. For a thicker cream, stir in 2 or 3 grated biscuits.

Baked Custards

Boil a pint of cream with some mace and cinnamon, and when it be cold, take four yolks and two whites of eggs, a little rose and orange-flower water and sack, and nutmeg and sugar to your palate. Mix them well together, and bake them in cups. (John Farley, 1783)

Serves 4

Basic Custard
1 PT (2½ CUPS) MILK OR CREAM
4 EGG YOLKS PLUS 2 WHITES
2 OZ (¼ CUP) SUGAR
½ TSP SALT

Heat the milk or cream. Beat the egg yolks and whites in a bowl with the sugar and salt. Add the hot milk in a stream. Pour into individual cups. Bake at 350° (Mark 4) in a bain-marie for 15–20 minutes, or until set.

Almond Custard
Use almond milk (*see p. 53*) instead of ordinary milk.

Spiced Custard
Cut down milk by 4 tablespoons (¼ cup); add 2 tablespoons each sherry and orange-flower water and 1 tsp nutmeg.

Orange Custard
Use ¾ pint (2 cups) milk, ¼ pt (½ cup) orange juice, 1 tablespoon each brandy and grated orange peel.

Lemon Custard
Use ¾ pint (2 cups) milk, ¼ pint (½ cup) lemon juice, and increase sugar to 4 ounces (½ cup). Then add 1 tablespoon each grated lemon peel and sherry.

Duke of Cumberland's Pudding

Take flour, grated apples, chopped suet and sugar, of each six ounces; six eggs, a little nutmeg and salt. Boil it two hours at least, and serve it with melted butter, wine and sugar. (John Farley, 1783)

Serves 4

4 OZ (1 CUP) FLOUR
½ LB (2 CUPS) APPLES, GRATED
4 OZ (1 CUP) MINCED SUET
4 OZ (½ CUP) SUGAR
6 EGGS
½ TSP NUTMEG
½ TSP SALT
2 OZ (4 TBS) MELTED BUTTER
2 TBS SUGAR
2 TBS WINE

Combine the flour, grated apple, suet, sugar, eggs, nutmeg and salt; blend well. Tie all in a cloth and boil for 2 hours. Combine the butter, sugar and wine and pour over the top just before serving.

Duke of Buckingham's Pudding

Take a pound of suet chopped fine, a quarter of a pound of raisins stoned and chopped, two eggs, a little nutmeg and ginger, two spoonfuls of flour, and sugar to the taste. Tie it close, boil it four hours at least, and serve it with melted butter, sack and sugar. (John Farley, 1783)

Serves 4

1 LB (4 CUPS) SHREDDED SUET
4 OZ (1 CUP) RAISINS
2 EGGS
½ TSP NUTMEG
¼ TSP GINGER
2 OZ (½ CUP) FLOUR
4 OZ (½ CUP) SUGAR

Sauce
2 OZ (4 TBS) MELTED BUTTER
2 TBS SHERRY
2 TBS SUGAR

Mix together all the first set of ingredients. Tie in a cloth and boil for 2–3 hours. Combine the melted butter, sherry and sugar and pour over the top just before serving.

To Make a Damson Dumpling

Make a good hot paste crust, roll it pretty thin, lay it on a bason, and put in what quantity of damsons you think proper, wet the edge of the paste and close it up, boil it in a cloth one hour and send it up whole, pour over it melted butter, and grate sugar round the edge of the dish; Note, you may make any kind of preserved fruit the same way. (*Elizabeth Raffald, 1769*)

Serves 8–10

Hot water pastry
6 TBS BOILING WATER
6 OZ (¾ CUP) LARD OR SHORTENING
9 OZ (2 CUPS) FLOUR
½ TSP BAKING POWDER
I TSP SALT

ABOUT 2 DOZEN DAMSONS OR PLUMS
2 OZ (4 TBS) MELTED BUTTER
2–4 TBS SUGAR

Pour the boiling water over the lard. Beat until creamy. Sift the flour, baking powder and salt. Combine the liquid and dry ingredients and shape into a ball. Chill until firm.

Roll out the pastry ¼ inch thick. Arrange the plums in the centre. Bring the ends to the middle and seal, wetting the edges. Wrap in cheesecloth or a tea-towel. Boil for 1 hour. Pour melted butter over the dumpling, grate sugar over the top and serve.

Prune Pudding

From a quart of milk, take a few spoonfuls, and beat in six yolks of eggs and three whites, four spoonfuls of flour, a little salt, and two spoonfuls of beaten ginger. Then by degrees, mix in all with the milk, and a pound of prunes. Boil it an hour tied up in a cloth, and pour melted butter over it. Damsons done this way, eat full well as prunes. (*John Farley, 1783*)

Serves 4–6

6 EGG YOLKS PLUS 3 WHITES
4 OZ (I CUP) FLOUR
½ TSP SALT
I TSP GROUND GINGER
I–I½ PT (2½–3 CUPS) MILK
I LB PRUNES, STONED AND CHOPPED
2 OZ (4 TBS) MELTED BUTTER

Beat the egg yolks and whites together. Add the flour gradually with the salt and ginger.

Then add milk a little at a time until you have a thick batter. Stir in the prunes. Tie the mixture in a floured cloth. Boil for 1 hour. Serve covered with melted butter.

Bread, Biscuits and Cakes

Bath Cakes

Take a pound of butter, and rub it into an equal weight of flour, with a spoonful of good barm. Warm some cream, and make it into a light paste. Set it to the fire to rise, and when you make them up, take four ounces of caraway comfits, work part of them in, and strew the rest on the top. Make them into a round cake, the size of a French roll. Bake them on sheet tins, and they will eat well hot for breadfast, or at tea in the afternoon. (John Farley, 1783)

Makes about 24 cakes

½ PT (I CUP) MILK
3 TBS SUGAR
3 OZ (6 TBS) BUTTER
3 OZ (2 PACKAGES) YEAST
½ PT (I CUP) WARM WATER
1½ LB (5–6 CUPS) FLOUR
I TBS SALT
I–2 TBS CARAWAY SEEDS

Scald the milk and add the sugar and butter. Dissolve the yeast in the warm water. Mix the flour and the salt in a bowl; make a well in the centre of the flour and add the milk mixture, the yeast and water and the caraway seeds and blend well. Knead for 10 minutes, until smooth and elastic, adding more flour if needed. Leave to rise in a warm place until the volume has doubled and then punch the dough down. Shape it into buns. Place these on a greased biscuit sheet and leave to rise, again until they are double the size. Bake at 375° (Mark 5) for 15–20 minutes.

Eighteenth-century Biscuits

Common Biscuits

Makes 20–30 biscuits

8 OZ (I CUP) SUGAR
¾ LB (2½ CUPS) SELF-RAISING FLOUR
4 EGGS
2 TBS ROSEWATER

Mix the sugar and flour in a bowl. Beat the eggs and rosewater together until smooth, add to the flour mixture and blend to make a stiff dough. Add a little more rosewater if it is too stiff. Drop by heaped tablespoonfuls into greased muffin tins and bake at 350° (Mark 4) for 15 minutes or until golden.

Naples Biscuits

Naples biscuits are the foundation for many desserts, including that wicked English temptation, trifle! The two most popular biscuits in the eighteenth and nineteenth centuries seem to have been these and Savoy biscuits or fingers. Their Italian names probably came from the fact that the Italians were noted confectioners and owned pastry shops the world over. The word 'biscuit', which means 'twice-cooked', was originally applied to unfermented dough that had been twice baked to make it dry enough to keep for some time.

Add 2 oz (½ cup) flour to the basic recipe to make a stiff dough that is not sticky. Roll out on a floured board 1 inch thick. Cut into oblongs about 8 inches long, 3 inches wide and 1 inch thick. Put on greased or paper-covered baking sheets and bake as above.

Cake Biscuits

I TSP ORANGE ESSENCE
2 TBS SHERRY
I TBS ORANGE PEEL, GRATED
I TSP CINNAMON
I OZ (¼ CUP) GROUND ALMONDS

Add these ingredients to the basic recipe.

Ratafia Biscuits

Ratafia is a name for the essence of bitter almonds and for a liqueur, now quite rare, that is flavoured with the kernels of various fruits such as peaches, apricots, or plums. The French used to talk of '*un doigt de ratafia*' – only a finger, as it is very strong. These little biscuits would be served with ratafia or with sack (sherry).

1 OZ (¼ CUP) GROUND ALMONDS
½ TSP BITTER ALMOND ESSENCE OR RATAFIA
   ESSENCE
1 TBS ROSEWATER

Add these ingredients to the basic recipe.

Spanish (or Sponge) Biscuits

Add 1 tablespoon grated lemon peel to the basic recipe.

Gingerbread Cakes

Mrs Glasse is so well known, and her book *The Art of Cookery* exists in facsimile, so we have not given the original recipe, but you can find it on page 310 of the facsimile edition. This is a very satisfactory recipe to give your child to make before a childrens' party at home, or when packing home-made delights as Christmas presents. It is so easy to do and you have all the fun of rolling up the little balls or making different shapes with them, the delicious smell of spices from the oven and the bonus of being able to concoct no less than eighty-two little treasures from such a small, inexpensive list of supplies.

1 LB (3½ CUPS) FLOUR
1 TSP SALT
1 TBS GROUND GINGER

148

1 TSP NUTMEG
6 OZ (¾ CUP) BUTTER
6 OZ (¾ CUP) CASTER (CONFECTIONER'S) SUGAR
¾ LB (1 CUP) TREACLE (OR CORN SYRUP)
2 TBS CREAM

Sift the flour, salt and spices together. Cream the butter, add the sugar, and beat until light and fluffy. Put the treacle and cream together in a saucepan and heat until the treacle melts, stirring to blend the two together. Add the flour mixture and the treacle/cream mixture alternately to the butter and sugar, stirring lightly. Allow to stand for 10 minutes. Form 1-inch balls of this mixture in your floured hands and put them on a floured baking sheet. sheet. Bake at 350° (Mark 4) for 10–15 minutes or until they are a spicy golden brown.

Portugal Cakes

In the seventeenth century Charles II brought home a Portuguese bride, which possibly accounts for the spate of such delicacies as Portugal broth, Portugal water and these Portugal cakes.

Take a pound of fine flour, and mix it with a pound of beaten and sifted loaf sugar. Then rub it into a pound of pure sweet butter till it be thick like grated white bread. Then put to it two spoonfuls of rosewater, two of sack, and ten eggs. Whip them well with a whisk, and mix into it eight ounces of currants. Mix all well together, butter the tin pans, and fill them about half full, and bake them. (*John Farley, 1783*)

Makes about 12

14 OZ (3 CUPS) FLOUR
1 LB (2 CUPS) SUGAR
6 OZ (1½ CUPS) CURRANTS
½ LB (1 CUP) SWEET BUTTER
1–2 TBS ROSEWATER
4 EGGS

Mix the flour and the sugar together; cut in the butter until the mixture is crumbly. Stir in the currants. Add the eggs, lightly beaten, and

the rosewater, and blend. Pour into buttered crumpet or small cake tins until they are half filled. Bake at 350° (Mark 4) for 10–15 minutes.

Saffron Cake (or Bread)

(*Hannah Glasse, 1747*)

This makes a delicious tea-bread or cake; it keeps beautifully for a week or ten days and makes excellent toast.

⅛ TSP SAFFRON
2 TBS ROSEWATER
1 TSP SUGAR
4 TBS LUKEWARM WATER
½ OZ (1 PACKAGE) YEAST
1¼ LB (4½ CUPS) FLOUR
4 OZ (½ CUP) SUGAR
½ TSP GROUND CLOVES
½ TSP GROUND MACE
1 TSP CINNAMON
2 EGGS
¼ PT (½ CUP) MILK
2 OZ (¼ CUP) BUTTER, SOFTENED

Put the saffron and rosewater into your smallest saucepan, heat them together, stirring to dissolve the saffron, and let them infuse off the heat. Dissolve the sugar in the water, add the yeast and stir until blended. Prove the yeast. (Let the mixture stand in a warm place until the mixture bubbles; this is your proof that the yeast is active; if it doesn't bubble, buy new yeast.)

In a large bowl combine 1 pound (3½ cups) of the flour, the sugar and the spices. Make a well and into it break the eggs, then add the yeast mixture, the rosewater, butter and saffron, and lastly the milk, blending them all together. Knead them in the bowl until the dough is smooth and elastic, adding flour as needed. Cover the bowl with a dishcloth and leave to rise in a warm (not hot) place for about 45 minutes. Punch down and put into an 8-inch spring-form tin, or shape into a football. Let it rise till it is double in size and bake at 350° (Mark 4) for 40 minutes. Leave to cool on a rack.

Shrewsbury Cakes

Beat half a pound of butter to a fine cream, and put in the same weight of flour, one egg, six ounces of beaten and sifted loaf sugar, and half an ounce of caraway seeds. Mix them into a paste, roll them thin, and cut them round with a small glass or little tins; prick them, lay them on sheets of tin, and bake them in a slow oven. (John Farley, 1783)

Makes about 24
½ LB (1 CUP) BUTTER, SOFTENED
4 OZ (½ CUP) CASTER (CONFECTIONER'S) SUGAR
1 EGG, BEATEN
1 TBS CARAWAY SEEDS
9 OZ (2 CUPS) FLOUR

Soften the butter and beat it with the sugar until fluffy. Add the beaten egg and the caraway seeds. Stir in the flour, adding enough to make a stiff paste, and roll the dough out on a floured cloth. Cut into circles with a tumbler. Bake on a greased pan at 350° (Mark 4) for 10 minutes. Serve hot, preferably spread with raspberry jam and topped with vanilla ice cream.

Sugar Puffs

Beat the whites of ten eggs till they rise to a high froth. Then put them in a marble mortar or wooden bowl, and add as much double refined sugar as will make it thick; then rub it round the mortar for half an hour, put in a few caraway seeds, and take a sheet of wafers, and lay it on as broad as a sixpence and as high as you can. Put them into a moderately heated oven half a quarter of an hour, and they will look as white as snow. (John Farley, 1783)

Makes 8–10
4 EGG WHITES
6 OZ (¾ CUP) CASTER (CONFECTIONER'S) SUGAR
1 TBS CARAWAY SEEDS

Beat the egg whites until frothy. Gradually add the sugar, a tablespoon at a time, and sprinkle

in the caraway seeds a few at a time to distribute them evenly throughout. Continue beating until the mixture is stiff and glossy and forms unwavering peaks. Put a sheet of brown paper on a baking sheet and spoon dollops of the mixture onto it. Bake at 300° (Mark 2) for 30–40 minutes, or until dry. Serve with fruit fools, mousses or ice cream.

These early meringues are quite delicious and can be flavoured in various ways:

Chocolate Puffs
Fold 4 tablespoons cocoa into the beaten egg whites and make the puffs about the size of an old sixpenny piece.

Almond Puffs
Fold 2 ounces (½ cup) ground almonds into the beaten egg whites and make the puffs slightly larger.

Lemon Puffs
Fold 1 tablespoon grated lemon peel and 1–2 tablespoons lemon juice into the beaten egg whites and make the puffs quite small, the same size as chocolate puffs.

For Icing Fine Cakes

Take the whites of eight or nine eggs, and beat them up into snow; put to them a little orange-flower or rose water; put to them double refined sugar, and beat it mighty well together till it comes glutinous and thick; if you please you may put in a little musk and amber prepared: and when your cakes are baked, lay your icing over thick with a thin knife, and just harden it in the oven; you may put over citron, or what you please. (Charles Carter, 1730)

4 EGG WHITES
4 OZ (8 TBS) CASTER (CONFECTIONER'S) SUGAR
1 TSP ORANGE-FLOWER WATER OR ROSEWATER
A PINCH OF MUSK OR AMBER

Beat the egg whites until soft peaks form. Add

the sugar gradually and beat until stiff peaks form. Fold in the orange water and musk. Spread over the cakes. Transfer to a 300° (Mark 2) oven to set.

Sauces

Egg Sauce
(*John Farley, 1783*)

2 HARD-BOILED EGGS
¼ LB (½ CUP) BUTTER

Chop the egg yolks and whites separately. Melt the butter and mix with the chopped eggs. Serve over boiled cauliflower, salt cod or smoked haddock, or plain boiled cod or haddock.

Bechamel Sauce
(*John Farley, 1783*)

¼ LB (1 CUP) MUSHROOMS, SLICED
2 OZ (4 TBS) BUTTER
1 SLICE HAM, CHOPPED
4 SPRING ONIONS (SCALLIONS), CHOPPED
¼ TSP GROUND MACE
1 CLOVE, CRUSHED
3-4 CORIANDER SEEDS, CRUSHED
1 TBS FLOUR
¼ PT (½ CUP) STOCK
½ PT (1 CUP) CREAM
1 TBS LEMON JUICE

Cook the sliced mushrooms in the butter with the ham, spring onions and spices. Cook very gently in a covered pan, stirring occasionally, for 5-10 minutes. Then stir in the flour, the heated stock and the cream, which you have just brought to the boil. Simmer gently for 10-15 minutes, stirring occasionally. Add salt, pepper and lemon juice to taste. Serve with boiled poultry.

White Sauce
(*John Farley, 1783*)

When English 'white sauce' is mentioned, it usually makes one think of nursery glue, station hotels, boarding-house food. Here is the true eighteenth-century version and what a delightful surprise it is! Try it over boiled chicken, with plain rice and a little stewed celery.

A FEW CHICKEN NECKS AND FEET
A PIECE OF SCRAG END OF VEAL OR VEAL BONES
   WITH SCRAPS OF MEAT
½ TSP GROUND MACE
6 BLACK PEPPERCORNS
1 ANCHOVY
1 STALK CELERY
1 SLICE LEMON PEEL
3-4 SPRIGS MIXED HERBS (PARSLEY, THYME,
   SAVORY)
2 PINTS (5 CUPS) WATER
1 OZ (2 TBS) BUTTER
2 TBS FLOUR
1 TBS PICKLED MUSHROOMS, CHOPPED (*see p.* 198)
   OR ½ TSP MUSHROOM KETCHUP (OPTIONAL)
2 EGG YOLKS
¼ PT (½ CUP) CREAM
¼ TSP GRATED NUTMEG

Put the chicken pieces, veal, mace, peppercorns, anchovy, celery, lemon peel and herbs in a deep pot with the water. Bring to the boil and boil until the contents have reduced to about ½ pint (1 cup). Strain and thicken with the butter and flour, mixed to a paste and stirred in small pieces over gentle heat. Cook for 4-5 minutes, stirring often, until the sauce is perfectly smooth. Then add the pickled mushrooms and the egg yolks, beaten with the cream. Season with grated nutmeg and cook for a few moments without allowing it to boil.

Mushroom Sauce
(*John Farley, 1783*)

¼ LB (1 CUP) MUSHROOMS, SLICED
2 OZ (4 TBS) BUTTER

¼ TSP SALT
¼ TSP GROUND MACE
½ PT (1 CUP) CREAM
1 EGG YOLK
A SQUEEZE OF LEMON JUICE

Cook the sliced mushrooms in the butter in a
covered pan with the salt and the mace. Stew
very gently for 10 minutes, then pour in the
cream, which you have just brought to the boil
and beaten into the egg yolk. Cook gently,
without allowing it to boil, until the sauce is
slightly thickened. Add the lemon juice, season
with pepper to taste, and serve with boiled
chicken.

Sauce for Capon

(*An Eighteenth-century Kitchen*)

1 TBS FLOUR
¾ PT (2 CUPS) LIGHT ALE
5 OZ (½ CUP) PICKLED CUCUMBERS, DICED
½ LB (½ CUP) CHICKEN LIVERS, FRIED IN BUTTER
   AND CHOPPED

Brown the flour in an iron frying-pan. Put into
a blender with the ale and blend. Transfer to a
saucepan with the cucumbers and chicken
livers, adding seasoning to taste. Reheat.
Serve with chicken.

Sauce for Boiled Chicken

(*An Eighteenth-century Kitchen*)

½ LB (½ CUP) COOKED SPINACH, CHOPPED
½ LB (½ CUP) COOKED SORREL, CHOPPED
4 TBS VINEGAR
2½ OZ (½ CUP) COOKED GOOSEBERRIES OR SEEDLESS
   GRAPES
1 OZ (2 TBS) BUTTER

Boil all the ingredients together, add sugar,
salt and pepper to taste and put through a
food mill. Return to the pan. Heat through and
stir in the butter. Serve over carved chicken.

Pickles and Preserves

Elder Buds

Having procured your elder buds, which must be gathered when they be about the size of hop buds, put them into a strong salt and water for nine days, and stir them two or three times a day. Then put them into a pan, cover them with vine leaves, and pour on them the water they came out of. Set them over a slow fire till they be quite green, and then make a pickle for them of allegar, a little mace, a few shallots, and some ginger sliced. Boil them two or three minutes, and pour it upon your buds. Tie them down, and keep them in a dry place for use. (John Farley, 1783)

½ PT (1 CUP) ELDER BUDS

Pickle
A PINCH OF ALLUM (sold in pharmacies)
½ PT (1 CUP) VINEGAR
2–4 TBS SUGAR
1 TSP MACE
4 SHALLOTS, CHOPPED
4 SLICES GINGER

Bring all the pickle ingredients to the boil. Put the buds in a sterilized preserving jar, pour over the pickle mixture and seal.

Pickled Grapes

Let your grapes be of their full growth, but not ripe. Cut them into small bunches, fit for garnishing, and put them into a stone jar with vine-leaves between every layer of grapes. Then take spring water, as much as will cover them, put into it a pound of bay salt, and as much white salt as will make it bear an egg. Dry your bay salt and pound it, before you put it in and that will make it melt the sooner. Put it into a pot and boil and skim it well; but take off only the black scum. When it has boiled a quarter of an hour, let it stand to cool and settle; and when it be almost cold, pour the clear liquor on the grapes, lay vine-leaves on the top, tie them down close with a linen cloth, and cover them with a dish. Let them stand twenty-four hours, then take them out, lay them on a cloth, cover them with another, and let them dry between the cloths. Then take two quarts of vinegar, a quart of spring water, and a pound of coarse sugar. Let it boil a little, skim it very clean as it boils, and let it stand till it be quite cold. Dry your jar with a cloth, put fresh vine-leaves at the bottom and between every bunch of grapes, and on the top. Then pour the clear of the pickle on the grapes, fill your jar that the pickle may be above the grapes, fill your jar that the pickle may be above the grapes, and having tied a thin piece of board in a piece of flannel, lay it on the top of the jar, to keep the grapes under the liquor. Tie them down with a bladder and a leather, and when you want them for use, take them out with a wooden spoon. (John Farley, 1783)

2 LB GRAPES, CUT INTO BUNCHES
16–20 VINE LEAVES
2 OZ (½ CUP) BAY SALT
2 PT (5 CUPS) WATER

½ PT (1 CUP) VINEGAR
2 OZ (½ CUP) SUGAR
¼ PT (½ CUP) WATER

Arrange the grapes and half the vine leaves in alternate layers in a preserving jar. Bring the salted water to the boil to dissolve the salt. Skim and leave to cool. Pour over the grapes and leave for 24 hours.

Drain and rinse. Bring the vinegar, sugar and water to the boil, then leave to cool. Arrange the grapes and the remainder of the leaves in layers in a clean, sterilized jar. Pour the pickling mixture over and seal the jar.

Pickled Nasturtiums

Seeds
Put your nasturtium berries, which must be gathered soon after the blossoms be gone off, into

cold salt and water, and change the water for three days successively. Make your pickle of white wine vinegar, mace, nutmeg, sliced shallots, peppercorns, salt, and horseradish. Your pickle must be pretty strong, as you must not boil it. When you have drained your berries, put them into a jar, and pour the pickle to them.
(*John Farley, 1783*)

¼ PT (½ CUP) WINE VINEGAR
2–4 TBS SUGAR
½ TSP MACE
¼ TSP NUTMEG
2 SHALLOTS
2 PEPPERCORNS
I TSP SALT
I TSP HORSERADISH
½ PT (I CUP) NASTURTIUM SEEDS

Bring all the pickling ingredients to the boil and then pour, boiling, over the seeds. Allow to cool, then spoon into a sterilized jar and seal.

Leaves
Keep them a few days after they are gathered; then pour boiling vinegar over them – they will not be fit to eat for some months, but by then are finely flavoured and by many preferred to capers.

The pickled leaves, chopped, can indeed replace capers for flavour, though not for appearance. A better idea is to stuff them as you would vine leaves, with rice, nuts, herbs and a little forcemeat if you wish. Nasturtium leaves are very common in English gardens and suitable recipes can be found in books on Greek cooking.

Preserved Peaches
(*Hannah Glasse, 1747*)

6 MEDIUM PEACHES
6 CLOVES
¾ PT (2 CUPS) WATER
¾ LB (I½ CUPS) SUGAR
A 2-INCH PIECE OF CINNAMON STICK
¼ TSP GROUND MACE
⅓ PT (¾ CUP) BRANDY

Drop the peaches in boiling water for 2–5 minutes. Drain and peel. Stick a clove in each one. Combine the water, sugar, cinnamon and mace in a saucepan; bring to the boil and cook until the sugar has dissolved. Add the peaches and cook for 5–10 minutes or until tender. Place the peaches in a wide-mouthed jar; stir the brandy into the syrup and pour over the fruit. Leave to cool.

Cover tightly and leave to stand in a cool place for about 3 days before using.

THE NINETEENTH CENTURY

THE NINETEENTH CENTURY opened with the Napoleonic Wars and short harvests, and the peace of 1815 brought no real relief. A fiery Chartist, Feargus O'Connor, wanted to establish a colony near Rickmansworth where each labourer would have 'three acres and a cow'; but his dream was never realised. In the working man's cottage fresh meat was a luxury seen only on Sunday, when there might be enough for a meat pudding or a 'toad' encased in a suet crust and boiled; butter had to be replaced with home-made lard flavoured with rosemary leaves. In 1845 a potato disease and a poor corn harvest brought England to its closest brush with revolution.

Revolt was sidestepped by the repeal of the Corn Laws in 1846, which lowered the price of bread and other staples. The next twenty years brought radical changes with huge industrial growth and the development of scientific farming that outstripped the experimental methods of the previous century. Now even the most conservative farmer could double his crop with chemical fertilizers; and there were all sorts of new ways to feed cattle during the winter with cottonseed, linseed cakes and similar concentrates. Ironically, the situation was finally turned around by the increasing imports. The demand for cheap food and the growth of free trade ended English agriculture based on wheat for ever. Within fifty years most of the English were eating food they had bought, rather than grown or reared themselves – the greater part of it imported.

The rise of free trade was only partly due to the growing Empire. Greater Britain had begun in 1583, when Sir Humphrey Gilbert took possession of Newfoundland. The first permanent colony in America – Jamestown, Virginia – had been founded in 1607. During the seventeenth century the English had imposed their authority on several Caribbean islands, in the Honduras, West Africa and India. In the eighteenth century they had extended their sway to Canada and India, also taking over Ceylon; they had acquired the Cape of Good Hope and sent their first convict settlers to Australia. Now, in the nineteenth century the Empire expanded in Africa, and also took in New Zealand, Fiji, North Borneo and much of Malaya.

It was trade that had led the early settlers to India, and Indian spices, Indian-grown tea (for tiffin – the colonial tea break) and such dishes as kedgeree became a permanent feature of English cooking. And trade or no, returning travellers must have brought recipes back from the colonies. In the nineteenth century also Australian beef began to arrive, posing a few problems in the kitchen. All meat varies in flavour and texture depending on the food the animal eats and the exercise it has taken. Thus steers reared in Australia were tougher than homegrown English cattle.

Much more influential to the Englishman's table were Mr McAdam's method of surfacing roads and the advent of the railway locomotive: as England became industrialized, feeding became heavily involved with transport. No one knew much about keeping large quantities of food fresh while shipping it about the nation. The problem of wheat spoiling on the way was finally solved by the roller mill which was brought from the Continent in 1870. The mill removed both the bran and the germ, producing flour which looked whiter, kept better and – of course – had lost most of its nutritious substances. Today health-food enthusiasts are trying to remedy this lack with stoneground flour and pure wheat germ. Bread became even whiter when millers started bleaching the flour.

Pasteurization of milk came to England in 1890 – not so much to save people from disease but to enable the milk to make a long railway journey without going sour. Replacement of the old sailing ships by steam trawlers improved the fish supply. As early as 1820 George Dempster, a London fishmonger, got a high price for a Scotch salmon transported that way; and salted and pickled herrings gave way to fresh fish as the railroads improved. Technology nearly destroyed the oysters, though; dredging was so reckless that by 1840 the beds were nearly exhausted and only the very rich could afford oysters. Artificial oyster beds turned out to be the answer.

Near the end of the eighteenth century a Frenchman, Nicholas Appert, developed a method of preserving food in glass bottles by heat-processing. In 1807 Thomas Saddington, an Englishman, made his addition with a similar method of preserving fruit. It was Bryan Donkin, of the Dartford Iron Works, who brought to England the use of tinned metal containers for this purpose, in about 1813. The bad reputation that English cooking has acquired may be credited in part to these men. The French complain – justifiably – that the English pour their sauces out of bottles instead of making them in saucepans. Harvey's, Lea & Perrins, A-1 and Roberts sauces, as well as anchovy essences and mushroom ketchups, can be used discreetly to flavour a sauce, but in the nineteenth century the housewife with no domestic help began to splash the sauce right out of the bottle and to tip the vegetables out of a tin. The medieval English love of spices and seasonings became bastardized in bottled flavouring and tinned meat. Coffee essence, excellent for flavouring a coffee mousse, was constantly used to make one of the worst drinks in the world when mixed with hot water and a splash of 'evap' (evaporated milk), a travesty that reached its nadir during the Second World War.

Refrigeration, technology which really is a boon to cooks, was given a boost towards the end of the century by the invention by a Scottish immigrant in Australia, James Harrison, of the first practical ice-maker, based on an earlier model by Jacob Perkins. The first load of refrigerated meat was transported from Australia to England in 1880 on the ss *Strathleven*.

One nineteenth-century achievement was the 'typical English breakfast'. The leisured were content with coffee and rolls or toast; and some old-fashioned people stuck to the eighteenth-century repast of cold meat, cheese and beer; but the majority of the English adopted the copious meal of porridge, fish, bacon and eggs, toast and marmalade that has appeared on English breakfast tables for a hundred years.

The old supper disappeared, to be replaced by luncheon in the middle of the day, which began as a glass of wine and a biscuit and developed into a full meal. City merchants and bankers had been lunching at taverns or clubs since John Farley's time. Late supper at 9 or 10 became tea or coffee with cakes or a punch or light wine.

Dinner, having settled at about 7, underwent a change too. Since medieval times the courses of an English dinner had been spread out on the table, all the dishes of one course at the same time. Some old charts of table setting suggest that the dishes, called 'removes', near the ends of the table could be replaced, but the others were stationed there until the course ended.

Prince Puckler-Muskau, writing in the 1820's, described his reaction to the English table, where the soup was in the plates when the guests sat down: 'After the soup is removed, all the covers are taken off, every man helps the dish before him and offers some of it to his neighbours . . . If he wishes for anything else, he must ask across the table; or send a servant for it – a very troublesome custom in place of which some of the most elegant travelled gents have adopted the more convenient German and French fashion of sending the servants round with the dishes'. Though the Prince's hosts may not have adopted it, the French system of service had in fact been gaining ground in England since the days of Charles II. By the 1850s it had replaced the Saxon style completely and for some reason was known as 'dinner *a la Russe*'. Guests were often seated at a number of small tables, instead of a single vast one, and servants would bring the dishes round. Between meals the chairs were ranged around the walls of the room with their back legs behind a chair rail. This custom accounts for the fact that most English chairs of the period have very plain back legs.

Another foreign fashion taken up early in the century was the custom of an aperitif before dinner, in imitation of the Russian or Scandinavian habit of taking a little vodka or aquavit before meals. Fashions in wine changed little; champagne, introduced in England in 1650 but long a rarity, became popular with the rich. The French, who themselves drank a sweeter wine, developed dry champagne in response to English taste. The fad for champagne made all carbonated drinks popular.

New vegetable luxuries arrived in nineteenth-century England. North Carolina sent the tomato, or 'love apple', which was first grown as a decoration; and vegetable marrows and pumpkins appeared.

Mayhew tells us of the rich variety of foods hawked on the streets of London in the mid-nineteenth century: oranges, nuts, watercress, pickled whelks, oysters; hot eels, sheeps' trotters, pea soup, fried fish; ham sandwiches; hot green peas, kidney puddings, boiled meat puddings; beef, mutton or kidney pies; baked potatoes; tarts of rhubarb, currants, gooseberries, cherries, apples, damsons, cranberries and mince pies; plum duff (dough) and plum cake; other cakes, gingerbreads, Chelsea buns, muffins and crumpets; candy rocks, sticks, lozenges and hard-bakes; cough-drops and horehound; ices and ice creams; tea, coffee, coca, ginger beer, lemonade, Persian sherbert; hot elder cordial or wine; peppermint water; curds and whey; water; rice milk; and milk straight from the cow in the parks.

The nineteenth century in England produced one of the strangest cookery books ever written. In 1817 Dr William Kitchiner published *Apicius Redivivus, or The Cook's Oracle*, which gave not only his own recipes but a three-century list of other texts he had consulted. Some of his recipes do not need modern adaptations, but he writes with such glorious pretension that his work is very amusing.

Dr Kitchiner had his own ideas about the dinner hour, refusing admittance to guests who were tardy. Here is one of his invitations:

Dear —
   The honour of your company is requested, etc. The first specimen will be on the table at five o'clock precisely, when the business of the day will immediately commence.

He never asked less than four or more than eight guests, and he locked the door at five o'clock. His motto was 'Better never than late'. When he gave his weekly *conversazione*, a sign placed over the mantelpiece read: 'Come at Seven, Go at Eleven'. 'In "The Affairs of the mouth" ' he wrote, 'the strictest punctuality is indispensable – the GASTRONOMER ought to be as accurate observer to Time as the ASTRONOMER. The Least Delay *produces fatal and irreparable Misfortunes*'.

One of Dr Kitchiner's quirks was to give his recipes quaint names. One called 'Tewadiddle' turns out to be a pint of beer with a tablespoon of brandy, a little grated nutmeg or ginger and a roll of very thin lemon peel. (The American working man's version of this is called a 'Boilermaker'.)

The most fascinating thing about one nineteenth-century cooking tome – Kettner's *Book of the Table*, published in 1877 and thought to be the work of Auguste Kettner, a Soho restaurateur – is that its author later turned out to be E. S. Dallas. He claimed to have published the work as Kettner's because the recipes were Kettner's and because his name would help to sell the book. Dallas was born in Jamaica in 1828, of Scottish descent. He spent his childhood in England and studied philosophy at Edinburgh. At first a critic for the *Edinburgh Guardian*, he wrote a book on poetics and for a time thought about entering the Church, but later wrote anonymously for *The Times* and became the leading reviewer of his day.

It is possible that his work on the *Book of the Table* was paid for in meals at Kettner's restaurant, for his fortunes declined sadly before his death at fifty-one in 1879. The book was a quick success in 1877 and was reprinted by Kettner's restaurant in 1912. It is organized like an encyclopaedia and is a marvel of research, literary allusions and practical cooking advice. But his excursions into philology lead him into some strange arguments based on very shaky premises. He contends, for instance, that the term 'galantine' is derived from the use of galingale. In fifteenth-century cookery manuscripts there are indeed many references to both, but they rarely coincide. Later scholars trace the word through Middle English and Old French to the Latine *gelata*, something jellied. But anyone who loves both words and eating will find Dallas's work a rich dish.

Another resounding nineteenth-century culinary name was that of Alexis Soyer. When George III's infirmities forced him to surrender his throne in 1811 to his son George, then Prince of Wales, the Prince had already incurred his father's anger by his extravagant living. His years as Prince Regent (which saw the creation of the Brighton Pavilion in 1784), until he was crowned George IV in 1820, were years of high living and great French chefs in England – Carême, Escoffier, Ude, Francatelli and Soyer.

A French chef in the classic tradition, Soyer spent most of his professional life in England. Born in Neaux-en-Brie, he was the son of a shopkeeper. He was sent off to be a chorister at the cathedral but amused himself by tolling the call to arms on the cathedral bells, which got him expelled and apprenticed to a chef. No one ate out in nineteenth-century France before the Revolution except travellers who dined at inns or taverns; meals were not served as a form of entertainment. After his five-year apprenticeship, Soyer's first job was in one of the earliest restaurants: M. Douix on the Boulevard des Italiens; but when the Revolution came Soyer fled to London, and attained a good deal of celebrity in his first job. He obtained a commission equal to his organizational genius when he was asked to design the kitchen quarters for the

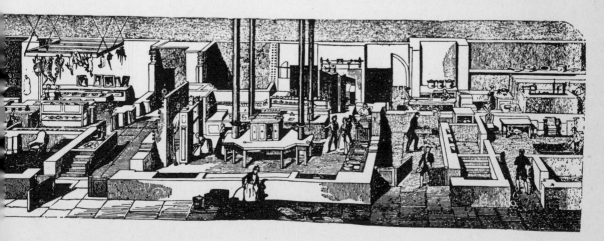

new Reform Club. Every convenience was provided for the food (though not for the staff) and tours of the kitchen with Soyer himself as guide became fashionable.

The breakfast for two thousand produced by Soyer at the Reform Club for Queen Victoria's coronation in 1837 was a triumph. His reputation soared. His book *The Gastronomic Regenerator* (1846) is a text for professionals, not for the housewife; but some of the recipes he created for the Reform Club became, in their Frenchness, as English as any roast beef ever carved. His famous '100-Guinea Dinner' in honour of Prince Albert included turtles, quails, capons, turkeys, chickens, grouse, pheasants, partridges, plovers, woodcocks, snipes, pigeons, larks, ortolans, etc., garnished with truffles, cockscombs, mushrooms, crawfish, olives, asparagus, sweetbreads, quenelles, green mangoes, and 'a new sauce'.

In 1847 Soyer – apparently on his own initiative – decided to soothe the strain between Louis-Philippe in his homeland and Victoria, his adopted queen. He sent off a bouquet ten feet high framed in Christmas greens and centered with twenty-two head of winged game. Soon after this sally, he received his first public commission and designed the galleys for a Royal Navy ship bound for Cuba. His marvellous design for a 17' × 8' kitchen became a model for future shipbuilders. The same year, he also intervened in Irish famine relief, raising money and opening a soup kitchen in Dublin, where he sold his new book, *The Poor Man's Regenerator*, for a penny a copy. The recipe he used at the soup kitchen was said to be tasty, but its economy is a far cry from the cullis he prepared for his richer clients; it was published in the London papers:

Put three ounces of dripping into a two-gallon pan with ¼ pound of boneless beef cut to ½-inch slices. Set over a coal fire and stir until lightly browned. Have then ready washed the peelings of two turnips, fifteen green leaves of celery and the green parts of two leeks (the whole of which are usually thrown away). Cut these into small pieces, throw them into the saucepan and stir occasionally for another ten minutes; then add half a pound of flour and half a pound of pearl barley, mixed well together. Add two gallons of water, three ounces of salt, a quarter of an ounce of brown sugar, stir occasionally till boiling, and simmer gently for three hours.

The Modern Housewife, Soyer's next book, was not a success; his was not middle-class cooking; but these were the years of bottled sauces, and in 1848 he had a hit with Soyer's Lady and Gentleman's Sauce – followed by Soyer's Relish and a bottled fruit juice called Soyer's Nectar. Opening his own establishment in 1849, he drew aristocratic crowds to unfashionable Charing Cross Road with demonstrations of his Patent Magic Stove. Still flaming in expensive restaurants, the stove drew this notice in *The Times*: 'At the ball given on the evening of her Majesty's departure from Castle Howard, one of the greatest attractions was afforded by M. Soyer's cooking various dishes on the supper tables with his Lilliputian Magic Stove, surrounded by Lords and Ladies not a little surprised to see, for the first time, part of their supper *cooked in a ballroom*'.

After his final departure from the Reform Club in 1850 Soyer opened a lavish restaurant, but Londoners were not ready for it, and it failed. To raise money for the London poor he gave a grand ball and demonstrated another new machine – the gas stove. And, to the poor, he

SOYER'S SAUCE,

offered his latest book, *A Shilling Cookery for the People*. His most ambitious work, *The Panathropheon, or The History of Cooking through the Ages*, a discussion of food from Roman times to his own, was published in 1855. During the Crimean War he revolutionized the kitchens of Florence Nightingale's hospital at Scutari; he did the same for the army at Balaclava. This finally ruined his health and led to his death at 49, while he was still trying to improve army food.

Despite the ubiquitous and enterprising Soyer, most cookery books were still written by women in the nineteenth century. Eliza Acton, who first made her reputation as a poet, is now better remembered for her *Modern Cookery In All Its Branches*, first published in 1845 (with a 'last edition' in 1905). Excerpts were published in 1968 as *The Best of Eliza Acton*.

Eliza was the eldest daughter of a brewer and grew up at Bramford Hall in Suffolk. She began to publish poetry in her mid-twenties. As an unmarried woman, living a life of her own and writing poetry, she was a living affront to Victorian convention. Still, when her cookery book came about at the suggestion of her publishers (who had seen a rival's profits from Maria Rundell's book) it was an instant success with middle-class housewives who would never be able to make their way through Soyer's highflown recipes. Well organized, clear and really useful, her book sold steadily for years until displaced by that almost supernatural force, Mrs Beeton.

The Book of Household Management by Isabella Beeton, first serialized in the *Englishwoman's Domestic Magazine* and published in book form in 1861, is possibly the most widely known of English cookery books, partly because it is still in print and partly because a facsimile of the first edition, published in 1968, sold in America as well as England, thus introducing the redoubtable Mrs Beeton to transatlantic readers.

Isabella Mary Mayson was the eldest of twenty-one children – siblings and step-siblings – and her step-father, Henry Dorling, was the manager of the grandstand at Epsom in its heyday. The family actually lived in the grandstand and Isabella must have been her mother's chief aide in household management. Just before Derby Day in 1855 Isabella was married to Samuel Beeton, an ineffectual publisher whose best property was the *Domestic Magazine*, a righteous sheet whose unrelenting theme was 'womanliness'. Young Mrs Beeton was soon indentured as an editor on her husband's magazine. She proved to be a prodigious editor, and her *Book of Household Management*, with its coverage of every detail of family life, has proved a rich lode for social historians. It does provide some lively reading, but as an English cookery book its reputation has been somewhat overrated. Many of the recipes are not English at all, even though they are offered under Anglicized names – some of them misspelt. Still, hers is the first cookery book to include colonial dishes – Indian and Australian – and it has seasonal menus with lists of dishes keyed to the available produce.

Overwork and childbearing wore Mrs Beeton out; paying her husband's debts and bearing her fourth child led to her death in 1865 at the age of twenty-nine. But her book now over one hundred years old, carries on her good work.

If middle-class Victorian households were preoccupied with food, imagine the eating that went on at the Palace. At Buckingham Palace there were daily deliveries of two hundred necks of mutton; two hundred and fifty shoulders of lamb; pheasants, partridges, quail, plovers, woodcock and snipe – all pouring in from the royal estates. Fruits and vegetables came in huge quantities, along with prawns, oysters, Italian truffles and enormous hothouse grapes that were used as decoration. Queen Victoria regularly served her guests quail stuffed with pâté de foie gras, surrounded by oysters, truffles, prawns, mushrooms, tomatoes and croquettes. She considered the Welsh lamb the most tender and would have no other served.

Ten or twelve courses were the rule at both luncheon and dinner; to refresh the palate (and, in theory, to aid the digestion) sorbets were served half way through, a survival of the *doucetye* that rounded out the courses in medieval times. These were often flavoured with port, brandy or rum. Here is a menu served at Buckingham Palace in 1899; consommé, thick soup, salmon, cutlets of chicken, saddle of lamb, roast pigeons, green salad, asparagus in white sauce, a fruit *macédoine* in champagne, ham mousse and lemon ice cream. The sorbets were served just before the roast pigeons. At Balmoral the next year Victoria's guests dined on pheasant

ST. JAMES'S PALACE, 1789.

Her Majesty's Dinner
TUESDAY, 26TH MARCH, 1889.

———— POTAGES. ————
A la Tortue. ———— Au Printanier à la Royale.

———— POISSONS. ————
Le Saumon, sauce homard et persil.
Les Rougets à l'Italienne.

———— ENTRÉES. ————
Les Petits pâtés de Homard à l'Indienne.
Les Kromeskys de Volaille.
Les Côtelettes d'Agneau aux pois.

———— RELEVÉS. ————
Les Poulardes à la Toulouse.
Les Jambons au Madère.
Roast Beef. ———— Roast Venison.

———— RÔTS. ————
Les Cailles. ———— Les Gelinottes..

———— ENTREMÊTS. ————
Les Asperges à la sauce. — Les Salades à l'Italienne.
Les Poudings à la Combacerès.
Les Eclairs au Chocolat et Café
Les Gelées Mosaïque. — Les Ramequins au Parmesan.

WINDSOR.

DRINK Cadbury's Cocoa

MAKERS TO THE QUEEN

Pure Refreshing.

consommé, cauliflower pureé, cod with egg sauce, trout, ham mousse with cucumbers, chicken, roast beef, braised cauliflower, roast turkey, haricot beans, sprouts, a sweet and a savoury. On the side table were hot and cold poultry, tongue, beef and salad. The servants had the same meal as the guests; but they also expected to eat most of the contents of the side table. On this occasion they were said to be disappointed, since the queen's guests had devoured the beef and poultry too.

Before the invention of the electric or gas refrigerators the iceman was a household familiar. In London ice was bought from the tradesmen, but the queen considered it inferior. At Balmoral and Windsor Castle ice was therefore chopped from ponds on the estate in winter and stored for use in the royal iceboxes, with the Royal Iceman in charge.

The Royal Chef was M. Ménager. In 1890, when apprentices lived at the palace and received £15 per year, Ménager drew a salary of £400 with an additional £100 living allowance. Every morning at 8 am he arrived at the palace in a hansom cab, wearing a top hat and frock coat as badges of his office, ready to provide meals for the queen and her guests, there or at any of the royal residences or on the royal yacht – where meals had as many courses as they did on dry land.

Prince Albert had brought a *gemütlich* German touch to English menus – the popularity of Christmas pudding owes a good deal to him – but after his death in 1861 the queen felt so deprived that she turned towards a blandness – almost a prudery – that deprived English cooking of its spicy, sensual character. As Victoria grew older it is said that she ate less and less. Rumour has it that towards the end of her life her breakfast consisted of a single boiled egg – served, however, in a gold egg cup and eaten with a gold spoon, while two Indian servants stood behind her chair should she wish for anything else. Meanwhile the rest of the family fed on a more robust English breakfast, including egg dishes, bacon, grilled trout or turbot, cutlets, chops or steak of beef, roast woodcock, snipe or chicken. But the queen's Indian cooks and servants ate the spiciest meals at the palace. They killed all their own sheep and poultry and prepared their own flavourings, grinding the spices for curries between two large stones. A part of the household was given over entirely to their use. Curiously, Edward VII, though a great gourmet, dispensed with their services when he came to the throne.

Soups

Scotch Barley Broth

(*Traditional*)

This is a very inexpensive dish and the perfect
lunch for a cold day in the country. You will
not need a main dish. It keeps quite well in
the refrigerator but as the barley swells you
must add extra liquid when it is reheated.
Puréed in a blender, it makes excellent baby
food. The same recipe, but with lamb ribs
instead of the beef, makes a delicious sort of
Irish stew.

Serves 6–8

1–2 LB SHIN OF BEEF
2 BEEF MARROW BONES
½ LB (1 CUP) PEARL BARLEY
5 PINTS (12½ CUPS) WATER
2 MEDIUM ONIONS, SLICED
1 LARGE PARSNIP, PEELED AND SLICED
1 BAY LEAF
2 CARROTS, SLICED
4 STALKS CELERY, SLICED

Combine the water, beef, bones and barley in
a deep pan and bring to the boil. Skim. Add
the onions, parsnip and bay leaf. Simmer for
2½ hours. Add the carrots and celery and then
simmer until the carrots are just tender.

Remove the meat, cut it into small pieces
(or shred it) and stir it into the soup.

Oxtail Soup

(*Traditional*)

Serves 6–8

3 OXTAILS (DIVIDED AT THE JOINT BY YOUR
   BUTCHER)
8 CLOVES
2–3 ONIONS
1 TBS SALT
¼ TSP ALLSPICE
¼ TSP BLACK PEPPER

Leave the oxtails to soak in warm water. Put
cloves, onions, allspice, black pepper and the
tails (which can be fried) into an 8-pint (20
cup) braising-pan. Cover with cold water. Bring
to the boil, skimming carefully until no more
scum rises. Then cover tightly and set on a
low flame for about 2 hours, until the meat is
tender and comes away from the bone easily.
When the meat is done, take it off the bone and
cut it into small pieces. Skim the broth and
strain it through a sieve. Replace the meat.

Pea Soup with Bacon and Herbs

(*from an unsigned manuscript, 1811*)

Serves 8–10

1 PT (2½ CUPS) OLD PEAS, SHELLED
4 PT (10 CUPS) STOCK
¼ LB PIECE BACON
1 LB SORREL, COARSELY CHOPPED
2 ENDIVES, SLICED
1½ OZ (½ CUP) SPEARMINT, CHOPPED
2 OZ (4 TBS) BUTTER
4 TBS (¼ CUP) CREAM

Boil the peas in the stock with the bacon,
sorrel, endives and spearmint. When the peas
are tender, remove the bacon and chop it into
small dice. Put the soup through a food mill
or coarse sieve and return it to the cleaned
pan. Reheat, stir in the butter and cream, add
a little pepper and then put back the chopped
bacon. Pour into a tureen and serve.

Eel Soup

Kitchiner recommends serving this soup in
the following manner:
*Then put your soup on in a clean stew-pan, and
have ready some little square pieces of fish fried
of a nice light brown, either eels, sole, skate or
plaice will do; the fried fish should be added
about ten minutes before the soup is served up.
Forcemeat balls are sometimes added.*
(*Adapted from William Kitchiner, 1817*)

Serves 6–8

3 MEDIUM ONIONS, QUARTERED
½ OZ (1 TBS) BUTTER
1 TBS OIL
½ EEL, BONED BUT NOT SKINNED, CUT INTO
    CHUNKS (OR SOLE, OR SKATE)
2 TBS FLOUR
2 SCANT PT (4–5 CUPS) WATER
2 TSP SALT
6 PEPPERCORNS
1 TBS LEMON BALM, CHOPPED
½ TSP ALLSPICE
2 TBS PARSLEY, CHOPPED
½ TSP TARRAGON, CHOPPED
1 TSP GRATED LEMON PEEL
1 TBS CAPERS, CHOPPED
FRESHLY GROUND PEPPER TO TASTE
FINELY CHOPPED PARSLEY FOR GARNISH

Toss the onions in the butter and oil until
golden. Dust the eel pieces in the flour.
Brown lightly in the fat. Add the water, salt
and herbs and cook gently, uncovered, for
30 minutes. Remove the eel pieces. Reduce
the stock to thicken. Replace the eel, rewarm
and serve. A little finely chopped parsley
sprinkled on top improves the rather drab
colour, but the taste needs no improving.
Serve in small bowls, as the soup is so rich
that you should not serve too much at a time.

Shellfish Soup

(*Traditional*)

Serves 6–8

1 LARGE POTATO, PEELED AND CHOPPED
1 ONION, CHOPPED
1 OZ (2 TBS) BUTTER
2 PT (5 CUPS) SHELLFISH
2½ PT (6 CUPS) FISH STOCK OR WATER
1 BUNCH PARSLEY, CHOPPED
1 BAY LEAF
2 CLOVES GARLIC, MINCED
1 PINCH SAFFRON
1 BUNCH EDIBLE SEAWEED, FRESH OR DRIED
½ PT (1 CUP) THICK CREAM
FINELY CHOPPED PARSLEY

Cook the chopped potato and onion gently in
the butter for a few minutes. Add the shellfish,
the stock or water, the herbs, garlic and saffron
and the seaweed. Bring to the boil and simmer
until cooked. Remove the fish from their shells
and return to the soup. Reheat, stir in the
cream and sprinkle with chopped parsley.

Smoked Fish Soup

(*Traditional*)

Serves 4–6

2 ONIONS, CHOPPED
2 CARROTS, CHOPPED
1 LARGE POTATO, PEELED AND CHOPPED
1 OZ (2 TBS) BUTTER
1½–2 LB SMOKED HADDOCK, CUT INTO 4 PIECES
2½ PT (6 CUPS) FISH STOCK OR WATER
1 BUNCH PARSLEY
1 BAY LEAF
1 SPRIG THYME
½ PT (1 CUP) THICK CREAM
½ TSP GRATED NUTMEG

Cook the chopped onions, carrots and potato gently in the butter. Add the fish, stock or water and the herbs and simmer until cooked. Remove the bones from the fish and return the flaked flesh to the pan. Reheat. Stir in the cream and sprinkle with grated nutmeg.

Eggs

Buttered Eggs

This way of cooking eggs, so that they are in contact with a hot surface for very short periods, makes creamy scrambled eggs, of a very even consistency and very light, which seem to remain creamy for longer than usual on a sideboard. They are excellent with smoked salmon.

Beat 4 or 5 eggs, yolks and whites together, put ¼ lb fresh butter in a basin, then set it in boiling water, stir it till melted, then pour it with the eggs into a saucepan, keep the basin in one hand and hold the saucepan in the other over a slow fire, shaking it one way as it begins to warm, pour the mixture into the basin, and then back again, hold it over the fire, stirring it constantly in the saucepan, and pouring it frequently into the basin to prevent it curdling,

and to mix the eggs and butter till they are boiling hot. Serve on toasted bread, or use it as a sauce to salted fish and red herrings.
(*Ann Miller, 1845*)

Serves 2

4–5 EGGS
¼ LB (½ CUP) BUTTER
PEPPER AND SALT

Follow the original recipe exactly, adding pepper and salt to taste.

Ox-eyes

(*Mrs Beeton, 1861*)

The average cost of this dish in 1891 was 2d a head. It can also be made with thick, drained yoghurt instead of cream, in which case some chopped chives, chervil, dill, tarragon or parsley are delicious mixed with it.

Serves 6

6 SLICES BREAD, ¾ INCH THICK
BUTTER FOR FRYING
6 TBS (⅓ CUP) SOUR CREAM
6 EGGS

Garnish
3 LB (1½–2 CUPS) FRESH SPINACH, BOILED,
   DRAINED AND CHOPPED
PARSLEY OR WATERCRESS

Cut the bread into 3-inch circles with a biscuit or doughnut cutter, then cut 1½-inch holes in the centre. Fry the bread until it is a very light golden colour. Butter a dish, lay the croutons in it, and spoon 1 tablespoon of sour cream into each hole. Put a raw egg on top of the cream and sprinkle with pepper and salt. Bake at 350° (Mark 4) for 10–15 minutes, until the whites are set but not browned. Garnish with parsley or watercress and the cooked spinach, tossed in butter.

Fish

Cod Pie

(*Domestic Cookery, 1843*)

Serves 4

1½–2 LB PIECE OF COD
¼ TSP PEPPER
2 TSP SALT
¼ TSP GROUND NUTMEG
1 OZ (2 TBS) BUTTER, CUT INTO SMALL PIECES
4 TBS (¼ CUP) FISH STOCK, MADE FROM COD
    TRIMMINGS
½ LB PASTRY

Sauce
1 OZ (2 TBS) BUTTER
2 TBS FLOUR
4 TBS (¼ CUP) FISH STOCK
¼ PT (½ CUP) CREAM
½ TSP GRATED LEMON PEEL
¼ TSP GROUND NUTMEG
½ PT (1 CUP) OYSTERS (OPTIONAL)
2 TBS PARSLEY, FINELY CHOPPED (OPTIONAL)

Take a piece from the middle of a small cod
and salt it well for 12 hours. The next day
wash it, season it with pepper, salt and
ground nutmeg and put it in a baking dish.
Cover with little pieces of butter and fish stock.
Cover with the pastry and bake for 20–30
minutes at 375° (Mark 5).

While it is cooking make the sauce. Melt
the butter, blending with the flour, and add
the stock and cream. Flavour with the grated
lemon peel and nutmeg and simmer until
thickened. Oysters may be added, or chopped
parsley. When the pie is cooked, cut a hole in
the centre of the crust and pour the sauce
through a funnel.

Cornish Bream Pie

(*Ann Miller, 1845*)

Serves 2–3

1 BREAM
2 OZ (1 CUP) BREADCRUMBS
2 TBS PARSLEY, FINELY CHOPPED

4 TBS MIXED FRESH HERBS, CHOPPED
½ LB PASTRY
2 TBS GRATED CARROT (OPTIONAL)
2 TBS CARROT JUICE (OPTIONAL)

The original recipe says that you should bone
the fish and then fold it over a stuffing of
breadcrumbs, parsley and herbs. But it is
easier to have it filleted by the fishmonger and
to put the stuffing between the layers of
fillets. Finely grated raw carrot adds a
surprisingly pleasant taste and a crunchy
texture to the stuffing. Moisten with fresh
carrot juice.

Line an 18-inch pie dish with pastry. Pre-
bake it for 10 minutes at 400°. Make layers of
fish with breadcrumbs, herbs and grated
carrots in between. Season and moisten with
carrot juice. Cover with the pastry lid and bake
at 375° for 20–25 minutes or until the crust is
golden.

Grilled Mackerel

*Clean a fine large mackerel, wipe it in a dry
cloth, and cut a long slit down the back; lay it
on a clean gridiron, over a very clear, slow fire;
when it is done on one side, turn it; be careful
that it does not burn; send it up with fennel
sauce; mix well a little finely chopped fennel and
parsley, seasoned with a little pepper and salt, a
bit of fresh butter, and when the mackerel is
ready for the table, put some of this into each
fish. (Ann Miller, 1845)*

Serves 4–6

4–6 MACKEREL
4 OZ (½ CUP) MELTED BUTTER
4 SPRIGS FENNEL, CHOPPED
4 SPRIGS PARSLEY, CHOPPED
½ TSP SALT
⅛ TSP PEPPER

Grill (broil) the fish, basting them with half
the melted butter. Heat the remaining butter
in a saucepan, add the chopped herbs and
seasonings and cook for 2–3 minutes. Pour
the sauce over the fish and serve.

Mackerel Pie

(*Ann Miller, 1845*)

This dish is particularly good if you use fennel and gooseberry sauce instead of water. It will look pretty if you cut out a mackerel shape from the pastry scraps and stick it to the lid of the pie with cold water. The lid can also be glazed with a wash of egg yolk beaten with a little water.

Serves 2–3

2 MACKEREL
¼ TSP GRATED NUTMEG
4 TBS WATER OR FENNEL AND GOOSEBERRY SAUCE
   (*see p.* 192)
½ LB PASTRY
1 EGG YOLK

Clean the fish, cut off the heads and tails and cut each into three pieces crossways. Lay in a pie dish with a seasoning of pepper, salt and the nutmeg and the water, or sauce. Cover with a pastry lid and bake for about 30 minutes.

A Maigre Fish Pie

(*William Kitchiner, 1817*)

Serves 6

1½ LB PASTRY

Forcemeat
6 OZ (1 CUP) LOBSTER OR CRAB
1 SLICE BREAD, MOISTENED IN FISH STOCK
2 HARD-BOILED EGG YOLKS, MASHED
2 SHALLOTS, CHOPPED
1 TSP PARSLEY, FINELY CHOPPED
2 EGG WHITES, BEATEN

¾ LB HALIBUT, WHITING, SOLE OR BASS, FILLETED
1 ONION, THINLY SLICED
2 HARD-BOILED EGGS, THINLY SLICED
2 TBS FRESH HERBS, CHOPPED
½ TSP MUSHROOM KETCHUP
1 TSP PREPARED MUSTARD
¼ TSP PEPPER
1 EGG YOLK

Court-bouillon
2 PT (5 CUPS) WATER
4 PEPPERCORNS
1½ TBS SALT
1 SMALL ONION, SLICED

Roll out half the pastry and line a dish with it, reserving the rest for the lid. To make the forcemeat, put the lobster or crab into the blender with the moistened bread. Blend, mix with the egg yolks, shallots and parsley, then season with salt and pepper. Beat the egg whites until stiff but not dry and fold into the mixture.

Make the court-bouillon by bringing all the ingredients to the boil and simmering them for 15 minutes. Add the fish fillets and simmer gently for a further 2–3 minutes. Remove the fish but continue to boil the liquor until it reduces. Skin the fillets and flake them.

Spoon a thick layer of forcemeat into the pastry-lined dish. Lay the flaked fish, onion, eggs and chopped herbs on top. Mix ¼ pint (½ cup) of the reduced fish stock with the mushroom ketchup, mustard, salt and pepper in a cup and pour over the fish. Cover with the pastry lid and make some slits in the top. Paint with egg yolk. Bake at 350° (Mark 4) for 30 minutes.

Fried Sole

. . . An hour before you intend to dress them, wash them thoroughly, and wrap them in a clean cloth to make them perfectly dry, or the breadcrumbs will not stick to them.

Prepare some breadcrumbs by rubbing some stale bread through a colander.

Beat the yolk and white of an egg well together, on a plate, with a fork, flour your fish to absorb any moisture that may remain, and wipe it off with a clean cloth; dip them in the egg, on both sides all over, or, what is better, egg them with a paste-brush; put the egg on in an even degree over the whole fish, or the

*breadcrumbs will not stick it to even, and the
uneven part will burn to the pan. Strew the
breadcrumbs all over the fish, so that they cover
every part, take up the fish by the head, and
shake off the loose crumbs. The fish is now
ready for the frying pan.*

*Put a quart or more of fresh sweet olive-oil, or
clarified butter, dripping, lard or clarified
drippings; be sure they are quite sweet and
perfectly clean (the fat ought to cover the fish);
what we here order is for soles about ten inches
long; if longer cut them into pieces the proper
size to help at table; . . . when you send them to
table, lay them in the same form they were
before they were cut, and you may strew a little
curled parsley over them; . . . fry the thick
parts a few minutes before you do the thin, you
can by this means, only fry the thick part enough,
without frying the thin too much.*

*Set the frying pan over a sharp and clear fire,
watch it, skim it with an egg slice, and when it
boils, i.e., when it has done bubbling, and the
smoke just begins to rise from the surface, put in
the fish; if the fat is not extremely hot, it is
impossible to fry fish of a good colour, or to keep
them firm and crisp.*

*The best way to ascertain the heat of the fat,
is to try it with a bit of bread as big as a nut;
if it is quite hot enough the bread will brown
immediately. Put in the fish, and it will be
crisp and brown, on the side next to the fire, in
about four or five minutes; to turn it, stick a
two-pronged fork near the head, and support the
tail with a fish-slice, and fry the other side
nearly the same length of time.*

*When the fish are fried, lay them on a soft
cloth near enough to the fire to keep them warm;
turn them every two or three minutes, till they
are quite dry on both sides, this common cooks
commonly neglect.*

*There are several general rules in this recipe
which apply to all fried fish, we have been very
particular and minute in our directions, for,
although a fried sole is so frequent & favourite a
dish, it is very seldom brought to table in
perfection. (William Kitchiner, 1817)*

2 SOLES
2 EGGS, BEATEN
2 CUPS BREADCRUMBS
SALT AND PEPPER TO TASTE
OIL FOR FRYING

Season the fish inside and outside; dip it in the
beaten egg then roll it in breadcrumbs. Heat
the oil in a frying pan until very hot. Cook the
fish until golden and tender, about 5 minutes on
each side.

Dressed Crab

*To dress a crab cold;
Extract meat from a cold crab, remove every
particle of shell. Keep the dark creamy substance
separate, in different bowls. Mix both well with
the same dressing, but separately.
(Ann Miller, 1845)*

Serves 2
2 CRABS

Dressing
1 TSP PREPARED MUSTARD
2 TBS CHILI, TARRAGON OR PLAIN VINEGAR
CAYENNE PEPPER
6–8 TBS OLIVE OIL

Garnish
3 HARD-BOILED EGG YOLKS
4 TBS PARSLEY, FINELY CHOPPED
¼ TSP CAYENNE PEPPER

Remove the meat from the shells carefully
and separate the white from the dark. Mix
each with half the dressing, and fill the
carefully cleaned shells with white meat at the
sides and the dark creamy meat down the
centre. Garnish the latter with a sprinkling of
2 hard-boiled egg yolks and the parsley, both
very finely chopped. Sprinkle 1 riced hard-
boiled egg yolk and the cayenne on the white
meat. Stick four little claws in the corners and
a fat sprig of parsley under the top of the shell.

Buttered Lobster

Take two lobsters when they are boiled and cold, cut one of the bodies down the middle, take all the meat out of the rest of the shells and the other body. Mince it small, put it in a saucepan, add a glass of white wine, two tablespoonfuls of vinegar, a little grated nutmeg, pepper and salt; let it boil, then have ready half a pound of butter, melted with an anchovy and the yolks of two eggs, beat up and mixed into the butter. Mix all together, shaking the saucepan round till it is quite hot. Lay the body of the lobster in the middle of the dish and the minced lobster round it. (Ann Miller, 1845)

Serves 4
2 BOILED LOBSTERS

Sauce
½ PT (1 CUP) WHITE WINE
1 TBS VINEGAR
1 TSP NUTMEG
¼ TSP PEPPER
1 TSP SALT

2 EGG YOLKS
1 TSP ANCHOVY ESSENCE
1 OZ (2 TBS) BUTTER

Chop the lobster meat. Heat the wine, vinegar, nutmeg and seasonings. Beat the egg yolks in a bowl. Beat in the hot liquid and return to the pan. Add the anchovy essence and butter. Put the chopped lobster meat into the pan and heat it through. Toss well together.

Potted Lobster

This must be made with fine hen lobsters, when full of spawn, boil them thoroughly, when cold, pick out all the solid meat, and pound it in a mortar; it is usual to add, by degrees, (a very little) finely pounded mace, black or cayenne pepper, salt, and while pounding, a little butter. When the whole is well mixed, and beat the consistance of paste, press it down hard in a preserving pot, pour clarified butter over it, and cover it with a wetted bladder.
(William Kitchiner, 1817)

Serves 4–6

1 LB LOBSTER MEAT (FRESH OR FROZEN)
6 OZ (¾ CUP) UNSALTED BUTTER
¼ TSP GROUND MACE
¼ TSP GROUND BLACK PEPPER
2 HARD-BOILED EGGS, FINELY CHOPPED
1 TBS PARSLEY OR DILL, FINELY CHOPPED

Chop the lobster meat, reserving the claws for garnish, if available. Add one-third of the butter in small pieces. Pound all together in a mortar or chop with a heavy knife. Add the mace and pepper and mix well together. Add the eggs and the chopped herbs and blend thoroughly. (The eggs make the lobster go further, and also help to lessen the rather salty taste of frozen lobster.)

Pack the paste lightly into an earthenware or china bowl. Melt the rest of the butter, let the sediment sink to the bottom and pour the clarified butter over the lobster in the pot. Arrange the claws round the top in a pattern. Chill until set. Serve as a first course.

Collared Eel

(*William Kitchiner, 1817*)

Serves 2

½ EEL
½ TSP PEPPER
½ TSP SALT
¼ TSP MACE
¼ TSP ALLSPICE
1 CLOVE, CRUSHED
½ OZ (¼ CUP) PARSLEY, CHOPPED
½ TSP THYME
½ TSP MARJORAM
¼ PT (⅔ CUP) VINEGAR
¼ PT (⅔ CUP) WATER

Clean and bone the eel but do not skin it. Mix together the pepper, salt, mace, allspice, crushed clove, parsley, thyme and marjoram. Stuff the eel with this mixture, roll it up and boil it in vinegar and water, salted. When it is cooked, leave it to cool and keep it in the pickling mixture.

Spitchcocked Eels

(*William Kitchiner, 1817*)

Serves 4

½ EEL (ABOUT 14 OZ), BONED AND SKINNED
½ TSP SALT
¼ TSP PEPPER
3 OZ (6 TBS) BUTTER
5 TBS (⅓ CUP) SHALLOTS, CHOPPED
4 TBS (¼ CUP) PARSLEY, FINELY CHOPPED
½ TSP SAGE
½ TSP THYME
2 EGG YOLKS
2 OZ (2 CUPS) FRESH LOW-DIET BREADCRUMBS
  (GLUTEN BREAD)

Cut the eel into 3–4 inch slices and sprinkle with salt and pepper. Melt the butter in a saucepan. Add the shallots and herbs, season and cook for 2 minutes. Remove from the heat and stir in the lightly whipped egg yolks. Dip the fish pieces into this mixture until well coated. Cover with the breadcrumbs. Grill (broil) for about 10 minutes on each side. The crumbs will not necessarily all turn brown, but all will get crisp; it is important to do the grilling fast, so that the whole thing is light, with the crumbs fluffy and crisp; the fish must not overcook and the herb and egg coating should merely heat through, not form a hard crust. Serve with soft boiled rice, lightly tossed in butter but not fried.

One good thing about this dish is that it improves if you do the dipping and breading earlier in the day, as 3 hours or so in the refrigerator crisps the sauce and the crumbs, which might otherwise go a bit soggy. The rice can also be cooked in advance and rewarmed in butter.

Poultry and Game

Season the inside of the bird with pepper and salt. Sew up one end with a darning needle and coarse thread. Fill the bird with the stuffing and sew up the other end. Bring the stock to the boil, put in the chicken, bring back to the boil and then simmer, covered, over low heat for about 1 hour or until tender. Take the bird out of the stock, drain it, pat it dry, rub it with butter and transfer to the oven at 375° (Mark 5) to brown for about 10–15 minutes. While browning the bird, melt the butter over low heat in a small saucepan, then add the mushroom ketchup.

Carve the bird into serving pieces and arrange them on a deep dish. Scoop out the stuffing and spoon it into a mound in the centre; pour the butter mixture over the top and serve.

Boiled Turkey

(*Domestic Cookery, 1843*)

Serves 8–10

1 12–14-LB TURKEY

Stuffing
½ LB (4 CUPS) BREADCRUMBS
1½ OZ (½ CUP) FRESH HERBS, CHOPPED
2 TSP EACH PEPPER AND SALT
1 TSP NUTMEG
1 TBS GRATED LEMON-PEEL
1 PINT (2½ CUPS) OYSTERS OR 1 ANCHOVY, CHOPPED
1 OZ (2 TBS) BUTTER
1 OZ (¼ CUP) SHREDDED SUET
1 EGG

Sauce
3 DOZEN OYSTERS
A PIECE OF MACE
PEEL OF 1 LEMON
2 OZ (4 TBS) BUTTER
1 OZ (4 TBS) FLOUR
JUICE OF 1 LEMON

Davenport Fowl

(*William Kitchiner, 1817*)

Serves 4–6

4 CHICKEN GIZZARDS (BOILED FOR 1 HOUR)
6 CHICKEN HEARTS (BOILED FOR 1 HOUR)
3 CHICKEN LIVERS (BOILED FOR 10 MINUTES)
1½ OZ (½ CUP) FRESH CLARY (A LITTLE LESS IF DRIED) OR SAGE
4 ANCHOVIES, MASHED
2 SMALL (½ CUP) ONIONS, CHOPPED MEDIUM FINE
½ TSP MACE
6 HARD-BOILED EGG YOLKS
1 LARGE CHICKEN OR CAPON
CHICKEN STOCK TO COVER
¼ LB (½ CUP) BUTTER
1 LARGE TBS MUSHROOM KETCHUP

Trim the hard skin off the gizzards and chop them fine with the hearts and liver. Chop the clary or sage finely and put with the anchovies, onion, mace and mashed yolks into a bowl. Mix well and season.

Combine the stuffing ingredients, spoon into the turkey's crop and tie it up. Wrap up the bird in a floured cloth, which makes it very white. Boil in seasoned water until tender and serve with the sauce.

Open the oysters in a hot pan, reserving the liquor. Pass this through a cloth. Put it back in a saucepan with the beards from the oysters, a bit of whole mace and the lemon peel. Meanwhile throw the oysters into cold water, then drain. Strain 1 pint (2½ cups) of the lemon-flavoured liquor and put it into a saucepan with a little white *roux*, made from the butter and flour cooked together, just enough to thicken the stock. Add the oysters, cook over a low flame, without boiling, for a few minutes then add the lemon juice and season to taste.

Turkey Rechauffe

(*Domestic Cookery, 1843*)

Serves 3–4
1 BREAST TURKEY, BOILED
3 OZ (6 TBS) BUTTER
1 OZ (4 TBS) FLOUR
½ PT (1½ CUPS) TURKEY OR CHICKEN STOCK
¼ PT (½ CUP) CREAM
2 TURKEY LEGS (DRUM STICKS), BOILED
½ TSP GRATED NUTMEG

Divide the turkey breast by pulling it apart with your fingers instead of cutting it. Melt two-thirds of the butter in a pan, stir in the flour and slowly add the heated stock and cream until the sauce is smooth and rather thick. Season with salt, pepper and nutmeg. Warm the turkey meat in this without boiling.

Meanwhile, score the turkey legs with a knife, rub them with the rest of the butter, salt and pepper and grill (broil) them until they are slightly scorched. Arrange the breast pieces in the cream sauce round the edge of a heated serving dish. Put the grilled (broiled) drumsticks in the centre and serve. The dark meat should be carved and divided among the guests.

Boiled vegetables, carefully seasoned and still crisp, can be served on the same dish, arranged between the drumsticks and the creamed turkey. Turnips, parsnips, carrots, pearl onions, slices of cooked and peeled marrow (or squash) will add colour and taste. They are all in season at turkey-time – Thanksgiving and Christmas – so this dish can be literally thrown together out of feast-day remains. Try steaming the vegetables in the nesting wicker and bamboo steamers that can be bought in Chinese shops, with the slowest-cooking ones below and the fastest above.

Cornish Hens

(*From an unsigned manuscript, 1811*)

Serves 2–3
Stuffing
3 OZ (½ CUP) RICE
½ PT (1 CUP) CHICKEN STOCK OR WATER
½ OZ (1 TBS) BUTTER
1 SMALL (¼ CUP) ONION, CHOPPED
½ TSP SALT
1–2 JUNIPER BERRIES, CRUSHED

2 2-LB CORNISH HENS OR GUINEA FOWL
3 TBS FLOUR
2 TBS OIL
1 OZ (2 TBS) BUTTER
½ PT (1 CUP) CHICKEN STOCK
½ PT (1 CUP) WHITE WINE
2 SHALLOTS, CHOPPED FINELY

To make the stuffing: cook the rice in the stock or water with the butter, onion and salt; when it is tender, stir in the juniper berries. Sprinkle the birds, inside and out, with pepper and salt and stuff them with the rice mixture. Secure the cavities. Dust the birds with the flour and brown them in a pan with the oil and butter mixed – this will stop the butter from blackening too quickly. Add the chicken stock and wine. Bring to the boil, lower the heat and simmer very gently, covered, for 1 hour. Adjust the seasoning if necessary, add the shallots and simmer for 1 hour longer.

Rabbits Surprised

(*Young Woman's Companion, 1806*)

Serves 3–4
1 YOUNG RABBIT, ROASTED OR BRAISED
½ OZ (2 TBS) BEEF MARROW
4 TBS PARSLEY, FINELY CHOPPED
1 TSP GRATED LEMON PEEL
2 HARD-BOILED EGG YOLKS, CHOPPED
1½ OZ (3 TBS) BUTTER
1–2 TBS CREAM
A LITTLE PAN JUICE TO MOISTEN

Gravy
1 OZ (2 TBS) BUTTER
1 TBS FLOUR
1 PT (2½ CUPS) JUICE OR STOCK, OR A
    MIXTURE OF BOTH

Cut the saddle meat off the cooked rabbit, without cutting the skin more than you can help. Chop finely. Combine with the other ingredients, except for 1 oz (2 tbs) of the butter, and enough juice to moisten it nicely. Put in a saucepan, and cook gently for 5 minutes. Put the mixture back in place on the saddle and re-cover with the skin. As the original says, 'Put them close down with your hands to make them appear like whole rabbits'. Rub with the rest of the butter and grill (broil) until golden (or brown in a hot oven if it is too deep to fit under the grill). Melt the butter, add the flour, cook for 1 minute, then stir in the juice and stock and cook until thick and creamy. Season and serve with the rabbit.

This recipe can also be cooked with a 4-lb chicken, in which case cut away the breasts, and mince as directed above.

My Great-Aunt Charlotte Winchester's White Devil

This was usually served at a shooting breakfast.

2 CHICKEN OR PHEASANT BREASTS, COOKED AND
    SLICED
1 CUP THICK (HEAVY) CREAM, WHIPPED
1 TBS HARVEY'S SAUCE
1 TSP WORCESTER SAUCE

Cut up the previously cooked meat and heat it in the oven. Whip the cream, add a little Harvey's and Worcester Sauce, pour over the meat and put in a casserole dish to brown in the oven. The more frothy the sauce the better.

Meat

Cold Cuts Rechauffe

(*Traditional*)

Serves 3–4
1 SMALL ONION, CHOPPED
1½ OZ (3 TBS) BUTTER
3 TBS FLOUR
½ PT (1 CUP) BEEF STOCK
¼ PT (½ CUP) RED OR WHITE WINE
1–2 SPRIGS THYME
1–2 SPRIGS PARSLEY
1 BAY LEAF
1 TSP SALT
½ TSP PEPPER
6–8 SLICES COOKED MEAT
A SQUEEZE LEMON JUICE
8 FINGERS TOAST
1 LIQUEUR GLASS BRANDY (OPTIONAL)

Brown the onion in butter and add the flour, then the stock and wine. Cook with the herbs and seasonings for 30 minutes. Put the cold slices of meat into a frying-pan and strain the sauce mixture over them. Simmer over the lowest possible heat, just enough to heat the meat. Add a squeeze of lemon juice. Serve the slices of meat on toast, with the sauce poured over the top. A glass of brandy will greatly enrich the flavour of the sauce.

If you are careful not to allow the butter to brown and use white wine, this recipe will make a very fine sauce in which to warm leftover cold chicken, veal, or any other white meat.

A Club Sandwich

(*Traditional*)

This was originally intended for a breakfast dish, but it is also fine for a quick lunch snack.

Serves 1

2 ½-INCH SLICES FILLET OF BEEF
3 SLICES BREAD
2 OZ (4 TBS) MELTED BUTTER
2 TBS PARSLEY, FINELY CHOPPED
Garnish
PARSLEY SPRIGS
CHUTNEY OR RELISH

Cut two ½-inch slices of meat and three of bread, about the same size and shape. Brush the meat all over with the melted butter and butter the bread thickly. Season the meat with pepper and salt and sprinkle with the parsley. Lay one slice of bread between two of meat, with the other two slices of bread on the outside; fasten together with short wooden skewers. Put this sandwich in a hottish oven (375°, mark 5) and cook for 15–20 minutes for rare beef, or 20–5 minutes for medium. Baste frequently with butter. The bread should get crisp and brown. Garnish with sprigs of parsley and serve a little chutney or relish with it.

Meat Balls, called Cecils

To dress beef, called cecils:
Mince any kind of meat, crumbs of bread, a good deal of onion, some anchovies, lemon-peel, salt, nutmeg, chopped parsley, a bit of butter warm, and mix these over a fire for a few minutes; when cool enough, make them up into balls the size and shape of a turkey's egg, with
an egg; sprinkle them with fine crumbs, and then fry them of a yellow brown.
(*Domestic Cookery, 1843*)

Serves 3–4 (16 meat balls)

1½ OZ (½ CUP) FINELY CHOPPED ONION
1 OZ (2 TBS) BUTTER
1 LB (2 CUPS) MINCED (GROUND) BEEF
1 TBS MINCED ANCHOVY
½ OZ (¼ CUP) SOFT BREADCRUMBS
1 TSP GRATED LEMON PEEL
2 TBS CHOPPED PARSLEY
½ TSP SALT
¼ TSP PEPPER
½ TSP NUTMEG
1 EGG, BEATEN
1 OZ (½ CUP) DRY BREADCRUMBS, FOR COATING
1 OZ (2 TBS) BUTTER, FOR FRYING

Brown the onions in the butter. Stir in the remaining ingredients except the breadcrumbs and butter for frying. Shape the mixture into 2-inch egg-shaped balls. Coat with the crumbs and fry in butter until golden.

Toad in the Hole

(*William Kitchiner, 1817*)

This is excellent served with lightly boiled cabbage, well drained and pressed and then lightly tossed in butter with a touch of garlic.

Serves 2–3

2 OZ (4 TBS) BEEF DRIPPING
5 OZ (1 CUP) FLOUR
2 EGGS
½ PT (1 CUP) MILK
1 LB BEEF STEAK, CUT INTO SMALL STRIPS

Pour the dripping into a roasting pan. Mix the flour, eggs and milk and beat with a rotary whisk. Season. Put a quarter of this batter into the roasting pan and cook in the oven at 400° (Mark 6) until it is lightly set. Lay the well-seasoned strips of beef on top of the batter in the pan and cover with the rest of the batter. Bake for 45–50 minutes or until golden. It should be crisp, brown and puffy, like Yorkshire pudding. Cut into wedges and serve.

Bubble and Squeak

For this, as for hash, select those parts of the joint that have been least done; it is generally made with slices of cold, boiled, salt beef, sprinkled with a little pepper, and just lightly browned with a bit of butter in the frying pan; if it is fried too hard it will be hard. Boil a cabbage, squeeze it quite dry, and chop it small; take the beef out of the frying pan, and lay the cabbage in it; sprinkle a little pepper and salt over it; keep the pan moving over the fire for a few minutes; lay the cabbage in the middle of a dish, and the meat around it.
(*William Kitchiner, 1817*)

Serves 4
8–10 SLICES COLD SALT (CORNED) BEEF
1 OZ (2 TBS) BUTTER
¾ LB (2 CUPS) COOKED CABBAGE, CHOPPED

Sauce
1 OZ (2 TBS) BUTTER
2 TBS FLOUR
½ PT (1 CUP) BEEF STOCK
2 TBS MUSHROOM OR WALNUT KETCHUP

Fry the beef until golden and keep warm. Add the cabbage to the frying pan and fry until heated through. Spoon the cabbage into the centre of the dish and arrange the beef round it. Serve, piping hot, with the sauce, made as follows; add the butter to the pan in which the beef was fried; then add the flour and cook a little; pour in the beef stock and cook, stirring, until thickened. Before serving, stir in 2 tbs mushroom or walnut ketchup.

Rump of Beef

(*Young Woman's Companion, 1806*)

Serves 6–8
4–5 LB RUMP OF BEEF
3 TBS FLOUR
4 TBS OIL
6 LARGE OR 12 SMALL SHALLOTS
1 PT (2–3 CUPS) RED WINE
1 PT (2–3 CUPS) WATER OR STOCK
2–3 BLADES MACE

1 TBS LEMON PICKLE, CHOPPED
2 TBS PICKLED WALNUTS, CHOPPED, OR WALNUT KETCHUP
1 TBS BROWNING (OPTIONAL)
CAYENNE PEPPER TO TASTE
1 OZ DRIED MORELS OR DRIED CHINESE MUSHROOMS
¼ LB (1 CUP) FRESH MUSHROOMS
1 OZ (2 TBS) BUTTER
2 TBS FLOUR

Garnish
FORCEMEAT BALLS (*see p.* 136) (OPTIONAL)
HORSERADISH SAUCE (*see p.* 230)

Dust the meat with the flour and brown it in oil on all sides; brown the shallots. Put all in a braising-pan with the wine, water or stock, mace, lemon pickle, walnuts and browning. Season to taste with salt and cayenne pepper. Bring to the boil, then cover tightly, lower the heat and simmer gently for 3 hours. Remove the beef and mace; lay the beef in a deep dish and put in a warm oven, covered, until the sauce is ready.

Skim the fat off the stewing liquid and add the morels and mushrooms. Return to the heat and cook briskly, stirring, while the sauce reduces and thickens. Pour over the beef and serve with forcemeat balls and horseradish sauce.

Beef Olives

(*Traditional*)

Serves 4

2 OZ (4 TBS) BUTTER
¼ LB SIRLOIN OF BEEF, FINELY CHOPPED (GROUND)
1 OZ (½ CUP) STALE BREADCRUMBS

4 OZ ($\frac{1}{2}$ CUP) HAM, FINELY CHOPPED
2 TBS PARSLEY, FINELY CHOPPED
1 TSP THYME
2 TBS CHIVES OR ONION, FINELY CHOPPED
8 THIN SLICES SIRLOIN OF BEEF
1 EGG YOLK
ABOUT 4 TBS ($\frac{1}{4}$–$\frac{1}{2}$ CUP) RICH GRAVY
2 TBS FLOUR
2 OZ (4 TBS) BUTTER
1 PT ($2\frac{1}{2}$ CUPS) BEEF STOCK
6 OYSTERS, CHOPPED (OPTIONAL)

Put the butter in a thick frying-pan and gently
fry the meat, breadcrumbs and herbs, seasoned.
While this is cooking, pound the sirloin
slices very flat and slash them on both sides
with a knife. Put the contents of the pan into a
mixing bowl, combine with the egg yolk and
enough gravy to moisten. Put a spoonful of
this in the centre of each slice of meat, roll it up
and secure with thread or a skewer. Dust the
beef olives with the flour and brown in the
butter, then add the stock. Bring to the boil
and simmer gently for 1 hour. 6 chopped
oysters can be added to the gravy for extra
flavour. Cook covered.

When the olives are put into the gravy,
various vegetables can also be added, such as
small potatoes, carrots or sliced celery; any
vegetable that takes 1 hour to braise will do.

Florendine of Veal

(*From an unsigned manuscript, 1811*)

Serves 6
Forcemeat
2 EGGS
8 OZ (1 CUP) SHREDDED HAM

8 OZ (1 CUP) COOKED VEAL OR CHICKEN, FINELY
  CHOPPED
2 OZ ($\frac{1}{2}$ CUP) SHREDDED SUET
1 SMALL ONION, FINELY CHOPPED ($\frac{1}{4}$ CUP)
$\frac{1}{2}$ OZ ($\frac{1}{4}$ CUP) FRESH BREADCRUMBS
2 TBS PARSLEY, FINELY CHOPPED
1 TBS GRATED LEMON PEEL
1 TSP SALT
$\frac{1}{4}$ TSP NUTMEG OR MACE
$\frac{1}{8}$ TSP CAYENNE PEPPER
1 OZ (2 TBS) LARD

6 THIN VEAL ESCALOPES (SCALLOPS)
A PINCH OF MACE
6 THIN SLICES BACON
2 OZ (4 TBS) BUTTER
1 TBS FLOUR
$\frac{1}{2}$ PT (1 CUP) RED WINE
$\frac{1}{2}$ PT (1 CUP) COOKED (OR TINNED) OYSTERS WITH
  THEIR LIQUOR
$\frac{1}{2}$ LB PASTRY

Egg glaze
1 EGG YOLK
2 TBS MILK

Beat the eggs separately, making sure the
whites are quite stiff. Mix all the other
forcemeat ingredients together, folding in the
whites last. Form into balls and fry in hot lard
until golden brown.

Season the veal escalopes with pepper, salt
and mace. Lay a small slice of bacon on top of
each; roll them up and secure with skewers.
Brown them lightly in half the butter, then
put them into an oven-proof pie dish. Melt
the rest of the butter in a saucepan, stir in the
flour, cook for 1 minute, then add the wine
and oyster liquor, just enough to make a
syrupy sauce. Season well. Pour the sauce into
the pie dish containing the meat and add the
forcemeat balls and the oysters. Cover with a
pastry lid (you may need a funnel under the
centre). Crimp the edge of the pastry. Make a
vent in the lid, or cut out a little piece over the
top of the funnel. Wash with the egg glaze
and bake until the pastry is crisp and cooked.
You can add any left-over sauce, reheated
through the funnel before serving. 30–40
minutes at 350° (Mark 4).

Lancashire Hotpot

(*William Kitchiner, 1817*)

Serves 4

2 LB BEST END OF NECK OF MUTTON
1 OZ (2 TBS) BUTTER OR MUTTON DRIPPING
A LITTLE SUGAR
1 LARGE SPANISH ONION, SLICED
3 SHEEP'S KIDNEYS, SLICED
¼ LB (1 CUP) MUSHROOMS, SLICED
18–20 SHELLED (FRESH) OR TINNED OYSTERS
2 LB ROASTING POTATOES, THICKLY SLICED
1 PT (2½ CUPS) STOCK

Divide the meat into cutlets and trim off the fat and skin. Brown in the fat on both sides; add salt, pepper and sugar. Put them into a deep earthenware baking dish and cover with the onion, sliced into rings, then the kidneys, mushrooms and oysters in layers, with the thickly sliced potatoes neatly arranged to cover everything. Pour the stock over, cover with a tight lid and bake for 2 hours at 350° (Mark 4). Test the meat to be sure it is tender by pricking through the whole thing with a skewer. Then remove the lid for a final 15 minutes, cooking with the oven slightly hotter, to brown the potatoes crisply on top.

My Grandmother's Irish Stew

(*The author*)

Serves 4

3 LB NECK OF LAMB OR 8–10 VERY SMALL SKINNY CUTLETS
6 MEDIUM BOILING POTATOES
2 LARGE ONIONS, SLICED
A SPRIG EACH OF THYME AND PARSLEY
2 PT (5 CUPS) WATER OR LIGHT MUTTON STOCK
3 OZ (½ CUP) PEARL BARLEY

Take all the fat off the meat and cut it, through the bone, into 8–10 pieces, or buy 8–10 small cutlets with the fat trimmed off. (The bones add flavour to the stew.) Peel the potatoes; slice half of them and put these in the bottom of a casserole, leaving the others whole. Add some of the sliced onion and then the pieces of lamb. Season generously with pepper and salt, as lamb needs rather high seasoning. Add the thyme and parsley, the rest of the onion and then the whole potatoes, seasoned. Bring the water or stock to the boil, put in the barley as soon as it starts cooking and pour over the ingredients in the casserole, to come not quite to the top. Put this into the oven at no more than 350° (Mark 4) and bake gently for 1½–2½ hours. Add a little liquid if the swelling barley drinks it up.

Mutton-Ham

Choose a fine-grained leg of wether-mutton, of twelve or fourteen pounds weight; let it be cut ham-shape, and hang two days. Then put into a stew-pan half a pound of bay-salt, the same of common salt, two ounces of salt-petre, and half a pound of coarse sugar, all in powder; mix and make it quite hot; then rub it well into the ham. Let it be turned in the liquor every day; at the end of four days put two ounces more of common salt; in twelve days take it out, dry it, and hang it up in wood smoke a week. It is to be used in slices, with stewed cabbage, mashed potatoes or eggs. (Domestic Cookery, 1843)

Serves 6–8

A LEG OF MUTTON
½ LB (1 CUP) COARSE SALT
½ LB (1 CUP) LIGHT BROWN SUGAR
3 TBS SALTPETRE

I left the mutton-ham in its pickle for about a month, but I think I could safely have left it even longer. As smoking is not possible in modern homes, cook it very gently in simmering, unsalted water for almost 4 hours and then cook various vegetables in the broth from the meat, such as onions, potatoes, carrots, celery, parsley root, turnips and swedes, adding 2 tablespoons very finely chopped parsley and dill.

To Boil Marrow Bones

Special spoons for eating marrow are still to be found in antique shops and markets in England. They look like very long, narrow salt spoons.

Let the large ends of the bones be sawed by the butcher, so that when they are dished they may stand upright; and if it can be done conveniently, let them be placed in the same manner in the vessel in which they are boiled. Put a bit of paste, made with flour and water, over the ends where the marrow is visible, and tie a cloth tightly over them; take the paste off before the bones are sent to table, and serve them, placed upright in a napkin, with slices of dry toasted bread apart. When not wanted for immediate use, they may be partially boiled, and set into a cool place, where they will remain good for many days. (Eliza Acton, 1845)

Large marrow bones, 2 hours; moderate sized, 1½ hours. To keep: boil them 1½ hours, and from ½ to ¾ hour more when wanted for table.

Forcemeat and Stuffings

Forcemeat

(From an unsigned manuscript, 1811)

These little meat balls used to be served as a soup garnish, with 'ragoos' or inside savoury pies.

1 OZ (½ CUP) BREADCRUMBS
4 OZ (½ CUP) BOILED LEAN HAM, FINELY CHOPPED
4 OZ (½ CUP) COOKED VEAL OR CHICKEN, FINELY CHOPPED
1 OZ (2 TBS) BUTTER
2 TBS HERBS, FINELY CHOPPED
1 TSP GRATED LEMON PEEL
¼ TSP NUTMEG
4 TBS ONION, FINELY CHOPPED
1 EGG YOLK
1 EGG WHITE, BEATEN UNTIL STIFF

Combine all the ingredients together in a mixing bowl, adding the egg white last. Make the mixture into small balls and fry in lard or vegetable shortening until golden.

Veal Forcemeat

Chop one pound of lean veal with 1½ of beef suet – a little parsley, two anchovies and a small piece of fat bacon – grate into it a penny loaf – season it with cloves, mace, pepper and salt – beat them together in a morter and make it into balls. (From an unsigned manuscript, 1811)

½ LB (1 CUP) MINCED (GROUND) VEAL
¾ LB (3 CUPS) SHREDDED BEEF SUET
2 TBS PARSLEY, FINELY CHOPPED
2 ANCHOVIES, MASHED
1 SMALL PIECE FAT BACON, CHOPPED
1 OZ (½ CUP) BREADCRUMBS
⅛ TSP CLOVES
¼ TSP MACE

½ TSP PEPPER
I TSP SALT

Combine all the ingredients and shape the mixture into 1-inch balls.

Stuffing for Boiled Fowl

(*Domestic Cookery*, *1843*)

4 OZ (½ CUP) MINCED (GROUND) VEAL
2 OZ (¼ CUP) LEAN HAM, CHOPPED
2 OZ (¼ CUP) BACON, CHOPPED
2–3 TBS MIXED HERBS, CHOPPED
2 OZ (½ CUP) BEEF SUET, GRATED
I ANCHOVY, CRUSHED
A LITTLE CAYENNE PEPPER
2 OZ (I CUP) BREADCRUMBS
3 EGGS, BEATEN

Combine all the ingredients together, season and use to stuff poultry to be boiled. The bird should be boiled or poached in chicken or veal stock, and a sauce made from this stock, thickened with flour and butter and enriched with cream.

Vegetables

Dressed Beetroot

I remember this dish being served very often at home when I was a child, usually with rare roast beef. When they are cold, you can lift the beetroot out of the congealed butter, mash them with a little sour cream and serve them on small croutons with cocktails.

The same recipe, but with the beetroot chopped fine, mixed with thick cream and a dash of Worcester sauce or *sauce diable* and served on fresh toast used to be a popular savoury and is still good as a light supper dish.

Boil your beetroot until tender but still firm, Peel it. Put into a stew-pan with some butter, minced parsley, finely chopped onions, a little crushed garlic, a dusting of flour, a little vinegar, salt and pepper. Simmer fifteen minutes. (*Ann Miller*, *1845*)

Serves 2–3

I LB BEETROOT
2 OZ (4 TBS) BUTTER
4 TBS PARSLEY, FINELY CHOPPED
I MEDIUM ONION, FINELY CHOPPED
I CLOVE GARLIC, CRUSHED
I TBS FLOUR
I TBS VINEGAR
I TSP SALT
¼ TSP PEPPER

Directions as above.

Cabbage and Rice

Shred a large white cabbage, or whatever size you require. Weight it and take the same weight in rice. In a deepish, fireproof casserole dish place a layer of rice, season it and add a few little pats of butter to the surface. Add a layer of cabbage, season and interlard with bits of butter. Repeat the layers according to the quantity wanted. Add enough water to cover, about half a pint for a large cabbage. Season with salt, pepper and a little mace. Bring to a boil and then simmer very gently, covered on top of the stove until both rice and cabbage are tender, about 30 minutes. For knowing this, it is better to make the last layer of rice, as this is less good when overcooked. If the water evaporates too much, add a little more, but it should be boiling and lightly seasoned. (*Ann Miller*, *1845*)

½ HEAD WHITE CABBAGE (ABOUT ¾ LB)
6 OZ (I CUP) RICE
I OZ (2 TBS) BUTTER
½ TSP GROUND MACE

Follow the original recipe.

Stewed Celery

Salsify, Jerusalem artichokes, white onions and skirret (or goat's beard) can all be prepared in this way. Serve with roast meat and poultry or game, or with grilled fish, but never with a dish that already has a sauce.

*Remove the coarse outside leaves, and green
ends of heads of celery. Boil till tender with just
enough water to cover, add a little more if it
evaporates too fast. With a slotted spoon,
remove the celery and keep warm. To the
cooking juices add a little salt, some finely
sliced lemon, a little mace. Thicken with a good
lump of butter rolled in flour, and boil a little.
Beat the yolks of two eggs and grate into them a
teaspoonful of nutmeg. Mix this with a teacupful
of good cream. Add this to the cooking juices off
the fire and then cook over a very low flame
until thickened, be careful not to boil which
would curdle the eggs. Put the celery back in
this sauce, heat through a few minutes and serve.
(Ann Miller, 1845)*

Serves 4

2 LARGE OR 4 SMALL HEADS CELERY
½ PT (1 CUP) WATER OR STOCK
1 OZ (2 BS) BUTTER
2 TBS FLOUR
1 TSP GRATED LEMON PEEL
½ TSP MACE
½ TSP SALT
½ TSP NUTMEG
¼ PT (½ CUP) CREAM
2 EGG YOLKS

Follow the original recipe.

Stewed Cucumbers

(William Kitchiner, 1817)

Serves 4

3 CUCUMBERS, PEELED, SEEDED AND DRIED IN A
    CLOTH
4 TBS FLOUR
12 SMALL WHITE ONIONS, PEELED
1 OZ (2 TBS) BUTTER
2 TBS OIL
½ PT (1 CUP) CHICKEN OR VEAL STOCK
2 TBS PARSLEY, FINELY CHOPPED

Dust the cucumber pieces lightly with flour.
Brown them with the onions in butter and
oil mixed. Season. Add the stock, cover and
simmer for 15 minutes. Sprinkle with finely
chopped parsley.

This dish is really excellent either hot or
cold. Dr Kitchiner tells us that 'the above,
rubbed through a tamis, or fine sieve, will be
entitled to be called "cucumber sauce"'.

To Dress Dandelions like Spinach

*This common weed of the fields and highways, is
an excellent vegetable, the young leaves forming
an admirable adjunct to salad, and much
resembling endive when boiled and prepared in
the same way, or in any of the modes directed
for spinach. The slight bitterness of its flavour is
to many persons very aggreable ; and it is often
served at well appointed tables. It has also, we
believe, the advantage of possessing valuable
medicinal qualities. Take the roots before the
blossom is at all advanced, if they can readily be
found in that state ; if not, pluck off and use the
young leaves only. Wash them as clean as
possible, and boil them tender in a large quantity
of water salted as for sprouts or spinach. Drain
them well, press them dry with a wooden spoon,
and serve them quite plain with melted butter in
a tureen ; or squeeze, chop, and heat them afresh,
with a seasoning of salt and pepper, a morsel of
butter rolled in flour, and a spoonful or two of
gravy or cream. A very large portion of the leaves
will be required for a dish, as they shrink
exceedingly in the cooking. For a salad, take them
very young and serve them entire, or break them
quite small with the fingers ; then wash and
drain them. Dress them with oil and vinegar, or
with any other sauce which may be preferred
with them. (Eliza Acton, 1845)*

Serves 6

2½ LBS DANDELION SHOOTS
4 LBS BUTTER
2 LBS FLOUR
½ TSP SALT
½ TSP PEPPER

An Herb Pie

Pick two handfuls of parsley from the stems, half the quantity of spinach, two lettuces, some mustard and cresses, a few leaves of borage, and white beet-leaves; wash and boil them a little; then drain, and press out the water; cut them small; mix and lay them in a dish, sprinkled with some salt. Mix a batter of flour, two eggs well beaten, a pint of cream, and pour it on the herbs; cover with a good crust and bake.
(*Domestic Cookery, 1843*)

Serves 3–4

½ OZ (½ CUP) PARSLEY
¼ OZ (¼ CUP) SPINACH
2 LETTUCES
¼ OZ (¼ CUP) MUSTARD LEAVES
¼ OZ (¼ CUP) WATERCRESS
¼ OZ (¼ CUP) BORAGE
¼ OZ (¼ CUP) WHITE BEET LEAVES
1 TSP SALT
1 TBS FLOUR
2 EGGS
1 PT (2½ CUPS) CREAM
A 9-INCH PASTRY CASE

Follow the original recipe and bake the pie at 325° (Mark 3) for 35 minutes.

Laver (Seaweed)

This may not seem very practical to us today, but if you happen to have some laver, which grows on rocks near the sea on the west coast of England and Ireland, this is what was done with it almost a century and a half ago. The silver bowl was in a fact a silver saucepan and would not taint the salty seaweed. An enamelled pan will do as well.

Put it in a silver bowl with fresh butter and the juice of a Seville orange well stirred till it is quite hot; vinegar may also be added. Serve with roast meats. (*Ann Miller, 1845*)

Potato Pudding

(*From an unsigned manuscript, 1811*)

This was a delightful surprise when I tried it. It rose like a soufflé and was very light and fluffy. The orange flavour is unexpected and the texture of the nuts made a perfect contrast with the soft potato.

Serves 4

1½ LB POTATOES
4 OZ (½ CUP) BUTTER
2 OZ (¼ CUP) SUGAR
1 TSP SALT
½ TSP GROUND NUTMEG
6 EGGS
4 TBS SHERRY
2 TBS FLOUR
1 TSP ORANGE ESSENCE
2 OZ (½ CUP) SLICED ALMONDS

Peel the potatoes and boil them for 20 minutes, or until tender. Put them through a food mill and purée. Stir in the softened butter, the sugar and seasonings and blend well. Beat the eggs and stir them in. Make a paste from the sherry, flour and orange essence and mix this in too. Finally stir in the almonds. Bake in a soufflé dish for 40–45 minutes at 350° (Mark 4).

In the original recipe, hand-written in the fine copperplate of the time, it is recommended to serve it with a sauce of 'melted butter, sevil orange and sugar'.

Turnip Tops

Turnip tops are not always easy to get in towns, but the beetroot tops that are so often thrown away in supermarkets are delicious, and radish tops have the same peppery taste as their bulb. They make a splendid dish, full of natural minerals, and are improved by the addition of a small lump of butter on top, or a little gravy, once they have been drained.

These are the shoots which grow out (in the Spring) of the old turnip roots. Put them into cold water an hour before they are to be dressed; the more water they are boiled in, the better they will look; if boiled in a small quantity of water they will taste bitter; when the water boils, put in a small handful of salt, and then your vegetables; if fresh and young they will be done in about twenty minutes; drain them on the back of a sieve. (William Kitchiner, 1817)

Tomatoes stuffed with Mushrooms

(Eliza Acton, 1845)

Tomatoes were accepted as wholesome at this period, although until then people were undecided as to whether they were a vegetable or a fruit and they were treated with some suspicion. They were always cooked, however, and never eaten raw.

Serves 8

8 RIPE TOMATOES
I OZ ($\frac{1}{4}$ CUP) FINE BREADCRUMBS
2 TBS BUTTER
A LITTLE CAYENNE PEPPER
A LITTLE GRAVY OR STOCK
$\frac{1}{4}$ LB (I CUP) BUTTON MUSHROOMS

Slice off the tops of the tomatoes and scoop out the insides. Sieve the pulp and mix with the breadcrumbs, the butter, cut into small pieces, cayenne, salt and pepper. Add the mushrooms, which you have previously cooked in a little butter. Fill the tomatoes with the mixture and bake at 350° (Mark 4) for 10–15 minutes.

Desserts

Apple Fritters

Take some of the largest apples you can get, pare and core them, and then cut them into round slices. Take half a pint of ale, and two eggs, and beat in as much flour as will make it rather thicker than a common pudding, with nutmeg and sugar to your taste. Let it stand for three or four minutes to rise. Dip your slices of apple in the batter, fry them crisp, and serve them up with sugar grated over them, and wine sauce in a boat. (Young Woman's Companion, 1806)

Serves 6

6 OZ (I$\frac{1}{2}$ CUPS) FLOUR, SIFTED
3 OZ ($\frac{1}{3}$ CUP) SUGAR
$\frac{1}{2}$ TSP GROUND NUTMEG
2 EGGS, SEPARATED
$\frac{1}{2}$ OZ (I TBS) BUTTER, SOFTENED
6 FL OZ ($\frac{3}{4}$ CUP) FLAT ALE
4 LARGE APPLES
4 TBS ICING (CONFECTIONER'S) SUGAR
8–10 LUMPS SUGAR, GROUND IN THE BLENDER
A LITTLE GROUND CINNAMON (OPTIONAL)

Sift together the flour, sugar and nutmeg. Beat together the egg yolks, butter and ale. Gradually add this to the flour and blend until smooth. Leave to rest for 2 hours before using.

Peel, core and slice the apples into round slices half an inch thick. Toss them in a bowl with the icing sugar. Beat the egg whites until stiff and fold into the batter. Dip the sugared apple slices in the batter and deep fry in oil heated to about 360° for 5–7 minutes, or until golden brown and puffy. Drain well and serve sprinkled with lump sugar, grated in the blender (the texture will be much nicer than granulated sugar). A little cinnamon can also be sprinkled on top. Serve very hot.

"AT HOME" in the NURSERY, or The Masters & Misses Twoshoes Christmas Party

Cranberry and Rice Jelly

Boil and press the fruit, strain the juice, and by degrees mix into it as much ground rice as will, when boiled, thicken to a jelly; boil it gently, stirring it, and sweeten to your taste. Put it in a basin of form, and serve to eat, turned out of the mould onto a dish. Serve with cream.
(*Domestic Cookery, 1843*)

Serves 4

1 LB (4 CUPS) CRANBERRIES
3–4 TBS GROUND RICE
½ LB (1 CUP) SUGAR

Proceed exactly as in the original recipe.

Currant Fool

(*Ann Miller, 1845*)

Serves 4

1 PT (2½ CUPS) RED OR BLACK CURRANTS, STRIPPED
  FROM THE STALK

½ PT (1 CUP) RASPBERRIES
¼ LB SUGAR
1 PT (2½ CUPS) CREAM

Put the currants and raspberries into a stone jar and place in a saucepan of water. Simmer gently for 15 minutes, then allow to cool. When cold add the sugar and cream by degrees, stirring all the time. Strain through a fine sieve and serve in a crystal bowl.

Lemon Patties

(*From an unsigned manuscript, 1811*)

Serves 6–8

½ PT (1 CUP) MILK
2 OZ (1 CUP) BREADCRUMBS
GRATED RIND OF 2 LEMONS
¼ LB (½ CUP) BUTTER, MELTED
3 EGGS, WELL BEATEN
2 OZ (¼ CUP) SUGAR

Pour the boiling milk on to the breadcrumbs in a mixing bowl and leave to cool. Add the grated lemon rind, the melted butter, the beaten eggs and the sugar. Blend well, but lightly. Pour into greased cake-cups and bake at 350° (Mark 4) for 10–15 minutes.

Orange Trifle

(*Ann Miller*, *1845*)

Serves 4–6

8 MACAROONS
4 TBS BRANDY OR SHERRY
I TBS ORANGE JUICE
2 SEEDLESS ORANGES, PEELED AND SECTIONED
½ PT (I CUP) CREAM, WHIPPED
ABOUT 12 GLACÉ CHERRIES

Custard
2 EGG YOLKS
2 OZ (¼ CUP) SUGAR
½ PT (I CUP) CREAM

Soak 8 macaroons for 1 hour in brandy or sherry and a little orange juice, then leave to stand for 10 minutes. Divide the seedless oranges into their natural segments and arrange the oranges and macaroons in circles in a shallow dish. Pour over the custard, made from combining the yolks, the sugar and the cream over gentle heat. Cover with whipped cream and decorate with glacé cherries. Chill until ready to serve.

Chocolate Pudding

(*Mrs Beeton*, *1861*)

Serves 4

¾ PT (2 CUPS) MILK, OR MILK AND CREAM MIXED
¼ LB CHOCOLATE
3 OZ (⅓ CUP) SUGAR
5 OZ (2½ CUPS) BREADCRUMBS
3 EGGS, SEPARATED
A FEW DROPS VANILLA FLAVOURING

Boil the milk with the chocolate and sugar and pour it over the breadcrumbs. Add the egg yolks and flavouring and beat well. Then butter a mould thoroughly. Beat the egg whites to a froth and fold them in. Pour into the greased pudding basin and steam for 1 hour, or until it is firm, and serve with custard or cream sauce flavoured with vanilla.

The Duke's Custard

Drain well from their juice, and then roll in dry sifted sugar, as many fine brandied Morello cherries as will cover thickly the bottom of the dish in which this is to be sent to table; arrange them in it, and pour over them from a pint to a pint and a half of rich cold boiled custard; garnish the edge with macaroons or Naples biscuits, or pile upon the custard some rose-coloured whipped cream, highly flavoured with brandy. (*Eliza Acton*, *1845*)

½ PT (I CUP) BRANDIED CHERRIES, DRAINED
2 OZ (¼ CUP) FINE SUGAR
I PT (2½ CUPS) COLD CUSTARD
10 SMALL MACAROONS OR NAPLES BISCUITS
  (*see p.* 147)
½ PT (I CUP) THICK CREAM
2–3 DROPS COCHINEAL
2 TBS BRANDY

Proceed exactly as in the original recipe.

Lowndes Pudding

(*From an unsigned manuscript*, *1811*)

This is not a steamed pudding but a delicious custard with redcurrant jelly in it.

Serves 4–6

4 EGG YOLKS
4 OZ (½ CUP) SUGAR
I PT (2½ CUPS) CREAM
4 TBS LEMON JUICE
¼ TSP GROUND MACE
SAUCE:
½ LB (½ CUP) REDCURRANT JELLY
2 TSP GRATED LEMON PEEL

Pour the mixed ingredients, well beaten together, into a greased oven-proof mould and bake at 350° (Mark 4), in a dish of hot water, for 15–20 minutes, or until set. Chill. Turn out on to a serving dish and serve with hot, melted currant jelly in a sauceboat. A little grated lemon peel can be added to this sauce.

A Tansy Pudding

Take a quart of cream, 20 eggs (leaving out half the whites), the juice of spinnage and a little tansy, ¼ lb of melted butter and bake it. You must serve it with the juice of Seville-oranges squeezed over it and 1 or 2 cut in sliced and lai'd round the dish.
(From an unsigned manuscript, 1811)

Serves 4

1 PT (2½ CUPS) CREAM
2 TBS SPINACH JUICE
2 TBS TANSY JUICE
3 EGGS PLUS 2 YOLKS
1 OZ (2 TBS) MELTED BUTTER

Beat the eggs and yolks in a bowl, add remaining ingredients and blend well.

Bake in a bain-marie for 20–30 minutes at 350° (Mark 4) until set.

Iced Sweet Pudding

Lay dried cherries or jar raisins ston'd at bottom of mould. On them put slices of stale sponge cake ½ inch thick soak'd in Noyau brandy. Then another layer of cherries & rough broken almonds; over them another layer of Noyau cake & so on till ye mould is 3 parts full.

Then pour in unboil'd custard, lukewarm, to fill ye shape. Cover it hermetically. Bury it in ice & salt 2 hours.

Place ½ pint custard on y ice meantime so as to get quite cold.

When y pudding is to be served up dip it in milk-warm water. Turn it out on an ic'd dish & over it pour the cold custard, on which sprinkle some rough pounded almonds.
(Old Master Cookery Book, 1841)

Serves 4–6

¾ LB (2 CUPS) PITTED CHERRIES (FRESH, FROZEN OR TINNED)
½ LB SPONGE CAKE, SLICED
4 TBS CHERRY BRANDY OR KIRSCH
2 OZ (½ CUP) COARSELY CHOPPED ALMONDS

Custard
1¼ PT (3 CUPS) MILK
6 EGG YOLKS
½ LB (1 CUP) SUGAR
A FEW DROPS OF VANILLA ESSENCE

Put half the cherries in a mould. Cover with half the sponge cake and sprinkle with half the liqueur. Cover with another layer of cherries and then the almonds, reserving 1 tablespoon for the sauce. Arrange the remaining slices of cake on top and sprinkle with the rest of the liqueur. Make the custard and pour two-thirds of it over the mould. Freeze for 3 hours.

Serve with the rest of the cold custard, chilled but not frozen, sprinkled with chopped almonds.

Whim-Wham

(Mrs Dalgairns, 1829)

This is one of the best trifles I have ever tasted but much firmer than most, almost the consistency of a shortcake, as it does not contain the usual custard.

Serves 6–8

½–¾ PT (1½ CUPS) THICK CREAM
2 TBS WHITE WINE
2 TBS ICING (CONFECTIONER'S) SUGAR
PEEL OF 1 LEMON, GRATED
6 NAPLES BISCUITS, (*see p. 147*), OR HARD SPONGE FINGERS THINLY SLICED
½ LB (½ CUP) CURRANT JELLY
1 OZ (¼ CUP) CANDIED ORANGE PEEL, FINELY CHOPPED

Put the cream, wine, sugar and lemon peel into a chilled bowl and whip until stiff. Spoon layers of whipped cream, biscuits and jam alternately in a glass or crystal bowl, ending with a layer of cream. Sprinkle the candied peel on top. Chill overnight.

Walnut Pudding

(From an unsigned manuscript, 1811)

Serves 6

4 EGG YOLKS
4 OZ (½ CUP) SUGAR
1¼ PT (3 CUPS) CREAM
4 OZ WALNUTS, GROUND IN THE BLENDER (1 CUP GROUND WALNUTS)
1 TSP GROUND CINNAMON

2 NAPLES BISCUITS (*see p.* 147), OR HARD SPONGE FINGERS, GRATED

Beat the egg yolks and sugar together in a bowl. Heat the cream and stir it in, in a stream, beating continuously. Add the walnuts, cinnamon and biscuits. Stir over simmering water until thickened. Pour into a bowl and chill.

Sauces

Basic Fish Sauce

This is a good basic fish sauce. It can be used as a stock, and as a fish jelly, without the addition of the flour and butter. Cream can be added to turn it into a savoury cream sauce for fish. Chilled and beaten into mayonnaise, it makes an elegant sauce for masking cold fish and sets to a smooth paste.

Strong fish gravy :
Skin two or three eels, or some flounders; gut and wash them very clean; cut them into small pieces and put into a saucepan. Cover them with water, and add a little crust of bread toasted brown, two blades of mace, whole pepper, sweet herbs, a piece of lemon-peel, an anchovy or two and a teaspoonful of horseradish. Cover close, and simmer; add a bit of butter and flour and boil with the above. (Domestic Cookery, 1843)

2 PT (5 CUPS) WATER
1 EEL, CUT INTO CHUNKS OR 1–1½ LB ANY
    FLAVOURSOME FISH OR FISH HEADS
1 SLICE DARK TOAST
2 BLADES OR ½ TSP MACE
6 BLACK PEPPERCORNS
½ TSP THYME
1 BAY LEAF
1 TSP BASIL
1 TSP TARRAGON
3 SPRIGS PARSLEY
1 TWIST LEMON PEEL
2 ANCHOVIES, CRUSHED
1 TSP GRATED HORSERADISH
1½ OZ (3 TBS) BUTTER
¾ OZ (3 TBS) FLOUR

Combine all the ingredients except the butter and flour in a pan; bring to the boil and simmer quite briskly, uncovered, for 30 minutes. Strain. Melt the butter in the bottom of a saucepan, stir in the flour and cook for 1 minute. Strain in the fish gravy gradually, continuing to stir until the sauce is

the consistency of thin cream. Season with pepper and salt to taste.

Gooseberry Sauce
(Alexis Soyer, 1846)

2 OZ (1 CUP) GOOSEBERRIES
½ PT (1 CUP) MELTED BUTTER SAUCE (*see p.* 53)
⅛ TSP GROUND GINGER
1 TSP LEMON PEEL, GRATED } (OPTIONAL)
1 TBS FENNEL LEAVES, CHOPPED

Top and tail the gooseberries and cook them lightly in a little boiling water. Drain them well and put into the melted butter sauce. Add a pinch of ginger and grated lemon peel if you like, or some minced fennel, and serve with mackerel.

Cockle Sauce
(Ann Miller, 1845)

1 OZ (2 TBS) BUTTER
1 TBS FLOUR
¾ PT (2 CUPS) LIQUID FROM THE COCKLES
1–2 TBS TARRAGON VINEGAR
1 PT (¾ CUP) COCKLES

Make a sauce with the butter, flour and the liquid from the cockles. Add a little vinegar to taste, throw in the cockles and stir until well heated. Season with salt and pepper. Serve with cod or haddock.

Fennel and Gooseberry Sauce
(Ann Miller, 1845)

I have found an almost identical recipe to this nineteenth-century English one in a French book of Arab cooking called *La Cuisine Arabe,* which shows that like so many others this very 'English' dish actually came from the Near East many centuries ago.

½ OZ (½ CUP) FENNEL LEAVES, FINELY CHOPPED
1 OZ (2 TBS) BUTTER
2 TBS FLOUR
¾ PT (2 CUPS) FISH STOCK OR WATER
½ TSP NUTMEG
1 OZ (½ CUP) GOOSEBERRIES

Cook the fennel leaves gently in the butter for
a few minutes. Stir in the flour and blend
with the fish stock or water. Season with
pepper, salt and grated nutmeg; when well
blended stir in the lightly cooked gooseberries.
Reheat and adjust the seasoning. Serve with
mackerel.

Bread Sauce

(*Mrs Beeton, 1861*)

This is traditionally served with roast
pheasant and other game birds, and to
children for Sunday lunch with a beautiful
roast chicken with crisp golden skin. It is a
real carbohydrate feast, for with it are served
crisp roast breadcrumbs and sometimes even
roast potatoes. A steaming sauce bowl of
chicken pan gravy adds the final touch of pure
bliss to this treat.

ABOUT ½ PT (1 CUP) MILK, OR CHICKEN STOCK
    MADE FROM GIBLETS
1 MEDIUM ONION
6 PEPPERCORNS
6 ALLSPICE BERRIES
1 BLADE MACE OR ¼ TSP GROUND MACE
1 OZ (⅔ CUP) BREADCRUMBS
2 TBS CREAM OR MELTED BUTTER

Heat the milk or stock with the onion and
spices; when it is boiling pour over the crumbs.
Cover and leave to infuse for 30 minutes.
Remove the onion and the spices and beat
over gentle heat to remove any lumps. Boil for
3–4 minutes, stirring until quite thick and
smooth, then add the cream or melted butter
and serve immediately. If it has become too
thick, thin with a little extra milk.

Chocolate Sauce

(*Mrs Beeton, 1861*)

2 OZ SEMI-SWEET OR BITTER VANILLA CHOCOLATE
½ PT (1 CUP) CREAM
½ PT (1 CUP) MILK
4 EGGS, SEPARATED
ABOUT 2 TBS SUGAR

Grate the chocolate into the top half of a
double boiler into which you have put
the milk and the cream, and enough sugar to
sweeten. Beat the egg whites to shiny peaks
with 1 tablespoon sugar. Transfer the pan with
the chocolate mixture on the heat and bring to
the boil, stirring. As soon as it boils, put the
pan into the lower half of the double
boiler, containing simmering water. Whisk
in the egg yolks beating until a good froth
rises. Fold in the whites, taking care not to
break up the frothy appearance.

Serve at once before the froth subsides. It is
a sort of chocolate zabaglione and is good with
almost any pudding.

Lemon Sauce (for sweet puddings)

(*Mrs Beeton, 1861*)

This is delicious with fruit tarts where one
longs for a lemony flavour.

3–4 LUMPS SUGAR
1 LEMON
1 OZ (2 TBS) BUTTER
1 TBS FLOUR
4 TBS (¼ CUP) SHERRY
¼ PT (½ CUP) WATER
SUGAR TO TASTE
4 EGG YOLKS

Rub the sugar lumps on to the lemon peel
until most of the peel has been absorbed.
Squeeze the juice from the lemon and strain it.
Put the butter into a saucepan, melt it, stir in
the flour, and when the mixture is pale brown
add the sherry, water and lemon juice. Crush
the lumps of sugar that you have rubbed on the

lemon and stir them into the sauce, which
should be very sweet. Mix well, simmer over
low heat until the sugar has dissolved and come
to the boil. Then remove from the heat and stir
in the beaten egg yolks. Return to very low
heat, stir until thickened, without boiling, and
serve.

Sauce for Cold Chicken or Partridge

(*Ann Miller, 1845*)

2 HARD-BOILED EGG YOLKS
I ANCHOVY
I SHALLOT, FINELY MINCED
PINCH OF CAYENNE PEPPER
I TSP MUSTARD
I TBS SHALLOT VINEGAR
4 TBS OLIVE OIL

Pound the dry ingredients in a mortar, then
add the vinegar gradually and the oil last of all.

Liver and Parsley Sauce

(*William Kitchiner, 1817*)

I CHICKEN LIVER
5 TBS WATER
2 TBS PARSLEY
½ PT (I CUP) MELTED BUTTER SAUCE (*see p.* 53)

Wash the liver and simmer it for 5 minutes in
the water. Chop it finely or pound it in a small
quantity of the cooking liquid. Rub through a
sieve. Blanch the parsley leaves in a little
boiling water, drain and chop very finely. Mix
the liver and parsley together and blend into
the melted butter sauce. Serve with chicken.

Currant Sauce for Venison

(*Ann Miller, 1845*)

2 OZ (½ CUP) CURRANTS
½ PT (I CUP) PORT
½ OZ (¼ CUP) BREADCRUMBS
4 OZ (½ CUP) SUGAR

I OZ (2 TBS) BUTTER
½ TSP GROUND CINNAMON
½ TSP GROUND CLOVES

Soak the currants in ½ pint (I cup) of hot water
for 10 minutes, then drain. Combine the
remaining ingredients in a pan and bring to
the boil. Reduce by boiling until thickened
and syrupy. Add pepper and salt to taste.
Throw in the currants, simmer for 10 minutes
and serve.

Caper Sauce

(*William Kitchiner, 1817*)

2 TBS CAPERS
I–2 TBS VINEGAR
½ PT (I CUP) MELTED BUTTER SAUCE (*see p.* 53)
I SPRIG PARSLEY OR CHERVIL OR TARRAGON
  or
JUICE OF ½ ORANGE OR LEMON

Chop the capers and add them to the melted
butter sauce, adding the vinegar by degrees
and tasting as you do so. Either blanch the
herbs, chop them finely and add to the sauce
or substitute the orange or lemon juice. Serve
with veal, chicken or cod.

Cream Sauce

(*William Kitchiner, 1817*)

SCANT 2 OZ (¼ CUP) BUTTER
SCANT 2 OZ (½ CUP) FLOUR
¾ PT (I¼–I½ CUPS) LIGHT BEEF AND VEGETABLE
  STOCK, STRAINED
3 TBS MUSHROOM KETCHUP (*see p.* 199)
¼ PT (½–¾ CUP) THICK CREAM
I SMALL BUNCH PARSLEY
I SMALL ONION

Melt the butter, stir in the flour and moisten
gradually with the beef stock. Stir in the
mushroom essence and cream and mix well.
Add the parsley, tied together with thread,
and the onion. Simmer on an asbestos mat

SOYER'S MODERN HOUSEWIFE'S KITCHEN APPARATUS.

over low heat, covering the pan with a sheet of greaseproof paper. Simmer for 20 minutes. At the last moment, remove the onion and parsley. Serve with roast veal.

Sauce for Tripe, Calves' Head or Cow Heel

I TSP MUSTARD
I TSP BROWN SUGAR
I TSP BLACK PEPPER
I TBS GARLIC VINEGAR
3 OZ (⅓ CUP) MELTED BUTTER

Mix the dry ingredients to a paste with the vinegar, then stir into the melted butter.

Almond Cream Sauce

(*E. S. Dallas,* Kettner's Book of the Table, *1877*)

I OZ (¼ CUP) GROUND ALMONDS
¼ TSP BITTER ALMOND ESSENCE
4 OZ (½ CUP) SUGAR

I TBS ORANGE-FLOWER WATER
¼ PT (½ CUP) CREAM
2 EGG YOLKS

Combine all the ingredients and put into the top of a double boiler over simmering (not boiling) water. Whip until thick and frothy.

Apricot Sauce (for sweet puddings)

(*Mrs Beeton, 1861*)

I DOZEN APRICOTS, FRESH OR DRIED
I–2 TSP FLOUR OR ARROWROOT
4 TBS (¼ CUP) SHERRY
SUGAR TO TASTE

Cut the apricots in half, remove the stones and crush the kernels in a mortar. Put the kernels with the fruit in a braising-pan with just enough water to cover them. Mix the arrowroot with water until very smooth and add to the pan with the sherry and sugar. When the apricots are well stewed, the sauce is ready. Strain and serve.

Apricot stones are very hard to crack, so to save time you can soak or simmer blanched almonds in Noyeau apricot brandy or kirsch and use them instead, though the flavour will not be quite as strong. In this case purée the apricots in a blender when they are cooked, return them to the pan, add a little more water and sherry if they are too thick and then the liqueur-soaked almonds.

A thick version of this sauce, without sugar or liqueur, is very good with roast pork. Add a little of the pork gravy and pepper and salt to taste.

Raspberry Sauce (for simple puddings)

(*Mrs Beeton, 1861*)

This sauce is delicious over a cold vanilla or chocolate soufflé. It is also heavenly by itself, served in tall-stemmed glasses, when it becomes a sort of fruit-flavoured zabaglione, light as swansdown. It can be made with the juice of any berries that are too soft to serve and is particularly good with blackberries.

4 EGGS
2–3 TBS FLOUR
¼ LB (½ CUP) LUMP (LOAF) SUGAR
1 PT (2½ CUPS) FRESH RASPBERRY JUICE

Beat the eggs. Mix the flour to a smooth paste with a little water. Put the eggs and the flour paste into a saucepan, add the sugar and juice and place over a very low flame or in a double boiler so that the contents will not boil. Whisk until the mixture thickens. It will be light and frothy and should be served at once.

Bread, Biscuits and Cakes

Sally Lunns

Sally Lunn was a celebrated personage in Bath who, at the close of the nineteenth century, used to make and sell in the street a kind of tea biscuit that came to be known by her name.
(*Traditional*)

Makes about 18 buns
½ OZ (1 PACKAGE) YEAST
4 TBS (¼ CUP) LUKEWARM WATER
1 LB (4½ CUPS) FLOUR
3 OZ (⅓ CUP) SUGAR
⅛ TSP SALT
3 EGGS
4 OZ (½ CUP) BUTTER, SOFTENED
¼ PT (½ CUP) MILK

Dissolve the yeast in the warm water. Mix the flour, sugar and salt in a bowl; make a well in the centre and put in the eggs, butter and milk and the yeast mixture and blend thoroughly. Beat with an electric mixer at high speed for 2 minutes. Stir in more flour if necessary, to make a stiff dough. Cover and put in a warm place to rise for about 1 hour, until the dough has doubled in bulk. Punch down and knead until smooth. Shape into small round buns, space these out on a greased baking sheet and let them rise again for 1 hour, or until they have doubled in size. Bake at 325° (Mark 3) for 20–25 minutes.

German Puffs

(*Old Master Cookery Book, 1841*)

½ LB (1 CUP) BUTTER, SOFTENED
4 EGGS, SEPARATED
1 PT (2½ CUPS) CREAM
1½ OZ (⅓ CUP) BLANCHED ALMONDS, GROUND
　　RATHER FINE
1 TSP ROSEWATER
4 TBS FLOUR, SIFTED
2 OZ (¼ CUP) SUGAR

Cream together the softened butter and the egg yolks. Beat in the cream, almonds and rosewater. Beat the egg whites until they are very stiff and form peaks; fold them into the mixture with the flour. Spoon on to greased biscuit tins or baking sheets. Bake at 350° (Mark 4) for 10–15 minutes, until golden.

Pickles and Preserves

Sauce a la Walesby

(*Ann Miller, 1845*)

Judge Walesby was Deputy Assistant Judge to the Middlesex Sessions. I can't help wondering if he was as peppery as his sauce! Anyway, it is delicious over steaks, or mixed into the gravy with roast beef.

¼ PT (½ CUP) VINEGAR
¼ TSP CAYENNE
2 TBS SOYA SAUCE
2 CLOVES, CRUSHED
1 CLOVE GARLIC, CRUSHED
2 SHALLOTS, MINCED
1 HOT CHILLI, SEEDED AND MINCED

Mix all the ingredients together and put them into a wide-mouthed jar. Seal. Shake the jar occasionally and in 2 weeks the sauce will be ready for use. Strain and rebottle it.

To Pickle Melons and Cucumbers like Mangoes

Take them before they are ripe – cut out a long slice and take out all the seeds – make a strong brine of salt and water and put it to them boiling hot – let them lay 48 hours – strain them – cover them with boiling vinegar and let them stand a day or two – take a ¼ oz of cloves – and mace, as much pepper, a little ginger and some shalots cut small, ½ a pint of mustard seed and spread it on them and lye it on the piece – cover them with vinegar and simmer over the fire till they are green.
(*From an unsigned manuscript, 1811*)

Makes 5 pints (12½ cups)
½ LARGE HONEYDEW MELON (about 1½ LB)
1 CUCUMBER
5 OZ (⅔ CUP) SUGAR
6 TBS WATER
¼ PT (½ CUP) VINEGAR
10 CLOVES

4 PEPPERCORNS
¼ TSP GROUND GINGER
½ TSP DRY MUSTARD
½ TSP GROUND MACE

Cut the melon open and remove the seeds. Remove the skin and the inner rind and cut the flesh into 2-inch pieces. Remove the seeds from the cucumber, but do not peel it. Cut into 2-inch pieces. Pack the melon and cucumber pieces into sterilized jars. Make the syrup by combining the sugar, water, vinegar and spices in a saucepan. Bring to the boil and stir to dissolve the sugar. Simmer for 5 minutes, then pour over the melon and cucumber pieces to cover. Seal.

Pickled Mushrooms

(*From an unsigned manuscript, 1811*)

Makes 2 pints (5 cups)

2 PT (5 CUPS) WATER
1 TBS SALT
2 LB (8 CUPS) MUSHROOMS
1 PT (2½ CUPS) VINEGAR
4 OZ (½ CUP) SUGAR
1 TSP SALT
4 TBS WHITE WINE
5 WHOLE PEPPERCORNS
10 CLOVES
½ TSP GROUND GINGER
½ TSP GROUND MACE
½ TSP GROUND NUTMEG

Bring the water to the boil with the salt. Put in the mushrooms for 2 minutes to blanch them; drain and cool. Bring the vinegar and seasonings to the boil in a saucepan. Pack the mushrooms tightly into sterilized jars, pour the vinegar mixture over the top to cover them and seal the jars. Keep sealed for at least 2 weeks before using.

Pickled Onions

This recipe, like several others in this section, comes from an unsigned notebook I found in the Kensington Market in London. The watermark is 1811. It is the best recipe I have come across for this brightener-up of cold meat dishes.

Makes 2 pints (5 cups)

2 LB SMALL WHITE ONIONS, AS EVEN IN SIZE AS POSSIBLE
2 OZ (½ CUP) SALT
1 PT (2½ CUPS) VINEGAR
4 OZ (½ CUP) SUGAR
½ TSP GROUND GINGER
1 TSP MUSTARD SEED
2 TBS MIXED PICKLING SPICE
10 PEPPERCORNS
5 CLOVES

Drop the onions into boiling water and boil for 1 minute. Drain immediately and then pour cold water over them. Peel. Place in a bowl and toss with the salt. Cover and leave to stand in a cool place for 8 hours.

Drain, wash and dry the onions. Bring all the other ingredients, which constitute the pickling mixture, to the boil and cook for 5 minutes. Add the onions and boil for another 10 minutes, or until they are still crisp but tender. Pack the onions into sterilized jars, pour the hot pickling mixture over them to cover, leave to cool a little and seal. Keep for a couple of weeks before using.

Anchovy Essence

There are many, many recipes for this English essence *par excellence*. It is said to have been introduced by the Romans, whose *liquamen*, made from rotting fish, was described by Apicius. Anchovies are as essential to English cooking as truffles are to the French. There are excellent bottled varieties and you can also buy Gentleman's Relish, a thick paste with a distinct lemony flavour, which this version closely resembles. We concocted this recipe from a combination of nineteenth-century recipes. This seemed the easiest way to make it and it produced the most delicately perfumed essence. A little goes a long way, and it should be diluted with a little water or broth.

Makes 2 tablespoons

1 TIN ANCHOVIES IN OIL
1 TBS WINE VINEGAR
1 TBS WATER
½ TSP GRATED LEMON PEEL
⅛ TSP CAYENNE PEPPER

Chop the anchovies and rub into a pulp with the back of a spoon. Put all the ingredients into a saucepan and cook over low heat until they have dried out. Rub through a sieve and pack into a little jar. Keep refrigerated.

Mushroom Ketchup

One could make a fat volume from nothing but English recipes for mushroom ketchup! It was one of the culinary passions of the eighteenth and nineteenth centuries. We tried a lot of them and this one, from an unsigned notebook of 1811, really seemed to work the best, because it had been made at home so often, I suppose. It is much thinner in consistency than the commercial brands, though these are also very good. It looks more like very strong coffee and should be labelled, as reheated and with cream and sugar added it can be a nasty surprise for breakfast! It's a valuable asset to home cooks: it adds enormously to the taste of grilled meats when it is added to the hot pan, with a little butter, before serving and can be used in gravy, in soups, home-made or tinned, and in cold mousses of mushrooms or ham; it also restores youth and flavour to fried or stewed mushrooms.

2 LB (8 CUPS) MUSHROOMS
2–3 TBS SALT
½ PT (1 CUP) PORT WINE
½ TSP GROUND ALLSPICE
¼ TSP GROUND CLOVES
½ TSP GROUND MACE
¼ TSP PEPPER

Mash the mushrooms. Toss them with the salt and leave them in a bowl in the refrigerator for 2 days until the juices are extracted, stirring each time you open the door. Drain

the juice through a fine sieve; it should make about ¾ pint (2 cups). Put in a saucepan, add the port and seasonings, bring to the boil and simmer for 5–10 minutes. Cool and then bottle.

A Fish Sauce

24 anchovies chopt with the bones small –
12 shallots – a handful of horse-radish – a lemon
cut in slices – 12 cloves – as many pepper corns –
4 blades of mace – a quart of white wine – a pint
of red wine – a pint of water, ½ pint anchovy
liquor – boil these together until reduced to
1 quart – strain into a bottle and cork it up –
[use] three spoonfuls to a pound of butter.
(From an unsigned manuscript, 1811)

½ PT (1 CUP) WHITE WINE
¼ PT (½ CUP) RED WINE
¼ PT (½ CUP) WATER
4 TBS ANCHOVY ESSENCE
6 ANCHOVIES
3 SHALLOTS
4 TBS GRATED HORSERADISH
A BLADE OF MACE
½ LEMON, SLICED

Boil all the ingredients together, and reduce by half. Bottle. Use 1 tablespoon to half a pound of melted butter. Keep refrigerated.

Relish for Lamb Chops

(Ann Miller, 1845)

This is one of my great favourites. A bottle of it makes an excellent present for a man who likes cooking.

½ TSP GROUND PEPPER
1 TSP ALLSPICE
½ TSP SALT
1 TSP GRATED HORSERADISH
2 SHALLOTS
2 CLOVES, CRUSHED
¼ PT (½ CUP) MUSHROOM KETCHUP

Combine all the ingredients, then let them

stand in a bottle for 2 weeks, shaking occasionally. Strain and rebottle.

Flavoured Vinegars

Burnet or Cucumber Vinegar
Dry and pound a ½ oz of cress seed, or burnet seed. Pour upon it 1 quart of best vinegar, let steep 10 days, shaking it up every day. Good for salads and cold meat.

Tarragon or Elder Flower Vinegar
Dry the freshly picked leaves, they should be picked between Midsummer and Michaelmas, just before flowering. Cover with best vinegar, steep 14 days. Strain through a flannel jelly-bag and bottle.

Basil Vinegar
Sweet basil is in perfection in the middle of August. Fill a wide-mouthed bottle with the fresh green leaves of basil and cover with vinegar or wine, let steep 10 days,. For strong liquor, strain liquor, put in fresh leaves and steep again for 14 days. Good for mock-turtle soup. (William Kitchiner, 1817)

Horseradish Mustard
Boil some scraped horseradish in white wine or vinegar, drain and use the liquid with dry mustard to make the paste. It can be mixed with sherry, Madeira or beer for a milder flavour. (William Kitchiner, 1817)

Apple or Quince Jelly

Pour into a clean earthen pot two quarts of spring water, and throw into it as quickly as they can be pared, quartered and weighed, four pounds of nonesuches, pearmains, Ripstone pippins, or any other good boiling apples of fine flavour. When all are done, stew them gently until they are well broken, but not reduced quite to pulp; turn them into a jelly bag, or strain the juice from them without pressure through a closely woven cloth, which should be gathered over the fruit, and tied, and suspended above a deep pan until the juice ceases to drop from it; this, if not very clear, must be rendered so before it is used for syrup of jelly, but for all other purposes once straining, it will be sufficient. Quinces are prepared in the same way, and with the same proportions of fruit and water, but they must not be too long boiled, or the juice will become red. We have found it answer well to have them simmered until they are perfectly tender, and then to leave them with their liquor in a bowl until the following day, when the juice will be rich and clear. They should be thrown into the water very quickly after they are pared and weighed, as the air will soon discolour them. The juice will form a jelly much more easily if the cores and pips be left in the fruit.

4 LB APPLES OR QUINCES
4 PT (10 CUPS) WATER

Proceed exactly as in the original recipe.

Lemon Brandy

(Traditional)

This is a flavouring for custard sauces and was once much used in England as a sweet sauce to go with puddings, fruit pies and stewed fruit.

2 SMALL LEMONS
¾ PT (2 CUPS) BRANDY
2 OZ LUMP (LOAF) SUGAR
¼ PT (½ CUP) WATER

Peel the lemons rather thinly, taking care to leave none of the white pith. Put the peel into a bottle with the brandy and let it infuse for 24 hours, then strain. Now boil the sugar with the water for a few minutes, skim it and, when it is cold, add it to the brandy. Half a tablespoon is an excellent flavouring for boiled custards.

THE TWENTIETH CENTURY

EDWARD VII, THE symbol of opulence – a superbly attired overfed body, with heavy-lidded, protruding eyes and a sensual mouth, smoking an enormous cigar – was the most exciting figure of his time. He handled his official obligations with intelligence and relish, particularly in the diplomatic sphere (the French called him 'the uncle of Europe'), but his pleasures were those of the senses. When he took the throne he had indulged his tastes for magnificence, comfort, women and food for more than forty years. Once he became king, society was ready to model itself on him. Balls, dinners, country house parties, clothes, racehorses, shooting, yachting – extravagant living became the fashion of the moment.

One of the dishes that his father's German family had enjoyed was a turkey stuffed with a chicken, inside the chicken a pheasant, inside the pheasant a woodcock – the whole made into a pie and served cold. In Edward's reign cooking became even more elaborate, and – in the skilled hands of the perfectionist M. Ménager and his staff of forty-five in the kitchen – more French. Luncheons and dinners were expanded to ten or fourteen courses, tea was an elaborate affair and little snacks of lobster salad or cold chicken were served to the king at eleven in the morning. After dinner a plate of sandwiches, a quail or a cutlet went to the royal apartments in case of sudden need.

The picnic lunches for Ascot and Goodwood and the shooting luncheons for Sandringham were dazzling. When the king attended the opera, dinner was served in a room behind the royal box, prepared by his own chef, and as perfect as those he demanded at home: nine or ten courses, served cold, with clean plates for each guest for each course – footmen struggled with hampers carrying four hundred plates and an equivalent amount of silverware. These dinners were served during the interval – between 8.30 and 9.30 pm – and followed this pattern: cold consommé, lobster mayonnaise, cold trout, duck, lamb cutlets, plovers' eggs, chicken, tongue and ham jelly, sandwiches, several fruit dishes, French pastries.

French was the language of menus now, even in restaurants. The following breakfast,

served to Edward's queen, Alexandra, at Windsor Castle is a good sample of what could now be called 'breakfast franglais': petites soles frites, haddock à l'Anglaise, oeufs en cocotte, oeufs pochés, bacon à l'Anglaise, bécassines sur canapés, les viandes froides à la gelée.

Edward considered grilled oysters the ideal supper dish, following it with Poulet Norvégienne, cold quails and Quails à la grecque. Queen Alexandra had a small number of preferences: the Danish fruit sweet of currants and raspberries called *Rod grod*, freshwater crayfish cooked in Chablis, chicken served on a bed of pasta with a rich white sauce. And certain dishes became traditional for special occasions: pigeon pie at Ascot, turtle soup and white bait for the Derby Night dinner, shrimps and local lobster for yachting lunches at Cowes, haggis once a week for Scots friends at Balmoral and deer pudding as a savoury at least four times a week.

The high-living society of Edward's day was fond of eating in clubs and restaurants. When the landed aristocracy came to London for three months, after the hunting and shooting had ended and the yachting and deer-stalking not begun, they might be seen in the kind of grand clubs that once had had Ude and Soyer in their kitchens. As Prince of Wales, Edward joined White's. Mott's and the Cremorne were packed, with champagne and pretty girls both in liberal supply. Crockfords, United Service Club, The Travellers Club, The Athenaeum, The Garrick, The Arts Club – they all flourished. Big hotels and restaurants flourished, too, with high standards and French food. Simpson's, already venerable, was serving excellent joints, turbot, delicious pies and puddings. Lieut-Col Newnham-Davis, writing in 1899, said about the waiters at the unchanging Simpson's: 'The waiters at Simpson's are Britannic and have that dignity which sits so well on the chairman of a company addressing his shareholders, or an M.P. entertaining his constituents, or the genuine English waiter taking an order. It is an undefinable majesty; but it exists.

But while all this good eating was going on from expensive French menus, there was at the same time more malnutrition in England than had occurred since Tudor times. The poor lived mostly on tea and bread – and white bread at that. Vitamins were finally defined in 1912, but it was years before they began to be added to processed foods. During the 1914–18 war, English scientists had their first chance to study nutrition by precise methods. The success of the government in solving the food problems was actually a bonus in the victory. But the rationing and control of foods during the war years were a blight on English cooking; and a second blow dealt by the war was the disappearance of the domestic servants into the factories.

The new factory jobs robbed many an English household of its staff and left many English women faced with the gas stove and a worn copy of 'Mrs Beeton'. Lucky indeed were those

country houses where well-trained and dedicated cooks still turned out real English meals. One such family are the Stirlings of Keir, in Perthshire: Alice Thomson, who cooks for them, is a remarkable source of English and Scottish recipes, some of them in this book.

Born in the Highlands, on the Beaufort estate, Alice Thomson came to Keir in her teens, and began work in the sculleries. She was later trained in the kitchen by two successive cooks, the second, Mrs Edwards, was an instructor 'so particular', said Alice, that she made her pupil write up each night the dishes she had learned that day – and repeat the dish if an error were discovered. From Mrs Edwards she learned to make her stocks and glazes and sauces. Alice's game glaze is so thick it looks like a sheet of toffee or leather; and a bit of it goes into all her meat sauces.

When she was twenty-one, Alice Thomson became the cook at Keir. She was often sent to London to help in the kitchens of friends of the Stirlings when they had big parties where famous cooks were in residence and by working with them, and with her excellent training by Mrs Edwards, she was able to handle the meals for the parties of twenty or more guests at Keir during the shooting season. Food was needed for the guests, the servants they brought with them, the family, the staff of the house, and the gillies. But Alice finds this wide-scale cooking normal and handles it all with no confusion.

Today Alice is happy to have four large deep freezes to keep her glazes and game etc. and to hold the salmon she gets 'straight out of the water'. She splits the fish down the back and removes the spine before freezing it. To cook the salmon, she only partially thaws it and rubs a little butter on it before she cooks it under a very hot grill.

One of Alice's secrets is her native economy. Everything gets used up – a bit of nice sauce goes into the thick vegetable soup. And although her recipes are classic, it is those little additions that enliven the dish and intrigue the diner.

One development in English dining habits between the World Wars was that synonym for frivolity – the cocktail. 'Tea dancing' really meant cocktail dancing (with a chaperon for the girls) and the thirties were the years of intricate, glamorous mixed drinks. Harry Craddock reigned in the Savoy bar and gave this advice:

A FEW HINTS FOR THE YOUNG MIXER
1. Ice is nearly always an absolute essential for any cocktail.
2. Never use the same ice twice.
3. Remember that the ingredients mix better in a shaker rather larger than is necessary to contain them.
4. Shake the shaker as hard as you can: don't just rock it: you are trying to wake it up, not send it to sleep!
5. If possible, ice your glasses before using them.
6. Drink your cocktail as soon as possible.

Craddock was once asked what was the best way to drink a cocktail: 'Quickly', replied the great man, 'while it's laughing at you!'

Cocktails faded away in the 'fifties, when serving drinks 'on the rocks' became the fad, but there are signs of their returning in the 'seventies.

The Second World War continued the dismal processes of bringing government regulation to the food industries to improve the health of the population but shrinking still further the possibilities of enjoying those lavish English dinners of the past. One curious consequence of the Second World War was a renewed English taste for coffee, especially the dark French and Italian brews, brought back by the armed forces who served on the Continent and in North Africa.

In the post-war years, manufacturers placed every sort of tinned, packed, bottled and frozen food in the hands of the servantless housewife. Fish-and-chip shops proliferated (no recipe needed for this English dish; it is always eaten at the shop); and restaurants became relentlessly foreign – not only French but also Italian, Pakistani, even – or else 'ye olde' English, aping the past for the tourists without serving the real food of the past. It is not surprising that English people welcomed spicier foods after the war years of rationing, Spam, powdered eggs, and coffee essence with 'evap'.

Postwar technology, however, was not all bad for English food. Electrical helpers such as freezers and blenders are boons to the home cook, and today's rapid transport brings a variety of fresh foods impossible in any other age. All sorts of fruits and vegetables can be had at any season, if one is willing to pay the price asked. One must shop carefully, though, for fruit that has been picked too green for shipping may be visually lovely but rock hard and completely tasteless. The best fruit is ripened on the tree, bush, or vine.

Fresh, non-farinaceous vegetables taste best, I find, if cooked in very little water, which evaporates down to a rich broth by the time they are ready to serve. I serve the liquid along with the vegetables, hoping to preserve all their minerals. Any larger amounts of vegetable broth are chilled and served instead of fruit juice at breakfast; they are much less acid for the empty stomach. With the exception of potatoes, vegetables should be rather undercooked and crisp; if not, they should be puréed. Cooking carrots with their tops, which need not be eaten, adds flavour. The tops of many root vegetables are delicious when cooked; radish leaves have a particularly good peppery flavour. To cook root vegetables quickly, grate them on a mandolin grater and sauté in butter.

Twentieth-century technology has brought us fish and shell fish quick-frozen on board the fishing boat, making them available everywhere. The result is often that the closer one lives to the sea the less available and more expensive the fish is; it seems almost impossible at times to buy fresh fish at the source. But fish that is fresh and not frozen is also shipped now with amazing speed, or you may catch your own. We can take our cues on flavouring from the fish's source: fennel grows along many estuaries where salmon run; marjoram grows by hill streams where mountain grayling can be caught; watercress beds grow in trout streams. Freshwater fish need more delicate asesonings than sea fish. Oatmeal, barley and other cereals are used to absorb the oily flavour of smoked fish.

Farley in the eighteenth century gave us the right tips for choosing the freshest fish at the market, 'by observing their gills which should be of a lively red . . . , the standing out of their eyes . . . ' Any fish should be cooked to the split second of being done; poached, grilled, or baked, it is ruined by the slightest overcooking. An exception is eel, which is very firm and can absorb flavours by stewing. If you plan to serve a fish cold, poach it by just boiling up and simmering for a very short while; then let it cool in its own herb-scented broth.

Andrew Boorde in the seventeenth century quoted this proverb: 'God may send a man good meat, but the devyll may send an evyll coke to destrue it.' Good meat is the foundation of English cooking and can be bought today in abundance, but care must be taken not to destroy it.

Roasts should never be carved the minute they come from the oven, or they will seem tough. One must allow the meat to sit in a warm place, such as on the open oven door, for five to ten minutes. The pleasure of eating steaks and roasts is increased by providing very sharp knives at the table. Many a rather tough piece of meat has been made to seem tender by paper thin carving and supplying guests with razor-sharp knives.

It will always be impossible for the home cook to produce steaks and chops seared black all over on the outside, a tender pink on the inside, without the tremendous heat produced by restaurant equipment. I have found the next best thing to be a heavy iron skillet or griddle. Rub it with oil and heat for about fifteen minutes on a high flame. A scattering of herbs will burn to a powder, improving the taste of the meat and smell of the kitchen. Rub the meat with oil, then slap down on the iron and turn as soon as the first side has blackened (about one to one and one-half minutes); when the second side is dark, turn off the flame, and add butter mashed with herbs. The remaining heat in the pan will usually cook the meat rare without blackening the butter.

To get good crackling, score the skin of a pork roast about thirty minutes before removing it from the oven. Pork should be well done; 'dropping from the bones' is nice, if the meat is well basted and kept very moist. Cold pork can be as uninteresting as cold turkey unless you slice it paper thin and serve it with a sharp and spicy sauce. Ham is a delicious flavourer of sauces, stocks, soups and salads. The secret is to chop it so fine that it is almost a powder.

English beef is justly famous. For tender beef, the meat must be well hung. Many inexpensive cuts have more flavour than those that are more popular and so sell at higher prices; a friendly relationship with the butcher can provide an education in meat buying. Beef intended for grilling may be painted first with mustard or marinated in Worcester sauce.

Boiled leg of mutton is a true English dish, though it is now the pride of the Jockey Club in Paris; but the pickling and salting of mutton is becoming a lost art. Mutton ham (page 182) is delicious and can be made easily at home. Lamb has almost replaced mutton in the United States, but the true mutton is obtainable at Sam's Meat Market on Ninth Avenue in New York City. The good meat of lambs grazed on salt marshes gives the key to flavourings: anchovies and oysters are natural accompaniments for mutton.

Every recipe in this book is for good English food. Some dishes were almost forgotten, some have been abused and unfairly scorned. But the English tradition of comfort is strong; and real English food is wholesome and delicious and surprisingly spicy and exotic, drawing on the best of our varied history, reflecting English taste and good English ingredients. There is no better way to enjoy our past than through the back, or kitchen, door.

Soups

Maxime's Curried Apricot and Fresh Mint Soup

Serves 6

I LB (2 CUPS) COOKED, BONED CHICKEN OR
    PHEASANT, CHOPPED
4 DRIED APRICOTS, COOKED AND DRAINED
1¼ PT (3 CUPS) CHICKEN OR PHEASANT STOCK
I OZ (2 TBS) BUTTER
I TBS CURRY POWDER
2 TBS FLOUR OR RICE FLOUR
½ PT (1 CUP) THICK CREAM
4 TBS FRESH MINT, FINELY CHOPPED

Purée the chicken and apricots in a blender
with ½ pint (1 cup) of the stock. Melt the
butter in a soup pan and add the curry
powder; cook for 1 minute, stirring. Stir in the
flour and cook for another minute. Add the
remaining chicken stock and the puréed
chicken and apricot mixture. Simmer, stirring,
for 10 minutes to heat and to blend the
flavours. Stir in the cream and simmer for
15 minutes to thicken or until reduced slightly.
Stir in the mint; cover and leave on the
lowest possible heat for 2–3 minutes, to allow
the flavour of the mint to infuse.

Chilled Carrot Soup
(*from Drue Heinz*)

Serves 4–6

I MEDIUM ONION, SLICED
4 CLOVES GARLIC, CRUSHED
2 OZ (4 TBS) BUTTER
I LB CARROTS, SCRAPED
2 PT (5 CUPS) GOOD STOCK OR TINNED CONSOMMÉ
½ PT (1 CUP) CREAM
4 TBS WHIPPED CREAM
I TBS CHOPPED PARSLEY

Fry the sliced onion with the garlic in the
butter in a covered pan until very soft, but
not browned. While the onions are cooking
chop up the carrots and add them to the onions.
Add the hot stock and simmer for at least an
hour. Allow to cool. Put through the blender,
then stir in the cream. Add salt and pepper to
taste. If the garlic is too elusive, add another
crushed clove or two; the soup must not have
a strong garlic flavour – a good hint but no
more. Chill. Serve with small dollops of
whipped cream and a sprinkling of
chopped parsley.

Maxime's Raw Carrot Soup

This makes a lovely, healthy, speedy cold soup
and can be prepared with all sorts of different
vegetables and leftover scraps. The carrot
juice can be made at home in a juice extractor
or bought from a health-food shop, but must
be kept in a completely airtight container
before you make the soup, and well covered
while chilling, or it will discolour. If you buy
a juice extractor, get a large, solid one. The
extra expense is well worth-while. I started
out with a 'portable' which starts to leap up
and down and growl ominously after about 3
carrots have been fed to it, and then has to be
taken apart and cleaned.

Serves 6

1½ PT (4 CUPS) RAW CARROT JUICE
6 TBS THICK YOGHURT
2 TBS FINELY CHOPPED PARSLEY

2 TBS FINELY CHOPPED MINT
PEPPER AND SALT TO TASTE

Combine all the ingredients with a whisk,
season with pepper and salt to taste, chill
and serve.

Alexis's Chestnut and Apple Soup

(*from my son, Alexis de la Falaise*)

Serves 4
1 LB CHESTNUTS
4 PT (10 CUPS) WATER, SALTED
1 STICK CELERY
2 APPLES
1½ OZ (3 TBS) BUTTER
2 OZ (4 TBS) BOILING MILK
A PINCH OF PAPRIKA
BREAD CROUTONS FRIED IN BUTTER

Throw the chestnuts into the boiling water
and cook for 2 minutes. This will make them
easier to peel. Put the peeled chestnuts to boil
in the water with the celery stick. Cook until
tender.

Slice the apples and cook them gently in a
small frying pan in the butter, with a seasoning
of salt and pepper, until soft.

Press the cooked chestnuts and apples
through a sieve or blend in an electric mixer
for 30 seconds. Put the purée back into the
water in which the chestnuts were cooked, stir
well and add the boiling milk. Sprinkle
paprika on top. Serve with small bread
croutons fried in butter.

Chicken and Ham Soup

(*from Drue Heinz*)

Serves 8–10
4 PINTS (10 CUPS) CHICKEN STOCK
A 4–5 LB CHICKEN (OR CAPON)
1 HAM BONE
2 TBS PEARL BARLEY
5–6 SPRIGS PARSLEY, TIED IN A BUNCH
1 SPRIG THYME
1 BAY LEAF
⅛ TSP POWDERED CLOVES

⅛ TSP POWDERED MACE
1 PEPPERCORN
5 OZ (1 CUP) CARROT, CHOPPED
5 OZ (1 CUP) ONION, CHOPPED
A LITTLE CHOPPED PARSLEY

Bring the stock to the boil, and add the
chicken, ham bone, barley, herbs and spices.
Lower the heat and simmer for ¾ hour. Add
the chopped vegetables and continue to simmer
until the chicken is tender. This generally
takes 1 hour, but you will know when it is
ready because the leg will feel soft and
springy under the pressure of your finger. Turn
off the heat and leave the bird to 'set' for
10 minutes in the liquid.

Remove the chicken (which can be served as
the main course next day), the ham bone,
parsley, thyme and bay leaf. Taste for seasoning
and add pepper and salt if necessary. Serve
with a good sprinkling of parsley.

Maxime's Chicken Giblet Soup

Serves 6–8
1 LB CHICKEN GIBLETS AND HEARTS
4 PINTS (10 CUPS) CHICKEN STOCK OR 2 PINTS
(5 CUPS) STOCK AND 2 PINTS (5 CUPS) WATER
1 TSP OREGANO
1 BAY LEAF
1 ONION, STUCK WITH 2 CLOVES
2 OZ (½ CUP) BOILED RICE
1 EGG YOLK
GENEROUS ½ PT (1½ CUPS) THICK CREAM
JUICE OF 1 LEMON
CHOPPED PARSLEY

Put the giblets and hearts (and any scraps of
leftover chicken) into a large pan with the
stock and bring to the boil. Skim off the
surface scum. Add the herbs and onion. Cook
until the giblets are tender (about 2 hours),
adding the rice during the last half-hour. Rub
the cooked rice through a sieve and stir well
into the strained soup. Bring back to the boil
and stir. Mix the egg yolk with the cream and
lemon juice in a warmed soup tureen. Stir
the soup in gently and sprinkle with the

chopped parsley. Little pieces of chopped giblets may also be served with the soup.

=====

Maxime's Duck Soup

This soup can be made economically only if you have served ducks previously and have reserved the carcases, necks and gizzards.

Serves 6–8

.1–5 DUCK CARCASES
1 EGG YOLK
A HANDFUL OF CHIVES, FINELY CHOPPED
A LITTLE DOUBLE (HEAVY) CREAM (OPTIONAL)

Gently boil the duck carcases in enough salted water to come to double the height of the solid contents of the pot. Cook for as many hours as possible over low heat. This can successfully be done over a period of several days: cook at the back of the stove each evening while you are preparing dinner; refrigerate at night and then skim off the fat before reheating. As the soup boils down, pour off the stock and replenish with an equal amount of water. Add salt. Most of the duck bones will gradually become soft and melt into the stock.

To serve: place the egg yolk in a heated soup tureen, and gently pour in the soup, stirring all the while. Serve with finely chopped chives. A little double cream may also be added (stir it into the egg yolk) if the soup seems too thin.

=====

Chilled Mint Soup

(*from my mother, Rhoda Birley*)

Serves 4–6

¼ LB (1½ CUPS) CHOPPED MINT
4 TBS CHOPPED PARSLEY
A FEW SPRIGS FRESH OR BOTTLED TARRAGON
2 OZ (¾ CUP) CHOPPED WATERCRESS
A FEW SPRIGS FRESH FENNEL LEAVES
¼ PT (½ CUP) RAW GREEN PEAS
¼ PT (½ CUP) TINNED PETITS POIS, DRAINED
1 PT (2½ CUPS) MILK
4 TBS ROSEWATER
1 PT (2½ CUPS) SINGLE CREAM

A PINCH OF INDIAN CURRY POWDER
A PINCH OF PAPRIKA

Chop the herbs and watercress finely. Place a little at a time in a blender with the peas, both fresh and tinned. Add a few tablespoons of milk and the rose water. Blend at medium speed for 30 seconds. Pour the contents through a fine sieve into a soup tureen, pressing stubborn herbs and peas through with a wooden spoon. When all the ingredients have been strained, stir in the remaining milk and the cream. Make sure all is well mixed. If the texture is too thick and creamy, add more milk. Add the curry powder and paprika and season with salt and pepper. Before serving, the soup should be thoroughly chilled in the refrigerator. Serve in small chilled soup cups.

=====

Robin McDouall's Peanut Soup

Serves 6

6 OZ (1½ CUPS) PEANUTS
1 MEDIUM ONION
1–1½ OZ (2–3 TBS) BUTTER
1½ PT (4 CUPS) CHICKEN STOCK
½ PT (1 CUP) CREAM OR EXTRA ½ PT (1 CUP) STOCK (*see recipe*)
A DASH OF SHERRY (OPTIONAL)

Shake the peanuts in a dry colander to get rid of the salt. If necessary, rub them in a cloth. Chop the onion finely and cook it until golden in just enough butter to stop it sticking. Stir in the nuts and push them round with a wooden spoon. Add the chicken stock and boil for 20 minutes. Leave to cool slightly and then put through the blender. Return to the pan and season; probably pepper alone will do – it is unlikely to need salt.

You can stop at this stage and merely add the extra chicken stock. To make it more of a party soup, add the cream. If you like, add a dash of sherry, but don't overdo it.

=====

Eggs

Green Eggs

(*from Sir Cecil Beaton*)

Serves 8

1 HARD-BOILED EGG PER PERSON
½ PT (1 CUP) HOME-MADE MAYONNAISE
1 DESSERTSPOON MELTED BUTTER
2 OR 3 DROPS TABASCO OR A PINCH OF CAYENNE
4 BUNCHES WATERCRESS
4 TBS FRENCH DRESSING
CHOPPED PARSLEY
LEMON SLICES

Cut the eggs lengthways. Press the yolks through a nylon sieve and mix them with a dessertspoon of the mayonnaise and the melted butter and tabasco, plus pepper and salt. Spoon back into the whites and reshape. Boil half the watercress in a little salted water, then liquidize in a blender. When cold, mix with the remaining mayonnaise. Chop the remaining watercress finely and cover the serving dish with watercress and French dressing. Place the stuffed eggs on top and cover with the green sauce, chopped parsley and slices of lemon.

Fried Eggs on Croutons with Escoffier Sauce

(*from Alice Thomson*)

Serves 2

½ LB MUSHROOMS
1½–2 OZ (3–4 TBS) SALTED BUTTER
1 TBS DOUBLE CREAM
4 ROUNDS OF BREAD
4 EGGS
¼ PT (½ CUP) THIN CREAM
A LITTLE EXTRA BUTTER, IF NEEDED
2 TBS ESCOFFIER SAUCE

Chop the mushrooms and fry in the butter; add the double cream after cooking, stirring slightly. Fry the rounds of bread in hot butter,

drain them on paper, arrange in a dish and transfer to a barely warm oven to keep warm. Break the eggs into the pan in which the bread was fried and fry them very slowly. Then cut round the edges of the whites and slide an egg onto each crouton in the oven. Put the remaining cream into the same frying pan, adding a little more butter if necessary and the Escoffier sauce. Stir together until the mixture is hot and well blended and has taken on a pale brown colour. Reheat the mushrooms, spoon them into the centre of the dish, arrange the croutons and eggs round and serve as hot as possible.

Charlston Manor Eggs with Haddock

This is my mothers' adaptation of an old favourite from the Savoy Grill in London. (*from my mother, Rhoda Birley*)

Serves 6

6 SLICES SMOKED HADDOCK
½ PT (1 CUP) THIN CREAM
1 SMALL CLOVE GARLIC, CRUSHED, OR
    2 SHALLOTS, MINCED
1 TSP POWDERED ANISE
6–8 EGGS
1½–2 OZ (3–4 TBS) BUTTER
1 TBS TARRAGON, OR OTHER FRESH HERB,
    CHOPPED

Poach the haddock in the cream, with the garlic or shallots and a seasoning of pepper and salt. When the fish is cooked and begins to flake, remove, drain and arrange on a serving dish. Keep warm.

Scramble the eggs with the herbs, seasoning with pepper and salt and keeping creamy and light.

Pile the eggs onto the haddock and serve.

Poached Egg and Haddock Souffle

(*from the author*)

Serves 6

2 OZ (¼ CUP) BUTTER

2 TBS DILL, FINELY CHOPPED
I TBS ONION, FINELY CHOPPED
2 OZ (½ CUP) FLOUR
2 TBS CURRY POWDER
½ PT (I CUP) MILK, WARMED
4 EGG YOLKS, BEATEN SEPARATELY
6 OZ (I CUP) HADDOCK, COOKED AND FLAKED
3 EGG WHITES, BEATEN TO MOIST PEAKS
6 EGGS, VERY LIGHTLY POACHED

Melt the butter, add the dill and onion and cook gently until the onion is soft and transparent. Sprinkle in the flour and cook, stirring, for 2–3 minutes. Blend in first the curry powder, then the milk, off the heat. Stir until creamy and smooth. Cook over very low heat until thickened. Remove from the heat and cool by standing the pan in a bowl of cold water for 5 minutes. Season. Stir in the egg yolks, one at a time, then the haddock, and fold in the egg whites. Pour one-third of the mixture into a buttered 3-pt (7½ cup) soufflé dish. Arrange the poached eggs on this mixture and fill up the dish with the rest of the soufflé mixture. The soufflé dish may need a greased paper collar attached to the rim. Stand the dish in a tin half filled with hot water and bake at 375° (Mark 5) for 35–45 minutes.

Fish

Iced Anchovy Cream

(*The Queen Cookery Books, 1913*)

Serves 2–3

6 ANCHOVIES
I HARD-BOILED EGG YOLK
I TBS OIL
¼ TSP CAYENNE PEPPER
A FEW DROPS OF CARMINE (RED COLOURING)
I½ TSP GELATINE
¼ PT (½ CUP) FISH STOCK
½ PT (I CUP) CREAM, WHIPPED

Mash the anchovies in a mortar with the egg yolk, oil, cayenne pepper and colouring. Soften the gelatine in the fish stock and let it dissolve. Leave to cool. Stir in the anchovy paste. Fold in the cream. Freeze in little moulds. 'Serve with a rose of cayenne flavoured (whipped) cream or good caviare on each little mould.'

Salmon Fish Cakes

(*from David Niven*)

Serves 6

I¼ LB SALMON, COOKED AND FLAKED
I LB MUSHROOMS, CHOPPED
I½–2 OZ (3–4 TBS) BUTTER
JUICE I LEMON
½ PINT (I CUP) VELOUTÉ OR WHITE SAUCE
2 EGG YOLKS
PEPPER AND SALT TO TASTE
⅛ TSP PAPRIKA
⅛ TSP GRATED NUTMEG
2 EGGS WELL BEATEN
4 OZ (2 CUPS) FINE BREADCRUMBS

Sauté the mushrooms in butter, add lemon juice, season lightly and cook until pan juices almost evaporated. Heat the white sauce gently, stir in egg yolks, cook without boiling until thickened. Season with salt, pepper, paprika and nutmeg. Stir in the mushrooms and then fold in the fish as lightly as possible to avoid crushing the flakes. Spread lightly on one sheet of buttered foil and cover with another. Chill.

Form into patties or croquettes, dip in egg and breadcrumbs and fry in a mixture of vegetable oil and butter until warmed throughout and golden brown.

Serve on a dish garnished with parsley.

Salmon Mousse with Cucumber

(*Traditional, adapted by the author*)

Serves 2–3

½ LB SALMON, FREE FROM SKIN AND BONE
I OZ (2 TBS) BUTTER, CUT IN SMALL PIECES
3 EGG YOLKS
½ OZ (¼ CUP) BREADCRUMBS
I TSP TARRAGON VINEGAR
I TSP ANCHOVY ESSENCE
5 EGG WHITES, BEATEN TILL STIFF
½ CUCUMBER, CUBED AND COOKED IN SALTED
    WATER UNTIL TENDER
SAUCE HOLLANDAISE

Pound the salmon in a mortar (or in the blender) with the butter, egg yolks, crumbs, vinegar and anchovy essence. Season with pepper and salt. When it forms a smooth paste, push it through a fine sieve and fold in the beaten egg whites. Butter a ring mould and fill it with the mousse; steam gently for 40 minutes. Turn out and fill the centre with the cucumber dice. Pour a little sauce over and serve the rest separately.

Lobster Merville

(*from my father, the late Sir Oswald Birley*)

Serves 2

I LOBSTER WEIGHING ABOUT 9 OZ
2 OZ (4 TBS) BUTTER
4 TBS (¼ CUP) GOOD BRANDY
¾ PT (2 CUPS) WHITE RHINE WINE
½ PT (I CUP) THICK CREAM
2 TBS CARROT, FINELY CHOPPED
2 TBS ONION, FINELY CHOPPED
2 TBS HAM, FINELY CHOPPED

6 OZ (¾ CUP) BUTTER
A SMALL PIECE OF BAY LEAF
A PINCH OF THYME
3 EGG YOLKS, BEATEN
18 TINY BUTTON MUSHROOMS
12 OYSTERS

Cut the lobster into thick pieces. Brown the chunks in very hot butter and pour over the brandy, which you have warmed in a ladle and ignited. Extinguish the flames with the wine. Spoon the cream all over the lobster and season with a sprinkling of pepper and salt. Add the following 'mirepoix' mixture; equal quantities of very finely chopped carrot, finely chopped onion and ham, all lightly browned in a little of the butter, with a small piece of bay leaf and a pinch of thyme. Cover the pan tightly and simmer very gently for about 30 minutes.

Remove the lobster shell, put the meat into a fireproof casserole and keep warm.

Mix the coral of the lobster with the rest of the butter and put it into the pan with the sauce. Cook over even lower heat than before. Stir in the egg yolks, button mushrooms and oysters. Pour this sauce over the lobster meat and serve with plain boiled rice.

Iced Lobster Curry, a starter

(*The Queen Cookery Books, 1913*)

Serves 4

¾ LB (2 CUPS) FINELY CHOPPED LOBSTER (OR
  CRAB)
½ PT (1 CUP) SAUCE TARTARE
2 TSP CURRY POWDER
2 OZ (½ CUP) COOKED RICE, CHILLED
4 TBS (¼ CUP) WHIPPED CREAM
½ TSP ANCHOVY ESSENCE

Combine the chopped lobster with the
tartare sauce and curry powder and spoon the
mixture into ice trays. Freeze.

When you are ready to serve, spoon the iced
lobster into small ramekins. Top with the
rice. Season the whipped cream with the
anchovy essence and pipe it on top.

Old-Fashioned Fish Pie

(*from Drue Heinz*)

Serves 3–4

1 LB SMOKED HADDOCK OR COD FILLET
½ PT (1 CUP) MILK
2 HARD–BOILED EGGS, SLICED
1 OZ (2 TBS) BUTTER
2 TBS FLOUR

Topping
1 LB POTATOES
½ OZ (1 TBS) BUTTER
2 TBS MILK
1 TSP SALT
¼ TSP PEPPER
4 TBS GRATED PARMESAN CHEESE

Place the fish in a buttered pie dish, add about
half of the milk and cover with a buttered
paper or lid. Bake in the centre of a moderately
hot oven (425°, Mark 5), for 10–15 minutes.
Strain and reserve the liquid in which the fish
has been cooked; bone and flake the fish and
place in a well-buttered 1½-pint (4 cups) pie
dish with the sliced hard-boiled eggs.

Melt the butter in a saucepan and stir in the
flour. Cook over low heat for 1–2 minutes but
do not allow it to brown. Gradually stir in the
reserved liquid in which the fish was cooked,
made up to ½ pint (1 cup) with extra milk if
necessary. Stir the sauce continuously until it is
smooth, thickened and boiling. Season well
with salt and pepper. Pour over the fish and
tap the dish gently so that the sauce coats all
the fish through to the bottom.

Plain boil the potatoes, then mash them;
season them with salt and pepper and beat
until smooth with the butter and milk. Spoon
over the fish, spread evenly then rough up with
a fork. Sprinkle with Parmesan cheese. Place
in the top of a hot oven 400° (Mark 6), for
about 20 minutes, until the pie is well heated
and the top is golden brown and crisp.

Kedgeree

(*from the author*)

This is one of many versions; one of our
favourite Indian 'imports' the original Hindu
word *khichri* came from the Sanskrit *k'ysara*.

Serves 4

1 LB HADDOCK, OR OTHER LEFT OVERS OF FISH,
  SUCH AS SALMON
¼ LB RICE, BOILED
2 HARD–BOILED EGGS, PEELED, SLICED
¾ PINT BÉCHAMEL SAUCE OR MELTED BUTTER
1 TSP CURRY POWDER
1 TBS PARSLEY, FINELY CHOPPED
GOOD PINCH OF CAYENNE
PEPPER AND SALT TO TASTE

Flake the fish, removing skin and bones; keep
warm in the oven. Warm the sauce or butter;
stir in curry powder, seasonings and parsley.
In a casserole dish, make layers rice, fish, egg
slices, with sauce in between and on top of
the last layer. Heat in oven and serve very hot,
for breakfast or for lunch.

Oyster Puffs

These make a delicious starter for a meal, or an

elegant garnish for a large poached fish. They can also be served with a roast shoulder of lamb. (*Traditional, adapted by the author*)

Serves 3
3 2½-INCH ROUNDS PUFF PASTRY
3 LARGE OYSTERS
3 TSP MELTED BUTTER
A DASH OF CAYENNE PEPPER

Bake the pastry rounds on a baking sheet until crisp and puffed. Pull off the top layer of each puff and into each cavity slide 1 oyster and 1 teaspoon butter. Sprinkle with a pinch of cayenne. Put the pastry lid back on and return to a hot oven for 1 minute, to heat the oysters without cooking them.

Creamed Kipper Fillets

(*from Drue Heinz*)

Serves 3–4
1 OZ (2 TBS) BUTTER
4 TBS FINELY CHOPPED ONIONS
½ PT (1 CUP) CREAM
1 LB KIPPER FILLETS
¼ TSP PEPPER
4 TBS CHOPPED PARSLEY

Melt the butter in a frying pan and sauté the onion until soft but not browned. Add the cream, bring to the boil and then add the kipper fillets and simmer for 5 minutes. Remove the fish and reduce the cream by boiling until it is thick. Season with the pepper and stir in the parsley. Pour over the fish and serve.

Poultry and Game

Chicken with Oysters

(*Traditional, adapted by the author*)

Serves 4
1 SMALL ONION
2 MUSHROOMS
1 CELERY HEART
4 TBS COOKING OIL
A 3-LB CHICKEN, CUT INTO SERVING PIECES
¼ PT (½ CUP) CHICKEN STOCK
12 POACHED OYSTERS
1 TBS PARSLEY, COARSELY CHOPPED

Sauce
1 OZ (2 TBS) BUTTER
2 TBS FLOUR
½ PT (1 CUP) CHICKEN STOCK

Slice the vegetables and cook them for a few minutes in the oil in a frying pan. Add the chicken pieces, brown them and cook with the vegetables, the chicken stock and a seasoning of pepper and salt until they are done. Remove to a cool oven to keep warm.

For the sauce: melt the butter in a saucepan, stir in the flour, then slowly add the stock until the mixture is smooth and creamy. Put the vegetables from the frying pan into a blender, purée them and add to the sauce. Check the seasoning. Reheat the oysters in this sauce, without boiling. Pour over the chicken, sprinkle with the chopped parsley and serve.

Chicken Stanley

This is adapted from a French version of a typical English chicken curry: an Indo-Franco-English dish! Omit the truffles if you want a strong curry and use peach chutney instead.

Serves 3–4
A 3–4 LB CHICKEN
¾ LB (3 CUPS) COOKED RICE
2 OZ (½ CUP) MUSHROOMS, SLICED

3–4 OZ TRUFFLES, CUT INTO STRIPS
2 MEDIUM ONIONS, SLICED
2–4 TBS CURRY POWDER
2 TBS FLOUR
1¼ PT (3 CUPS) CHICKEN STOCK
¼ PT (½ CUP) THICK CREAM

Season the cavity of the chicken with salt and pepper. Combine the rice, mushrooms and truffles in a mixing bowl and season with salt and pepper. Stuff the chicken with this mixture and close the cavity securely by sewing or with wooden toothpicks. Brown the chicken lightly on all sides in a little butter in a braising pan. Remove, and cook the onions until golden and soft. Sprinkle with curry powder and flour to taste. Add the chicken and enough stock to cover and simmer, covered, for about 1½ hours or until tender.

Remove the chicken, draining it back into the pot, remove the skin and carve it into serving pieces. Arrange the stuffing in the centre. Sprinkle it with a few teaspoonfuls of stock to stop it drying out, cover and put in a warm oven or on a plate-warmer while the sauce is being prepared.

Put ½ pint (1 cup) of the stock and the onions in a blender. Blend for a few seconds and return to a thick, wide pan. Add the cream and reduce the sauce over high heat, stirring, until it is quite thick. At this stage more curry powder can be worked in, if desired. Turn down the heat, add another 4 tablespoons (¼ cup) of cream and adjust the seasoning if necessary. Pour the sauce over the chicken (but not over the stuffing). Sprinkle the chicken and sauce with a little sifted curry powder or with finely minced parsley to add a touch of colour.

For an attractive garnish cut the chicken skin into strips with a pair of scissors, fry these until crisp in a little butter and arrange them round the edge of the dish.

Cold Chicken Pie

(*Traditional, adapted by the author*)

Serves 6

¾ LB PUFF PASTRY
6 COLD BOILED CHICKEN BREASTS
½ TSP SALT
¼ TSP PEPPER
2 TBS TARRAGON VINEGAR
1 PT (2¼ CUPS) DOUBLE CREAM, WHIPPED
FRESH TARRAGON LEAVES, WHEN AVAILABLE

Line a pie-dish with the pastry and crimp the edges. Line with foil and fill with uncooked rice. Bake blind (pre-bake) at 400° (Mark 6) for 8–10 minutes. Remove the foil and rice and cool to room temperature. Remove the skin from the chicken breasts and rub with the salt, pepper and tarragon vinegar. Whip the cream and spoon some into the bottom of the pie dish. Arrange the chicken breasts in a fan shape on top of the cream, covering them with the rest of the cream. Garnish the top with fresh chopped tarragon leaves arranged in an attractive pattern.

For extra flavour, whip the cream with very finely chopped, almost powdered, tarragon leaves and a little lemon juice.

Curried Pheasant or Chicken

(*from Alice Thomson*)

Serves 2–3

1 PHEASANT OR CHICKEN
1 ONION, SLICED
2 CARROTS, SLICED
1 BAY LEAF
1 SPRIG THYME

Sauce
4 OZ (½ CUP) BUTTER
2 ONIONS, SLICED
4 CARROTS, SLICED
1 APPLE, PEELED, CORED AND SLICED
2 TBS SULTANAS
2 TBS CURRY POWDER
1 PT (2½ CUPS) LIGHT GAME OR CHICKEN STOCK
ABOUT 1 TBS FLOUR

Cook the bird in a pan with the onion, carrots, bay leaf, thyme, a seasoning of pepper and salt and water to cover. Simmer gently for ¾–1 hour, until tender.

While it is cooking, make the sauce: fry the sliced onions in three-quarters of the butter for 2–3 minutes, then add the carrots, apple, sultanas and curry powder. Add enough stock to cover and cook until soft (about 30 minutes). Purée in the blender and put into a bowl. Melt the rest of the butter, add enough flour to thicken it slightly, then add the puréed mixture.

When the bird is tender, divide it into large pieces and put these into the sauce to reheat, but do not boil. Serve with plain boiled rice.

Croquettes of Chicken and Ham

(*Traditional, adapted by the author*)

8 OZ (1 CUP) COOKED CHICKEN, CHOPPED
4 OZ (½ CUP) HAM, CHOPPED
1 OZ (½ CUP) MUSHROOMS, CHOPPED
1 TRUFFLE (OPTIONAL)
1 OZ (2 TBS) BUTTER
2 TBS FLOUR
¼ PT (½ CUP) CREAM OR STOCK OR A MIXTURE
   OF BOTH
2 TBS CHOPPED PARSLEY
1 TSP GRATED LEMON PEEL

A SQUEEZE OF LEMON JUICE
CAYENNE TO TASTE
1 EGG, BEATEN
FINE BREADCRUMBS FOR COATING
DEEP FAT FOR FRYING

Mix the chopped chicken, ham and mushrooms, adding a finely chopped truffle if available. Melt the butter in a pan, stir in the flour and blend with the stock or cream. Put in the parsley and lemon peel and season to taste with salt, pepper and a little cayenne. When the mixture is thoroughly blended and well seasoned, stir in the meat and mushrooms. Continue to stir over gentle heat until all is well mixed, then turn out on to a dish to cool.

When the mixture is cold, shape it into balls, ovals or any other shape you fancy; roll them in beaten egg and then in fine breadcrumbs, and fry until golden in hot fat, as for fritters.

Casseroled Grouse

(*from Alice Thomson*)

Serves 8
6 OZ (¾ CUP) BUTTER
2 MEDIUM ONIONS, SLICED
4 GROUSE
12 CARROTS, SLICED

Sauce:
1½ OZ (3 TBS) BUTTER
3 TBS FLOUR
ABOUT ¾ PT (1½–2 CUPS) GAME STOCK

Melt the butter in a saucepan, fry the sliced onion in it, then add the whole grouse; brown them, add a little water and the carrots. Put the lid on the pan and simmer gently over low heat for 2 hours. Remove the grouse and keep them warm. Put the vegetables through a sieve, or liquidize in a blender. Melt the butter, stir in the flour and make the sauce with the game stock. Add the puréed vegetables. Cut the grouse in half, put them back into the casserole, season the birds and the sauce with pepper and salt to taste and pour the sauce over them in the casserole.

Three Pepper Chicken

(*from my daughter, Louise de la Falaise*)

I 2–3 LB ROASTING CHICKEN
I OZ (2 TBS) BUTTER ⎤
¼ TSP CAYENNE PEPPER ⎟
½ TSP PAPRIKA ⎬ STUFFING
¼ TSP BLACK PEPPER ⎟
½ TSP SALT ⎦
¼ TSP CAYENNE
I TSP PAPRIKA
½ TSP BLACK PEPPER
I TSP SALT
4 ONIONS, PEELED AND QUARTERED
4 WHOLE ENDIVES
¼ PT (½ CUP) CHICKEN STOCK

Mash the butter and peppers and salt together and put inside the chicken cavity. Dust the outside of the bird with the remaining seasonings. Put in baking dish in oven preheated to 500°. As soon as the butter starts to melt into the pan, add the hot stock and vegetables. Baste occasionally with the pan juices. Roast for 20–25 minutes: the vegetables should be a little crisp.

Serve with champagne.

Grilled Stuffed Chicken

(*Traditional, adapted by the author*)

This dish can be prepared with any small bird or with game. For game, use game forcemeat (*see p.* 136) instead and replace the lemon juice with a dash of Worcester Sauce, Harvey, Sauce Diable or a mixture of all three. Garnish with redcurrant jelly. The preparations can be made in advance, but the grilling must be done at the last moment.

I YOUNG CHICKEN (ABOUT 2 LB), BONED AND
    SPLIT OPEN DOWN THE BACK
¾ LB (1½ CUPS) GRILLING VEAL, MINCED (GROUND)
I TBS FRESH CORIANDER OR TARRAGON LEAVES,
    CHOPPED OR I TSP DRIED CORIANDER OR
    TARRAGON

I TSP SALT
¼ TSP PEPPER
4 TBS CREAM
I EGG
2 OZ (¼ CUP) BUTTER
JUICE OF ½ LEMON
BREAD SAUCE
WATERCRESS

Put the minced veal in a mixing bowl with some of the herbs; season, mix in the cream and bind with the egg. Paste this forcemeat on to the under side of the flattened chicken. Return to the refrigerator for half an hour to set.

Melt the butter and lemon juice, season lightly with pepper and salt and the rest of the herbs. Paint the chicken all over with this butter, then put it on a greased pan under the grill (4–5 inches from the heat). Grill on both sides, gently at first then with a sharper flame towards the end, basting frequently with the seasoned butter, for about 15–20 minutes on each side. Serve with bread sauce, the pan gravies and a garnish of watercress.

Pigeon Pie

(*adapted from the Guide Culinaire Escoffier*)

Serves 4

8 RASHERS OF BACON
4 SHALLOT CLOVES, FINELY CHOPPED
2 PIGEONS OR VERY SMALL CHICKENS, CUT INTO
    4 PIECES
PEPPER AND SALT TO TASTE
4 TBS PARSLEY, FINELY CHOPPED
TWO EGG YOLKS, HARD-BOILED, HALVED
3 CUPS STRONG CHICKEN, OR VEAL STOCK, OR A
    MIXTURE OF BOTH, THAT WILL SET TO A JELLY
    WHEN CHILLED
ENOUGH PASTRY FOR A 10 BY 8-INCH CASSEROLE,
    OVEN PROOF, ABOUT 4-INCH DEEP
A PIE FUNNEL

Line the casserole with the bacon rashers, sprinkle in the shallots. Arrange the pigeon pieces and egg yolks inside, season and add the parsley and stock. Place the funnel in the centre and cover with a pastry lid, cutting out a hole over the funnel. Flute the edges and scratch the surface with the prongs of a fork, to make a ripple pattern. Glaze with egg wash and bake at 350° for 1½ hours. Cover the lid with foil if it starts to burn. Add a little extra stock through the funnel, especially if the pie is to be eaten cold, as this will make nice jelly around the birds.

Salmis of Game

(*Traditional, adapted by the author*)

Serves 2

2 COLD COOKED GAME BIRDS
2 PT (5 CUPS) STOCK
1 BAY LEAF
1 SPRIG THYME
4 TBS (¼ CUP) MADEIRA
1 OZ (2 TBS) BUTTER
1 HEAPED TBS FLOUR
1–2 TBS MELTED GAME GLAZE
CROUTONS OF FRIED BREAD, CUT INTO TRIANGLES
A FEW TRUFFLE PEELINGS (OPTIONAL)

Remove the flesh from the birds and cut into strips. Put the carcases in a pan with the stock and bring to the boil. Simmer for 1–2 hours, then strain through a fine sieve. Remove all the grease and scum and boil until the stock is reduced to about half a pint (1 cup). Make a brown sauce with the butter, the flour and the reduced stock. Add the Madeira, the game glaze and the truffle peelings. Toss in the strips of game and reheat thoroughly, but without allowing to boil. Taste for seasoning, adding pepper and salt if required. Arrange the game strips on a warm serving dish, surround with the croutons, pour over some of the sauce and serve the rest separately in a warm sauceboat.

Plain boiled rice and a watercress salad are the perfect accompaniments to this dish.

Game Soufflé

(*Traditional, adapted by the author*)

Serves 2–3

½ LB (1 CUP) BREAST OF GROUSE OR OTHER GAME, CHOPPED AND POUNDED
1 SMALL ONION, VERY FINELY CHOPPED OR PUT THROUGH A GARLIC PRESS
2 TBS FINE BREADCRUMBS
1½ OZ (3 TBS) BUTTER
3 TBS FLOUR
½ PT (1 CUP) MILK
½ TSP SALT
¼ TSP CAYENNE
4 EGGS

Blend the pounded game and crushed onion to achieve an even texture and perfect blending of flavours. Butter the inside of a soufflé dish and sprinkle with the crumbs. Melt the butter in a saucepan, add the flour and cook for 1 minute. Then add the milk, salt and cayenne and cook until thickened. Beat the egg yolks in a bowl, then beat into them some of the hot sauce. Combine both preparations and cook until thick, but do not boil. Stir in the game and onion paste and mix well. Draw off the heat and leave to cool.

Beat the egg whites until they form soft, tiny white peaks; they should remain in the bowl when you turn it upside down. (If overbeaten the peaks will be sharp instead of glossy, and the whole mass will slide out of the bowl when it is reversed. This makes a dry, granulated soufflé.) Fold in the whites, pour into the soufflé dish to within 2 inches of the rim. Bake at 400° (Mark 6) for 40–50 minutes.

Quails in Pastry

(*Traditional, adapted by the author*)

Serves 4

4 QUAILS
1½ LB PASTRY
1 EGG YOLK
2 TBS MILK

Stuffing
¼ LB (1 CUP) CARROTS, FINELY CHOPPED OR GRATED
1½ OZ (½ CUP) ONION, FINELY CHOPPED
4 TBS PARSLEY, CHOPPED
1 TSP THYME

I TSP SALT
¼ TSP PEPPER
1½ OZ (3 TBS) BUTTER
3 SLICES BACON, CHOPPED

Tarragon Sauce
I PT (2½ CUPS) CLARIFIED STOCK OR TINNED
    CONSOMMÉ
4 EGG YOLKS
2 TBS FRESH TARRAGON, CHOPPED

Mix together all the stuffing ingredients
except the butter and cook gently in the butter
until almost tender. Stuff the birds and secure
them. Roll out the pastry and cut into 5-inch
squares. Sprinkle the birds with pepper and
salt and roll each in a square of pastry. Brush
the surface of the pastry with the egg yolk,
beaten with the milk, and cook in the oven at
450° (Mark 8) for 15–20 minutes.

To make the tarragon sauce, heat the stock
and stir into the well-beaten egg yolks. Cook
over low heat in the top of a double boiler
until thickened. Do not boil, or let the water
below boil. Stir in the chopped tarragon and
serve with the quails.

Marinated Roe Deer (or Hare)

(*from Alice Thomson*)

Serves 6–8

A 4–5-LB HAUNCH OF ROE DEER (OR A SADDLE
    OF HARE)
3 CARROTS, SLICED
2 ONIONS, SLICED
I TURNIP, SLICED
6 BLACK PEPPERCORNS
I BOTTLE WHITE WINE
I PT (2½ CUPS) SOUR CREAM

Put the haunch in a fireproof dish and cover
with the sliced carrot, onion and turnip and
the peppercorns. Cover with the wine and
leave for 2–3 days in a cool place, basting and
turning as often as possible.

Transfer to the oven, still in the marinade,
and cook for about 3 hours (or 1 hour for
hare) at 350° (Mark 4). When the meat is
tender, pour the marinade through a strainer,

discarding the vegetables. Add the sour cream
to the sauce, season with salt and pepper, and
scrape all the brown pieces from the edges of
the pan, mixing them into the sauce. Reheat
and serve the meat covered with the sauce.

Devilled Pheasant

(*from Robin McDouall*)

This recipe is for a cold devilled pheasant,
which is more suitable for a cold buffet on
Sunday night supper than for a dinner party.

*Take a young hen pheasant. Make the oven very
hot – 15–20 minutes. Turn it down to Regulo 7
(425°) and put in a baking tin with some butter
and some arachide oil in it (butter alone tends to
brown). Stuff the pheasant with butter – if
unsalted, with some salt. When you can hear the
butter, put in the pheasant, breast upwards, with
some more butter spread on it. Cook for
10 minutes. Lie it on its side and cook for another*

10 minutes. Turn it on its other side and cook for another 10 minutes. Lower the heat to Regulo 5 (375°) and put it breast upwards again. Baste every 5 minutes. As it browns, lower the heat to Regulo 3 (325°). Continue to baste. Stick a fork into the leg (where it doesn't matter losing some juice) to test when it is done. A pheasant should not be saignant like a grouse or partridge, but on the other hand, must not be overcooked or it gets hard.

When it is cold, cut it up, discarding skin and fat. If you are going to eat it with a knife and fork, carve the breast into four slices, take the bone out of the cuisses, and keep the drumsticks and the wing-bones for a rainy day. If you are going to have fork only, cut breast and cuisses into small pieces. Season with salt.

Take ½ pt thick cream. Whip it or not as you will. Chop very finely 2 tablespoonfuls chutney. Add it and a tablespoonful or two of Worcestershire sauce and a pinch or two of curry powder to the cream; add more curry powder and/or pepper if you want it hotter. Either pour this over the pieces of pheasant or put the pieces of pheasant into the cream to get them coated all round. Turn out into the middle of a dish.

Round the pheasant put a bank of rice salad or serve them separately, if you like.

Serves 4–6

A YOUNG HEN PHEASANT
¼ LB (½ CUP) BUTTER
3 TBS ARACHIDE OIL (PEANUT OIL)
½ PT (1 CUP) DOUBLE CREAM
2 TBS CHUTNEY
1–2 TBS WORCESTERSHIRE SAUCE
1–2 PINCHES CURRY POWDER

Directions as above.

Meat

Maxime's Braised Veal

Serves 8

5–6 LB BRAISING VEAL, IN ONE PIECE
5–6 VEAL BONES
4 CALVES' FEET, EACH SPLIT IN HALF
6 OLD CARROTS
2 ONIONS, STUCK WITH 2 CLOVES EACH
A TWIST OF ORANGE PEEL
1 STALK CELERY, CHOPPED
2 BAY LEAVES
1 TBS THYME
2–3 TBS DRIED TARRAGON
6 YOUNG CARROTS
6 SMALL ONIONS
10 POTATOES

Put the bones and calves' feet into the bottom of a very large deep braising pan. Cover with cold water; bring to the boil and skim until the water is perfectly clean. Add the meat and all the other ingredients except the young carrots, the onions, and the potatoes. Bring back to the boil and then simmer for about 2 hours, or until the meat is tender when pierced with a fork. Remove the meat to a covered dish, add a few spoonfuls of stock and keep warm.

Strain the rest of the stock, drain the calves' feet and leave to cool with a weighted plate over them. Reduce the stock by boiling uncovered for another hour; it should be rather syrupy, because of the bones and gelatine in the feet. Add the young carrots and onions about 20–30 minutes before the hour is up and remove them to the dish with the meat as soon as they are tender.

Serve the meat in a deep earthen casserole with the juice, the carrots and the onions. Boil the potatoes separately and add them to the dish before serving.

Roll the calves' feet in egg and breadcrumbs, grill them with a little butter and serve them next day with mashed potatoes and fried apple slices.

Lamb like Veal

(*from Nellie Gallaher*)

Serves 4

4 LAMB CUTLETS
2 TBS FLOUR
1 EGG
1 TSP LEMON JUICE
½ TSP SALT
⅛ TSP PEPPER
6–8 OZ (1½–2 CUPS) DRY BREADCRUMBS
1 TSP TARRAGON
1 TSP THYME
1 TSP CHERVIL
1 OZ (2 TBS) BUTTER
2 TBS OIL

Cut out the centre loin of the meat and pound to flatten it slightly. Dip in the flour, then in the egg, beaten with the lemon juice, salt and pepper. Mix the breadcrumbs with the herbs, coat the meat with the mixture and fry quickly in butter and oil on both sides.

Roasted Mince

(*from Drue Heinz*)

Serves 3–4

1 OZ (2 TBS) LARD OR DRIPPING
½ LB MINCED (GROUND) BEEF
½ LB MINCED (GROUND) PORK
4 TBS FRESH BREADCRUMBS
1 SMALL ONION, FINELY CHOPPED
2 TBS MILK
1 EGG
1 TBS CHOPPED PARSLEY
1 TSP SALT
¼ TSP GROUND PEPPER
1 TBS FLOUR
½ PT (1 CUP) STOCK OR WATER
4 TBS (¼ CUP) SOUR CREAM

Brown the onion in the fat until golden. Combine the meat, crumbs, onion, milk, egg, parsley, salt and pepper. Shape into a loaf. Put into a baking pan and bake at 350° (Mark 4) for 35–45 minutes. Remove the loaf from the pan. Stir the flour into the dripping. Cook for 1 minute. Stir in the stock and cook until thickened. Stir the sour cream into the sauce and serve.

Steak and Kidney Pudding

(*from Donald Smith*)

Serves 4

1 LB (4½ CUPS) FLOUR
8 OZ (1 CUP) BEEF SUET, FINELY CHOPPED
1½ LB SHIN OF BEEF
½ LB (1 CUP) OX KIDNEY

Mix the flour, suet and a pinch of salt with water, as for short pastry. Line a greased pudding basin with a layer of paste about ⅛ inch thick. Cut the beef and kidney into 1-inch dice. Dip into flour and place in the lined basin. Add salt and pepper to taste. Pour water over to come three-quarters of the way up the meat; cover with paste and tie a

pudding cloth over the top. Place in a pan of boiling water and cook for about 4½ hours.

Optional additions are thyme and a bay leaf, and a few mushrooms.

Kidneys, Chives and Bacon

(*from the author*)

Serves 2

6 LAMBS KIDNEYS, SLIT AND OPENED FLAT
4 RASHERS (SLICES) OF STREAKY BACON
6 SHALLOT CLOVES, FINELY MINCED

3 TBS FRESH CHIVES, SNIPPED SMALL
PEPPER AND SALT TO TASTE
4 TBS DRY WHITE WINE
4 BOILED POTATOES

Fry the bacon in an iron skillet until crisp.
Remove and keep warm. Throw the shallots
into the hot bacon fat and cook until coloured.
Add the kidneys and brown on both sides; add
the chives and seasoning. Pour in the wine and
cook down on a sharp flame for a few minutes,
turning the kidneys and scraping the coagulated
meat juices in the pan back into the wine
sauce. Serve very hot with the hot boiled
potatoes and the rashers of bacon.

Yorkshire Pudding

In Yorkshire this is served with any type of
roast meat, or sometimes before the meat with
gravy. In Lancashire it is sometimes eaten after
the meat course, with sugar sprinkled on top.
(*Traditional*)

2 TBS BEEF DRIPPING
2 EGGS
½ PT (I CUP) MILK
4 OZ (I CUP) SIFTED FLOUR
½ TSP SALT

Heat the oven at 425° (Mark 7). Pour the hot
dripping into a heated 10-inch pie plate or
small roasting pan and coat the surface with it.
Beat together the remaining ingredients in a
bowl with a rotary beater and pour into the
plate. Bake for 20–25 minutes, or until puffy
and golden.

Vegetables

Iced Artichoke bottoms with Cream and Tomatoes

(*The Queen Cookery Books*, *1913*)

Serves 6

½ PT (¾ CUP) TOMATO PURÉE (MADE FROM
  TINNED TOMATOES RUBBED THROUGH A SIEVE)
1½ TBS MAYONNAISE
1½ TSP TARRAGON VINEGAR
¼ PT (½ CUP) WHIPPED CREAM
2–3 DROPS COCHINEAL OR RED FOOD COLOURING
6 COOKED ARTICHOKE BOTTOMS, FRESH OR TINNED
A LITTLE CHOPPED ASPIC JELLY

Mix together the tomato purée and mayonnaise,
season with pepper and salt and the vinegar;
when all is well blended fold in the whipped
cream and the cochineal. Spoon into little
moulds of the same diameter as the artichoke
bottoms. (These can easily be made with silver
foil.) Freeze until set. Turn out and set one
mould on top of each artichoke bottom. Arrange
on a serving dish and garnish with the aspic
jelly. Keep refrigerated until you are ready
to serve.

Chestnuts as a Vegetable

This is a vegetable dish to serve with roast
meats or birds which produce their own
pan-gravy that can be used in the sauce; it
has the added advantage of associated flavours
in one course.
(*from the author*)

Serves 6

1 LB (OR 1 LARGE TIN) CHESTNUTS
1 OZ (2 TBS) BUTTER
2 TBS FLOUR
½ PT (1 CUP) COOKING LIQUID (OR THE LIQUID
  FROM THE TIN WITH A LITTLE CHICKEN OR
  VEGETABLE STOCK
½ TSP SALT
¼ TSP PEPPER
1 TBS LEMON JUICE
1 TBS MEAT GLAZE OR GOOD GRAVY

Peel the fresh chestnuts and cook until tender.
Melt the butter, stir in the flour and cook for
1 minute; gradually add the cooking liquid or
stock, the seasonings, glaze or gravy and
lemon juice. When all is well blended, add the
chestnuts and reheat.

Mushroom Bog

(*from my mother, Rhoda Birley*)

Serves 8

2 LB (8 CUPS) FIELD MUSHROOMS
2 OZ (4 TBS) BUTTER OR MARGARINE
I TSP FINELY CHOPPED GARLIC
½ PT (I CUP) MADEIRA
I TSP MUSHROOM ESSENCE OR MUSHROOM
  KETCHUP
I TSP WORCESTERSHIRE SAUCE
¼ PT (½ CUP) CREAM
I TSP SALT
¼ TSP PEPPER
I TSP LEMON JUICE
2 EGG YOLKS
I EGG WHITE, LIGHTLY BEATEN
A FEW WHOLE MUSHROOMS FOR GARNISH
I OZ (2 TBS) BUTTER
I TBS MADEIRA WINE

Cook the mushrooms whole in the butter or margarine, with the garlic, Madeira, mushroom essence (or mushroom ketchup) and Worcestershire sauce. Then add the cream and cook down a little until the cream is well coloured by the mushrooms and the sauce is well mixed. Mash or sieve most of the mushrooms, but leave some pieces intact to add texture to the soufflé. These should be coarsely chopped. Season all the mushrooms with pepper and salt, and add a squeeze of lemon juice. Put the sieved and chopped mushroom mixtures into the pan in which they were cooked, rewarm and add the egg yolks off the heat. Leave to cool.

Cook the egg and mushroom mixture over low heat, stirring until thickened but not boiling.

Pour into a soufflé dish, garnishing the top with whole mushrooms cooked in butter and Madeira. Chill.

Maxime's Quick Vegetable Toss-up

Serves 4

2 POTATOES, PEELED
I–2 TURNIPS, PEELED
I–2 PARSNIPS, PEELED
2 STALKS CELERY
2 LARGE CARROTS
I ONION, SLICED
2½ OZ (4–5 TBS) BUTTER
A LITTLE OIL
¼ TSP PEPPER
½ TSP SALT
A PINCH OF THYME

Using the corrugated side of a 'Waefa' grater (or mandoline), set to about ⅛ inch, grate the potatoes, turnips, parsnips, celery, carrots and any other crisp or root vegetables you want to use up. Slice the onion by hand. Melt the butter, with a little oil to prevent it from blackening, in a thick enamelled frying-pan. When the fat is hot, toss in the vegetables and stir them round until they are all fairly well coated with butter. Cover and let them cook over medium heat for about 5 minutes. Then stir the browned ones to the top and the raw ones to the bottom. Cover and cook for 5 more minutes. Now take the lid off and add the pepper, salt and thyme, plus extra bits of butter if the mixture starts sticking to the bottom of the pan. Cook until the vegetables are crisp, not too brown and just tender enough to eat.

Rice Salad

(*from Robin McDouall*)

Put a cupful of rice (preferably Patna) into a saucepan of boiling salted water. Cook rapidly, skimming, for 12 minutes, then test a few grains between your thumb and forefinger to see if they are cooked. Test every minute till the rice is done. Tip it into a colander and put that under the cold tap to separate the grains. Shake to dry – if you like, dry on a cloth or towel. Put the rice into a bowl and, while it is still warm, add some best olive oil – enough to coat the grains but not so much as to make the salad runny. Squeeze on some lemon juice. Add salt, pepper, cayenne, paprika, a pinch of curry powder, nutmeg, cinnamon – no saffron. Add a few raisins and some blanched, sliced almonds.

Add small quantities of any or all or some of the following : finely chopped cucumber (with the peel on); flesh only of tomatoes; celery; apple (very little); onion, garlic and chives (very important); pimento, red or green; red cabbage. Correct the amount of oil, lemon juice and salt. If it is too runny, drain some liquid off.

To a rice salad for chicken or fish, you can add a few shrimps or a chopped anchovy but I shouldn't with pheasant.

I CUP RICE, PREFERABLY PATNA
OLIVE OIL
LEMON JUICE
A PINCH EACH OF CURRY POWDER, CAYENNE
   PEPPER AND PAPRIKA
GRATED NUTMEG
GROUND CINNAMON
A FEW RAISINS
A FEW ALMONDS, SLICED AND BLANCHED

small quantities of any or all of the following :

CUCUMBER, FINELY CHOPPED
TOMATO SKINNED, SEEDED AND CHOPPED
CELERY, DICED
ONION, FINELY CHOPPED
GARLIC, FINELY CHOPPED
CHIVES, CHOPPED
PIMENTO, RED OR GREEN, CHOPPED
RED CABBAGE, CHOPPED

Iced Vegetable Creams

Savoury ices came into fashion in the early twenties. Frozen sauces were served in solid cubes or 'fingers', often as an accompaniment to hot dishes such as grilled meat, or with cold lobster, dressed crab or cold roast beef. Several of them can be made with different vegetables and colourings; they can be put into a mould in layers, in which case each must set before the next is added. They are then turned out and served sliced like Neapolitan ice-creams. The slices can be arranged attractively on a dish, glazed with half-melted aspic and rechilled until needed.
(*The Queen Cookery Books, 1913*)

Cook the vegetables very gently until they are tender enough to sieve or blend, adding milk, white stock or brown stock for peas, cucumbers or artichoke hearts, and brown stock for tomatoes. Season the pulped purée to taste, adding $\frac{1}{4}$ pint ($\frac{1}{2}$ cup) of good cream sauce or bechamel, velouté or espagnole sauce for the tomatoes. Add rather more than $\frac{1}{4}$ pint ($\frac{1}{2}$ cup) of rather strong, half-melted aspic jelly. Cool and stir in 2 tablespoons of whipped cream. If necessary, add a little vegetable colouring. Spoon into a single mould or individual moulds and chill.

Tomato Ice

(*The Queen Cookery Books, 1913*)

Serves 6
I LB (3 MEDIUM) RIPE TOMATOES
I PT (2$\frac{1}{4}$ CUPS) WATER
JUICE OF I LEMON
3 APPLES, PEELED, CORED AND SLICED
2 TBS APRICOT JAM
5–6 OZ ($\frac{3}{4}$ CUP) SUGAR
2–3 DROPS COCHINEAL OR OTHER RED FOOD
   COLOURING (OPTIONAL)
2–3 TBS RUM OR BRANDY

Slice down the tomatoes, which should be very red and ripe. Put into a saucepan with the water, lemon juice, apples, jam and sugar, bring to the boil and allow to simmer until tender enough to pulp; add the food colouring and rub through a hair sieve or 'chinoise' (a conical-shaped sieve obtainable at good kitchenware shops). When the mixture has cooled, flavour with rum or brandy and freeze in a mould or individual parfait glasses.

Tomato Soufflé

(*from Nellie Gallaher*)

Serves 3–4
$\frac{1}{2}$ OZ (I PACKAGE) GELATINE
$\frac{3}{4}$ PT (2 CUPS) TOMATO PURÉE
4 TBS ONION, MINCED
4 TBS ($\frac{1}{4}$ CUP) WATER
$\frac{1}{4}$ PINT ($\frac{1}{2}$ CUP) CREAM, WHIPPED

¼ PINT (½ CUP) MAYONNAISE
¼ LB (½ CUP) DICED TOMATO FLESH, CHOPPED
   PARSLEY AND SHREDDED LETTUCE, MIXED
¼ LB (½ CUP) ASPIC JELLY, CHOPPED

Dissolve the gelatine by heating it in ¼ pint
(½ cup) of the tomato purée with the water
over gentle heat; stir until dissolved and
blended. Combine with the remaining purée
and the minced onion, stirring frequently until
cooled. When the mixture begins to thicken
and set, fold in the whipped cream and the
mayonnaise. Oil a 1½-pint soufflé dish and the
outside of a narrow tumbler. Place an oiled
paper round the rim of the soufflé dish. Put
the oiled tumbler in the centre of the dish
and pour the soufflé mixture all round it,
leaving it to rise to the edge of the projecting
paper. Chill until set.

Remove the tumbler and fill the hole it
leaves with the diced tomato, lettuce and
parsley, seasoned with salt and pepper, and the
chopped aspic. Gently remove the paper; the
soufflé will appear to have risen above the edge
of the dish. Return to the refrigerator until
ready to serve. This dish can be prepared a day
in advance, but you must retain the paper and
the tumbler until the last hour or so.

Mustard Glazed Onions
(*from Drue Heinz*)

Serves 4
1 LB SMALL ONIONS
2 OZ (4 TBS) BUTTER
2 TBS MADE ENGLISH MUSTARD

Peel the onions but leave them whole. Cover
with cold water, add a little salt and bring
to the boil. Simmer gently for 15–20 minutes
or until the onions are tender – test them with
a sharp skewer or the point of a knife. When
they are ready, drain them. Melt the butter in
the hot pan and stir in the mustard. Add the
onions and toss to coat well. Serve at once.
They are particularly good with roast beef or
steak.

Desserts

Apple Charlotte
(*Traditional, adapted by the author*)

Serves 8
ABOUT 16 SLICES BREAD, CRUSTS REMOVED
3½ OZ (7 TBS) BUTTER, MELTED
5 LB APPLES, PEELED, CORED AND SLICED
½ LB (1 CUP) SUGAR
¼ PT (⅓ CUP) WATER
1 TSP GROUND CINNAMON

Brush a 3-pint (7½ cup) charlotte mould with
melted butter. Cut 10 slices of bread to fit the
mould, dip them in butter and arrange in the
mould, leaving no spaces between them and
overlapping them slightly where necessary.
Fry another 3 slices of bread in 1½ ounces
(3 tablespoons) butter until golden; cut into
1-inch squares and reserve. Cook the apples,
sugar and water in a covered pan until tender.
Remove cover and cook until thick. Stir in the
cinnamon and chill. Stir the browned bread
squares into the purée and pour into the
prepared mould.

Cut the remaining 3 slices to make a lid and
dip them in melted butter. Arrange carefully
on top of the mixture, to cover completely.
Bake at 375° (Mark 5) for 1 hour, or until
golden. Leave to cool for 30 minutes, then
invert the mould onto a serving dish. Leave
for another 30 minutes, then remove the mould.

Brown Betty
(*Traditional, adapted by the author*)

Serves 8–10
6 APPLES, PEELED, CORED AND SLICED
3 OZ (1½ CUPS) DRY BREADCRUMBS
¾ LB (1 CUP) GOLDEN SYRUP (OR CORN SYRUP)
2 TBS BROWN SUGAR
2 TBS LEMON JUICE

Sauce
4 OZ (½ CUP) SWEET BUTTER, SOFTENED
4 OZ (½ CUP) CASTER (CONFECTIONER'S) SUGAR
I EGG WHITE
I TSP VANILLA ESSENCE
½ TSP GROUND NUTMEG

Layer the apple slices and crumbs alternately
in a deep dish, finishing with a layer of crumbs.
Mix the syrup, brown sugar and lemon juice
and pour over. Bake covered at 350° (Mark 4)
for 40–45 minutes, remove the cover and raise
the heat to 400° (Mark 6) for 10–15 minutes,
to brown the top layer of crumbs. To make
the sauce, beat the butter to a cream, adding
the sugar gradually, then the egg white, and
beat until light and frothy; add the vanilla and
the nutmeg and chill.

This pudding can be served hot or cold,
but the sauce should always be chilled. It can
be turned out before serving, in which case the
dish should be well buttered and the layers of
apples should be covered with a sprinkling of
sugar. The whole Betty must then be browned
in the oven before serving.

Rhubarb Flummery

(*from Drue Heinz*)

Serves 3
6 OZ (¾ CUP) SUGAR
½ PT (I CUP) WATER
I LB RHUBARB, CUT INTO I-INCH LENGTHS
I TBS FLOUR
½ OZ (I PACKAGE) GELATINE
PEEL OF I ORANGE
2 TBS GRAND MARNIER
CLOTTED CREAM FOR GARNISH

Make a syrup from the sugar and water and cook
the rhubarb in this gently, until tender. Drain
and reserve the syrup. Mix the flour with I
tablespoon of the cooled syrup and blend into
the remainder of the syrup. Add the gelatine,
which you have soaked and then dissolved in
hot liquid. Add the grated orange peel and pour
into a very cold bowl, whisking hard as the
mixture cools and thickens. Fold in the stewed

rhubarb and the orange-flavoured liqueur.
Serve in individual glasses and cover with
clotted cream.

Redcurrants Charleston

(*from my mother, Rhoda Birley*)

Serves 4–6
I LB (2 CUPS) REDCURRANTS
WHITES OF 4 LARGE EGGS
½ LB (I CUP) SUGAR
2 OZ (¾ CUP) MINT, VERY FINELY CHOPPED
½ PT (I½–2 CUPS) WHIPPED CREAM
¼ TSP VANILLA ESSENCE
¼ TSP ALMOND ESSENCE
2 OZ (½ CUP) CRYSTALLIZED FRUIT

Pick small bunches of redcurrants and leave
them on their stalks. Mix equal quantities of
egg white and sugar in a shallow dish. Coat
the berries in this and put them in the
refrigerator. Chop some fresh mint very finely
and mix it with the remaining egg and sugar
mixture. Coat the berries again in this and
chill again very thoroughly. Strip the currants
from their stalks very quickly with a fork. Put
them into a cut-glass serving bowl, cover with
whipped cream flavoured with vanilla and
almond essence and arrange some small pieces
of crystallized fruit on top.

Atholl Brose

(*from Alice Thomson*)

Serves 4–6
I PT (2½ CUPS) STIFFLY WHIPPED CREAM
2 TBS LIQUID HONEY
3–4 TBS COARSISH OATMEAL
2–3 JIGGERS SCOTCH WHISKY

Stir all the ingredients together gently, adding
the whisky last. Serve at once.

Brown Bread Cream

(*Traditional, adapted by the author*)

Serves 4–6

1 PT (2½ CUPS) DOUBLE CREAM
3 OZ (1½ CUPS) COARSE BROWN BREADCRUMBS,
   DRIED IN THE OVEN
1 TSP VANILLA ESSENCE
2 TBS BRANDY
1 PT (2 CUPS) STRAWBERRIES OR STONED
   CHERRIES (FRESH, FROZEN OR TINNED)
LIQUEUR OF YOUR CHOICE, FOR STEEPING THE
   FRUIT

Whip the cream and fold in the breadcrumbs
lightly. Stir in first the vanilla, then the
brandy. Spoon into a glass dish and garnish
with strawberries or cherries that have been
steeped for a few hours in the liqueur.

   The liqueur used to steep the fruit can be
drained off, bottled and kept in the refrigerator
as a delicious flavouring for future desserts.

Nassau Tart

(*The Queen Cookery Books, 1913*)

Many of the early colonists and landowners in
Nassau were Scots, Irish and English. This is
obviously a marmalade pie from an early
Bahamian settler who moved out with a
standing order for marmalade at the Army &
Navy Stores in London:

Serves 6

A 9-INCH PASTRY SHELL, BAKED BLIND
   (UNFILLED)
½ LB (¾ CUP) MARMALADE
2 OZ (¾ CUP) BUTTER
3 EGGS

Melt the marmalade and butter in a saucepan.
Beat the eggs in a bowl and pour in the hot
jam and butter mixture, beating while you
do so. Pour the contents of the bowl into the
cooled tart shell. Bake for 20–25 minutes at
350° (Mark 4) until puffed, browned and set.
Serve hot.

Dorset Apple Cake

(*from Sir Frederick Warner*)

Serves 4–6

¼ LB (½ CUP) BUTTER OR LARD
½ LB (1¾ CUPS) FLOUR
3 OZ (⅓ CUP) SUGAR
1 TSP BAKING POWDER
3 HARD COOKING APPLES, FINELY CHOPPED
1 EGG, BEATEN
A LITTLE MILK, SCRUMPY, BRANDY, CALVADOS
   OR APPLEJACK
A LITTLE CASTER (CONFECTIONER'S) SUGAR

Rub the fat into the flour, add the other dry
ingredients and then the apples and the egg.
Care must then be taken to pour in only just
enough milk to blend the paste, because as the
apples bake they will release a good deal of
the moisture in them. In the Marshwood Vale
(in Dorsetshire) a small amount of scrumpy
brandy is used in the blending, but if you
cannot find this, calvados or applejack will do
as well. Grease a shallow baking tin, put in the
mixture and bake for half an hour in a moderate
oven. Turn out of the tin, dredge well with
caster sugar and serve cold.

Edinburgh Fog

*Beat half a pint of cream to a stiff froth with a
little pounded sugar and vanilla flavouring.
Mix thoroughly with a good handful of ratafia
biscuits and some blanched and chopped almonds.
Serve in a glass bowl or dish.*
(*F. Marian McNeill, 1929*)

Serves 4

½ PT (1 CUP) DOUBLE CREAM
2 TBS ICING (CONFECTIONER'S) SUGAR
A LITTLE VANILLA FLAVOURING (OR ORANGE
   ESSENCE)
2 OZ (½ CUP) TINY RATAFIA BISCUITS
2 OZ (½ CUP) BLANCHED ALMONDS, CHOPPED

Follow the recipe, but chill well before serving.

Welsh Amber Pudding

(*from my grandmother, the late Vava Lecky Pike*)

Melt the butter over a slow fire, stir in 6 oz finely powdered sugar and after it has boiled, take it off, and in a few minutes stir in the yolks of 6 eggs which have been well beaten. When cold, put into a dish lined with puff paste, adding a little orange or lemon peel and some ratafia. Let it be taken out of the oven ¼ of an hour before being sent to the table.

Serves 4–6

6 OZ (¾ CUP) BUTTER
6 OZ (¾ CUP) CASTER (CONFECTIONER'S) SUGAR
6 EGG YOLKS, WELL BEATEN
A PIE DISH LINED WITH PUFF PASTRY
1 TSP GRATED ORANGE OR LEMON PEEL
4 TBS RATAFIA ESSENCE

Brown Bread Ice Cream

(*The Queen Cookery Books, 1913*)

Serves 4
1½ PT (4 CUPS) CREAM
a 1½-INCH PIECE OF VANILLA POD
4 OZ (½ CUP) SUGAR
6 OZ (3 CUPS) FRESH BROWN BREADCRUMBS

Heat a quarter of the cream with the vanilla pod and the sugar until the sugar has dissolved. Remove the pod, scraping the seeds into the cream. Leave to cool. Mix the cooled cream with the rest of the cream and the breadcrumbs. Pour into an ice-cream freezer and crank until you can barely turn the handle. Remove the paddle, cover and repack with ice and salt. Leave for 1–2 hours before serving.

Caledonian Ice

This is also known as Stapag, or Iced Cream Crowdie.

Whip some cream stiffly; sweeten it and flavour with vanilla; set it to freeze. When nearly frozen stir in coarse toasted oatmeal, well dried in the oven without being browned. Serve in a glass dish or in individual glasses.
(*from F. Marian McNeill, 1929*)

Serves 3–4
½ PT (1 CUP) DOUBLE CREAM
SUGAR TO TASTE
A FEW DROPS OF VANILLA FLAVOURING
2–3 OZ (¼–½ CUP) COARSE OATMEAL, TOASTED

Almond Ice Cream

(*Traditional, adapted by the author*)

Makes about 3 pints (7–8 cups)
1 PT (2½ CUPS) CREAM
8 OZ (2 CUPS) ALMONDS, COARSELY GROUND
2 TBS ORANGE FLOWER WATER
4 EGG YOLKS
4 OZ (½ CUP) SUGAR
6–8 DROPS ALMOND ESSENCE
½ PT (1 CUP) WHIPPED CREAM

Heat half the cream until scalded. Stir in the almonds and orange-flower water and leave to stand until cool.

Make a custard by beating the egg yolks and sugar together in the top of a double saucepan. Add the remaining cream and cook over simmering water until the mixture thickens and will coat a spoon. Leave to cool.

Combine the custard and almond cream in an ice-cream freezer container. Put in the dasher and cover with a lid. Pack round with crushed ice and rock salt in the proportions recommended by the freezer manufacturer. Leave to stand for 3–4 minutes. Turn the handle and crank until you feel resistance in turning. Remove the lid. Add the almond essence and whipped cream. Place the lid back on and crank until you can barely turn the handle. Remove the lid and the dasher from

the container. Cover. Repack with ice and rock salt and leave to stand for 1–2 hours before serving.

Pittencrief Pudding

(*Traditional, adapted by the author*)

Serves 4

2 TBS NAPLES BISCUITS, (OR HARD SPONGE
    FINGERS) CRUMBLED
½ OZ (1 TBS) BUTTER, SOFTENED
4 OZ (1 CUP) SHREDDED SUET
2 OZ (½ CUP) FLOUR
2½ OZ (½ CUP) BROWN SUGAR
2 EGGS
4 TBS RASPBERRY JAM (OR ANY GOOD PRESERVE)
½ TSP BAKING-SODA
4 TBS MILK
A 10-OZ PACKET FROZEN RASPBERRIES
SUGAR TO TASTE

Rub a 2-pint pudding basin with butter and line it with biscuit crumbs. Mix the suet, flour, sugar, eggs, jam, baking-soda and milk and pour into the basin. Steam for 2½ hours. Turn out and serve hot with an iced purée of raspberries (made by puréeing the thawed raspberries in a blender with sugar to taste, then refreezing lightly) and a bowl of whipped cream.

Rhubarb Charlotte

(*from Drue Heinz*)

Serves 4
1 LB RHUBARB
½ PINT (1 CUP) WATER
6 OZ (¾ CUP) SUGAR

6 OZ (3 CUPS) WHITE BREADCRUMBS
2 OZ (4 TBS) BUTTER, MELTED
2 OZ (¼ CUP) BROWN SUGAR
½ TSP GROUND GINGER
¼ TSP GROUND NUTMEG
¼ TSP GROUND CINNAMON
GRATED PEEL OF 1 ORANGE
2 TBS GOLDEN SYRUP (CORN SYRUP)
½ TBS LEMON JUICE
½ TBS ORANGE JUICE
2 TBS WATER

Cut the rhubarb into 1-inch lengths. Cook the pieces in a syrup made of the water and sugar.

Toss the breadcrumbs in butter, shaking the pan so that they fry evenly. Spread a thin layer on the bottom of a 2-pint (5 cup) soufflé dish. Cover with the drained rhubarb. Mix together the sugar, spices and orange peel and add a little of the resulting mixture to the dish. Repeat the layers of rhubarb and flavourings until the dish is full. End with a crumb layer. Heat the golden syrup and the fruit juice with the water. Pour over the charlotte and chill.

Sauces

Scotch Egg Sauce

(*Traditional, adapted by the author*)

1 OZ (2 TBS) BUTTER
½ OZ (2 TBS) FLOUR
½ PT (1 CUP) BOILING MILK
A LITTLE GRATED NUTMEG

A FEW DROPS OF TABASCO
2 HARD-BOILED EGGS

Melt the butter in a saucepan, stir in the flour, mix and cook through for a few seconds over low heat; gradually add the boiling milk, stirring continually. Add the nutmeg and tabasco, season with salt and pepper, mix well and reboil. Add the whites of the eggs, finely chopped, and the yolks, riced, at the last moment. Serve with haddock, or with cauliflower and Jerusalem artichokes.

Eggs and Butter Sauce
(*Traditional, adapted by the author*)

6 OZ (¾ CUP) BUTTER, MELTED
A SQUEEZE OF LEMON JUICE
2 HARD-BOILED EGGS, DICED
I TSP PARSLEY, FINELY CHOPPED

Stir all the ingredients together over low heat until the butter has melted. Turn up the heat so that the butter foams and serve at once with large boiled fish, which have been poached (not boiled) in a spicy broth.

Northumberland Celery Sauce
(*Traditional, adapted by the author*)

2 LARGE STALKS CELERY, SLICED
THE GIBLETS OF THE BIRDS
½ PT (I CUP) CHICKEN OR GAME STOCK
I OZ (2 TBS) BUTTER
1½ TBS FLOUR
½ PT (I CUP) CREAM
¼ TSP GRATED NUTMEG
⅛ TSP CAYENNE

Put the celery into a saucepan, cover with cold water, bring to the boil and then drain. Put the celery, the giblets and the stock into a saucepan, bring to the boil and simmer, covered, for 40 minutes, or until the giblets are tender.

Remove the giblets and purée the stock and celery in the blender. Make a cream sauce by melting the butter in a saucepan, stirring in the flour, cooking for I minute and gradually adding the cream, stirring until smooth, creamy and thickened. Season with pepper and salt, add the celery purée and the giblets, finely chopped. Add the cayenne and nutmeg and serve with pheasant, duck or any other game bird.

Horseradish Sauce
(*Traditional, adapted by the author*)

¼ PT (½ CUP) THICK CREAM
2 TBS GRATED HORSERADISH
I TSP DRY MUSTARD
¼ TSP SALT
¼ TSP SUGAR
2 TBS VINEGAR

Whip the cream and fold in the grated horseradish, the seasonings and the vinegar. Serve with roast beef, grilled steaks and cold meat of any kind.

Mint Sauce
(*Traditional, adapted by the author*)

2 TBS MINT, FINELY CHOPPED
½ PT (I CUP) BOILING VINEGAR
4 TBS WATER
½ TSP SALT
¼ TSP PEPPER
I TBS BROWN SUGAR

Pour the boiling vinegar over the mint, add the cold water, salt, pepper and sugar. Stir until the sugar dissolves and leave in a cool place for at least I hour before serving, so that the mint can flavour the vinegar thoroughly.

Mustard Sauce
(*Traditional, adapted by the author*)

4 TBS CHOPPED ONION,
½ OZ (I TBS) BUTTER
½ TBS FLOUR
½ PINT (I CUP) MILK OR STOCK
½ TSP SALT

¼ TSP PEPPER
⅛ TSP SUGAR
2 TSP FRENCH OR ENGLISH MADE MUSTARD

Cook the onion in a braising pan with the butter until softened. Stir in the flour, mix well and slowly add the milk or stock, stirring until slightly thickened. Cook gently for 10 minutes, add the seasonings and stir well. Bring to the boil and serve. Serve with mackerel, grilled kidneys, liver or tripe.

Albert Sauce

(*Traditional, adapted by the author*)

4 TBS GRATED HORSERADISH
¼ PT (½ CUP) LIGHT BEEF AND VEGETABLE
   STOCK, STRAINED
¼ PT (½ CUP) MELTED BUTTER SAUCE (*see p.* 53)
¼ PT (½ CUP) CREAM
1 OZ (½ CUP) FINE WHITE BREADCRUMBS
1 EGG YOLK
½ TSP ENGLISH MUSTARD, MIXED TO PASTE
   WITH VINEGAR

Gently boil the grated horseradish in the beef stock for 20 minutes. Gradually stir in the melted butter sauce, then the cream and finally the breadcrumbs. Do not pack down. Put over low heat and reduce the sauce down to a creamy consistency, stirring all the time. Strain through a sieve, scraping hard with a wooden spatula. Replace in saucepan, rewarm, bind with the egg yolk over low heat. Do not reboil. Season. Add the mustard and mix well. Serve at once, with braised beef.

Mussel Sauce

(*Traditional, adapted by the author*)

3 DOZEN MUSSELS
½ LB (1 CUP) MELTED BUTTER
A PINCH OF CAYENNE
1 OZ (2 TBS) HARD BUTTER
4 TBS (¼ CUP) CREAM

Open the mussels in a saucepan over low heat. Discard the shells. Strain the juice

through fine muslin and transfer to a clean pan. Poach for a very few moments in their juice, then remove them and keep warm. Add first the melted butter to the juice, then the cayenne and the hard butter cut into small pieces, followed by the cream. Return the mussels to the pan, rewarm gently and serve at once, with fish.

This sauce can also be made with oysters, in which case substitute 1 dozen oysters for the mussels.

Oyster Sauce

(*Traditional, adapted by the author*)

12 OYSTERS
1 OZ (2 TBS) BUTTER
2 TBS FLOUR
¼ PT (⅔ CUP) MILK OR LIGHT CREAM
4 TBS (¼ CUP) CREAM
½ TSP SALT
A PINCH OF CAYENNE PEPPER

Poach the oysters in their own liquid, remove the beards and slice. Reserve the juice.

Melt the butter in a saucepan, stir in the flour and cook through for a few minutes, stirring, but without allowing the mixture to darken. Gradually stir in ¼ pint (⅔ cup) of the broth from the oysters, the milk and the cream, and season with the salt. Strain through a sieve and rewarm. Add the oysters and cook just long enough to heat through – no longer, or they will toughen. Sprinkle in the cayenne pepper and serve over boiled cod or hake.

A Sauce for Ham

(*Traditional, adapted by the author*)

2 TBS FINELY GRATED HORSERADISH
2 TBS REDCURRANT JELLY, MELTED
1 TBS PREPARED MUSTARD
GRATED RIND OF 2 ORANGES AND 1 LEMON
JUICE OF 2 ORANGES AND 1 LEMON
1 TBS VINEGAR

Cook all the ingredients together for 15–20 minutes until the mixture has reduced a little. This makes enough sauce for reheating 6 thin slices of cooked ham. They should be served with the sauce and a bland vegetable such as green beans or carrots, which go well with the spicy taste.

Apricot and Carrot Sauce

(*from the author*)

I LB (2 BOXES) DRIED APRICOTS
6–8 CARROTS
I½ OZ (2–3 TBS) BUTTER
2 TBS PARSLEY, FINELY CHOPPED

Put the apricots into a saucepan with enough water to cover and boil gently until fairly soft. Purée them in a blender, then season. Boil the carrots in salted water until cooked but still crisp. Drain and slice. Spoon the apricot purée, which should be quite thick, into an earthenware dish and arrange the sliced carrots on top, with the butter scattered over in small lumps. Sprinkle with parsley and heat through for a few minutes in the oven. Serve with pork.

Chocolate Sauce

(*from Drue Heinz*)

MAKES ABOUT ½ PINT (I CUP)

2 OZ (¼ CUP) SUGAR
¼ PT (⅓ CUP) THIN CREAM
4 OZ (⅔ CUP) SWEET COOKING CHOCOLATE, BROKEN INTO SMALL PIECES
I OZ (3 TBS) UNSWEETENED COOKING CHOCOLATE, BROKEN INTO SMALL PIECES

Cook the sugar and cream together in the top of a double saucepan. Stir in the chipped chocolate, then remove from the heat, but keep the top pan sitting in the hot water contained in the lower one. Beat in the rest of the cream and serve warm with ice-cream.

Cumberland Rum Butter

(*from Drue Heinz*)

4 OZ (½ CUP) SWEET BUTTER, SOFTENED
4 OZ (½ CUP) CASTER OR GRANULATED SUGAR
4 TBS RUM
¼ TSP GRATED LEMON PEEL
¼ TSP CINNAMON

Work all the ingredients together and then chill in a sauceboat. Serve with Christmas pudding.

Bread, Biscuits and Cakes

Banbury Cakes

(*The Queen Cookery Books, 1913*)

Makes 12–15 cakes

I OZ (2 TBS) BUTTER, MELTED
3 TBS SUGAR
2 OZ (½ CUP) CURRANTS
½ OZ (2 TBS) MIXED CANDIED FRUIT PEEL, FINELY CHOPPED
¼ TSP GROUND ALLSPICE
½ TSP GROUND CINNAMON
⅛ TSP GROUND NUTMEG

1 LADYFINGER BISCUIT (OR ANY PLAIN SWEET
BISCUIT), DRIED IN THE OVEN UNTIL VERY
CRISP AND GROUND IN THE BLENDER
1½ LB PASTRY
A DUSTING OF CASTER (CONFECTIONER'S) SUGAR
1 EGG WHITE

Combine the melted butter and sugar in a
bowl and stir in the currants, peel, spices and
biscuit crumbs. Roll out the pastry on a
floured board until it is ¼ inch thick. Cut into
3½-inch circles. Gather up all the scraps of
pastry, reknead them and roll them out again,
then cut into the same shapes. Place 1
tablespoon of the mixture on each circle of
pastry and fold the edges towards the centre
to seal in the filling. Turn them upside down
and flatten them a little with your rolling pin.
The currants should be just visible below the
surface of the dough. Slash an inch-long gash
on the surface in the shape of an X. Brush
with lightly whipped egg white and dust with
the sugar. Put on a floured baking sheet and
bake at 400° (Mark 6) for 10–15 minutes.

Alexis's Soda Bread or Maslin

(*from my son*, *Alexis de la Falaise*)

This bread must be very similar to the type
made in medieval times from the mixed
sowing of cereal grains.

2 LB (4 CUPS) FLOUR: ½ LB (1 CUP) WHITE;
¾ LB (1½ CUPS) WHOLEWHEAT AND THE
REMAINDER ANY MIXED FLOUR, RYE, BARLEY,
CORNMEAL OR OATS
1 TSP SALT
1 TSP BAKING SODA
½ OZ (1 TBS) BUTTER OR MARGARINE
ABOUT ½ PT (1–1½ CUPS) BUTTERMILK

Sift all the flours together with the salt and
soda until perfectly blended; rub in the butter
and add two-thirds of the buttermilk, to make
a soft dough. If it is too dry to form a ball,
add the remaining buttermilk, or as much of it
as you need. Knead lightly into a ball and
flatten down into a circle 1½ inches thick. Cut
an X on the top and put on a floured baking

sheet. Bake at 425° (Mark 7) for 35–40 minutes
and cool on a rack.

Brandy Snaps

(*Traditional, adapted by the author*)

Makes about 16

4 OZ (½ CUP) BUTTER
1 OZ (¼ CUP) ICING (CONFECTIONER'S) SUGAR
2 TBS TREACLE (CORN SYRUP)
2 OZ (½ CUP) FLOUR
4 TBS BRANDY OR WATER
2 TSP GRATED LEMON PEEL

Filling
¾ PT (2 CUPS) THICK CREAM
2 TBS ICING (CONFECTIONER'S) SUGAR
2 TBS BRANDY (OPTIONAL)

Put half the butter, the sugar and the treacle
into a heavy saucepan and bring to the boil.
Remove from the heat and stir in the flour,
brandy (or water for children) and lemon peel.
Drop the mixture by teaspoonfuls on to a
greased baking sheet, making sure that they are
4 inches apart. Bake at 350° (Mark 4) for
8–10 minutes, until golden and bubbly. Remove
one biscuit at a time with a spatula and wrap
round the buttered handle of a wooden spoon,
or round your finger. Slide off on to a cake
rack. Do this as fast as possible, before they
cool and become too brittle to curl. Leave
to cool.

To make the filling, whip the cream and
sugar together until fairly stiff and fold in
(for grown-ups only) the brandy. A little fruit
essence can replace the brandy for the nursery.

Crumpets

(*Traditional, adapted by the author*)

There are some very good crumpet pans on
the market now that are lined with Teflon and
all in one section, so that you do not need the
frying-pan. Crumpets freeze very well, so it is
worth making a large batch.

Makes about 10

½ OZ (1 PACKAGE) YEAST
2 TBS LUKEWARM WATER
4½ OZ (1 CUP) FLOUR
¼ TSP SALT
1 EGG
½ OZ (1 TBS) BUTTER
¼ PT (½ CUP) MILK
ABOUT 2 OZ (4 TBS) BUTTER

Dissolve the yeast in the water. Mix the flour
and salt together. Make a well in the flour
and add the yeast, egg, butter and milk. Mix
well. Cover and leave to rise for 1 hour or
until double in size.

Brush some crumpet rings with melted
butter and put them into a greased 10-inch
frying-pan. Put the pan over moderate heat,
then drop 1 tablespoon of the batter into each
ring. When they begin to bubble and the
undersides turn brown, remove the rings.
Turn over and brown on the other side.
Break them open with your fingers, toast and
butter them and serve very hot in a covered
crumpet-dish.

Gooseberry Layer Shortcake

(*from Drue Heinz*)

Serves 8

6 OZ (1½ CUPS) SELF-RAISING FLOUR
3 OZ (¼ CUP) CASTER SUGAR
½ TSP GROUND NUTMEG
3 OZ (6 TBS) BUTTER
1 LARGE TIN GOOSEBERRIES
ICING (CONFECTIONER'S) SUGAR FOR DECORATION

Sieve the flour into a mixing bowl, then add the
sugar and nutmeg. Add the butter in small
pieces and work in. Put half of the mixture
into a greased 7–8-inch round cake tin. Add
the drained gooseberries and cover with the
rest of the mixture. Spread the mixture evenly
and pat it down. Put the tin into the centre of
an oven heated to 400° (Mark 6) for 20–30
minutes. When the shortcake is baked, remove
and leave to cool in the tin for 5 minutes. Turn

out on to a plate, by putting the plate on top
and then turning plate and tin upside down.
Dust with the sifted icing sugar, cut into
wedges and serve warm, with cream.

Pickles and Preserves

Lemon Cheesecurd

(*The Queen Cookery Books*, 1913)

Makes 1 lb (1½ cups)

3 EGG YOLKS
6 OZ (¾ CUP) SUGAR
GRATED PEEL OF 1 LEMON
4 TBS (¼ CUP) LEMON JUICE
2 OZ (¼ CUP) SWEET BUTTER
2 NAPLES BISCUITS (OR HARD SPONGE FINGERS),
   GRATED

Beat the yolks in a saucepan. Gradually add
the sugar, the lemon peel and juice, the
butter and biscuit crumbs and cook over low
heat until the mixture has thickened. Do not
boil. Use for tart fillings. This cheesecurd
keeps very well in the refrigerator.

Corned Beef

(*Traditional, adapted by the author*)

1½ LB CHUCK ROAST
¼ LB (1 CUP) COARSE SALT
4 TBS (¼ CUP) SUGAR
1 PT (2 CUPS) WATER
1 TBS SALTPETRE
1 TSP BAKING SODA

Toss the meat with the salt in a bowl. Cover and refrigerate overnight.

Combine the sugar, water, saltpetre and baking soda in a saucepan. Heat until the sugar has dissolved. Pour over the meat. Store in a cool place (under 45°F) for 4–6 weeks. Turn the meat in the pickle every day.

Forcemeats and Stuffings

Beef Farce

(*The Queen Cookery Books, 1913*)

¼ PT (½ CUP) PANADE (THICK WHITE SAUCE)
¼ LB (½ CUP) MINCED (GROUND) BEEF
1 OZ (2 TBS) BUTTER
2–3 EGG YOLKS
A LITTLE CAYENNE PEPPER

Pound the panade and the minced beef in a mortar, or soften in a blender. Add the other ingredients and mix thoroughly until you have a smooth paste. Stuff this mixture into 'pockets' under the skin of meat for roasting or in meat pies.

Herb Farce

(*The Queen Cookery Books, 1913*)

4 OZ (2 CUPS) FRESH BREADCRUMBS, MADE IN A
  BLENDER

2 OZ (½ CUP) BEEF SUET, GRATED OR MINCED
2 TBS MIXED HERBS, CHOPPED
2 EGGS
FLOUR

Mix all the ingredients (except the flour) together. Form into tiny balls, roll in the flour, and then either boil gently in water for 10 minutes, or dip in beaten egg and fine breadcrumbs and fry until golden. Use as a garnish for veal or roast hare, as a stuffing for roast meat or inside pies.

Liver Farce

(*The Queen Cookery Books, 1913*)

½ LB CALVES', POULTRY OR GAME LIVER
¼ LB (½ CUP) BACON, CHOPPED
¼ LB (½ CUP) RAW VEAL OR CHICKEN
1 OZ (2 TBS) BUTTER OR RAW BEEF MARROW
2 BAY LEAVES
2–3 SPRIGS PARSLEY
1 TSP THYME
A LITTLE CAYENNE PEPPER
1 EGG YOLK
2–3 BUTTON MUSHROOMS OR 1 TRUFFLE,
  FINELY CHOPPED

Chop the liver and fry it with the bacon and the veal or chicken in the butter or marrow. Add the herbs and seasonings; cook for 5 minutes. Pound to a smooth paste while still hot, or purée in a blender. Beat in the egg yolk and stir in the mushrooms or truffle.

Use for stuffing pigeons or other small birds, or in savoury pies of poultry or game.

APPENDIX

Unusual Herbs, and where to find them

Burnet The plants and seeds can be bought from The Old Rectory Herb Garden (*see below*); the plants only from Laxton & Bunyard (*see below*). In the United States, the plants and seeds from Caprilands Herb Farm (*see below*).

Clary The plants and seeds can be bought from The Old Rectory Herb Garden (*see below*); dried clary is obtainable at Culpeper House.

Galingale A root much used in medieval cookery. It does not soften in the cooking and should be tied in a muslin and removed after it has flavoured the dish. Dried galingale root is obtainable from Culpeper House (*see below*).

Hyssop This is still fairly easy to find; the plants and seeds from The Old Rectory Herb Garden and Laxton & Bunyard (*see below*); dried hyssop is obtainable at Culpeper House (*see below*). In the United States it can be found at Aphrodisia (*see below*).

Marigold Flowers The flowers of the common marigold can be freshly picked from the garden; dried marigold flowers are obtainable from Culpeper House (*see below*), who also sell 'Broth Posies', a mixture of dried marigold flowers, parsley, thyme and bay leaf, for flavouring broth.

Purslane The seeds only are obtainable from The Old Rectory Herb Garden and Laxton & Bunyard (*see below*).

Rocket (or roquette, or scaragula) This cannot be found anywhere in England; in the United States, the seed can be bought at Caprilands Herb Farm (*see below*).

Samphire This is not obtainable commercially, as far as we can discover. It can be found growing wild on rocks near the sea on the coast of Devon and Cornwall, and the West coast of Ireland.

Tansy The plants and seeds are obtainable from The Old Rectory Farm (*see below*); dried tansy is stocked at Culpeper House (*see below*); in the United States the seed can be bought from Caprilands Herb Farm and Aphrodisia (*see below*).

Medieval Spices

Cubebs Much used in medieval cookery, this can only be found today in the United States in Aphrodisia (*see below*). It seems to have resembled a mixture of black pepper and allspice, and can be replaced in this way.

Sanders A red colouring made from powdered sandal wood, much used to satisfy the medieval love of colour in food. It can be replaced by carmine, cochineal, or other red food colouring.

Pouder-forte According to Dr Kitchiner (*The Cook's Oracle*, 1817) this was a seasoning made from a mixture of dried chives and mace, ground together. Pepper probably formed part of the mixture also.

Pouder-douce This seems to have been a blend of ginger, cinnamon and nutmeg. It must have resembled the classic French blend of spices known as *quatre-épices*, still much used in charcuterie. According to Jane Grigson, (*Charcuterie and French Pork Cookery*), this is a blend of pepper, nutmeg, cloves, and either cinnamon or ginger, in the proportions of 7 parts pepper to 1 part of each of the three others used.

Other Flavourings

Almond Milk A recipe for this is given on page 53.

Ground Almonds These were used constantly in medieval cooking, in both sweet and savoury dishes. They must have been coarser than the ground almonds sold today, so it is better to buy them whole and grind them oneself in the blender. In the United States there is a finely chopped almond packaged as 'nibbed almonds', which can be used at a pinch.

Elder and Orange flower water This is obtainable from Culpeper house and in the United States from Aphrodisia (*see below*).

Rosewater This is still obtainable from chemists everywhere, and from Culpeper House (*see below*).

Verjuice Advice about making this is given on page 53. It can be replaced at a pinch by a sharp cider, or cider mixed with cider vinegar, or a very mild cider vinegar such as one sometimes finds in health food stores. The sharpness can be mitigated by a little rose-hip juice, or syrup.

Unusual Game and Meat

Quail can be bought in London at Harrods, Jacksons, and Fortnum & Mason (*see below*). Venison is obtainable in London from Harrods and John Baily (*see below*). Sucking pigs can be bought in London at Harrods. Venison, quail, and unusual game of all sorts can be bought in the United States at The Maryland Gourmet Mart (*see below*).

Addresses of Stockists

In England

Harrods, Knightsbridge, London SW1.

The Old Rectory Herb Garden, Ightham, Kent.

Jacksons of Piccadilly, 171 Piccadilly, London W1.

Laxton & Bunyard Nurseries Ltd, Brampton, Huntingdon.

Culpeper Ltd, 21 Bruton Street, London W1.

Culpeper Ltd, 59 Ebury Street, London SW1.

Culpeper Ltd, 14 Crystal Palace Parade, London SE19.

John Baily, 116 Mount Street, London W1.

In the United States

The Caprilands Herb Farm, Silver Street, North Coventry, Conn.

The Maryland Gourmet Mart, 412 Amsterdam Avenue, New York, NY. 10024.

Aphrodisia, 28 Carmine Street, New York, NY. 10014.

Sam's Meat Market, 543 9th Avenue, New York, NY. 10018 'Ask for Gerry Shapiro'.

INDEX

237

SOURCES

The Middle Ages
*Two Fifteenth-century Cookery
　Books.*
　Thomas Austin, ed., published
　for the Early English Text
　Society by the Oxford Univer-
　sity Press (London, New York
　and Toronto 1888; reprinted
　1964), from Harleian MS 279
　and Harleian MS 4016, with
　additional extracts from
　Ashmole MS 1439, Laud MS 553
　and Douce MS 55.
The Rev. Samuel Pegge, *The
　Forme of Cury* (1378). Partly
　from an eighteenth-century
　handwritten transcript.
Ancient Cookery (1381).
A Noble Boke of Cookery,
　R. Napier, ed. (*1882*).

**The Sixteenth and Seventeenth
Centuries**
Andrew Boorde, *A compendyous
　regyment of a dyetary of helth,
　made in Montpylior (1542).*
Sir Kenelme Digbie, *The Closet of
　the Eminently Learned Sir*

*Kenelme Digbie Knight, Opened
　(1669; reprinted 1910).*
Gervase Markham, *A Way to
　Health (1660).*
Robert May, *The Accomplisht Cook
　(1660).*
Hannah Wolley, *The Cook's Guide
　(1664).*
The Family Dictionary (1695).
*The Good Huswife's Handmaid
　(1594).*
John Murrel, *A New Book of
　Cookerie (1617).*

The Eighteenth Century
Charles Carter, *The Compleat
　Practical Cook (1730).*
Charles Carter, *The Compleat City
　and Country Cook (1732).*
John Farley, *The London Art of
　Cookery (1783).*
Hannah Glasse, *The Art of Cookery
　Made Plain and Easy (1747).*
Elizabeth Raffald, *The Experienced
　English Housekeeper (1769).*
*An Eighteenth-century Kitchen
　The Family Cook (1738).*
*The Housekeeper's Pocket Book
　(1738).*

Collingwood, Francis and John
　Woolams, *The Universal Cook
　and City and Country
　Housekeeper,* 1797.

The Nineteenth Century
Eliza Acton, *Modern Cookery for
　Private Families (1845).*
Isabel Mary Beeton, *The Book of
　Household Management (1861);*
　published as *Mrs Beeton's Book
　of Household Management,* ed.
　J. Herman Senn, (*1906*).
Mrs Dalgairns, *The Practice of
　Cookery (1829).*
E. S. Dallas, *Kettner's Book of the
　Table (1877).*
William Kitchiner, *The Cook's
　Oracle (1817).*
Ann Miller, *A Practical Cook
　(1845).*
Alexis Soyer, *The Gastronomic
　Regenerator (1846).*
*A New System of Domestic Cookery
　(1843).*
Old Master Cookery Book (1841).
Young Woman's Companion (1806).

The Twentieth Century
Horace Cox, *The Queen Cookery
　Books,* 1913.
F. Marian McNeill, *The Scots
　Kitchen,* 1929.
The author.
The author's mother, Lady Birley.
The author's father, the late
　Sir Oswald Birley.
The author's grandmother,
　the late Vava Lecky Pike.
The author's son, Alexis de la
　Falaise.
The author's daughter, Louise
　de la Falaise.
Mrs Alice Thomson, cook to
　Mrs Stirling of Keir.
Miss Nellie Gallaher, cook to Mr
　Henry McIlhenny at Glenveagh
　Castle, Co. Donegal.
Mrs Henry J. Heinz II.
Robin McDouall.
Donald Smith, chef at Annabel's
　(owned by the author's brother,
　Mark Birley).
Sir Federick Warner.
David Niven.
Sir Cecil Beaton.